Barbara Sonnenhauser and Patrizia Noel Aziz Hanna (Eds.)
Vocative!

Trends in Linguistics
Studies and Monographs 261

De Gruyter Mouton

Vocative!

Addressing between System and Performance

edited by
Barbara Sonnenhauser
Patrizia Noel Aziz Hanna

De Gruyter Mouton

ISBN 978-3-11-048535-6
e-ISBN 978-3-11-030417-6
ISSN 1861-4302

Library of Congress Cataloging-in-Publication Data
A CIP catalog record for this book has been applied for at the Library of Congress.

Bibliographic information published by the Deutsche Nationalbibliothek
The Deutsche Nationalbibliothek lists this publication in the Deutsche Nationalbibliografie; detailed bibliographic data are available in the Internet at http://dnb.dnb.de.

© 2013 Walter de Gruyter GmbH, Berlin/Boston
Printing: Hubert & Co. GmbH & Co. KG, Göttingen
♾ Printed on acid-free paper
Printed in Germany
www.degruyter.com

Contents

Introduction: Vocative![*]

Barbara Sonnenhauser and Patrizia Noel Aziz Hanna

Abstract

The vocative has long been neglected in the linguistic literature. There is still no systematic approach to capturing the diverse language-specific ways of addressing others. The lack of morphological vocative marking in many European languages is one of the reasons for this neglect, in addition to the dual status of vocatives between system and performance. This volume intends to fill this gap by dealing with the various facets of the vocative from an onomasiological perspective, with special emphasis on the position of this phenomenon between system and performance.

In this introduction, the intricate nature of the vocative and the problems it poses for current linguistic analyses will be outlined. To this end, the main characteristics of the vocative will be distinguished and an overview will be given of the main theoretical approaches and lines of argument. In order to avoid any commitment to a specific theoretical framework, 'vocatives' will be defined functionally as 'forms and structures used for direct address'. This will also allow us to consider ways of marking the vocative structurally.

1. The 'vocative'

The onomasiological approach towards the vocative taken in *Vocative! Addressing between system and performance* implicates a variety of differing and diverging concepts, interpretations and theoretical positions concerning the term 'vocative'. Traditionally, and depending to a large degree both on the theoretical approach and the specific language studied, vocatives are classified either in purely formal terms as part of the language system, or as functional structures manifesting themselves in language use only. While the focus of research still lies on languages with morphologically marked vocatives, increasingly syntactic restrictions, pragmatic factors, and semantic characteristics are also becoming the focus of attention. In addition to the focus on morphology, another aspect that may have impeded a comprehensive discussion of vocatives in languages without overt vocative marking is their position between system and performance. Furthermore, most approaches refer to only one specific aspect of the vocative – i.e. its form (phonology, morphology, syntax) or function (address, call) – and take this aspect as the crucial and defining one.

As used within this article, the term 'vocative' is a mere label for linguistic addressing phenomena, without any commitment to specific theoretical assumptions or positions. This pretheoretical approximation is necessary considering the various possible definitions, theoretical treatments and language specific studies of this phenomenon in terms of its category status, its structure and function, etc. A few definitions shall suffice to demonstrate the impact of the theoretical background – predominantly formal or predominantly functional – on the classification of vocatives. Zwicky (1974: 787) defines the vocative in English by stating that it is "set off from the sentence it occurs in by special intonation […] and it doesn't serve as an argument of a verb in this sentence". In emphasizing the vocative's syntactic non-integration and its non-argument status, Zwicky's definition is primarily a syntactic one. Levinson (1983: 71) regards vocatives as "an interesting grammatical category", leaving open, however, what exactly he means by a grammatical category in terms of its systematic status. He then goes on to focus on the non-integrated nature of vocatives, defining them as "noun phrases that refer to the addressee, but are not syntactically or semantically incorporated as the arguments of a predicate; they are rather set apart prosodically from the body of the sentence that may accompany them". A more functional definition is given by Betsch and Berger (2009: 1023), who regard the vocative as 'a traditional means of marking nominal forms of address' ("traditionelles Mittel zur Markierung nominaler Anredeformen").

A functional approach is also taken by Daniel and Spencer (2009: 626), who define the vocative as "a form used for calling out and attracting or maintaining the addressee's attention […] by using a term referring to [her]". Lambrecht (1996: 267) describes the function of vocatives as serving "to call the attention of an addressee, in order to establish or maintain a relationship between this addressee and some proposition". In his attempt to give an exclusively semantic definition, Schaden (2010: 176) is concerned with vocatives "in a narrow sense", i.e. with "noun-phrases that identify or describe the addressee" and do not have any further, non-vocative functions. He considers "vocatives alone and in isolation", leaving aside "components of the meaning of vocatives that are not rooted in the linguistic system (i.e., Saussure's *langue*), but that seem to stem exclusively from the use that speakers make in context of that system" (Schaden

2010: 176). He classifies only NPs identifying or describing the addressee as vocatives. Other cases, such as pronominal expressions or formulae like the beginning of the Lord's Prayer – *Our Father in heaven* – can optionally be regarded as vocatives (Schaden 2010: 176). This seems to suggest that he assumes some kind of inherent feature marking certain NPs unambiguously as 'vocative'.[1] Moreover, he arrives at the conclusion that there are "three semantic functions" of vocatives (Schaden 2010: 183): identification, predication and activation. This differentiation is based on the question of "whether the (group of) addressee(s) is presupposed to be already established (this is the case with predicative and activational vocatives), or whether the addressee still has to be established as such (identificational vocatives)" (2010: 184). In regarding 'semantic' as "the part of meaning that is linguistically encoded" (2010: 176), Schaden's approach amounts to 'vocative' being an inherent semantic feature of specific NPs (not only nouns) and, as a consequence, to NPs being systematically ambiguous between vocative and non-vocative uses.

What these and other definitions (cf. Fink 1972) show is the non-distinct nature of vocative categorisation – it is regarded as a formal category, a functional structure, a semantic component or as a mere element of usage.

The vagueness of the term also accounts for the fact that, contrary to their importance in communication, and even though they are amongst the most basic and earliest acquired structures of language, vocatives have hardly ever been discussed in all their facets from a linguistic point of view. This is pointed out, e.g., by Levinson (1983: 71), who notes that "[v]ocatives in general are […] underexplored", and Floricic (2002: 151), who states that "force est de reconnaître que les études consacrées spécifiquement au vocative sont assez rares; à quelques exceptions près, tout au plus dispose-t-on à ce sujet d'observations fragmentaires et éparses". Hock (2006) stresses the neglect of vocatives in the linguistic discussion and particularly of their functional aspects. He ascribes this to the focus of traditional grammar on the status of the vocative within the case system, which means that the function of directly addressing an interlocutor is not duly taken into account.

The lack of interest in the syntactic and semantic aspects of vocatives in "traditional and generative grammar" is also noted by Lambrecht (1996: 267). He sees the reason for this in "the inherently deictic nature of vocatives and […] their grammatical status as non-arguments". Due to their non-argument status, vocatives "can be omitted from a sentence without influencing its syntactic well-formedness", and structures of this type "have traditionally been considered less worthy of syntactic theorizing than constituents whose presence is obligatory" (1996: 267). As can already be seen from this short outline of vocative definitions, discussions concerning the vocative illustrate the "power of theory over data" (van Schooneveld 1986: 17 on vocative case).

Taking seriously Ashdowne's (2002: 161) challenge – "[n]o longer should the vocative case be a source of puzzlement, but a topic for renewed enquiry" –, the contributions to this volume cover the diversity of vocative marking, vocative structures and vocative functions, the syntactic peculiarities of vocatives, the paths of vocative development in various languages, the pragmatic aspects associated with vocative use, and the difficulties in dealing with the vocative from a theoretical point of view. The volume brings together approaches from various linguistic disciplines in order to arrive at a more detailed picture of this structure between 'system' and 'performance' on a cross-linguistic basis.

2. Types of vocative marking

The vocative is structurally marked. In some languages, the marking is primarily morphological, in some it is prosodic, in others syntactic. A grammatical description of vocatives is usually closely related to overt morphological marking. This goes hand in hand with discussing whether the vocative is to be regarded as a case or not. By focussing on the notion of case, however, data in which the vocative is marked by means of particles or intonation are usually disregarded.

2.1. Morphology

With respect to the discussion of the vocative as a case, two main positions can be distinguished: 1) the vocative is regarded as a case in languages that have morphological marking (for Georgian cf. Abuladze and Ludden, this volume), and 2) the vocative is not analysed as part of the case system although there is morphological marking. Both approaches differ mainly in the hierarchisation of form and (syntactic and semantic/pragmatic) function. In the latter approach, the vocative is excluded from the case inventory, because its function is not that of a prototypical case; cf. Isačenko (1962: 83):

Der Vokativ ist eigentlich gar kein 'Kasus', wenn man unter der Kasusform den Ausdruck einer syntaktischen Beziehung zu anderen Wörtern versteht. Der Vokativ drückt nämlich keinerlei syntaktische Beziehung aus, er ist eine in die Rede eingeschobene 'Anredeform' mit deutlicher Appellfunktion.

[The vocative is not a case if one regards as a case form the expression of a syntactic relation to other words. The vocative does not convey any syntactic relation, it is a parenthetical 'form of address' with a clearly appellative function.]

On closer inspection, however, Isačenko's conclusion is not as absolute as it may seem at first glance, since it is restricted to a specific interpretation of prototypical case. Similar restrictions, either explicitly stated or merely implied, underlie most vocative definitions.

When focussing on the formal side of the vocative, i.e. on its morphological marking, many researchers' opinions run counter to Isačenko's. From a formal point of view, a morphologically marked vocative is regarded as part of the morphological system, more precisely, of the case inventory of a given language. Kiparsky (1967: 39) argues that the vocative belongs to the morphological system since it is marked by a special form, and Kottum (1983: 137) argues in his "defense of case status for the vocative" for the "primacy of morphological over syntactic criteria, as in any definition of case".

Skalička (1994) takes a somewhat different approach, regarding the vocative – which he considers a "really unhappy case" (1994: 56) – as a case not only on formal grounds, but also because of its syntactic non-integration. He argues that the position "outside the syntactic link" (1994: 56) is a feature which the vocative shares with the nominative. In doing so, Skalička seems to propose a broader conception of sentence integration. In this conception, case may be interpreted as specifying an integration parameter: Both syntactic integration and non-integration is indicated by case, and therefore the vocative can also be regarded as a case on functional grounds – "a case without syntactic link" (Skalička 1994: 60). To substantiate his argument, Skalička refers to the specific function he assumes for the vocative, i.e. the "exclamatory meaning [that] brings it into syntactic combinations" (1994: 60–61). Two further arguments for regarding the vocative as a case (1994: 56), which have been made by others as well, are its functional equivalence with the nominative in the plural[2] ("otherwise we could not explain e.g. why in Czech, Latin and Greek the nominative plural in the vocative function is a case – the nominative – whereas the vocative in the singular would not be"), and its formal marking ("We could also hardly explain why the vocative is not a case in spite of the fact that it is consistent with other individual cases and formally fits well into the case system.").

References to the functional equivalence of (certain uses of) the nominative and the vocative are usually linked to their equivalence of form in many languages (cf. e.g. Betsch and Berger 2009: 1024 on the Slavonic languages). Approaches that regard the vocative as a case even without specific morphological marking argue that its morphological make-up is that of the nominative, or that the nominative may take over the function of the vocative; thus, they suggest morphological syncretism (cf. Hjelmslev 1935: 116–117) with its non-arbitrary congruence of forms. The formal similarity of vocatives and nominatives may also lead to the reanalysis of the vocative as a nominative, both language-internally (on Russian cf. Kiparsky 1967: 40–41) and in language contact; this opens up a further perspective on form-function pairs (cf. Stifter, this volume).

Other approaches regard the vocative as an 'outlier case' (Daniel and Spencer 2009), or as "a case not like the others" (van Schoonefeld 1986: 185). Vairel (1981: 444) defines the vocative in terms of 'case' while at the same time acknowledging its special status: "it denotes the *role assumed by the referent of the noun as a participant in the act of speech*, whereas the other cases mark the *syntactic function of the noun as a constituent of the sentences*".

The diverging opinions on the status of the vocative as a case can partly be traced back to diverging assumptions concerning the notion of case in general. A rather traditional definition of case is given by Blake (2001: 1): "Case is a system of marking dependent nouns for the type of relationship they bear to their heads. Traditionally the term refers to inflectional marking, and, typically, case marks the relationship of a noun to a verb at the clause level or of a noun to a preposition, postposition or another noun at the phrase level." Whether the vocative is classified as a case or not is often discussed with reference to a conception of case like Blake's. However, Mel'čuk (1986) and Haspelmath (2009) point out various ambiguities related to the 'technical' side of the notion of 'case': It may denote a grammatical category, a grammatical meaning or the means of marking only.[3] Another aspect of this "terminological polysemy" (Haspelmath 2009: 505) pertains to the specific kinds of cases that are referred to according to the respective theoretical frameworks. As these diverging conceptions of case show, the 'case problem of the vocative' is actually a 'case problem' in its own right.

As a consequence, it seems doubtful whether discussions focussing on the case status of the vocative are indeed able to shed light on this phenomenon. These doubts are substantiated further by the linguistic facts in languages such as Bulgarian and Macedonian, whose nominal systems has lost morphological case marking – with the exception of the vocative, which may optionally be used for specific nouns (cf. Betsch and Berger 2009: 1024; on Bulgarian cf. Girvin, this volume). In any case, the fact that the morphological encoding of a 'peripheral' case prevails while 'prototypical' cases are lost, and vice versa (e.g. in the Germanic language family with vocative case marking only in extinct Gothic), is a severe problem for case system classification.

Morphological marking is usually considered the most important indication of vocatives. Anstatt (2008), for instance, speaks of 'vocative languages' only if the vocative is morphologically marked, whereas intonationally marked vocatives are not regarded as cases, even though their function seems to be the same. At the same time, however, Anstatt acknowledges that it is not only morphology that marks the vocative, but also intonation. The intonation of vocatives has been treated mainly in phonetic research (cf., e.g., Ladd 2008, Gussenhoven 1993, Varga 2008). It focuses on intonation contours, especially on the language-specific prosody of calls. Another observation is the markedness of prosodic vocative signalling, such as the vocative stress pattern in Turkish (Zimmer 1970). This in turn leads to the question of the linguistic status of prosodically marked vocatives.

2.2. Prosody

Qvonje (1986) assumes two general types of vocatives: the purely intonational type and the type with additional marking by inflection or external features such as word order. In the case of nominative-vocative syncretism, it is intonation that distinguishes vocatives from nominatives; thus intonation is represented as a categorical feature of vocatives:

> Unserer Meinung nach handelt es sich bei den Formen von vokativisch gebrauchten Substantiven (wie auch von Adjektiven und Pronomina), die im Schriftbild mit dem Nominativ zusammenfallen, um ebenso echte Erscheinungen des Vokativs, wie beispielsweise bei den Formen mit speziellen En-

dungen. Was nämlich den Vokativ vom Nominativ unterscheidet, ist immer die spezielle exklamatorisch-appellative Intonation, sowie eine Pause vor dem eventuell folgenden Satz. (Qvonje 1986: 86)

[In our opinion, forms of nouns (as well as adjectives and pronouns) in vocative usage which coincide in writing with the nominative are real instances of the vocative, just as e.g. forms with special endings. What distinguishes the vocative from the nominative is always a special exclamatory-appellative intonation, as well as a pause preceding any following sentence.]

Zwicky (1974) points out that nominative NPs are distinguished from vocatively-used NPs by means of intonational marking; intonation differentiates the referential use of NPs from their non-referential use. Morphological and intonational marking of vocatives may both be present in a language. This is emphasized by Vairel (1981) for Latin with the example of *pater / advenit* 'father, he has arrived' vs. *pater advenit* 'my father has arrived'. Judging from the present state in modern languages, she assumes the two sentences to have differed in intonation. Vairel proposes that, as a consequence, morphological marking became redundant, and "since a noun in the vocative was always melodically marked, an inflectional mark was superfluous, and could easily disappear" (1981: 446). This sketch of development is not uncontroversial, as the argumentation in Hock (2007) shows. The inconsistencies of the marking of suprasegmental features in Greek documents and their Church Slavonic translations pointed out by Hock also seem to suggest the possibility of the opposite direction.

However, intonational marking indeed plays an important role. It is a feature that manifests itself at the utterance level and thus applies to both morphologically marked and morphologically non-marked vocatives. Noel and Sonnenhauser (forthc.) argue that in written language this specific function of prosodic marking is rendered by means of punctuation. In German *Was hast du Peter gesagt?* 'What did you say to Peter?' vs. *Was hast du, Peter, gesagt?* 'What did you, Peter, say?' it is the commas that distinguish the use of *Peter* as indirect object from its vocative use.

If intonation is a systematic and inherent feature of vocative marking, vocatives can be considered part of an intonational paradigm and thus be anchored within a traditional conception of language system (cf. Göksel and Pöchtrager, this volume, for an intonational analysis of Turkish and German calls). In addition, empirical analyses of a direct relation between one-word intonational vocative marking and sentential intonation (with or without emphatic or emotional enrichment) are a desideratum (Noel Aziz Hanna 2011).

Furthermore, Zwicky (1974: 790) observes that "some vocative NPs do not occur as referential NPs" and "some referential NPs do not occur as vocatives". This can be seen with the NP *doctor*, which can be used both referentially and vocatively, whereas NPs such as *physician, pedestrian* or *surgeon* have a referential use only (1974: 790). Constraints like that lead Zwicky to ask another question: Which NPs may be used as vocatives? While this question can be answered quite easily for languages with morphological marking – it is mainly feminine and masculine nouns but not neuter nouns that can be marked for vocatives – the evidence is not that clear for languages where referential and vocative use are distinguished intonationally only. Even though some regularities can be observed, Zwicky (1974: 791) argues that "most vocative NPs" are idioms. Yet, contrary to idioms of the common type, i.e. idioms that can be regarded as lexicon items, the idiomaticity of vocative NPs manifests itself in language use only and thus can hardly be systematized in its entirety with respect to the lexicon.

2.2. Vocative syntax

The syntactic classification of vocatives concerns their external syntax, i.e. their position within the sentence, and their internal make-up, as well as their categorisation in terms of parts of speech.

Contrary to peculiarities of their – morphological or intonational – marking, the syntactic properties of vocatives have, for a long time, remained outside the focus of linguistic research. Stavrou (ms: 1) relates this to the "widespread view" that the vocative "is a noun form which does not carry any information about grammatical relationships, its purpose being entirely pragmatic". Therefore, she concludes, "[i]t doesn't come as a surprise [...] that syntactic accounts are almost non-existent" (ms: 1). The fact that vocative nouns do not seem to be syntactically integrated into the sentence structure (on the 'extra-sentential' nature of Latin vocatives cf. Ashdowne 2002: 153) is one of the most common arguments for excluding the vocative from the case inventory (cf. section 2.1). Syntactic non-integration is a criterion vocatives share with parenthetical structures (on parentheticals cf., e.g., Espinal 1991). Lambrecht (1996: 267–268), in contrast, regards vocatives as sentence constituents whose grammar resembles that of topic-NPs in right- and left-dislocated position. For French, he argues that both "belong to the same grammatical construction type" (1996: 269) not only in terms of syntactic position but also in terms of function insofar as "both serve to establish a RELEVANCE relation between a DISCOURSE REFERENT and a PROPOSITION" (1996: 269). Both lack a theta role in the sentence, and both are syntactically optional. Lambrecht also motivates the grammatical similarity between vocatives and dislocated topic-NPs on a functional basis: "In both constructions, a constituent coding a referent which is accessible from the speech setting or from the linguistic context is associated with a sentence via a pragmatic link of RELEVANCE" (1996: 277). This functional basis may also account for the fact that vocatives and dislocated topics assume some kind of twitter status with respect to clausal integration. On the one hand, they are syntactically optional, on the other hand, both may be linked to an argument within the clause (1996: 271–272). The question of whether the vocative is interpreted as a component of syntax can also be considered as a question of the nature of the relation holding between a verb and its arguments, which is still matter of debate (cf., e.g., Jacobs 1994).

Depending on their position in the sentence, vocatives can be ascribed three functions (cf. Osenova and Simov 2002): non-arguments, subjects and appositions. Osenova and Simov (2002) argue against assigning these three pragmatic and syntactic characterizations to vocatives. They regard them as "misleading and irrelevant on linguistic grounds" (2002: 2), providing a number of arguments for their view (2002: 2–3), such as the possible agreement between vocatives and other parts of the sentence (e.g. subject, object, possessives), or the fact that vocatives can be combined with all types of illocutionary force. In order to account for the interaction between the specific syntactic and pragmatic features of the vocative, Osenova and Simov (2002: 3) propose to regard them as both adjuncts and discourse particles.

In approaches treating vocatives as syntactic structures, the argumentation is built on reasons for their formal integration. The argumentation in Stavrou (ms) relies on the internal structure of vocatives as head of an NP vs. DP, and on syntactic similarities to syntactic structures like copular sentences. The vocative is not licensed in a sentence, but interferes with arguments and modifiers (Stavrou ms: 1). However, being "co-indexed with an argument of the verb coding 2nd person" it forms "part of the sentence" (ms: 2) and is embedded as VoP (vocative phrase) in a pragmatically oriented "Speech Act Phrase [+addressee]" (ms: 20) (cf. Hill, this volume, for RoleP). This functional projection lies outside of the CP domain. Syntagmatic observations like the one made by Longobardi (1994), who notices that indefiniteness is incompatible with the highly individualising nature of the vocative, add to the argumentation of the effect vocatives have on syntax.

Regarding vocatives as structures, similarities to other syntactic structures can be established as well. Espinal (this volume) investigates potential similarities to structures such as copular sentences. She thereby puts the vocative into a broader syntactic perspective and distinguishes it on both structural and functional grounds from allegedly similar phenomena (such as subjects of infinites, calls, pseudo-vocatives). Moreover, the syntactic position of vocatives matters. This can be taken as another argument against them being completely outside the clause. Lambrecht (1996: 267) calls vocatives "a kind of sentence constituent", whose position "correlates with the activation status of the representation" of the topic-NP's or the vocative's referent "in the mind of the hearer at the time of utterance" (1996: 278): Preclausal position signals the announcement, postclausal position the continuation of the relation between this referent – the addressee in case of the vocative – and the proposition. The correlation of the position of vocatives and their contribution to interpretation is also pointed out by Stetter (this volume).[4]

The close link between pragmatic function and syntactic status of vocatives is also emphasized by Stavrou (ms) and Hill (this volume). Stavrou argues that, in order to properly account for the vocative, the pragmatic factors that trigger its usage have to be considered, as well as "the syntactic environment and constraints that determine its integration into the clause" (ms: 1). The pragmatic aspects of vocatives relevant for syntax consist of their speech act character, which Stavrou (ms: 10) captures by embedding the vocative into a pragmatically oriented category 'Speech Act Phrase [+addressee]' (ms: 30; cf. also Hill 2007). The speech act character is also emphasised by Janson (this volume), who argues that 'vocatives' are ways of marking the utterance type 'call'. If marked within the NP, this marking may interfere with morphological case marking in the relevant language. If there is no specific marking within the noun phrase, calls are signalled by intonation.

Because of their addressing function, vocatives are put in close relation to imperatives (cf. also the discussion on Georgian in Abuladze and Ludden, this volume). Referring to this function, Jakobson (1971: 10) regards both the vocative and the imperative as being positioned outside the 'grammatical sentence' and the 'other verbal categories'. Both are to be classified as 'vocative sentences' which also share the same intonation:

Die Sprachwissenschaft hat eingesehen, dass der Vokativ sich nicht auf derselben Ebene befindet, wie die übrigen Kasus, und dass die vokativische
Anrede ausserhalb des grammatischen Satzes steht; ebenso ist der echte Imperativ von den übrigen verbalen Kategorien abzusondern, da er durch dieselbe Funktion wie der Vokativ gekennzeichnet ist. Der Imperativ darf nicht
syntaktisch als prädikative Form behandelt werden: die imperativen Sätze
sind, gleich der Anrede, volle und zugleich unzerlegbare 'vokativische ein-
teilige Sätze', und auch ihre Intonation ist ähnlich.

[Linguistic research has accepted that the vocative is not located on the
same level as the other cases and that the vocative address is situated outside the grammatical sentence; furthermore, the true imperative has to be
separated from the other verbal categories, because it is characterised by the
same function as the vocative. The imperative is not to be treated as a predicative complement form: imperative sentences are, just like addresses,
complete and, at the same time, indecomposable 'vocativic unitary sentences'; in addition, vocatives and imperatives have similar intonational
properties.]

Jakobson's argumentation seems to suggest an analysis of vocatives and
imperatives in terms of sentence mode. Another common feature of vocatives and imperatives pointed out by Jakobson (1971: 10–11) is their being
reduced to the word-stem in Russian, cf. *Maš!* (voc). vs. *Maša* (nom.) and
prostit' 'to pardon', *prošču* 'I pardon' vs. *prosti!* 'pardon me' (imperative).

The functional resemblance between vocatives and imperatives is also
taken as a basis for questioning the traditional parts of speech categorisation for vocative nouns. An extreme position is adopted by Fink (1972),
who regards the vocative "as a form for person rather than a case" (1972:
67). Accordingly, he draws up a paradigm accommodating "the double
function of the vocative as a noun form having person" (1972: 67), with the
vocative as second, and the nominative as first and third person, both in the
singular and in the plural (1972: 68; cf. also Kempgen forthc.). In this
sense, vocatives seem to contradict the traditional assumptions regarding
parts of speech since they are neither clearly 'nouns' (as case marked NPs)
nor 'verbs' (as referring to a second person). Thus vocatives are sometimes
classified together with imperatives as belonging to a higher category of
'appellative' (cf. Jakobson above), or classified as a separate part of speech.

As regards parts of speech, vocatives are also interesting insofar as they
may develop into interjections or discourse markers. In Russian, the old
vocative forms were lost except for forms such as *bože* 'God!' or *gospodi*
'Lord!', which are nowadays used as parts of formulae or as interjections

(e.g. Daniël 2008: 443). Another example is *güey* (originally *buey* 'ox') in Mexican Spanish, which developed from an imprecation to a form of address among adolescents and is now used as a discourse marker (Kleinknecht, this volume).

As has become evident from the discussion in this section, even in approaches that focus mainly on vocative forms, vocative functions are intimately connected to the analyses. Just like the form of vocatives, the question of vocative functions is approached from various perspectives.

3. Vocative function

Vocatives can be approached from an explicitly functional point of view, dealing with e.g. evaluation, expressivity (and its loss) as well as discourse functions. Special attention is paid to proper names and their being used as vocatives, and the connotations that arise with their interpretation. These functions manifest themselves in usage only, that is, they can be considered pragmatic aspects of the vocative.[5]

3.1. Calls and addresses

Zwicky (1974: 787) distinguishes two functions of vocatives: calls and addresses. Based on their position within the sentence, further subtypes of vocatives can be added; Portner (2007), for instance, classifies tags as sentence-final vocatives. Calls and addresses, the two main types recognized in the literature, differ in that "calls are designed to catch the addressee's attention, addresses to maintain or emphasize the contact between speaker and addressee", as Zwicky (1974: 787) illustrates with *hey lady* in *Hey lady, you dropped your piano* (call) and *sir* in *I'm afraid, sir, that my coyote is nibbling on your leg* (address). The address function can be regarded as more general than the call function, since "all address forms are usable as calls" (Zwicky 1974: 791). By 'address form' Zwicky understands specific NPs that may appear in a position other than the beginning of the sentence (this would be the position for calls). The notion of 'address forms' thus implicitly suggests some inherent or formal feature which unambiguously and context-independently marks specific forms as 'addresses'. Yet Zwicky regards address and call as two functions of the vocative that are distinguished in terms of position.

Hock (2006) shows the relevance of Zwicky's distinction on a speech act theoretic basis (monologue vs. dialogue) and proposes correlations between the pragmatic and the morphological level in languages that have morphological vocative marking. His hypothesis is that morphological vocative marking could serve as a touchstone for Zwicky's generalisation that all addresses can be used as calls. In languages that mark the vocative morphologically, this form is used for both calls and addresses. However, in some cases the nominative may be used instead of the vocative. Hock (2006) presumes that this is related to the distinction between calls and addresses. He argues that, with calls, the appellative character might be too strong to allow for a substitution by the nominative, whereas with addresses, either the gestural (appellative) or the symbolic (characterizing) use may be more important and hence both vocative and nominative could be used. And indeed, this assumption seems to be corroborated by Greek and Church Slavonic (Hock 2007), where the distinction between call and address is not so much one of intonation or position, but rather indicated by a difference in case.

Calls and addresses are vocative functions that in some way nominate the addressee (either by establishing contact or qualifying the addressee). Another function postulated in the literature (cf. Ivanova and Nicolova 1995: 24–29) is the mere reference function, which is carried out by vocative particles such as *hey* in English or *be* in Bulgarian (cf. Greenberg 1996 on appellative particles in Balkan Slavic).

3.2. Expressivity

Vocatives not only share their syntactic non-integration with parenthetical structures. In addition, the semantic contribution of both parentheticals and vocatives to the sentence and utterance meaning remains an open question. For parentheticals, the assumption that they do not contribute to the truth conditions and, hence, the overall sentence meaning is being challenged (cf. the argumentation in Asher 2000). The same holds for vocatives. Predelli (2008) shows that even if vocatives do not contribute to truth conditions, since "the addressee's identity does not affect the truth conditions of the uttered sentence" (2008: 98), their presence – i.e. their being used – does matter (for the relevance of being used cf. Hinrichs 1986 on parentheticals). Predelli's solution for vocatives is to categorize them as expressive expressions which are characterized by a specific contextual bias, i.e. their meaning is provided "by criteria relevant for the identification of the class of non-defective [contextually appropriate, the authors] uses" (2008: 103). In this sense, vocatives primarily make a pragmatic contribution to the inter-pretation. This expressive and pragmatic nature of vocatives is also em-phasized by Portner (2004, 2007), who relates vocatives to other structures such as parentheticals, appositions and topics. All of those structures can be analysed as 'separate performatives'. These performatives do not contribute to the semantic content proper, but rather give explicit instructions as to how this content has to be processed. The vocative encodes the information to whom the sentence is addressed. Accordingly, the expressive meaning of *John* as in *What are you doing, John?* can be paraphrased as 'I hereby re-iterate that John is my addressee', and the expressive meaning of *my lord* in *I don't know, my lord, if we have any potted meat in the house* has the ad-ditional separate performative interpretation 'I hereby address you as 'my lord''. Thus vocatives involve a description, which is why only address terms are felicitous here (Portner 2007: 10). The question remains how address terms can be identified, if not by testing their being felicitous in this specific context. The most unambiguous address forms are probably those that are already conventionalized and constitute the system of address for one specific language (on systems of address in the Slavonic languages cf. Betsch and Berger 2009).

The question remains as to where the expressive, separate performative meaning comes from. Portner (2007: 9) relates it to intonation, which he considers more relevant in this respect than syntactic position: "It's difficult to figure out whether the meaning of calls is associated with their intona-tion or their syntactic position. I will assume that the meaning ultimately comes from intonation, and that position plays a role only indirectly." Ac-tually, this seems to be the main issue involved in dealing with vocatives and their function: If there is no morphological marking, intonation can signal the vocative use of certain structures (cf. section 2.2.).

Besides the sense pointed out above, there is another sense in which vocatives relate to expressivity. This is not connected to the fact of them being used, but relates to expressivity ascribed to their lexical content (cf. Kleinknecht on lexical change from interpersonal to discourse level in Mexican Spanish, this volume), their morphological marking (cf. Girvin on the development of connotations related to morphological vocative marking in Bulgarian, this volume) or their internal make-up (cf. d'Avis and Mei-bauer on a syntagmatic vocative construction in German and Swedish, this volume).

4. Between system and performance

As the previous discussion on the status of the vocative has revealed, there are a number of classification problems associated with the vocative. These problems are attributed here mainly to the underlying assumption of 'paradigm'. Usually, the vocative is categorized within a specific paradigm, be it morphological (case), prosodic (intonation), or pragmatic (speech act). The importance of paradigms for the classification of vocatives can partly be attributed to the still prevailing tradition of classical, i.e. Greek and Latin, grammar (on this tradition cf. also Donati, this volume). This becomes evident, e.g., with Kiparsky's (1967: 39–40) statement that even though the vocative might not be a case 'in the traditional sense', it nonetheless belongs to the morphological system. He justifies this assumption by pointing out the – alleged – pedagogical advantage by remaining within the paradigm of classical grammar: "Schon pädagogische Rücksichten [...] verlangen die Behandlung des Vokativs an seiner in der traditionellen Grammatik üblichen Stelle." (1967: 39–40) [Even pedagogical considerations [...] call for treating the vocative in its usual place in traditional grammars.]

The preference for paradigmatic approaches might also be related to the alleged alternative: Paradigmaticity is a feature of the language system. Hence, if the vocative is not part of some paradigm, it is not always regarded as part of the language system, but as a phenomenon of language use. When the vocative is regarded as a phenomenon that manifests itself in language usage only, it can be excluded from grammatical reasoning, depending on the theoretical framework. This seems to be substantiated by the 'exceptional' nature of vocatives: They do not fit into the syntactic or prosodic patterns expected – they are non-integrated. However, even though vocatives contradict the traditional assumption of 'system' by being instantiated in language use only and by their non-integrated status, they are not just performance phenomena. This is indicated by two observations: First, they are morphologically and/or prosodically marked; this signals their non-integration, which again is functionally interpreted. Second, they show specific patterns in usage and interpretation (cf., e.g., the correlation between position and interpretation) that contradict assumptions of vocatives as mere ad hoc devices.

Vocatives, thus, seem to occupy a position between 'language system' and 'language use'. Therefore, the complexity of the issues involved in vocative studies is directly linked to the central concepts of 'language system' vs. 'performance'. The issue relates not only to the classification of vocatives as such, but also to the way they are approached from a language theoretical perspective. It is for this reason that a usage-based analysis of vocatives questions deeply entrenched linguistic concepts, such as the division of system and performance and their strict separation. Being recognizable only online, i.e. in the actual context of language production, vocatives challenge the separate treatment of language as a system and language as performance. Vocatives belong to a type of category which cannot be defined cross-linguistically in terms of paradigms (unlike, e.g., verbs or accusative objects), but which are syntagmatic in nature. The peculiar properties of syntagmatic categories still needs to be investigated in detail, the main difficulty being that they cannot be captured extensionally, since they do not constitute a closed class (cf. Noel Aziz Hanna and Sonnenhauser, this volume).

The answers given by various theoretical frameworks concerning categories between system and performance contribute to a larger current discussion. Recently, language usage has been focused on within connectionist models, theories on entrenchment, and usage-based models. At the other side of the system vs. performance spectrum, there is the ongoing innateness debate, and the notions of underlying structures. As syntagmatic, performance-based categories, vocatives are a testing case for these positions and are suitable for assessing the limits of both traditional and more recent approaches.

5. To sum up

As this short introduction has illustrated, the main problem in discussing the 'vocative' is the separation of levels – form vs. function and the subsystems of prosody, morphology, syntax, semantics, and pragmatics – as well as the differing assumptions about the structures constituting the object of observation – morphology only, or syntactic structures such as NPs, clauses, sentences or utterances, and the contribution of prosodic signalling. There is no consensus on their structure and no consensus on how to encompass vocative structure within a cross-linguistic approach. Nevertheless, the address function of vocatives is undisputed.

Furthermore, this discussion has shown that it is very doubtful whether the vocative can indeed be investigated by focussing only on one of its aspects. Quite the contrary: Vocatives need to be seen as phenomena which cannot be assigned to only one linguistic subsystem, and thus also challenge modular conceptions of language structure. Furthermore, vocatives are among the phenomena that challenge the theoretical construct of 'system' vs. 'performance' in a number of ways: They contradict the assumption of language being a 'system', because they are instantiated in language use only. They are not just performance phenomena, since they can be morphologically, prosodically, and syntactically encoded; the interaction of linguistic subsystems by which vocatives are signalled is language-specific. They are not necessarily integrated into a syntactic structure but still exhibit restrictions on syntactic position. They show specific patterns in usage and interpretation that contradict assumptions of vocatives as mere ad hoc devices.

It has been demonstrated that there is more than one reason for the neglect of vocatives in the linguistic literature. It is their 'oscillating' quality which is the reason for the onomasiological approach taken in *Vocative! Addressing between system and performance.*

Notes

*   We would like to thank the anonymous reviewers for their comments as well as William Tayler for his assistance in improving the English text.

1. The argumentation in Daniël' (2008: 445–446) seems to point into the same direction. Daniël' observes that in Russian, proper names, kinship terms, and specific common nouns (of the type *doctor*) hardly combine with vocative particles such as *ej* 'hey' or *ej ty* 'hey you'. When used together, the address receives some very specific interpretation, 'close to citation or imitation of some other's point of view'. He ascribes these effects to an inherent 'appellative potential' which precludes these lexemes from being used with further explicit appellative markers.

2. Delbrück (1883: § 62), for instance, who refers to Pāṇini, states that the nominative was not understood as subject case, but as a stem in Sanskrit grammar. The difference between nominative and vocative is that the latter is used for calls.

3. One example of the fusion of case form and case function is Lewis' (2000: 33–34) treatment of the vocative as one of the functions of the absolute case. The absolute case is "[t]he simplest form of a noun, with no suffixes", which "is used not only for the nominative and vocative, but also for the indefinite accusative" (2000: 26).

4. The same correlation between position and interpretation can be observed for parentheticals (cf. Noel Aziz Hanna 2009, Noel Aziz Hanna and Sonnenhauser forthc.). This can be taken as an argument for subsuming detached topic-NPs, vocatives and parentheticals – as well as further structures, such as citations – under one functional category. Noel Aziz Hanna and Sonnenhauser

(this volume) suggest 'functional performance structure' as a superordinate term.

5. This kind of context-dependency is independent of the type of vocative marking; it arises no matter whether the vocative is recognised because of its morphological marking or because a specific structure is contextually, i.e. in usage, identified as a vocative. Only vocatives that are recognized as such can receive one of the functions (e.g. call, address) and interpretations (expressivity).

References

Abuladze, Lia and Andreas Ludden
   this vol.   The vocative in Georgian.
Anstatt, Tanja
   2008   Der slavische Vokative im europäischen Kontext. In *Linguistische Beiträge zur Slavistik. XIV JungslavistInnen-Treffen in Stuttgart, 15.-18. September 2005*, Ljudmila Geist and Grit Mehlhorn (eds.), 9–26. München: Sagner.
Ashdowne, Richard
   2002   The vocative's calling? The syntax of address in Latin. In *Oxford University Working Papers in Linguistics, Philology and Phonetics*. Vol. 7, 143–161, Ina Hartmann and Andreas Willi (eds.). Oxford: Oxford University.
Asher, Nicholas
   2000   Truth conditional discourse semantics for parentheticals. *Journal of Semantics* 17: 31–59.
Betsch, Michael and Tilman Berger
   2009   Anredesysteme. In *Die slavischen Sprachen. Ein internationales Handbuch zu ihrer Struktur, ihrer Geschichte und ihrer Erforschung*, Sebastian Kempgen, Peter Kosta, Tilman Berger, and Karl Gutschmidt (eds.), 1019–1028. Berlin: de Gruyter.
Blake, Barry J.
   2001   *Case*. Cambridge: Cambridge University Press.
D'Avis, Franz and Jörg Meibauer
   this vol.   *Du Idiot! Din idiot!* Pseudo-vocative constructions and insults in German (and Swedish).
Danièl', Michael, A.
   2008   Zvatel'nost' kak diskursivnaja kategorija. Neskol'ko gipotez. In *Grammatičeskie kategorii v diskurse*, Valentin Ju. Gusev, Vladimir A. Plugnjan, and Anna Ju. Urmančieva (eds.), 439–466. (Issledovanija po teorii grammatiki 4.) Moskva: Gnozis.

Daniel, Michael and Andrew Spencer.
 2009   The vocative – an outlier case. In *The Oxford Handbook of Case*, Andrej Malchukov and Andrew Spencer (eds.), 626–634. Oxford: Oxford University Press.

Delbrück, Berthold
 1893   *Vergleichende Syntax der indogermanischen Sprachen. Erster Teil*. Strassburg: Trübner.

Donati, Margherita
 this vol. The vocative case between system and asymmetry.

Espinal, Teresa
 1991   The representation of disjunct constituents. *Language* 67: 726–762.

Espinal, Teresa
 this vol. On the structure of vocatives.

Fink, Robert O.
 1972   Person in nouns: is the vocative a case? *The American Journal of Philology* 93: 61–68.

Floricic, Franck
 2002   La morphologie du vocatif: l'exemple du sarde. *Vox Romanica* 61: 151–177.

Girvin, Cameron
 this vol. Addressing changes in the Bulgarian vocative.

Göksel, Aslı and Markus Pöchtrager
 this vol. The vocative and its kin: marking function through prosody.

Greenberg, Robert D.
 1996   *The Balkan Slavic Appellative*. München: Lincom.

Gussenhoven, Carlos
 1993   The Dutch foot and the chanted call. *Journal of Linguistics* 29: 37–63.

Haspelmath, Martin
 2009   The terminology of case. In *The Oxford Handbook of Case,* Andrej Malchukov and Andrew Spencer (eds.), 505–517. Oxford: Oxford University Press.

Hill, Virginia
 2007   Vocatives and the pragmatics–syntax interface. *Lingua* 117: 2077–2105.

Hill, Virginia
 this vol. Features and strategies: The internal syntax of vocative phrases.

Hinrichs, Uwe
 1986   Die Parenthese im Slavischen. In *Festschrift für Herbert Bräuer zum 65. Geburtstag*, Reinhold Olesch and Hans Rothe (eds.), 125–143. Köln: Böhlau.

Hjelmslev, Louis
1935   *La Catégorie des Cas.* München: Fink.
Hock, Wolfgang
2006   Kann jede Anrede auch ein Anruf sein? In *Between 40 and 60 Puzzles for Krifka,* Hans-Martin Gärtner, Sigrid Beck, Regine Eckardt, Renate Musan, and Barbara Stiebels (eds.), Berlin. http://www.zas.gwz-berlin.de/fileadmin/material/40-60-puzzles-for-krifka/pdf/hock.pdf, 07.02.2012.
Hock, Wolfgang
2007   Das große *O!* Omega bei Anruf, Anrede und Ausruf im nach-klassischen Griechisch und im Kirchenslavischen. In *Darъ slovesьny. Festschrift für Christoph Koch zum 65. Geburtstag,* Wolfgang Hock and Michael Meier-Brügger (eds.), 135–153. München: Sagner.
Isačenko, Alexander
1962   *Die russische Sprache der Gegenwart. Formenlehre.* München: Hueber.
Ivanova, K. and Ruselina Nicolova
1995   *Nie, govoreštite chora.* Sofia: Sveti Kliment Ochridski.
Jacobs, Joachim
1994   *Kontra Valenz.* Trier: Wissenschaftlicher Verlag.
Jakobson, Roman
1971   Zur Struktur des russischen Verbums. *Roman Jakobson, Selected Writings. Vol. II,* 3–15. The Hague: Mouton.
Janson, Tore
this vol.   Vocative and the grammar of calls.
Kempgen, Sebastian
forthc.   Bože moj - der Vokativ ist ja gar kein Kasus! Forthcoming 2013 in *Slavistische Linguistik 2011.*
Kiparsky, Valentin
1967   *Russische historische Grammatik.* Vol 2. *Die Entwicklung des Formensystems.* Heidelberg: Winter.
Kleinknecht, Friederike
this vol.   Mexican *güey* – from vocative to discourse marker. A case of grammaticalization?
Kottum, Steinar E.
1983   In defense of the vocative: The case of modern Polish. *Scando-Slavica* 29, 135–142.
Ladd, Dwight Robert
2008   *Intonational Phonology.* Cambridge: Cambridge University Press.

Lambrecht, Knud
    1996   On the formal and functional relationship between topics and vocatives. Evidence from French. In *Conceptual Structure, Discourse and Language*, Adele Goldberg (ed.), 267–288. Stanford: CSLI Publications.

Levison, Stephen
    1983   *Pragmatics*. Cambridge: Cambridge University Press.

Lewis, Geoffrey
    2000   *Turkisch Grammar*. Second Edition. Oxford: Oxford University Press.

Longobardi, Giuseppe
    1994   Reference and proper names. *Linguistic Inquiry* 25: 609–666.

Mel'čuk, I. A.
    1986   Toward a definition of case. In *Case in Slavic*, Richard D. Brecht and James Levine (eds.), 35–85. Columbus: Slavica Publishers.

Noel Aziz Hanna, Patrizia
    2009   Der Wackernagelkomplex im Deutschen: Zur Interaktion der linguistischen Subsysteme Phonologie, Syntax und Informationsstruktur. Habilitationsschrift, University of Munich.

Noel Aziz Hanna, Patrizia
    2011   Vocativ im Deutschen? Paper given at the University of Vienna.

Noel Aziz Hanna, Patrizia and Barbara Sonnenhauser
    forthc.   Verschriftlichung zwischen System und Rede. Zur interpunktorischen Kodierung von funktionalen Performanzstrukturen. Forthcoming 2013 in *Sprachwissenschaft*.

Noel Aziz Hanna, Patrizia and Barbara Sonnenhauser
    this vol.   Vocatives as functional performance structures.

Osenova, Petja and Kiril Simov
    2002   *Bulgarian vocative within HPSG framework*.
            http://www.bultreebank.org/papers/ bgvocativeOS.pdf, 18.10.2011

Portner, Paul
    2004   Vocatives, topics, and imperatives. Paper given at the *IMS Workshop on Information Structure*. Bad Teinach.
            http://www9.georgetown.edu/faculty/portnerp/my_papers/ Stuttgart_handout.pdf, 18.10.2011.

Portner, Paul
    2007   Instructions for interpretation as separate performatives. In *On Information Structure, Meaning and Form*, Kerstin Schwabe and Susanne Winkler (eds.), 407–426. Amsterdam, Philadelphia: Benjamins.

Predelli, Stefano
    2008   Vocatives. *Analysis* 68 (2): 97–105.

Qvonje, Jørn Ivar
    1986   *Über den Vokativ und die Vokativformen in den Balkansprachen und im europäischen Sprachareal*. Copenhagen: Dep. of Modern Greek and Balkan Studies, Univ. of Copenhagen.

Schaden, Gerhard
    2010   Vocatives: a note on addressee-management. *University of Pennsylvania Working Papers in Linguistics* 16 (1): 176–185. http://repository.upenn.edu/pwpl/vol16/iss1/20, 18.10.2011.

Schooneveld, Cornelis H. van.
    1986   Is the vocative a case? Jørgen D. Johansen and Harly Sonne (eds.). *Pragmatics and Linguistics. Festschrift for Jacob L. Mey*. Odense: Odense University Press, 179–186.

Skalička, Vladimír
    1994   On case theory. In *Praguiana 1945-1990*, Philip A. Luelsdorff (ed.), 45–70. Amsterdam: Benjamins.

Stavrou, Melita
    Ms.   About the vocative phrase.

Stetter, Christian
    this vol.   On the case of the vocative.

Stifter, David
    this vol.   Vocative for nominative.

Vairel, Helene
    1981   The position of the vocative in the Latin case system. *The American Journal of Philology* 102 (4): 438–447.

Varga, Lázló
    2008   The calling contour in Hungarian and English. *Phonology* 25: 469–497.

Zimmer, Karl E.
    1970   Some observations on non-final stress in Turkish. *The American Oriental Society* 90: 160–162.

Zwicky, Arnold
    1974   "Hey, Whatsyourname". In *Papers from the Tenth Regional Meeting, Chicago Linguistic Society. April 19-21, 1974*, Michael La Galy, Robert A. Fox, and Anthony Bruck (eds.), 787–801. Chicago: Chicago Linguistic Society.

The vocative in Georgian

Lia Abuladze and Andreas Ludden

Abstract

As the title indicates, this paper presents the vocative markers of nouns, adjectives and pronouns as well as different forms of address in modern Georgian. The authors analyze in detail kinship terms and their vocative cases as well as other forms of address, paying special attention to truncated and inverse forms of address and their functions. They emphasize the affective role which these forms play in communication between speaker and hearer, especially when interlocutors are representatives of different generations. The authors also shortly discuss the position of vocative and address forms in sample sentences and the types of clauses with which they occur, designating the close connection between vocative and imperative. Simultaneously, they provide evidence for the assumption that Georgian has, like some other languages, 3rd person imperatives too, but leave this question for future investigation.

1. Introduction

All our speech acts are explicitly or implicitly directed to somebody (the recipient), i.e. they suppose an addressee. Some languages have special forms of address, and among these forms the vocative case plays a leading role. It names the addressee explicitly, by using a noun referring to him, her or it.

There are different opinions on the vocative in linguistics, and not all linguists regard this form of a noun as a case (Trubezkoj 1937; Hjelmslev 1972). This problem has also been discussed in Georgian linguistics (Topuria 1956; Šanidze 1956; Oniani 1987).

1.1. Vocative markers in Georgian

From a purely morphological point of view the vocative in Georgian is a case, because it has its own forms, namely the following:

(1)   *-o* after consonant-final stems of common nouns:

nominative	vocative		
k'ac-i	*k'ac-o*[1]	'man',	'human being'
kal-i	*kal-o*	'woman'	
bat'on-i	*bat'on-o*	'sir',	'master'
kalbat'on-i	*kalbat'on-o*	'Mrs',	'mistress'

The vocative marker of monosyllabic nouns whose stems end in the vowels *-a* or *-e* is also *-o*, whereas in the case of polysyllabic stems the vocative suffix *-o* is reduced to *-v*:

(2)

nominative	vocative	
da	*da-o*	'sister'
mze	*mze-o*	'sun'
ocneba	*ocneba*, ocneba-v*	'dream'
mebaǧe	*mebaǧe*, mebaǧe-v*	'gardener'

*These forms occur chiefly in colloquial Georgian

There are also some exceptions, mostly in poetry, in which the vocative of a polysyllabic noun may have a suffix *-o*, e.g. in the case of the above-mentioned noun *ocneba* in Galaktion Tabidze's poem *Tetri pelik'ani* ('The white Pelican'):

(3)   *ocneba-o   čem-o   dzvel-o,   v-ar   ǧame-ta   mteveli...*
      dream-VOC   my-VOC   old-VOC   1S-be   night-GEN.PL   awake
      'My old dream, I am awake overnight... '

Children sometimes use the vocative marker *-o* instead of the stem final vowel *-a*; they drop the final vowel *-a* and use the vocative suffix *-o* in its place as if the stem of the noun ended in a consonant, e.g. in the word *mankana*: nom. *mankana*, voc. *mankan-o* 'car' (cf. nom. *burt-i*, voc. *burt-o* 'ball').

The vocative of monosyllabic as well as polysyllabic nouns whose stems end in the vowels *-o*, *-u* and *-i*[2] today is likely not to have any suffix at all (so the nominative and the vocative are identical), or very rarely *-o* (if the stem is monosyllabic: nom. *qru*, voc. *qru-o* 'deaf') or *-v* (if the stem is polysyllabic: nom. *samšoblo*, voc. *samšoblo-v* 'native country').

The plural suffix in Georgian is *-eb-*; in Old Georgian it was *-n-*, which sometimes is still in use today. Both plural forms have the suffix *-o* in the vocative: *bavšv-eb-o* 'children', *xalx-n-o* 'people'.

In Old Georgian the nominative sometimes fulfilled the function of the vocative, too. In his grammar of Old Georgian, Fähnrich (1994: 184) gives numerous relevant examples, among them

(4) *sul-i*   *ege* *arac'mida-j,* *gan-ved*   *k'ac-isa* *mag-isgan!*
     spirit-NOM this   impure-NOM PREV-go.away.IMP man-GEN that-from
     'Impure spirit! Go away from that man!'

1.2. The vocative of proper nouns

In the case of proper nouns there is a difference between geographical and personal names. The vocative of geographical names whose stems end in a consonant has the suffix *-o* (*tbilis-o*), whereas that of the first names of persons has no suffix at all (*tamar!*, *guram!*, *nodar!*), so the names appear in the form of the bare stem, and that of surnames ending in consonants has *-o* or *-i* (as in the nominative): *cagarel-o!* or *cagarel-i!*, *iašvil-o!* or *iašvil-i!*. When a name ends in a vowel, there is no difference between the nominative and vocative cases, both these cases appear in the form of the bare stem: *nana* (NOM), *nana* (VOC); *elene* (NOM), *elene* (VOC); *dodo* (NOM), *dodo* (VOC); *giorgi* (NOM), *giorgi* (VOC); *irakli* (NOM), *irakli* (VOC). Unlike common nouns the first names of persons often have stems ending in *-i*: *lali*, *dali*, *k'axi*, etc.

Sometimes the vocative of a first name with consonant-final stems also has the suffix *-i* or *-o*: *levan-i!*, *temur-i!* and *otar-o!*, *merab-o!*, particularly in the Western dialects of Georgian. In some Eastern mountain dialects first names ending in the vowel *-a* obtain the suffix *-u* or *-v* in the vocative: *matia-u!*, *matia-v!* (Apridonidze 2001: 23).

Truncation is widespread in first names: *giorgi* > *gio*, *gia*; *nik'oloz* > *nik'o*, *nik'a*; *guram* > *guri*, *guro*; *vaxt'ang* > *vaxo*, *vat'o*; *ketevan* > *keto*, *keti*, *keta*; *ek'at'erine* > *ek'a*, *ek'o*; *aleksandre* > *alek'o*, *ale*. All these truncated forms are not only used for addressing someone, but also in other cases. When used for addressing somebody, first names often have the diminutive suffixes *-ik'o* or *-una*: *tinik'o!* (from *tina*), *zurik'o!* (from *zurab*), *datuna!* (from *david*), *tamuna!* (from *tamar*); these forms also occur in other cases.

There is a specific form of addressing a person in the Mokhevian dialect – the first name with the suffix *-is-i* (*maqvala-is-i*, *onise-is-i*). This suffix consists of the genitive case marker *-is* + the nominative suffix *-i*. Some linguists (Apridonidze 1991) regard this *-i* as an emphatic vowel. According to Apridonidze (1991: 143) *maqvalaisi* < *maqvalais gaxarebam* 'Maqvala's joy (ERG)' is "a case of the substantivization of the genitive modifier with the loss of the modified noun". Substantivization of a consonant-final stem (*Maqvalais*), however, needs the ending *-i* to mark the nominative, so this final *-i* is not, as Apridonidze states, an emphatic vowel, but the marker of the nominative case.

Geographical names with stems ending in a vowel have no suffixes in the vocative, or very rarely *-v* (*ač'ara, ač'ara-v; sačxere, sačxere-v*). The suffix *-o* is an exception, e.g. in the poem *Sxva sakartvelo sad aris?* ('Where is another Georgia?') by Ana Kalandadze:

(5) *sakartvelo-o   lamaz-o,   sxva   sakartvelo   sad   ari-s...*
     Georgia-VOC beautiful-VOC other Georgia.NOM where be-3S
     'Oh, beautiful Georgia! Where is another Georgia...'

1.3. The vocative forms of adjectives and pronouns

The vocative forms of adjectives have the same suffixes as those of nouns. Like nouns, their stems may end either in consonants or in vowels. Attributive adjectives with stems ending in vowels, which usually precede the noun, never change according to case or number, whereas the vocative of adjectives with stems ending in consonants has the suffix *-o*. Numerals have no vocative suffix at all.[3] As regards possessive pronouns, there are the following peculiarities: Only 1st person pronouns have vocative suffixes: *čem-o* 'my!', *čven-o* 'our!' The possessive pronoun of the 2nd person (pl.) *tkveni* 'your' has a vocative suffix only in such expressions as *tkven-o udidebulesoba-v* 'your Highness!', *tkven-o ağmatebuleba-v* 'your Eminence!', *tkven-o uc'mindesoba-v* 'your Holiness!'; these are all calques from Russian.

The personal pronouns of the 2nd person *šen* 'you' (sg.) and *tkven* 'you' (pl.) have the vocative forms *šen* and *še, tkven* and *tkve* respectively. The short forms (*še* and *tkve*) are used only with adjectives or nouns: *še sac'qalo* 'you poor one!', *še sulel-o* 'you silly one!', *še vir-o* 'you ass!', *tkve oxreb-o* 'you rascals!'. Cases like these can be regarded as extended uses of the vocative. It has to be mentioned that the adjectives and nouns in these expressions almost always have a negative (pejorative) connotation.

A sequence consisting of a noun preceded by the vocative *še* may obtain a stylistic effect, as for instance in the well-known Georgian film *Džarisk'acis mama* ('The Father of a Soldier', 1964). The hero of this film, an old Georgian peasant, sees a vine on the battlefield and addresses it saying *še* but then instead of using the pejorative expression for which the audience is probably waiting, uses a positive one: *madlian-o* 'good, noble', so that this expression obtains the effect of unexpectedness and becomes highly impressive. The pronouns *šen* and *tkven* are also used for addressing people, but these forms of address are regarded as impolite. The personal pronouns of the 1st and 3rd persons have no vocative at all.[4] There is only one vocative form of the 3rd person, namely *imano!* (*ima-n-o* 3P.OBL-ERG-VOC = ergative case of the 3rd person + vocative suffix *-o* 'he-ERG-VOC'), which is used for addressing a person whose name is unknown to the speaker. It is used mostly in West Georgian dialects when the speaker does not know or does not remember the name of the person in question, and it is regarded as impolite.

1.4. Lexemes compatible with forms of address

Having considered the different forms of the vocative in Georgian, we should point out that not all nouns have the vocative case simply because not all referential nouns can be addressed. As Bonnenkamp (1971: 17) mentions, "the number of lexemes which can have vocative morphemes is smaller than the number of lexemes with nominative morphemes. The vocative case implies an 'appeal' and thus a person as the addressee of speech. The lexemes that have vocative morpheme include not only the names of persons, professional titles etc., but also other names which may be identified with persons".[5]

In theory, one could probably identify all nouns with persons, but it is certainly more common to address people (and animals) than inanimate objects. Besides the proper nouns or names of human beings, the vocative case in Georgian is used mostly in abstract nouns – e.g. *ocneba* 'dream', *siqvaruli* 'love', *sixaruli* 'joy' etc. (frequently when addressing children or beloved persons with the possessive pronoun *čemi*: *čem-o sixarul-o* 'my joy!', *čem-o siqvarul-o* 'my love!'); the names of celestial phenomena: *mze* 'sun', *mtvare* 'moon', *varsk'vlavi* 'star' (in the same contexts as above: *čem-o mze-o* 'my sun!', *čem-o mtvare-(v)* 'my moon!'); names of animals – *viri* 'ass', *dzaγli* 'dog', *lomi* 'lion', *arc'ivi* 'eagle' etc., which are very frequently used in the vocative form (*vir-o*, *arc'iv-o*) in fairy-tales and fables. In addition, certain concrete inanimate objects may also appear in the vocative case: *xmali* 'sabre', *supra* 'tablecloth', *xališa* 'carpet', *k'alami* 'pen' etc., or such nouns as *kari* 'wind', *kveqana* 'country', *samšoblo* 'native country', e.g. in Ilia Č'avč'avadze's (1987: 126, 155) famous poems *Čemo k'argo kveqanav* ('My good country') and *Čemo k'alamo* ('My pen'):

(6) *čem-o   k'arg-o   kveqana-v,   ra-zed   mo-gi-c'qenia?...*
    my-VOC   good-VOC   country-VOC what-on   PREV-2S-grieve
    'My good country, why are you so sad?'

(7) *čem-o   k'alam-o, čem-o   k'arg-o,   ra-d   gvi-nda   taš-i?*
    my-VOC   pen-VOC   my-VOC good-VOC, what-ADV   1S.PL-want applause-N(
    'My pen, my good one, why do we need applause?'

Here we have another example from the poem *C'qaltubodan Kutaisši*
('From Tsqaltubo to Kutaisi, 1956') by Galak't'ion Tabidze:

(8) *c'qaltubo-dan   kutais-ši   mimaval-o   kar-o,   tu mais-is*
    C'qaltubo-from   Kutaisi-to blowing-VOC   wind-VOC   if may-GEN
    kutais-ma   g-kitxo-s   vina x-aro...
    Kutaisi-ERG   2IO-ask-3S who 2S-be
    'Wind blowing from C'qaltubo to Kutaisi, if Kutaisi in May asks you
    who you are...'

1.5. The forms of address of kinship terms

The vocative case as well as other forms of address of Georgian kinship
terms are especially interesting. Terms as *deda* 'mother', *mama* 'father',
bebia, dideda 'grandmother', *babua, p'ap'a* 'grandfather' have no suffixes
in the vocative: *deda!,*[6] *mama!, bebia!, dideda!, babua!, p'ap'a!* But there
are other possible forms of address, too, e.g. *dedi!* or the truncated *de!,*
mami!, bebi!, beba!, bebo!, bebe! or the truncated *be!, babo!* (in Eastern
Georgia), *baba!, didi!* (truncated form of *dideda*), or *babu!*
    According to Šanidze (1955: 73) the forms *dedi* and *mami* originate
from *dedilo* and *mamilo*, in which *-il* is the diminutive suffix and *-o* the
marker of the vocative. Apridonidze (1991: 141) points out that we might
also regard *dedik'o* and *mamik'o* as the sources of *dedi* and *mami* because,
according to her, the form of address *švili!* originates from *švilik'o!* ('oh
child!') and is not the result of a contraction of the suffix *-ilo*. The form
*švililo does not exist at all. We think, however, that the source of *švili!* is
not necessarily *švilik'o* (see below). These affixes have certain dif-
ferentiating functions. *Dedi!* and *dedilo!* are often used when addressing
one's own mother or an elderly woman. The form of address *dedik'o!* or
the vocative *deda!* with no affix are used referring to one's own mother or
mother-in-law.
    We think that the forms *dedi, mami,* and *švili* are the results of the same
modifications that we also notice in forms as e.g. German *Mami* and *Papi*,

Vati in German children's language. We may add that the vocative form *bebi!* does not originate from *bebilo or *bebik'o*, which is extremely uncommon.

Furthermore, among all the above-mentioned forms of addressing, *dedi*, *mami* and *bebi* are exclusively forms of address, i.e. they can be used only for this purpose, whereas all other forms are also used as common nouns in other cases, e.g. *deda-m*, *deda-s* or *dedik'o-m*, *dedilo-s* but not *dedi-m, *dedi-s*:

(9) *me   v-c'er   c'eril-s   deda-s / dedik'o-s / dedilo-s (*dedi-s)*
    I   1S-write   letter-DAT mother-DAT
    'I'm writing a letter to (my) mother.'

(10) *mama-m/mamik'o-m/mamilo-m (*mami-m) gamo-mi-gzavn-a c'eril-i*
     father-ERG   PREV-1IO-sent-3S letter-NOM
     '(My) father sent me a letter.'

In colloquial Georgian the suffix *-i* instead of *-o* generally tends to mark the vocative case more and more frequently. We might name forms as *bič'-i!* 'boy!', which is synonymous with *bič'-o!*, and *gogon-i!* 'girl!', a synonym of *gogona!*. Considering the diminutive meaning of the suffixes *-un-a* and *-un-i-a*, we should not exclude that the vocative *gogon-i!* is a truncated form of *gogo-un-i-a > gog-on-i-a > gogon-i!*; nor that the vocative *bič'-i!* is a truncate form of *bič'-ik'-o > bič'-i!*. But we might also think of sound symbolism here, as the suffix *-i* mainly designates small objects.

As we mentioned before, *-ik'o*, as well as *-ilo*, are diminutive suffixes. Šanidze (1955: 73) thinks that in these suffixes the final vowel *-o* is a marker of the vocative case. The suffix *-ilo* is used only with the nouns *deda* (*dedilo*) and *mama* (*mamilo*) in Eastern Georgian dialects. Boeder (1985: 57) compares the vocative form *dzm-ob-il-o!* 'friend!' with *ded-il-o* and concludes that these words "can also be used in the nominative case without a vocative marker, retaining their hypocoristic suffix *-il-: dzmobil-i*".[7] We have to consider, however, that there is no such form as *dedil-i in Georgian, but there are nouns like *dobil-i* '(female) friend, a friend regarded as sister' (from *da* 'sister'), *dedobili* (from *deda*) 'adoptive mother', *mamobili* (from *mama*) 'adoptive father', or *švilobili* (from *švili*) 'adoptive child'. We think instead that the *-il-* in *dzmob-il-i* is a suffix indicating a past participle, as e.g. in *šob-il-i* 'born'. In Georgian there is the verb *idzmob-s* 'to make someone one's brother', so the *-il-* in *dzmobili* is no hypocoristic suffix, and the word *dzmobil-i* itself is not a derivative of *dzmobil-o*.

The nouns *deda* and *mama* have the vocative forms *deda-o* and *mama-o*, too, but in these cases the meanings of the nouns change: *deda-o* is a form of address for the Mother of God (cf. *deda-o ǧvtisa-v, mze-o mariam!* 'mother-VOC God.GEN-VOC, sun-VOC Mary!' (Galak't'ion Tabidze, from his poem *Silažvarde anu vardi silaši* 'The Azure or the Rose in the Sand') or a nun, *mama-o* is the form of address for a priest or a monk.

Boeder (1985: 57) notes that *deda!* can lose the status of a noun: "The categorial state of a 'noun' can be lost so only the pragmatic meaning associated with the original vocative remains. The Georgian word *deda*, for example, means 'mother', but *deda!* as an exclamation expresses dread, astonishment and the like."[8] We would like to add in this context that the word *genacvale*, a form of address that means approximately 'I would suffer/die in your place', changes to *genacva(t)* and is also used as an interjection expressing astonishment, e.g. *genacvat* (or *deda), es ra momxdara!* 'oh, what has happened!'. Moreover, the Georgian interjection *ka* is the truncated form of the vocative *kal-o* 'woman!' and expresses astonishment.

1.5.1. Inverse addresses

It is characteristic of Georgian kinship terms denoting members of the elder generation that their forms of address do not only have a straightforward meaning but also a reversed one: A woman, for example, can address her child (or any other young person) in two ways: *švil-o!, švil-i!* and *deda!* (the last one combined with various suffixes denoting affection). Apridonidze (1991: 137) calls this form of address an "expressive address" as opposed to the neutral address, i.e. the "direct appellative mention of the addressee". Boeder (1989: 12) speaks of "Vokativinversion" 'vocative inversion' or "reziproke" 'reciprocal' or "bipolare Anrede" 'bipolar address'. Other kinship terms that may have reversed meanings are *mama, bebi(a), babua, deida* 'aunt' ('mother's sister'), *(bi)dzia* 'uncle', *mamida* 'aunt' ('father's sister'), *bicola, dzalo,* and *dzalua* 'aunt' ('uncle's wife'). Here are some examples:

(11) *ra   gi-nda,   mama   (mamik'o),   ra   gi-qid-o?*
    what   2S-want   father.VOC   dad.VOC   what   2IO- buy-OPT
    'What do you want, father [addressing son, daughter or any other child], what shall I buy for you?'

(12) *bebi,   rodis   mo-x-val   čem-tan?*
    grandma.VOC   when   PREV-2S-come   me-to
    'Grandmother [addressing grandchild], when will you come to me?'

(13) *ra-s   ak'eteb,   deida,   ak?*
what-DAT 2S.do   aunt.VOC here
'What are you doing here, aunt [addressing nephew or niece or any other young person]?'

(14) *sad   mi-di-xar,   bidzik'o,   mart'o   am   sibnele-ši?*
where PREV-go-2S uncle-VOC alone   this darkness-in
'Where are you going, uncle [addressing nephew or niece or any other young person], alone in the darkness?'

(15) *mo-di   ak,   mamida,   rat'om m- e-malebi?*
PREV-2S.IMP.come here aunt.VOC why   1IO-R-hide.2S
'Come here, aunt [addressing nephew or niece], why are you hiding from me?'

(16) *ar ga-m-agon-o,   bicola,   šen-i   t'iril-i!*
not PREV-1IO-hear-OPT aunt.VOC your-NOM crying-NOM
'Don't let me hear you crying, aunt [addressing nephew or niece of husband]!'

Forms of address like these are characteristic of other languages, too, e.g. of Arabic in Jordan and Lebanon, of Albanian, Armenian, Bulgarian, Southern Italian etc. (Boeder 1989: 14; Braun 1985: 83). In Arabic, for example, a mother may address her son *jumma* 'mother', a grandfather may address his grandchild *dzeddi* 'my grandfather', and an uncle his nephew or any other young man *ammi* 'my uncle' (Braun 1985: 81–82). The similarity to Georgian is easily seen.

There are different points of view on these inverse addresses.[9] Some linguists (Ayoub 1964; Beyrer and Kostov 1978; Wills 1977) assume that parents teach their children parental words, use 'baby talk' or take on the role of the child aiming to obtain a symmetrical address and to achieve equality with the child by approximating the levels of adults and children to each other.

Apridonidze (1991: 138–139) explains the Georgian way of inverse addressing (which she calls 'self-address') as an ellipsis. The expression *deda g-e-nacval-o-s* > mother-NOM *g-2IO-e-R-nacval*-instead-of/*o*-OPT-*s*-3S 'the mother would suffer/die in place of her child', for example, is used very frequently. She writes (Apridonidze 1991: 138):

Yet, the Georgian way of self-address is specific and is reflected in the peculiarities of its grammatical structure, the polypersonalism of the Georgian verb being of considerable importance here. The realisation of the system of address in question becomes possible only through verbs of relative structure that is by omission of nouns of self-address. Ellipsed verbs are etymologically symptomatic: *genacvalos* and the verb designating a circular movement *šemogevlos*. Such verbal forms mark a relationship between the 2nd and the 3rd persons. Only the participation of the 3rd person could have the trace of parental words in the phraseological solution containing the noun and the verb.

Boeder (1989: 18), too, considers this idea as well as its counterarguments; he states that: 1) in Georgian, inverse forms of address are used only between members of different generations, but not within one generation although expressions like *da* 'sister', *genacvalos* or *dzma* 'brother' are possible; 2) the inverse forms of address sometimes have vocative forms, too, but an expression as **deda! genacvalos* is impossible. He concludes that the self-address in Georgian cannot be explained as ellipsis.

We should add that Georgians often use these inverse forms of address with diminutive suffixes such as *dedik'o*, *dedik'una* when they address children, whereas an expression as **dedik'o* (or *dedik'una*) *genacvalos* is unnatural.

We think that inverse forms of address are possible because the vocative case as well as other forms of address fulfill interpersonal functions maintaining relationships between the interlocutors.[10] As Braun (1985: 85) puts it,

> a form of address primarily signalizes that it is directed to an addressee. When we assume that effects like the identification of the addressee or the activation of her/his attention and suchlike are side effects which a form of address often is able to fulfill but not necessarily does so, then we see that the most important task of a form of address is to define the relationship between a speaker and a hearer.

So when a mother addresses her son, how can she designate their relationship? Probably the shortest way is to say simply – 'mother', which means that she is his mother, and at the same time this word, *deda* 'mother', expresses all the feelings that a mother usually has for her child.

The affection is an element of the relationship between the speaker and the hearer and probably an important one too. When a mother addresses her son or the grandmother addresses her grandchildren using the word *deda* 'mother' or *beba* 'grandmother' respectively, by using these forms of address they express their attitude towards them: the relation between mother and child or the relation between grandmother and children and at the same time their emotions, i.e. their love for them, and this applies not only to forms of address with diminutive suffixes, but to all of them. Boeder (1989: 13) is right when he writes that "it is quite natural to recognize that different motivations or circumstances may lead to reciprocal expressions".[11]

2. Vocative and imperative

Having discussed the vocative in Georgian we may summarize that it is marked morphologically (it has its own suffix -*o*, which sometimes will be reduced to -*v* or fully deleted). We have observed that first names and kinship terms often have a truncated vocative, and that almost all truncated forms end in the vowels -*o*, -*a*, or -*i*.

The position of a vocative (or any other form of address) in a Georgian sentence is by no means determined: it may come at the beginning of a clause, at its end or in the middle of it, i.e. interpolated into various points of a clause.[12] Vocatives in Georgian are typically separated from the rest of the clause by a break in the intonation, the so-called comma intonation, which means that they are isolated from other parts of the sentence; their reference is limited to the addressee. They occur with all types of clauses, and do not necessarily correspond to an argument.

The evaluation of clauses with vocative forms will invariably lead to the conclusion that vocatives are mostly found in imperative and interrogative clauses, but sometimes in declarative clauses too. In imperative clauses vocatives have to correspond to the subject, since they refer to the addressee and the subject of an imperative has to refer to, overlap with or quantify the set of addressees. This means that vocative and imperative are closely connected.

The close connection between vocative and imperative is widely discussed in linguistics. Jakobson (1971: 10–11) emphasizes the similarities between vocative and imperative.[13] He specifies these similarities as a result of a tendency to use only the bare stem and the capability to constitute a complete utterance without any other phrasal elements, and says that both share an appellative function ('Auslösungsfunktion'), as opposed to the representative function ('Darstellungsfunktion').

The similarities between vocative and imperative are discussed by other linguists, too, among them by Winter (1969) and Lomtatidze (1994). Their works both exclusively refer to the 2nd person as subject of the imperative, as the imperative can only be used for addressing somebody, so the subject of an imperative sentence has to be the 2nd person or addressee.

In Georgian the subject of an imperative clause is always interpreted as coinciding or overlapping with the set of addressees, e.g.:

(17) *gogo-eb-o,*   *dac'ere-t*   *savardžišo-eb-i!*
      girls-PL-VOC   PREV-write.IMP.2S-PL   exercise-PL-NOM
      'Girls, write the exercises!'

The vocative form *gogoebo* refers to the addressee, it is isolated from the component parts of the imperative clause, which contains no subject that refers to the 2nd person. This 2nd person, which here is mentioned implicitly, coincides with the set of addressees, i.e. in this sentence with *gogoebi* 'girls'.

As Lomtatidze (1994: 479) puts it, "the imperative mood is a category of the 2nd subjective person only" and "the main point of this problem is that the 2nd subjective personal marker disappears in the imperative mood […] e.g. Georgian *c'adi!* 'go!' (cf. indicative *c'a-x-vedi* PREV-2S-go 'you have gone')". To the question "What is the cause of the loss of the 2nd subjective personal marker in the imperative mood?" she answers that "since the imperative mood implies only the 2nd person, the interlocutor – who is present and visible – needs no general indicator" (Lomtatidze 1994: 480). In other words, the 2nd person pronoun (sg. or pl.) is the implied subject of any imperative sentence. Hence there is no distinct 2nd person pronoun or personal marker in the imperative clause. The verb *c'adi!* is the only one in Georgian that has a separate imperative form. All other verbs use the forms of the 2nd person in the aorist tense, e.g. *da-art'qi burt-s!* 'PREV-kick-2S the ball-DAT'. This example shows that an imperative clause does not require an overt subject. The subject is understood to be the addressee or the 2nd person, which can be confirmed when we insert the vocative: *bič'o* (VOC), *(šen) daart'qi burts!* 'boy, (you) kick the ball!'.

Moreover, the vocative marks the 2nd person only. Apridonidze (2001: 141) states that the vocative corresponds to the imperatives, which supposes a 2nd person, "but in reality the vocative form of the noun is substituted with the pronoun of the 3rd person"; this appears to be wrong, because when the speaker uses a noun in the vocative case, (s)he converts (transforms) it (whether it denotes a person or an animal or an inanimate object) into an addressee and the addressee can only be a 2nd person, i.e. it can only be substituted with *you* – the 2nd person pronoun. So both forms – the vocative case as well as the imperative mood – are substitutable by the 2nd person.

2.1. 3rd person imperatives

Recent studies show that there are exceptions to the generalization made in the preceding section. Some languages also have 3rd person imperatives. Georgian is one of them:

(18) *vinme-m*   *da-u-dzaxe-t*   *ekim-s!*
     someone-ERG   PREV-R-call.IMP.2S-PL   doctor-DAT
     'Someone call a doctor!'

(19) *bič'-eb-i*   *c'a-di-t*   *saxl-eb-ši,   gogo-eb-i   da-rči-t!*
     boy-PL-NOM   PREV-go.IMP.2S-PL   house-PL-in   girl-PL-NOM   PREV-stay.
                                                                 IMP.2S-PL
     'Boys go home, girls stay!' [boys and girls in the nominative case definitely are 3rd persons]

(20) *qvela-n-i*   *c'a-di-t*   *šin!*
     all-PL-NOM   PREV-go.IMP.2S-PL   home
     'Everybody go home!'

What is most interesting in these cases is that there is no agreement between subject (3rd person) and verb (2nd person). Such mismatches between syntax and morphology can also be seen in interrogative clauses, e.g.:

(21) *bič'-eb-i*   *mi-di-xar-t*   *saxl-ši*   *tu*   *gogo-eb-i?*
     boy-PL-NOM   PREV-go.2S-PL   house-in   or   girl-PL-NOM
     'Are the boys going home or the girls?'

(22) *qvela-m*   *še-a-srule-t*   *davaleba?*
     everybody-ERG   PREV-R-perform.2S-PL   homework-NOM
     'Has everybody done his homework?'

Boeder (2009) examined such cases in Kartvelian languages, yet imperatives are not the topic of his investigation.

We think that imperatives with a 3rd person subject are examples of an anaphoric 'mismatch' or ellipsis of the 2nd person, as in the above imperative:

(20) a. *(tkven)   qvela-n-i*   *c'a-di-t*   *šin!*
        (you)   all-PL-NOM   PREV-go.IMP.2S-PL   home
        'Everybody go home!'

But whether it is possible or not to explain all examples of imperatives with 3rd person subjects in such a way, is another question and really quite a different subject that deserves a separate investigation, so we will not discuss it now in detail.

We may point out, however, that though the vocative is syntactically different from the other cases, it still has a certain syntactic function, at least in imperative phrases, and can be regarded as a grammatical category of a case, especially in Georgian, since in this language it also has its own morphological markers.

3. Conclusion

To sum up, the Georgian vocative has its own morphological marker (*-o* and the phonetic variety *-v*). These forms are typically isolated from other parts of the sentence. In the imperative clauses the vocative corresponds to the subject, therefore one can say that the vocative has a certain syntactic function and consequently can be regarded as a grammatical category of a case. But it would be wrong to analyze the vocative without paying any attention to other forms of address, so the full description of the vocative would have to discuss not only its grammatical but also its pragmatic aspects.

Notes

1. In colloquial Georgian this expression (*k'aco*) is used very frequently so it has become a general designation of Georgians in Russian slang.
2. By the way, no original Georgian stem ends in the vowel *-i*, but only a few borrowed nouns (e.g. *čai* 'tea', *t'ramvai* 'tram', *t'aksi* 'taxi').
3. Hewitt (1995: 55–56) mentions vocative forms such as *as or-o kal-o* '102-VOC women-VOC', *sami atas-o kal-o* '3000-VOC women-VOC', *sam-o milion-o kal-o* '3-VOC million-VOC women-VOC', but such forms sound artificial and are usually not used.
4. Boeder (1985: 74) mentions the vocative suffix *-o* following the pronoun *me* 'I': "Im westgeorgischen Imerischen kann nach Auskunft von N. Džanelidze der Vokativ auch in der ersten Person auftreten, da es sich um eine Art Selbstanrede handelt, also: *me sac'qal-o!* „Ich Bedauernswerter-Vokativ!" wie: *še sac'qal-o!* Selbstanreden werden im Georgischen durch Periphrasen ausgedrückt; *me* „ich" wird [...] mit *čemi tavi* "mein Kopf" umschrieben, das grammatisch gesehen eine dritte Person ist", so for addressing him/herself a

Georgian would say *čem-o tav-o* 'my-VOC head-VOC', as can be seen in a poem by Ak'ak'i C'ereteli (C'ereteli 1990: 231): "Čemo tavo" ('My head'): *čem-o tav-o, bedi ar gic'eria* 'my-VOC head-VOC, you have no luck'.

5. "Die Menge der Lexeme, bei denen eigene Vokativmorpheme auftreten können, ist viel geringer als die Menge der Lexeme, bei denen Nominativmorpheme zu finden sind. Der Vokativ unterstellt einen „Appell" und damit eine Person als Adressaten einer Rede. Zu den Lexemen (bei denen eigene Vokativmorpheme auftreten können) gehören damit nicht nur alle Personennamen, Berufs- und Standesbezeichnungen usw., sondern auch alle sonstigen Bezeichnungen, welche Identifizierungen mit Personen zulassen." (Bonnenkamp 1971: 17).

6. Although Šanidze (1955: 41) and Čxenk'eli (1958: 21) do mention the form *deda-v*, this form is extremely uncommon and appears only in 19th century literature.

7. "Diese Wörter (*dzmobilo* and *dedilo* – L.A., A.L.) können auch im Nominativ ohne Vokativendung und unter Beibehaltung ihres hypokoristischen Suffixes *-il-* gebraucht werden, z.B. *dzmobil-i* 'als Bruder betrachteter Freund'."

8. "[D]er kategoriale Status ("Nomen") kann verlorengehen und nur die mit dem ursprünglichen Vokativ verknüpfte pragmatische Bedeutung übrigbleiben. So bedeutet z.B. georgisch *deda* „Mutter", aber *deda!* als Ausruf drückt Furcht, Erstaunen u. dgl. aus" (Boeder 1985: 57).

9. Cf. the discussion of this problem in Boeder (1989) and Braun (1985).

10. „Eine Anredeform zeichnet sich primär dadurch aus, dass sie an den Adressaten gerichtet ist. Geht man davon aus, daß Leistungen wie Identifizierung, Aufmerksamkeit-Erregen und dergleichen Nebeneffekte sind, die eine Anredeform oft erfüllen kann, aber nicht notwendigerweise erfüllen muß, so bleibt es wichtigste Aufgabe einer Anredeform, die Beziehung zwischen Sprecher und Hörer zu definieren." (Braun 1985: 85).

11. "Es ist ganz natürlich, anzunehmen, daß ganz verschiedene Motive oder Bedingungen für reziproken Ausdruck gelten können." (Boeder 1989: 13).

12. The position of vocative lexemes in Georgian sentences is considered in detail by Boeder (1985: 62).

13. „Die Sprachwissenschaft hat eingesehen, dass der Vokativ sich nicht auf derselben Ebene befindet, wie die übrigen Kasus, und dass die vokativische Anrede außerhalb des grammatischen Satzes steht; ebenso ist der echte Imperativ von den übrigen verbalen Kategorien abzusondern, da er durch dieselbe Funktion wie der Vokativ gekennzeichnet ist [...] auch ihre Intonation ist ähnlich. Das Personalpronomen beim Imperativ ist seiner Funktion nach eher Anrede als Subjekt."

References

Apridonidze, Šukia
   1991   Literary and dialectal forms of address in Georgian. *Studia Lin-
                  guistica* 45: 136–146.
Apridonidze, Šukia
   2001   C'odebiti brunva tu mimartvis porma? Xelaxali cda da zogi axali
                  argument'i [The vocative case or the form for addressing? New
                  effort and some new arguments]. *Arnold Čikobavas sak'itxavebi*
                  XII: 19–23.
Ayoub, Milicent R.
   1964   Bi-polarity in Arabic kinship terms. In *Proceedings of the Ninth
                  International Congress of Linguists*, Horace G. Lunt (ed.), 1100–
                  1106. The Hague/Paris: Mouton de Gruyter.
Beyrer, Arthur and Kiril Kostov
   1978   Umgekehrte Anrede im Bulgarischen und Rumänischen?.
                  Balkansko ezikoznanie 21 (4): 41–53.
Boeder, Winfried
   1985   Der Vokativ in den Kartwelsprachen. In *Studia Linguistica. Dia-
                  chronica et Synchronica: Werner Winter sexagenario anno
                  MCMLXXXIII gratis animis ab eius collegis, amicis disciulisque
                  oblata*, Ursula Pieper and Gerhard Stickel (eds.), 55–80. Berlin/
                  New York/Amsterdam: Mouton de Gruyter.
Boeder, Winfried
   1989   Über einige Anredeformen im Kaukasus. *Georgica. Zeitschrift
                  für Kultur, Sprache und Geschichte Georgiens und Kaukasiens*
                  11: 11–20.
Boeder, Winfried
   2009   Sint'aksisa da morpologiis šeusabamobis teoriuli problemebi
                  kartvelur enebši [Problems of mismatch between syntax and mor-
                  phology in Kartvelian.] *Kadmosi. Journal of Studies of Hu-
                  manities* 1: 43–66.
Bonnenkamp Udo
   1971   Der Vokativ im Romanischen. In *Interlinguistica. Sprachver-
                  gleich und Übersetzung. Festschrift zum 60. Geburtstag von
                  Mario Wandruszka*, Karl-Richard Bausch and Hans-Martin
                  Gauger (eds.), 13–25. Tübingen: Max Niemeyer.
Braun, Friederike
   1985   Umgekehrte Anrede im Arabischen. In: *Studia Linguistica. Dia-
                  chronica et Synchronica: Werner Winter sexagenario anno
                  MCMLXXXIII gratis animis ab eius collegis, amicis disciulisque*

oblata, Ursula Pieper and Gerhard Stickel (eds.), 81–92. Berlin/ New York/Amsterdam: Mouton de Gruyter.

Č'avč'avadze, Ilia
1987   *Txzulebata sruli k'rebuli* [Collected Writings]. Tbilisi: Sabčota Sakartvelo.

C'ereteli, Ak'ak'i
1990.   *Lirik'a* [Lyrics]. Tbilisi: Merani.

Čxenk'eli, K'i'ta [Tschenkéli, Kita]
1958   *Einführung in die georgische Sprache. Band 1: Theoretischer Teil*. Zürich: Amirani.

Fähnrich, Heinz
1994   *Grammatik der altgeorgischen Sprache*. Hamburg: Buske.

Hewitt, Brian G.
1995   *Georgian: A structural Reference Grammar*. Amsterdam: Benjamins.

Hjelmslev, Lui
1972   *La catégorie des cas. Étude de grammaire générale*. Munich: Fink.

Jakobson, Roman
1971   Zur Struktur des russischen Verbums. *Selected Writings II*, 3–15. The Hague/Paris: Mouton.

Lomtatidze, Ketevan
1994   On the Imperative Mood. In *Indogermanica et Caucasica. Festschrift für Karl Horst Schmidt zum 65. Geburtstag*, Roland Bielmeier and Reinhard Stempel (eds.), 479–485. Berlin/New York: de Gruyter.

Oniani, Aleksandre
1987   C'odebiti brunvis sakitxisatvis tanamedrove salit'erat'uro kartulši [On the vocative case in contemporary literary Georgian]. *Ak'ak'i Šanidze–100. Saiubileo k'rebuli 1*. [Centennial Collection], Tbilisi: Mecniereba.

Šanidze, Ak'ak'i
1956   C'odebitis pormis adgilisatvis gramat'ik'aši [The position of the vocative form in grammar]. In *Saxelis brunebis ist'oriisatvis kartvelur enebši*. Vol. 1 [On the history of the declension of nouns in Kartvelian. Vol. 1], Varlam Topuria (ed.), 36–47. Tbilisi: TSU gamomcemloba.

Šanidze, Ak'ak'i
1955   *Kartuli enis gramat'ik'a*. Vol. 1. [Grammar of the Georgian language. Vol. 1]. Tbilissi: TSU gamomcemloba.

Topuria, Varlam
   1956   C'odebiti brunvisatvis [On the ergative case]. In *Saxelis brunebis ist'oriisatvis kartvelur enebši*. Vol. 1 [On the history of the declension of nouns in Kartvelian. Vol. 1], Varlam Topuria (ed.), 36–47. Tbilisi: TSU gamomcemloba.

Trubezkoj, Nikolaj
   1937   Gedanken über die slovakische Deklination. *Sbornik matice slovenskej* 15: 39–47.

Wills, Dorothy Davis
   1977   Participant deixis in English baby talk. In *Talking to children. Language input and acquisition*, Catherine E. Snow and Charles A. Ferguson (eds.), 271–295. Cambridge: Cambridge University Press.

Winter, Werner
   1969   Vocative and Imperative. In *Substance and Structure of Language. Lectures delivered before the Linguistic Institute of the Linguistic Society of America, University of California, Los-Angeles, June 17–August 12, 1966*, Jaan Puhvel (ed.), 205–223. Berkeley/Los Angeles: University of California Press.

Vocative for nominative[*]

David Stifter

Abstract

This study examines the use of morphologically marked vocative forms, mostly of personal names, as new nominatives or inflectional base forms, language-externally in situations of linguistic contact and, to a lesser extent, language-internally. This phenomenon (*Vocatiuus pro Nominatiuo* = VpN) has received some attention in previous scholarship, but it is here for the first time studied in a wide typological context, involving appr. two dozen languages of various genetic affiliation from Europe, Northern Africa and the Near East, and covering a period of almost 4.000 years. The aim of this paper is to collect a large sample of VpN and to draw typological conclusions about its development and the situations in which it normally occurs. VpN emerges as a frequent phenomenon, especially in situations of linguistic exchange, and not as a rare and marginal one.

1. Introduction

This study takes its starting point in the observation that in several languages forms, mostly of personal names, are encountered which look like vocatives, either in those same or in neighbouring languages, but which are used in functions and syntactic positions other than those of address. Less cautiously formulated, under certain circumstances vocatives of personal names have been reinterpreted as new nominatives or unmarked base forms. With a term that is meant in a purely descriptive sense the phenomenon can be called *Vocatiuus pro Nominatiuo* (VpN; after Wackernagel 1920: 310). This paper has two aims: to collect examples of VpN from a wide range of languages in time and space, and to try to highlight its development and the situations in which it typically occurs. Before that, an overview of the research history will be given, and VpN as understood in a narrow sense in this article will be delimited against related phenomena.

2. Research history

References to VpN are extant in works as early as those of Greek and Latin grammarians of the Roman imperial period. Apollonius Dyscolus, living in the 2nd c. A.D., states in his *Syntactica* 214 b, 3 ff.:

ἢ ἀνεστραμμένως, ὅτε ἡ κλητικὴ ἀντ' εὐθειῶν παραλαμβάνεται κατὰ Μακεδονικὸν ἔθος ἢ Θεσσαλικόν, ὡς οἱ πρὸ ἡμῶν τὸ τοιοῦτον ἐπιστώσαντο:
αὐτὰρ ὃ αὖτε Θύεστ' Ἀγαμέμνονι [λεῖπε φορῆναι; add. DS]

[Or in a contrary fashion, when the vocative is used in a Macedonian or Thessalian manner instead of the nominative, like our predecessors have recognised:
autàr hò aũte T^hýest' Agamémnoni [leĩpe p^horēnai]][1]

Apollonius' 'predecessors' are likely to be Aristarchus of Samothrace (220?–143? B.C.) and Aristonicus of Alexandria (Augustan period), whose treatises on the Homeric poems are lost. Similar statements can be found in the works of other Greek grammarians, e.g. in *De Vita et Poesi Homeri* 2, 48, by the roughly 1st-century Plutarch, or as late as in the works of the 12th-century Eustathius of Thessalonica (see Hedberg 1935: 76–77, 80 for quotations). This tradition was also taken up in the Latin world; the immediate use of Apollonius is palpable in book 17 of the *Institutiones Grammaticae* 'Grammatical Foundations', a Latin grammatical handbook by the early medieval Priscianus Caesariensis (around 500 A.D.):

Macedones autem et Thessali e contrario uocatiuos solebant pro nominatiuis proferre. Homerus: "αὐτὰρ ὃ αὖτε Θύεστ' Ἀγαμέμνονι δῶκε φορῆναι". hic uocatiuus est pro nominatiuo: Θύεστα dixit pro Θυέστης. unde Romani frequentissime huiuscemodi nomina, et maxime appellatiua per uocatiuum Graecum etiam pro nominatiuo suo proferunt: sophista, citharista, poeta, Scytha, Sarmata, Sosia. Persius tamen indubitanter uocatiuum pro nominatiuo posuit: "censoremue tuum uel quod trabeate salutas?" trabeate pro trabeatus. et Horatius: "macte uirtute esto" pro mactus uirtute. (*Institutiones Grammaticae* 17, 190 = *Corpus Glossarum Latinarum* 3, 208)

[In a contrary fashion, moreover, the Macedonians and Thessalians used vocatives for nominatives. Homer (said): "*autàr hò aũte T^hýest' Agamémnoni dõke p^horēnai*". Here, the vocative stands for the nominative: he said *T^hýesta* for *T^hyéstēs*. For this reason, the Romans use very often names of this sort, and especially appellative nouns in the Greek vocative

for their nominative: *sophista, citharista, poeta, Scytha, Sarmata, Sosia.*
Persius, however, undoubtedly placed the vocative for the nominative:
"censoremue tuum uel quod trabeate salutas?"[2] [*Saturae* 3, 28; DS] ([voc.]
trabeate for [nom.] *trabeatus*). And Horace: *"macte uirtute esto"*[3] [*Satira* 1,
2, 31; DS] for [nom.] *mactus uirtute.*]

Actually, these apparent ancient instances of VpN are mostly of a different
nature from the phenomenon discussed here. While some Greek forms in
-τᾰ (*-tă*) do probably continue earlier vocatives (Brugmann and Delbrück
1892: 651; Sihler 1995: 274; differently Schwyzer 1939: 560–561), in other
cases, notably in Latin where words in *-ta* systematically correspond to
Greek ones in *-tēs*, we are simply looking at different inflectional morphology. The endings of the nominative of the one group of languages are
incidentally similar to those of the vocative of a culturally dominant idiom,
i.e. Greek, thereby prompting a false etymological conclusion by the
grammarians. In Priscian's quote from Persius, a Roman poet, voc.
trabeate instead of nom. *trabeatus* is a poetic licence. While usually in
Latin the nominative serves as the case of predication after the copula,[4] in
this instance the nominative is exceptionally attracted to the vocative in the
context of address, thereby creating a predicative vocative (see Brugmann
and Delbrück 1892: 647, 1893: 398; Wackernagel 1920: 308–309; Löfstedt
1956: 103–106; Svennung 1958: 406–409; Hofmann and Szantyr 1965:
25–26). The same is true for *macte uirtute esto* 'be blessed by excellence',
a phrase originating in the religious sphere, but transferred to mundane
usage as an exclamation of praise or approval. Such rare examples of case
attraction occur mainly in syntagms involving second-person verbs, but are
not re-interpretations of vocatives as nominatives in the strict sense. The
vocative has not taken over the full set of functions of the nominative, but
only functions as a predicative case in a stylistically very highly marked
construction when dependent on second-person verbs.

   In contrast to those ancient examples, this paper will be concerned with
examples where new inflectional base forms are derived from vocatives in
all, not only in a single syntactic context. The number of previous studies
of the problem is limited. In various studies and grammars of Indo-European languages of the 19th and 20th centuries the observation is made that
the attested nominatives of the names of humans and gods can be traced
back to earlier vocatives. Typically mentioned in this context are Latin
Iuppiter 'Jupiter' (see paragraph 8.1. below) and personal names like
Μεννει, Τιμολλει in Boeotic, a dialect of Ancient Greek (see 9.1. below).
The underlying process is that of hypostasis or conversion (Brugmann and
Delbrück 1892: 651; for the term 'hypostasis', see Bloomfield 1933: 148,
180; pers. comm. Paul Widmer), the transference and re-interpretation of a

form that originally belonged to one grammatical category to another one. As far as I can see, the first person who devoted more than a passing remark to the phenomenon was Heinrich Zimmer (1893: 190–196). The first full and truly profound treatment of VpN is an article by the famous orientalist Enno Littmann from 1916 in which he formulated a number of fundamental insights into the involved processes. He discussed both the transference of forms of address to new base forms, as well as the re-interpretation of vocatives as nominatives in contact situations. Littmann adduced a large collection of examples mainly from languages of the Near East and north-western Africa. Most of what was said about VpN in the following years and decades is directly or indirectly derived from Littmann, as can easily be recognised from the fact that only rarely new forms were introduced into the discourse (e.g., Wackernagel 1920: 309–310; Löfstedt 1956: 102–103; Svennung 1958: 394–403). While isolated references to VpN are scattered throughout the 20th century, only the nineties of the last and the first decade of this century saw the resurgence of interest in it, and new languages and original observations were added to the discourse (e.g., Rix 1963, 1994; Petersmann 1998; Dunkel 1998; Malzahn 2000; Adams 2003: 512–515, 2007: 97–100, 570–571; Schumacher 2004: 295–296; Straxov 2004; despite its late appearance, the observations in Stifter 2008 [2010] date from 2001). However, hardly anyone discussed the phenomenon in a wider typological, cross-linguistic context.

3. Definitions

Several of the early studies mention VpN as part of the broader phenom-enon of using forms of address outside their original domain, that is, as subjects, objects or other phrases. In fact, the terms 'forms of address' (*Anredeformen*) and 'vocatives' may be used interchangeably, and they often are.[5] However, in the present study a distinction will be made between the two. Only such forms of address that are morphologically, i.e. inflectionally marked with overt endings[6] will be called 'vocatives'. All vocatives are by their nature forms of address, but the reverse is not true, not all forms of address are morphologically marked vocatives.

One can distinguish broadly the following types of re-interpretation of forms of address:

1. Transference of a true vocative → nominative:[7] the previous studies make one expect that this happens mostly language-externally, i.e. in situations of language contact, but instances of language-internal developments can be found, too.[8]

2. Transference of other forms of address → nominative: very often, this involves collocations with first-person possessive pronouns followed by kinship terms, titles or terms of deference. Cross-linguistically, it is particularly frequent with words for 'master' or 'mistress'. Many examples are found with reference to rulers or religious leaders and dignitaries, e.g. Hebrew *rabbī* 'lit. my lord' → 'teacher'. In the strict sense, such expressions are proper only to situations of personal communication, but they can become stereotyped, and can turn into titles themselves or into mere referential terms, e.g. when French *madame* 'lit. my lady' on its own is used in German conversation as a pointer to a particular person, almost like a pronoun. Such constructions may on occasion form the basis of proper names, e.g. Welsh *Angharad* < *(f)y ngharad* 'my beloved', Old Irish *Mérnóc* < *mo Érnán-óc* 'my little Érnán' (Zimmer 1893); or English *Ned* < *mine Edward*, *Nol* < *mine Oliver* (Wackernagel 1920: 310; Svennung 1958: 394). Littmann (1916) and Svennung (1958: 395–403) provide wealthy collections for this phenomenon from a wide range of languages. This kind of transference is likely to happen both language-internally and externally, but of course the detachment of such expressions from their original pragmatic constraints is easier in loan situations. In language-internal examples, it has been observed that there is a preference for certain superlatives in acts of address:

(1)   German   *(mein / ihr)*   *Lieb-st-er*
               1sg.poss / 3sg.f.poss   dear-superlative-m.nom.sg
               '(my/her) dearest'

(2)   Greek   φέριστ-ε *(pʰérist-e)*
               good.superlative-m.voc.sg.
               'best one'

Such expressions could then be transferred to other contexts, without necessarily transferring vocative morphology (Leumann 1939: 10).

3. Transference of vocatives and other forms of address → interjections: because of their high emotive value, forms of address, especially of transcendental entities, can be detached from their original uses and can become semantically depleted phrases and interjections whose primary

function becomes to reflect the high degree of emotional involvement of the speaker in a particular situation, e.g.

(3) Hungarian   *jó   Isten-em*
                  good   God-1sg.poss
                  'my good God!'

(4) Latin   *me-hercl-e*
                  1sg.acc-Hercules-voc.sg
                  'by Hercules'

or Austrian German *Oida* 'old man', a form originating in slightly derogatory situations of direct address,[9] but having by now turned into an empty phrase of amazement or a call for attention. In such stereotyped expressions, morphologically marked vocatives may survive as isolated relics even in languages that have lost vocatives as an inflectional category, e.g. Russian Боже мой (*Bože moj*) 'my God' or Slovenian *bože* 'God', beside nom. *bog* 'God' in both languages.

This paper will be limited to cases of type 1 where morphologically marked vocatives are re-interpreted as nominatives or as morphologically un-marked base or citation forms (VpN). Unless otherwise stated, the dis-cussion will always focus on the singular. For convenience's sake, the term 'nominative' will be used throughout, even for languages with little or no inflection where the term 'nominative' is not strictly appropriate. VpN is something entirely different from the rather common, if not trivial use of the nominative in place of the vocative, a use which is basically the ex-tension and generalisation of the unmarked base form to a pragmatically marked environment. This phenomenon will not be treated here. As shall be seen, the use of the vocative for the nominative is fundamentally dif-ferent in its character. It has nothing to do with the loss of markedness or with the shift of markedness from morphology to syntax, and unlike the use of nominatives for vocatives, VpN is not a primarily language-internal process, but one that is more at home in situations of linguistic contact and borrowing.

The following survey will partly consist of previously identified examples, partly of new cases that have not yet been mentioned in the literature. Because of my background in Indo-European historical lin-guistics, many examples will be taken from past contact situations in Eu-rope and its vicinity, but a number of modern examples will also be cited.

The examples mostly involve the vocatives of nouns that belong to the Indo-European *o*-stem declension. In Proto-Indo-European, the vocative singular of this class ended in the bare stem-class vowel, which, probably for suprasegmental reasons connected with the placement of the stress, surfaces as *-e* in absolute final position. There is no particular system in the arrangement of the following chapters. Sometimes the languages given in the titles will refer to the recipient, sometimes to the donor languages. No consistent system was adhered to in this, but the arrangement is oriented to practical aspects.

4. Etruscan

The survey will start with Etruscan, partly because the documentation of this language is much better than that of other fragmentarily attested languages of antiquity, partly because VpN has been especially well studied for this language before and can therefore be demonstrated in an exemplary fashion. Etruscan is a non-Indo-European language spoken in the early historic period, i.e. in the 1st mill. B.C., over a large area in Northern Italy. It was eventually superseded by Latin around the beginning of the Common Era. Prior to its disappearance, it had extensive and long-standing contacts in particular with the Indo-European languages Greek, Umbrian, Latin, both belonging to the Italic sub-branch of Indo-European, and Gaulish. Through these contacts, a very large number of personal names were borrowed into Etruscan. It has been long observed that Greek *o*-stem names borrowed into Etruscan regularly appear as *e*-class nouns, e.g. Gr. Δίφιλος (*Díp^hilos*) → Etr. *tiφile*, Λύκανδρος (*Lýkandros*) → *licantre* (de Simone 1970: 94–95). Likewise, Etruscan names in *-e* have a large number of correspondences in Latin or Osco-Umbrian names in *-us/-os* and are indeed best regarded as loans from those languages (Rix 1963: 226–238), e.g. Etr. *tite* ← *Titus*, *prute* ← *Brutus*, *palpe* ← *Balbus*, *macre* ← *Macer* etc. (see also Rix 1995: 723; Steinbauer 1993: 288). The case of Italic ***_io_-stems is slightly more complex. In early loans, Etruscan *-ie* represents Italic ** -iio-* (Wallace 2008: 93), e.g. Etr. *numesie* continues Latino-Faliscan **Numesios* (Lat. *Numerius*), *spurie Spurius*, etc. In younger loans, Etruscan has an *-i* where Latin gentilic names end in *-ius*, e.g. *fapi* ← *Fabius*, *φisi* ← *Fisius* (Rix 1963: 258–260, 1994: 63–64; Kaimio 1970). But not only Greek and Latin names were treated in this manner, it also applies to loan names from Celtic languages, e.g. Etr. *eluveitie* ← Celtic ethnonym **elu̯eiti̯ios* 'Helvetian' used as a personal name, *nemetie-ś* (*-ś* = genitive ending added to the base form) ← Gaulish **Nemeti̯os* (de Simone 1980).

It has been suggested (e.g., de Simone 1970: 142) that these correspondences are due to a mechanical morphological transformation, i.e. to
the transference of Indo-European *o*-stems to the Etruscan *e*-class. Etruscan
possessed an inherited class of words ending in overt *-e*, e.g. *flere* 'divinity'
(Rix 1963: 230–231). In addition to this, there was another, only diachronically tangible, *e*-class where the final vowel had been dropped in
consequence of "a prehistoric sound change that eliminated word-final
vowels" (Wallace 2008: 44–45). In such words, the original class is recognisable only in those cases where the stem vowel is protected by a consonantal ending, e.g. **aise* > Etr. *ais* 'god', but pl. *aiser* 'gods',[10] or gen.
meθlumes vs. nom. *meθlum* 'city' (Wallace 2008: 45, 49). However, this
hypothesis cannot explain why Latin gentilic names in *-ius* are represented
by Etruscan *-i*. Therefore according to an alternative solution, widely accepted today, this is not the substitution of the suffix of one language by a
functionally corresponding one of another, but rather the re-interpretation
of the Italic vocative ending as that of a new nominative in the recipient
language (Rix 1981: 124, 1994: 63 fn. 32; Steinbauer 1993: 288; Adams
2003: 514, 2007: 97–100). The speakers of Etruscan, which had no vocative in its grammatical system, were not sensitive to the pragmatic role of
the forms in *-e* and could employ it for other functions. This hypothesis not
only accounts neatly for the preponderance of *-e* in loan names over other
possible stem endings, but it also explains why sometimes *-ie*, sometimes *-i*
is found for Italic names ending in **-iio-*: **-iie* is the Common Italic, *-ī* the
regular Latin reflex of the vocative of these stems,[11] and the distribution
reflects diatopically and diachronically different layers of loans.

It is of course possible that we are looking at a complex phenomenon
whereby the vocative of the donor language was preferred because of its
compatibility with an already existing inflectional class which in turn was
awarded greater pragmatic prominence in the recipient language and
eventually became productive even inside native Etruscan word-forms
(Adams 2003: 514, 2007: 97–98; Wallace 2008: 93 with reference to the
onomastic suffix *-ie*).

The correspondence described above pertains to personal names only.
Although quite often they can be traced back to descriptive adjectives or
ethnonyms (see the lists in Rix 1963: 227–228, 231), it is apparent that
these words had been in use as personal names in their original languages.
Names of Italic gods, on the other hand, were taken over in the nominative.
This is evident from Etruscan *neθuns* (corresponding to Latin *Neptūnus*)
whose name was perhaps borrowed from hypothetical Umbrian **Nehtuns*
(de Vaan 2008: 406), and from Etruscan *selvans*, a god of the nature corresponding to Latin *Siluānus*. In the same vein, *velχans* may be an equivalent of Latin *Vulcānus*. It seems that no common nouns in **-os* were bor-

rowed from Indo-European languages into Etruscan (except for the possible but special case of **aisos* 'god' mentioned above). Thus it remains unclear whether these would have been treated differently from personal names. Neuter *o*-stem nouns in ** -om* or *-ov* were taken over in a form that is reminiscent of the nominative/accusative singular of the original language, e.g. Greek κῶθον (*kôîʰon*) 'drinking vessel' → Etruscan *qutum*, λήκυθον (*lékytʰon*) 'oil flask' → *leχtumuza*, πρόχουν (*prókʰoun*) 'jug' → *pruχum*, Italic (?) *uīnum* 'wine' → *vinum*, and perhaps Italic **pōtlom* 'drinking ves-sel' → *putlumza* (Wallace 2008: 127–129).[12] The lack of substitution of **-om* by something like **-e* may indicate that this substitution pertained to personal names only, thereby lending support to the theory of its origin in the vocative.

In Etruria, the re-interpretation of Lat. vocatives as new Etruscan nomi-natives was occasionally carried even a step further in that the use of voca-tive forms was extended even to Latin funeral inscriptions composed, in some likelihood, by native speakers of Etruscan with insufficient command of Latin (Adams 2007: 98–99), e.g.

(5) *Sex.   Gegan-i   P.   f.   Gall-e*
Sextus Geganius-voc.sg Publius-gen.sg. son-nom.sg. Gallus-voc.sg.
a(nn-os)   u(ix-it)   LXX
year-acc.pl live.pst-3sg 70
'Sextus Geganius Gallus, son of Publius, lived 70 years' (CIL 11, 2979)

From a sociolinguistic point of view it is worth noting that the contacts to the different languages correspond to different types of social and linguistic relationships. Speakers of Greek, often traders and artisans, represented a culture that exerted considerable influence on Etruscans and from which Etruscans borrowed intentionally cultural artifacts and words. Relations with speakers of Italic languages were much more imbalanced, in that es-pecially Umbrians formed part of the lower class of Etruscan society. They held subjugated positions where they were able to exert substratum in-fluence. A very early cultural superiority by Etruscans over Italic peoples is also evident from the fact that several of them took over the art of writing from Etruscans. Despite this, the main mode of communication would of course have stayed oral, and with this the pragmatic prominence of voca-tives. With the rise of Roman power Etruscans came to be on the receiving end and Latin became the dominant language. While evidence for the early period is lacking, it seems that mutual knowledge of the languages seems to have been surprisingly limited in the historical period (Adams 2003: 159–183). With Celtic peoples, relations, as far as we can judge them, seem to have been hostile initially, but the possibility must be granted that after the initial period of Celtic invasions more peaceful exchange situations arose. In any case, despite these very different types of contact, the mechanics of how names were borrowed into Etruscan remained the same in all situations, giving evidence of the persistence of the fundamental principle underlying the borrowing of names.

5. Raetic

After Etruscan, it is convenient to look at a closely related language next, Raetic. It is attested in short inscriptions in an epichoric alphabet in the Alpine valleys of Northern Italy and the Tyrol, dating to the 2nd half of the 1st mill. B.C. Its affiliation had remained a mystery until rather recently it was demonstrated on the basis of morphofunctional correspondences to be a cognate of the non-Indo-European language Etruscan (see Rix 1998; Schumacher 2004: 294–318). The small surviving corpus of Raetic contains a handful of names that have the appearance of having been borrowed from neighbouring Indo-European languages like Venetic, Celtic or some other language. The inscription from Steinberg in the Tyrol contains two names that could be of Celtic origin (Schumacher 2004: 300, 353). One is *esimnesi* (ST-3), the pertinentive of *esimne**, corresponding to *Essimnus/Essibnus*. This latter name, which is attested several times in Latin inscriptions, shows a strong connection to the probably Celtic-speaking Vindelici in modern-day Bavaria.[13] The other name is *rit'auiesi* (ST-2), the pertinentive of *rit'auie**, whose Latinised cognate *Ridaus* is known from Gaimersheim near Ingolstadt (CIL III 5905), again in the Vindelician area. *Kat²iave* in Sanzeno (SZ-8) is possibly of Celtic origin (cp. Middle Welsh *Keidyaw*, Schumacher 1998). *Klevie* (MA-17) evidently continues the Indo-European formation **kleu̯ios* 'having fame' (cp. *Cleuius* in CIL 5, 4717, Brescia, and *Cleuia* in CIL 5, 1816, Friuli), but the identity of the donor language is unknown, it could be any old Indo-European language. With a good deal of speculation, one could see behind *φeluriesi φelvinuale* (NO-13) two formations from the Proto-Celtic base **φelu-* 'many' (= Gaulish *elu-*); the first name could then be set up as Proto-Celtic **φelurios* (= Gaulish **elurios*). For more Raetic names ending in -*e* see Schumacher (2004: 295–296 fnn. 172–173), but their possible external relations are not so clear.

6. Iberian and Basque

The Iberian Peninsula provides valuable insights into the processes at work in anthroponymic borrowing, depending on the morphological character-istics of the borrowing languages.

6.1. The treatment of several Celtic, Latin and Greek names in Iberian, an ancient non-Indo-European language spoken in the east and southeast of the peninsula, attested in epichoric texts from the 4th/5th–1st c. B.C., follows the pattern established above for Etruscan and Raetic. The affiliation of Iberian had remained a mystery for a long time, but it is starting to emerge now that it may have been an early relative or even precursor of modern Basque. The Iberian numerals show striking similarities with those of Basque (Orduña Aznar 2005), and there seem to be correspondences in the verbal system (pers. comm. Kim McCone). Foreign names in the Iberian corpus are recognisable not only from parallels or etymons in languages like Latin, Gaulish, etc., but sometimes also by sound combinations that are foreign to the other Iberian material (Untermann 1980: 47; e.g., *u* before a vowel, the sequences *śk* and *ŕn* in the names below). Two factors com-plicate the identification of foreign names: sound substitutions (e.g., Iberian had no sound *m*, but wrote *b* or the digraph *m̃b* in substitution for it; and it made no phonemic distinction between voiceless and voiced consonants) and the unsuitability of the semisyllabic Iberian script for writing con-sonant clusters (consonants were either omitted in writing or empty vowels had to be written). In consequence, some of the identifications below may be circular, and not all equations can lay claim on an equal amount of cer-tainty. Still, it is clear that Iberian *-e* systematically replaces the masculine endings Latin *-us*, Celtic and Greek *-os* in the donor languages (Untermann 1980: 48; Ruiz Darasse 2010: 341–342, following Correa 1993, regards this as a phonetic process). Relatively regularly, *-i* can be found for Latin *-ius*; very rarely Iberian shows *-oś*,[14] apparently corresponding to the nominative singular ending of the donor languages. The following Latin names have been identified (here and below, identifications by Untermann 1980: 48,[15] unless otherwise stated; for southern France, sigla of the type B.x.x, the examples are comprehensive): *[.]uke kořneli* [C.1.1] = *Lucius Cornelius* (*-e* for *-ius*!), *balante* [B.1.125] = *Blandus*, *kai* [C.7.6, C.11.5] = *Caius*, *luki* [A.6–11, D.1.1] = *Lucius*, *m̃basi* [B.1.125] = *Massius*, *m̃baske* [B.1.269] = *Mascus*, *seśte* = *Sextus* or *sextus* (a monetary unit)? (Ferrer i Jané and Giral Royo 2007: 96), *tibeŕi* [A.12–17] = *Tiberius*. In one case, fragmentary *]itoŕ* [F.11.8] seems to correspond to Greco-Latin *Isidorus* in a bilingual text.[16] From Celtic, the following loan names have been proposed: *anetilike* [B.1.39] = *Aneχtlicos*, *aśetile* [B.1.42] = *Assedilos*, *auŕtem̃baŕe*

[B.1.258] = -*māros*? (unclear first element), *betukine* [F.17 2,B] = *Medugenos*? (my suggestion; but perhaps Iberian, see Stifter forthc.), *eśkinke* [B.1.268] = *Eχscingos*, *itutilte* [B.1.9] = *Indutillos*?, *kaŕate* [B.1.33] = *Carantos*, *kasike* [B.1.33] = *Cassicos*, *katubaŕe* [B.1.373] = *Catumāros* (Solier and Barbouteau 1988: 61), *katuŕe* [B.1.51] = *Caturos*, *kobakie* [B.1.53] = *Comagios*?, *latubaŕe* [B.1.364] = *Latumāros*, *]mbaŕe[* [B.1.174] (uncertain) = -*māros*?, *ośiobaŕe* [B.1.59] = *Oχsiobarros* or *Oχsiomāros*, *śeŕtubaŕe* [B.1.257] = -*māros*? (unclear first element).

The situation resembles very strongly that of Etruscan. The equivalents in Iberian of Indo-European *o*-stem names are names ending in -*e*, homomorphous with the vocatives of the donor languages, with the exception of Latin names in -*ius* which are mostly represented by names in -*i*, incidentally the ending of the vocative in this sub-type of names. This rule of equivalence seems to pertain to anthroponyms only; so far no common nouns have been identified with certainty. The sole possible exception would be *seśte* if it stood for the monetary unit *sextus*, which is far from certain. In one respect, the situation in Iberian differs from that in Etruscan. Whereas in the latter there arguably pre-existed in the recipient language an inflectional class ending in -*e*, this is not so in Iberian. The words in -*e* are an entirely new morphological class specifically for loan names.

6.2. Two features of loan names on the Iberian Peninsula make them even more valuable for this study. Celtic names that belong to other than the *o*-stem declension and which therefore have no vocative that would formally differ from the nominative, are most revealingly borrowed in a form resembling their nominative: *atetu* [B.1.26] = *Ateχtū*, *auetiŕiś* [B.1.15] = *Adueχtirīχs*, *kabiŕilo* [B.1.272] = *Cabril(l)ō*, *kaŕtiŕiś* [B.1.28] = -*rīχs* (unclear first element), *tiuiś* [A.1–5, B.1.331] = *Dīuiχs*, *untikoŕiś* [B.1.333] = perhaps *Tincorīχs* (unclear first element); de Hoz (2008) added the name *smertaz* = *Smertans* [B.1.2].

This means that if there was a morphologically distinct vocative of a name in Celtic, it was borrowed into Iberian, but if there was not, the nominative was used, which is thus shown to have served as the case of address in the donor language as well.[17] The other observation relates to the treatment of loan names in different languages. In a few instances, the same Greek and Latin names were borrowed both into Celtiberian, a Celtic language spoken in the centre of the peninsula, and into Iberian. The Greek name Φιλόνικος (*P*[h]*ilónikos*) was borrowed into Iberian as *bilonike* [K.1.7], as could be expected. However, in Celtiberian texts it appears as *bilonikos* [K.1.3, III-28, -51]. Latin *Licinus* appears as *likine* [E.7.1 = K.28.1, K.5.3] in Iberian, but six times as *likinos* in Celtiberian [K.1.3, I-29, -40, II-6, -35, III-49, IV-36]. Again, this double treatment of the names in the two languages is significant and revealing. Celtiberian, as an old Indo-European language, most likely possessed a vocative and had an inflectional system that was recognisably cognate to that of Greek and Latin. Therefore, speakers of Celtiberian either borrowed the nominative directly from those languages or, if they, too, were primarily exposed to vocatives of such personal names, were able to decode them in their communicative function and identified them with the appropriate grammatical category of their own speech. For speakers of Iberian, which most likely did not have a vocative, this option was not open and they reverted to the vocative as the *Nennform* at face value, the one they were most frequently exposed to.

6.3. Basque, which is spoken in northeastern Spain and southwestern France today, is famous for being the sole survivor of the pre-Indo-European languages of Europe. Like Iberian, to which it is perhaps related, it has no morphologically marked vocative case. For areal and typological reasons, one could *a priori* expect the same to have happened to Latin loan names and words like in Iberian, but I could find only very few examples for this. The old accusative underlies most of the countless loanwords of Latin into Basque (Trask 2008: 62). Only Basque *done* 'saint' can be derived from Proto-Romance **donne* via syncope and assimilation of the Latin vocative *domine* 'lord'[18] (Meyer-Lübke 1935: nr. 2741; Michelena 1961; Trask 1997: 338; 2008: 157), and Basque *agure* 'old man' comes from the Latin vocative *auule* 'grandfather' (Trask 2008: 79). Everything else is open to doubt: the Latin agentive suffix *-ārius* was borrowed into Basque as *-ari* (Trask 2008: 104), but this could be the regular outcome of **-āriu(m)* and need not reflect the Latin vocative in *-ī*. If the medieval Basque names *Martie* or *Mikele* do indeed exist, as claimed by Trask (1997: 348), at least the first of the two can be straightforwardly derived from the Latin vocative *Martine* via regular loss of intervocalic *n*, i.e. Michelena's Law, but I could find no independent support for those names.[19]

7. Punic

Even though the power of the Punic town of Carthage was broken by the Romans in the 3rd Punic War (149–146 B.C.), the Punic language, a daughter of Phoenician and thus a member of the Semitic family of languages, continued to be spoken in North Africa for a long time afterwards, at least until the 5th c. A.D. For the most part, it was written in the autochthonous Punic script, but in the final period the Roman script was also used.

7.1. The extended contact with Latin over more than half a millennium meant that Punic and Neo-Punic, its late variant, experienced linguistic influence from the dominant language in various areas of the grammar (Adams 2003: 214–235). Since Punic possessed no vocative case, it can by now be expected that it showed VpN in relation to names borrowed from Latin, and this is exactly what is found. Adams (l.c.) provides many examples for monolingual Punic and bilingual Punic-Latin texts where Roman names are rendered in Punic by forms that reflect the Latin vocative. "The ending *-e* instead of *-us* is represented by *-'* and *-i* instead of *-ius* by *-y*" (Adams 2003: 218 fn. 428). For example, in the bilingual KAI 117, what corresponds to Latin

(6)   *Q. Apule-us*   *Maxssim-us*   *qui   et*
      Quintus Apuleius-nom.sg Maximus-nom.sg   rel   con
      Ride-us   *uoca-ba-tur*
      Rideus-nom.sg   call-impf-3sg.pass
      'Quintus Apuleius Maximus who also was called Rideus'

is *'pwl'ẏ m'k[šm]' ryd'y* = *Apulei Maxime Ridai* in Punic, with endings that resemble those of the Latin vocative. The same inscription demonstrates another peculiarity, already observed in Iberian (section 6.2.), namely that names which belong to inflectional classes of the donor language without a morphologically marked vocative are borrowed in a form that reflects the nominative. The sons of Q. Apuleius Maximus Rideus are called *Pudens*, *Seuerus* and *Maxsimus* in the Latin part of the text. As could be expected, the latter two appear as *š'w'w'r'* = *Seueuere* [sic!] and *m'k[šm]'* = *Maxime* in the Punic section, whereas the first of the three is written *pwdnš* = *Pudens* (Adams 2003: 217–218). The same pattern is encountered in the bilingual epitaph KAI 142 (= CIL 8, 793). *Gadaeus* and *Saturius* are rendered in Punic as *g'[d]'y/g'dy* = *Gadai* and *š'ṭry* = *Saturi*, but *Felix* as *plkš* = *Felix* (Adams 2003: 225). Like in the case of the Iberian inscriptions, this different treatment, depending on the stem-class of the names in the donor language, is an indicator that the names were not merely adapted to inflectional classes of the recipient language, but rather directly reflect morphological properties of the names in the donor language.

There is some evidence that the borrowing of vocatives as base-forms occurred in the living language, in the communicative interchange of people. Latin names that do not belong to the everyday life of the average speakers of Punic, notably the titles and names of members of the Roman imperial families, with which they would be more familiar in official, written form, are rendered in Punic in forms that reflect the Latin nominative: *grm'nyqs* = *Germanicus, dr'ss* = *Drusus* (Adams 2003: 218 fn. 428).

In the latest phase of the language, Neo-Punic, written in Roman letters, when the language was under great pressure from Latin and bilingualism and good knowledge of Latin became widespread, Latin nominatives were more regularly employed as base-forms in Punic (Adams 2003: 233), although even at this stage the forms reflecting the Latin vocative are in preponderance.

7.2. If Latin influenced Punic, the reverse could be expected to be true, too. Indeed, substitution of the vocative for the nominative in vulgar texts has been claimed to be a feature of African Latin since the end of the 19th century. Marx (1894: 2) discusses the expression *Romaniane uiuat* 'may Romaniane (vocative for nominative Romanianus) live' in the subscription of a manuscript, syntactically wrong according to the grammatical rules of standard Latin, and compares it with seven instances of vocatival forms instead of nominatives[20] among the approximately 30.000 lapidar inscriptions from the Roman province of Africa. He then uses this parallel to ascribe the subscription to an African author. Referring to the same seven texts, Adamik (1987: 1) maintains that the statistically very small number of examples should not be used to draw conclusions about the grammatical features of spoken African Latin. Instead of accepting them as instances of VpN, Adamik (1987: 5) connects these grammatically aberrant inscriptions with the so-called *signa*, super-nomina that are infrequently found on Roman inscriptions in addition to the civil names of the deceased. They sometimes stand – unsyntactically – in the vocative[21] and represent clearly some kind of pet names by which the deceased were known during their lifetimes. Adamik is quite vague about the exact usage and the formal side of the *signa*. Furthermore, he mixes quite diverse phenomena, i.e. true vocatives addressing the deceased, possible cases of VpN, and pet names stereotyped in the vocative (= *signa*), to support his hypothesis that those African names are true vocatives, intended as forms of address of the dead. Adamik's account is briefly reviewed by Petersmann (1998: 133–134) who critically remarks that Adamik overlooked several more inscriptions where the interpretation as true vocatives is excluded on syntactical grounds. Adams (2003: 512–514), too, notes that the important corpus of texts from Sirte had apparently been unknown to Adamik. These texts, written in Neo-Punic and Latin, contain a substantial number of vocatival names in unambiguous nominative function. Nevertheless, in (2007: 570–571, 574–575) Adams does not want to make a decision and takes an ultimately cautious position regarding VpN in Punic and African Latin by maintaining that the case has not been decisively proven yet.

8. Latin and Romance

8.1. Having discussed numerous examples of external relations of Latin above, it is time to take a brief look at Latin and her Romance daughter languages themselves. The case of the nominative *Iūpiter*, *Iuppiter*, alluded to in the introduction, has served as the classical example of VpN in most of the literature devoted to the phenomenon since the end of the 19th century (Wackernagel 1920: 310; Svennung 1958: 395; Hofmann and Szantyr 1965: 23–24; Hermann 1937: 72–73, to name but a few). *Iūpiter* directly continues the PIE vocative collocation **dịeụ ph₂ter* 'oh father sky!'[22] (cp. Greek vocative Ζεῦ πάτερ [*Zeû páter*]), instead of the expected nominative [†]*Diuspiter* < [†]*Dịoụs patēr* (Leumann 1939: 9–11).[23] Furthermore, Leumann makes the valuable observation that the use of certain superlative attributes accompanying divine names must have originated in acts of addressing the divinities. Fixed expressions such as *Iuppiter Optimus Maximus* 'best, greatest Jupiter' would thus have been formed on the analogy of vocatives like *Iuppiter Optime Maxime*.

The only other relevant example in Latin that I have come across is the generalisation of the collocation *domine deus*[24] 'Lord God' outside of addresses to the Christian god, thus giving rise to Romanian *dumnezeu*, Italian *domineddio*, Old Fr. *damnedeu*, *damledieu*, Provenzal *dompnedeu*, all 'God' (Meyer-Lübke 1935: nr. 2734; Svennung 1958: 398–399). A similar use of *domine* as base form of words referring to clerics or other venerable, learned persons like schoolmasters, e.g. in English, German, Dutch or Italian, is frequently cited in the early literature about VpN (e.g., Brugmann and Delbrück 1892: 651, 1893: 398; Littmann 1916: 95; Wackernagel 1920: 309; Svennung 1958: 398; Straxov 2004: 125), notably with reference to the novel *Guy Mannering* by Sir Walter Scott where this expression found its way into world literature.

8.2. To conclude the survey of Latin and Romance, and to demonstrate how careful one has to be, I want to draw attention to two only apparent examples of VpN, the Spanish names *Lope* < Latin *lupus* 'wolf' and *Felipe* < *Philippus*. Instead, they are the product of the so-called 'apocope extrema', a phonological phenomenon in Castillian in the 11th century. The final vowel had first been weakened and become a mere prop vowel in the 10th century (cp. the record *Lope Garsea*, 978 A.D.), eventually to become completely apocopated in proper names in the 11th century. In the case of **Lobo* > **Lob* this also entailed devoicing of the now final consonant, i.e. *Lop*. This phenomenon first occurred when the names stood in proclitic position, but it was then extended to other positions as well (e.g., *Don Lop*). Apocope extrema appears to have been a diastratic phenomenon, perhaps confined to the higher layers of society. Some of the forms thus created are still in use, e.g. *Hernan* < *Fernando*. When the social factors that had favoured apocope extrema changed, the effects of the sound change were undone. While most names that were so affected were refurbished with their original *-o*, in the case of *Lope* and *Felipe* an unetymological *-e* was added, after the model of words like *prinçep* > *principe* 'prince' where the *-e* is historically justified (Lapesa 1951, 1975). This process has nothing to do with VpN.

9. Greek

We will turn to various instances of VpN involving Greek next.

9.1. The possibly language-internal case of the Boeotian nominatives in ⁻ε (*-e*) (6th century B.C.), then ⁻ει (*-ei*; both = [ɛː]), later also -ι (*-i*; reflecting the development of the vowels to [iː]), and finally also sigmatised -η(ς) (*-ē(s)*) and -εις (*-eis*; Vottero 1985: 407) was already pointed out in the introduction; cf. examples like Θιττε (*Tʰitte*), Πτωιλλει (*Ptōillei*), Μεννει (*Mennei*), Τιμολλει (*Timollei*). It is widely agreed that these names are backformed from vocatives in -ε (*-e*), by lengthening the vowel in the nominative (e.g., Zimmer 1893: 190–197; Brugmann and Delbrück 1893: 397–398; Wackernagel 1920: 309; Schwyzer 1939: 636; Sihler 1995: 224; critical Kretschmer 1895 and Solmsen 1906: 181–182). An indicator for the origin of those names in forms of address is that almost all of them display geminate consonants, typical of hypocoristics and terms of endearment (Vottero 1985: 407).

9.2. Greek forms ending in -ă (*-ă*) like ἱππότα (*hippóta*) 'rider', δέσποτα (*déspota*) 'lord' or νύμφα (*nýmpʰa*) 'nymph' probably continue earlier vocatives of *ā*-stems (Brugmann and Delbrück 1892: 651; Sihler 1995: 274; differently Schwyzer 1939: 560–561), but, as mentioned in section 2, this explanation must not be extended to similarly-looking forms in other languages like Macedonian or Latin where the ⁻a has different origins. It is notable that this case does not involve personal names, but common nouns with animate reference.

9.3. In a small number of cases there is evidence that the base forms of theonyms were influenced by their respective vocatives. Whereas the usual Greek name of the god Apollo is Ἀπόλλων (*Apóllōn*), in the Thessalian dialect he is called Ἄπλουν (*Áploun*). This has been explained as regular accent retraction in the vocative with subsequent syncope of the medial vowel in allegro style, i.e. *Ἄπελλον (*Ápellon*) > *Ἄπλον (*Áplon*). This stem was eventually generalised (Kretschmer 1905: 134; Fraenkel 1956: 83–84; Dunkel 1998: 80). Fraenkel even argues that the Attic form Ἀπόλλων (*Apóllōn*) itself instead of older Ἀπέλλων (*Apéllōn*; attested in the Doric dialect) owes its medial *o* to the assimilation in unstressed position to the following vowel in the vocative *Ἄπελλον (*Ápellon*). Finally, Dunkel (1998: 79–81, with reference to previous literature) explains the peculiar vocalism of compound names like Ποσειδῶν (*Poseidôn*), Ποτειδάων (*Poteidáōn*) and Ἡρᾰκλῆς (*Hēraklês*) as original vocatives of divine names.

9.4. Now to examples of VpN in situations where names were borrowed from Greek into other languages, in particular in the context of Christianisation. In Syriac, the vocatives of Greek names like *Paule, Aleksandre* etc. serve as nominatives beside *Paulōs* and *Aleksandrōs*, etc. (Littmann 1916: 97; Adamik 1987: 4). Since final -*ī* was lost in Syriac, names going back to Latin vocatives in -*ī* or Greek vocatives in -ιε (-*ie* > *-*ī*) end in plain consonants, e.g. *mwryk* beside *mwrykys* < Μαυρίκιος (*Mauríkios*). When the knowledge of Greek as a spoken language waned and Syriac itself developed into a written, learned language, these 'popular' forms retreated from the literature and the number of Greek names in -*os* increased (Littmann 1916: 98).

9.5. In Coptic, Greek and Latin loan names continuing the vocative like *Geōrge, Maximine* etc. are very frequent, even though in high, literary style forms in -*os* also occur (Littmann 1916: 102; Adams 2003: 515). This reinforces the impression that VpN is a phenomenon originating in spoken language contact.

9.6. In Georgian, nominatives like *iv k'e* = *Iesu K'riste, iowane, pawle, petr^e* are again based on Greek vocatives (Littmann 1916: 101; Wackernagel 1920: 310), whereas in neighbouring Armenian Greek names in -*os* preponderate, although occasionally forms occur that could go back to Greek vocatives (Littmann 1916: 101).

9.7. The preceding examples come from countries with more or less intensive linguistic contacts with Greek. Ethiopia lies on the margins of the ancient Greek cultural sphere and the exchange was more via the written than the spoken word. Therefore it comes as no surprise that Greek names in Ethiopian (Amharic) sources generally have the 'learned' ending -*ōs* (Littmann 1916: 104–105).[25]

9.8. Finally, a modern instance of VpN. Except for masculine *o*-stems, which mostly retain the inherited ending *-e*, the vocative of Modern Greek is identical with the accusative and ends in the bare stem vowel (Ruge 1997: 32–37). Only one subclass of masculine *o*-stem nouns forms its vocative according to the same, clearly productive, pattern. This includes γέρος (*géros*) 'old man', but also many personal names, like Αλέκο (*Aléko*), Γιόργο (*Giórgo*), Πέτρο (*Pétro*). The linchpin for the extensive merger of accusative and vocative may perhaps be sought in the question πως σε λένε (*pōs se léne*) 'what's your name?', which literally means 'how does one call you?' and asks for the accusative. Alternatively, the identity of vocatives and accusatives in stem-classes with vowel-final base forms may have been the trigger for this phenomenon. In any case, the Modern Greek vocative underlies the names of many Greek emigrants in modern Germany: countless people with the name Γιάννης (*Giánnēs*, pronounced [janis]) are more or less officially known as *Janni* in German; the German pop singer *Costa Cordalis* was born in Greece as Κονσταντίνος Κορδάλης (*Konstantínos Kordálēs*). Κόστα (*Kósta*) is the vocative of Κόστας (*Kóstas*), the hypocoristically shortened form of the first name. It is noteworthy that the surname, which is not used in familiar forms of address, is retained in the nominative in the German version of the name.

10. Slavic

The Slavic languages, medieval and modern, provide numerous and diverse examples for VpN, some of them certain, some more hypothetical and amenable to alternative explanations. This makes research into aspects of the Slavic vocative a particularly interesting field because many Slavic languages retain it as a vivid and morphologically rich category, whereas those languages that do not have it any more lost it relatively recently in the historic period. Thus its demise can be studied in the extant documents. Neither is VpN restricted to situations of language contact in Slavic, but there are more or less clear examples of language-internal cases as well.

10.1. A language that is said to have lost the vocative very early is Russian. First traces of this process have been claimed to be observable as early as the 11th century (see the literature cited in Strakov 2004: 111–112). Strakov (2004) subjects the problem of the interchange of vocatives and nominatives, and of vocative morphology, to a detailed investigation and comes to the dissenting conclusion that the alleged cases of early loss of vocatives are rather due to certain practices in the translation and transliteration of Greek texts into Russian and other Church Slavonic traditions (Strahov 2004: 111–115). Of interest for the present study are those cases where vocatives appear in positions where nominatives or other cases would be expected. Again, Strahov's approach is the same: partly, the examples have nothing do to with linguistic phenomena as such, but are due to the slavish translation and mechanical transliteration from Greek into Russian (Strahov 2004: 115–116),[26] or they result from misunderstandings (Strahov 2004: 117), or they find some other bookish explanation. For example, he argues that the abbreviation *апло* (*aplo*) referring to the female saint Thekla, renders the Greek masc. *ἀπόστολος* (*apóstolos*; with omission of the final -*s*) and must not to be understood as the feminine Church Slavonic vocative *апостоло* (*apostolo*; Strahov 2004: 118–119). In some instances, vocative forms in place of other cases seem to be triggered by a laudatory context, that is to say, in a context that is fundamentally that of eulogy, whereby the name of the praised saint may be syntactically attracted to the address inherent in the situation (Strahov 2004: 122). As Strahov puts the matter, the question of these apparent vocatives is not one pertaining to 'language', but to 'texts' and to the mechanics of textual translation and transmsission. It is noteworthy that the phenomenon seems to be restricted to the names of Christian saints in hymnography and literature derived from it (Strahov 2004: 119–120).

10.2. In the second part of his study, Strahov (2004: 124–133) makes reference to another, related phenomenon that is more *sprachwirklich* than the previous ones. In various medieval Slavic church traditions, members of the clergy bore names that were properly the vocatives of their patron saints' names. These names could be used in all syntactic functions in written documents. Examples of this type can be explained by the transposition of forms by which the saints were addressed in the church service, first to anthroponomy, then into written texts. Unlike the examples described in the preceding paragraph, such names are genuine examples of VpN. Their learned origin, however, is betrayed by their morphology. Names like *Геωргиѥ* (*Geōrgije*) or *Николае* (*Nikolae*) are formally Greek vocatives; the proper Slavic vocatives would be *Геωргию* (*Geōrgiju*) or *Николаю* (*Nikolaju*). For a subgroup of such names, a predilection for 'vocatival' forms may have been prompted because of phonotactic reasons: after the loss of final -*ъ* (-*ŭ* = 'yor') in the spoken Slavic languages, names like *Петре* (*Petre*), *Павле* (*Pavle*), *Митре* (*Mitre*) etc. had the advantage of ending in an open syllable instead of a consonant cluster.

10.3. In Bosnian-Croatian-Serbian epic poetry, vocatives can be used in subject position, but this is restricted to masculine nouns, overwhelmingly personal names and titles, rarely animals or things, ending in consonants, e.g.

(7) *vino   pije   silan-ø   car-ø   Stjepan-e*
wine.acc.sg drink.3sg strong-nom.sg emperor-nom.sg Stjepan-voc.sg
'the strong emperor Stjepan is drinking wine'

(only *Stjepane* being in the vocative, but not the title *car*, nor the adjective *silan*),

(8) *netko   bješe   Strahinić-u   ban-e,*
someone.nom.sg be.pst.3sg Strahinić-voc.sg ban-voc.sg
bješe   ban-e   u   malen-oj   Banjsk-oj
be.pst.3sg ban-voc.sg in little-loc.sg Banjska-loc.sg
'there was a Ban Strahinić, he was Ban in little Banjska'

(both the name *Strahinić* and the title *ban* are in the vocative). This usage, which is not a feature of the spoken language, may have its origin in performances during which the praised hero was actually present and addressed by the singer, but it developed into an artificial device with the practical metrical advantage of providing the desired trochaic rhythm where the nominative would not yield it (Leskien 1870: 174; Brugmann and Delbrück 1893: 398; Vondrák 1906–1908, 2: 261–262; Vaillant 1977: 24; Vermeer 1994: 152). Svennung (1958: 410) mentions the same phenomenon also for Ukrainian popular songs.

10.4. Less certain and, at any rate, more complex is the possible case for VpN in the Slavic language of medieval Novgorod and neighbouring towns. This North-Russian dialect has been transmitted on birch bark letters from the 11th–15th centuries. In these documents, the ending of the nominative of masculine *o*-stem nouns is unexpectedly *-e*, in contrast to *-ъ* (*-ŭ*) in all other Slavic languages (Zaliznjak 2004: 99–106). Numerous explanations have been proposed for which at first sight looks like a mysterious ending. Relevant for the present study are the ones advocated by Vermeer (1991, 1994) and recently by Kwon (2009). Both scholars argue for the analogical introduction of the ending *-e* of the vocative into the nominative, albeit with differences in the paths chosen. The starting point for both explanations is the paradigm of masculine *o*-stem nouns in Proto-Slavic. The inherited Proto-Indo-European nominative singular *-os* developed regularly into Proto-Savic *-o* (or *-ă* at an early period), the accusative *-om* into short *-ŭ*, traditionally written *-ъ* in Slavic linguistics. This state of affairs is not attested in Slavic as such, but it can be reconstructed fairly securely for Proto-Slavic.[27] Since the resulting masculine ending *-o (*-ă) was identical with that of the neuter o-stems, there was pressure within the system to differentiate the two categories, in order to maintain a morphological distinction between masculines and neuters. In all Slavic languages with the exception of the dialect of Novgorod and the surrounding area, this end was achieved by introducing the nominative ending of the u-stems -ъ (see Majer 2011 for various hypotheses relating to this replacement). Only occasionally have traces of the earlier ending -o survived (for one of them, see section 10.5. below).

The solution for the origin of nominative -e in the dialect of Novgorod, proposed by Vermeer (1991, 1994), is that this ending had been taken over analogically from the i̯o-stems. The reason why speakers of Slavic in Novgorod did not proceed in tandem with the rest of Slavic, is, according to Vermeer (1994: 148–149), that the language of Novgorod built on a strong Finnic substrate. Although Finnic languages possess an elaborate case system, this system differs from that of Slavic in two essential points: the Finnic system has no vocative, but uses the nominative in situations of address; and in Finnic, the object is usually marked by an overt ending different from that of the nominative in the singular (Vermeer 1994: 149; Hakulinen 1957: 62). Common Slavic -ъ for the nom. would have obliterated the distinction between the nominative, the subject case, and the accusative, the object case, which was also -ъ < *-om. Therefore *-e, the nominative of the masculine i̯o-stems, suggested itself, which in the situation of language shift had the advantage for speakers of Finnic of introducing the familiar formal identity of nominative and vocative into the o-stems. Note, however, that the ending *-e of the i̯o-stem nominative and vocative required by Vermeer's analogy is merely reconstructed. Although its previous presence in the language is not implausible, the fact remains that it is not attested as such.

Therefore a different explanation, likewise invoking the vocative as linchpin for the change, was proposed by Kwon (2009). He makes the observation that the nominative singular ending -e of the o-stems is best attested among personal names, and is longest retained there, whereas the standard Russian ending -ъ/-Ø encroached slowly upon common nouns. He argues that the vocative ending was introduced as an animacy marker on personal names in this dialect, i.e. as a differential subject marker, to rescue masculines from being confused with neuters, at an early period when the nominative ending of o-stems was still inherited *-o. There is further evidence that animacy had a great – and early – salience in the dialect of Novgorod, in contrast to the other Slavic languages (Kwon 2009: 50–51). During a liminal period, when the vocative as a morphological category faded out, that is, at a time when some speakers still used the morphologically marked vocative in its original function, but when it had already disappeared from the active grammar of others, "the ending could have embraced all *o*-stem nouns and further agreeing parts of speech" (Kwon 2009: 49), in a process of over-generalisation. Like Vermeer (1994), Kwon reckons with the substratal influence of speakers of Finnic.

Even though Vermeer's and Kwon's accounts differ in the details, the precise details are of no concern for the present study. What is important is that both accounts reckon with a situation of language shift to Slavic by speakers of Finnic languages who were unfamiliar with the distinction between nominative and vocative in their original languages, and for whom therefore the formal identity of the two cases would have been no matter for concern. Thus, if one of these two explanations of Novgorodian *-e* is correct, we are not looking at a simple case of VpN, but rather at the spread of the vocative ending within the paradigm, triggered by complex inter-paradigmatic analogies, possibly crossing linguistic borders.

10.5. Leskien (1870: 173–174) cites Russian dialectal forms like *(о)ратаюшко* (*(o)ratajuško*) 'dear ploughman', which is not only used as the regular *ā*-stem vocative of *(о)ратаюшка* (*(o)ratajuška*) 'ploughman' (term of endearment beside unmarked *оратай* (*orataj*)), but which gave rise to a new paradigm *(о)ратаюшко*, gen. *-ка* (*(o)ratajuško, -ka*), i.e. inflecting like a neuter *o*-stem. To this may perhaps be added the Ukrainian surnames in *-nko* that may ultimately find their origin in a similar process. Furthermore, Leskien (l.c.) suggests that Bosnian-Croatian-Serbian masculine names in *-o*, like *Ivo, Mirko, Ranko*,[28] be regarded as original vocatives of *ā*-stems, used in hypocoristic function for male persons (cp. *Ivo* beside *Ivica*, both from *Ivan*, or *Joško* beside *Joška*, both from *Josip*).[29] An argument against this explanation is that even though Bosnian-Croatian-Serbian is a language where the inflectionally marked vocative is quite alive, in the current grammar the vocative is identical with the nominative exactly in the masculine hypocoristic names ending in *-a*. Furthermore, relatively few variant forms in *-o* and *-a* can actually be found side by side of each other, derived from the same onomastic base (like *Ivica* beside *Ivo*). Leskien (l.c.) provides the alternative explanation that the feminine vocative ending *-o* had been analogically transferred to masculine names, for which he adduces further support from Modern Bulgarian (e.g. *безаконико* (*bezakoniko*) as vocative of *безаконик* (*bezakonik*) 'lawless man'). Vondrák (1906–1908, 1: 401) provides more Bosnian-Croatian-Serbian words of this structure, not restricted to anthroponyms, but all, often in a derogatory manner, referring to persons: *gúbo* 'mangy one', *gúšo* 'cankery one', *krézo* 'toothless one', *bráto* < *brät* 'brother', *médo* <

mèdvjed 'bear', but he does not specify whether these words can be inflected.

However, an altogether different explanation is available for those names. The *-o* could simply be the regular outcome of Proto-Indo-European **-os*, the ending of the masculine *o*-stems (see section 10.4. above), which survived marginally in anthroponomy, whereas the inherited ending was replaced by analogical **-ъ* elsewhere. Similar-looking names like *Marco* in Romance languages in contact with South Slavic may have reinforced the resilience of the names in *-o* against the spread of the new ending **-ъ*. In the same manner, the Serbian nominatives *Miloje, Blagoje*, for which Leskien also assumes a vocative origin, can be regarded as the regular outcomes of names in **-ịos*.

10.6. In Slovene, which lost the vocative some time after the 14th century (Vaillant 1977: 22), there is a group of names that have an *-e* in the nominative, but whose stems end in ⁻*et*- in the oblique cases, e.g. *France* (gen. *Franceta*), *Tone, Lojze*, but also *oče* 'father'. The straightforward explanation of such forms is that the productive suffix *-et-* < **-ęt-*, which attached to words for little animals in Proto-Slavic, was extended to names of persons as well. A more circuitous way to account for them is to assume that when the inherited vocative became obsolete in Slovene, the forms ending in *-e*, the erstwhile vocatives of *o*-stem nouns, were no longer understood as such and were accordingly reinterpreted as nominatives of *et*-stems. Straxov (2004: 131 fn. 31) makes a similar observation regarding the anthroponyms of 15th-century Dubrovnik, but seems to decide against the origin of names like *Лавре* (*Lavre*), *Жоре* (*Žore*), *Марює* (*Maroje*) etc. in vocatives.

10.7. In colloquial Polish, the vocative can be used as subject, e.g.

(9) *Lechu   nie   przyszed-ł*
     Lech-voc.sg   neg   come.pst-m
     'Lech has not come'

vs. standard *Lech nie przyszedł* (Kwon 2009: 48 fn. 6).

10.8. Modern Russian and its dialects provide a few further examples of VpN. High dignitaries of the Russian orthodox church are addressed as *владыко* (*vladyko*), the vocative of *владыка* (*vladyka*) 'ruler'. This vocative is often incorrectly used for the nominative with reference to bishops and patriarchs. Straxov (2004: 125) quotes an example of VpN from dialectal Russian of the 20th century:

(10) *шчо-бы*   *да-л*   *тибе*   *Господ-и*
    ščo-by   da-l   t'ib'e   Gospod'-i
    that.subj   give.pst-m   2sg.dat   Lord-voc.sg
    'may the Lord give you'

where *Господи* (*Gospod'i*) is vocative. Even though these examples from Russian may look like language-internal instances of VpN at first sight, they are more correctly ascribed to language contact. The vocatives do not originate in Russian itself, but rather have been borrowed from Church Slavonic, the language of the church, a related but nevertheless foreign idiom in which the vocative as a grammatical category still survives.

11. Finnish

In Finnish, which in the course of its history absorbed a large number of loanwords from its neighbouring languages, I identified two or three possible instances of VpN. Whereas Slavic words of the *o*-declension are usually borrowed as words ending in *-a* or *-u* in Finnish (see footnote 22 above), Slavic **păpъ*, later *popъ* 'priest', appears in Finnish as *pappi* 'cleric'. In view of the change of final **-e > -i*, which Finnish underwent in its prehistory (Hakulinen 1957: 22), the explanation suggests itself that the word for 'cleric' was borrowed from the Proto-Slavic vocative **păpe*. Since Finnish does not have a vocative case, this reinterpretation can be considered trivial by now. Something similar may underly the personal name *Petri* 'Peter' < **Petre* (cp. what was said about *Petre* in section 10.4. above). Finally, perhaps this explanation extends also to the common noun *risti* 'cross', which is usually derived from Old Russian *крьстъ* (*krьstъ*) 'cross', itself a loan from Old High German *krist* 'Christ, crucifix' (Kallio 2006: 156). However, perhaps the borrowed form was rather the vocative **kriste*, the form of address of the crucified 'Christ'. A difficulty with this explanation of *pappi* etc. resides in the fact that the stem vowel of those nouns remains *-i-* throughout the paradigm, e.g., gen. *papin, Petrin, kristin*, whereas in inherited '*e*-stems' *-i* in the nominative alternates with *-e-* elsewhere, e.g., *vesi*, gen. *veden* 'water'. In order for the present explanation to be correct, it must be assumed that the vowel *i* of the nominative was generalised throughout the paradigm. Seeing that the '*i*-stem' declension has become productive in Finnish, especially for loanwords, the explanation advanced here is a reasonable alternative to an exclusively phonological account of equations like *popъ ~ pappi* (see, e.g., Kallio 2006: 156).

12. Old Prussian

Old Prussian is an extinct Baltic language, closely related to Lithuanian and Latvian, spoken east of modern Gdańsk. It died out in the 17th or 18th century. The earliest extensive document about Prussia is the 14th-century *Cronica Terre Prussie*, an account of the Teutonic Order's crusade against the non-Christian Prussians, written by the German Peter of Dusburg. The chronicle contains a considerable number of Old Prussian male personal names (collected in Stifter 2008: 291–293), a large portion of which ends in -*e*. This is surprising, inasmuch as Old Prussian had no inflectional class that ended in -*e* in the nominative. However, like all Baltic languages, Old Prussian possessed a vocative case, while Middle High German did not. Therefore I proposed to regard at least a subset of those names in -*e* as Old Prussian vocatives, most probably of the *o*-stem declension, mistaken for nominatives by the Teutonic knights. Such an explanation suggests itself, for example, for the name *Wilke*, which looks like the expected Old Prussian vocative of *wilkis* 'wolf'.

13. Old English

Old English provides one somewhat uncertain example of VpN. The 8th-century manuscript N of *Caedmon's Hymn* uses the noun *scepen* 'creator' for the subject in line 6, where the other manuscripts have the grammatically expected form *sceppend*. Notwithstanding the divergence in the single *p*, Jiriczek (1912: 279) refers to other examples of OE vocatives in ⁻*n* (identified by Bülbring 1896) and suggests that scribe N, writing in the Northumbrian dialect of Old English, had used the form of the vocative for the nominative in this particular instance. However, this instance of VpN is different from most others discussed in this paper in that it is not a case of simple transference of the vocative form to the nominative, but in that it is rather due to the analogy of other stem classes where the two cases were identical, so that the formal distinction between them could get blurred. Furthermore, it is not completely ruled out that -*n* < -*nd* is simply an early example of a phonetic development that became more widespread in later Middle English.

14. Celtic

From the Neo-Celtic languages, i.e. the medieval Middle British and the modern Gaelic languages, several examples of VpN can be cited, both of language-external and language-internal nature.

14.1. The British Celtic languages lost all final syllables, i.e. the endings inherited from Proto-Celtic, in their prehistory. Nevertheless, on occasion these lost endings have left synchronic effects, inasmuch as grammatical categories that historically ended in a vowel trigger lenition (or 'soft mutation') on a following word. While masculine nouns and names typically continue non-leniting categories, male personal names (but also place names) – in all syntactical contexts – may trigger lenition on nouns and adjectives standing in apposition to them, e.g. Welsh *Dafydd frenin* 'King David' (< *brenhin* 'king'), *Hywel Dda* 'Hywel the Good' (< *da* 'good'), *Llandeilo Fawr* 'Great Llandeilo' (< *mawr* 'big, great'), *Llundain dref* 'London town' (< *tref* 'town'); Middle Breton offers *Ian Vadezour* 'John the Baptist' (< *badezour*) (Strachan 1909: 12; Morris Jones 1931: 42–43; Evans 1964: 15; Hemon 1975: 17). This behaviour could find its explanation in a generalised vocative form of the personal name,[30] the vocative having ended in **-e* in Proto-Celtic *o*-stem nouns. But caution needs to be applied: this special rule of lenition "only applies when the noun is a title or epithet specially applicable to the proper name; when it is an adventitious addition, inserted as it were parenthetically by way of explanation, it is generally not mutated" (Morris-Jones 1931: 43), e.g. unmutated *Paul gwas Duw* 'Paul, the servant of God' (not [†]*was*), *Rolant tywyssawc lluoed* 'Roland, the leader of the hosts' (not [†]*dywyssawc*).[31] Furthermore, in very old names, the adjectival epithet is also often unmutated, e.g. *Rhodri Mawr* 'Rhodri the Great' or *Dyfnwal Moelmud* 'Domnall the Bald and Silent'; names of major religious significance like *Iesu* 'Jesus' and *Duw* 'God' also show exceptional behaviour. Williams (1938: lxxix–lxxx) makes similar remarks about the fact that the presence of lenition after personal names is not as regular in early Middle Welsh as it appears in the classical language. Taking this as his starting point, Zimmer (1997: 1038–1044) proposes that the synchronically rather unpredictable presence of lenition after names in early texts could reflect the complex mutational effects of the names according to their syntactic function, i.e. lenition after old genitives, datives and vocatives, but non-lenition after nominatives and accusatives of male names, parallel to the systematic distribution of these effects obtaining in Old Irish. Even though Zimmer's statistics, derived from the early Middle Welsh tale *Culhwch ac Olwen*, are slanting towards his suggestion, the evidence does not unequivocally bear out the idea and could perhaps be explained differently. Ultimately, because of the complex distribution of the phenomenon in British, the situation is not easy to assess. However, even Zimmer is ready to accept that VpN may be invoked as the explanation at least for the lenition following divine or mythical names (1997: 1041).

14.2. The re-interpretation of vocatives as nominatives is not restricted to the pre-modern period, cp. the recent case *Hamish*, a name current in modern Scotland, which is the anglicised spelling of *á Sheumais* [(ə) he:maʃ], the Scots-Gaelic vocative of nominative *Seumas* [ʃe:mas] 'James'. A similar process lies behind the anglicisation *Vaughn* ← Welsh *fychan* [vəxan], vocative of *bychan* 'small one', and the anglicisation *Vevin* ← Irish *á Bhéibhinn* [(ə) vʲe:vʲənʲ], vocative of *Béibhinn* [bʲe:vʲənʲ], Old Irish *Bé Find* [b⁽ⁱ⁾e: v⁽ⁱ⁾ind] 'fair woman', and its modern and purely superficial association with the Norman name *Vivian*.

15. Tocharian

For the Indo-European branch of Tocharian, a family comprising the two extinct languages Tocharian A ('Turfanian') and Tocharian B ('Kuchean'), spoken in the 1ˢᵗ mill. A.D. in the Tarim Basin, Malzahn (2000) made the pertinent proposal that in Tocharian B the three duals *ñaktene* 'pair of gods', *eṅwene* 'pair of men', *pacere* 'parents (lit. pair of fathers)' show the unexpected ending *-e*. Whereas the regular ending, i.e. various allophonically conditioned reflexes of Proto-Tocharian $*-\ddot{a}$ [ə], can be traced back directly to the PIE *o*-stem nominative dual ending $*-oh_1$, this is not possible for *-e*. Malzahn suggests that it continues the allomorph *-o*, regularly shortened from $*-oh_1$ in pausa, i.e. in vocative usage. This explanation is phonologically possible, but see below for the plausibility of this explanation against the typological background.

16. Varia

Finally, I want to refer to a few isolated instances of VpN or phenomena that are reminiscent of it:

16.1. In Assyrian, the vocative of divine names, consisting of the bare stem, has become the usual form of those names, cp. *Bēl* 'God Lord', but *bēlu* 'lord' or *Šamaš* 'God Sun', but *šamšu* 'sun' (Littmann 1916: 96; Wackernagel 1920: 310).

16.2. In Hittite 'naming constructions', endingless forms, identical with the vocative, are used to introduce new names. This applies to names of persons, e.g. *MUNUS-aš ŠUM=šet ⁱŠintalimeni* '(there was) a woman, her name was Šintalimeniš' (KUB 33.121 ii 5), as well as to non-anthroponyms, e.g. *URU-aš ŠUM-an=šet* ᵁᴿ[ᵁŠ]*udul*, '(there was) a town, its name was Šudul' (KUB 24.8 i 7) (Hoffner and Melchert 2008: 244–245).

16.3. It is possible that the hypocoristic suffix *-i* of South German, which can be attached to almost any truncated name (e.g., *Michaela → Michi*, *Rudolf → Rudi*, *Eleonora → Elli*, *David → Dadi*),[32] finds its origin in the Latin vocative of such *i̯o*-stem gentilic names which became recycled as individual names after the demise of the classical Latin naming formula. The pattern could have been set by *Antonius*, vocative *Antoni → *truncated *Toni* (Petersmann 1998: 134) whence it became extremely productive.

17. Evaluation

We can now proceed to an assessment of the material collected in the preceding sections. The examples have been taken from a relatively small area (Europe, North Africa, Near East). They span almost 4,000 years and are taken from the Indo-European, Afro-Asiatic, Finno-Ugric and Tyrsenian language families and from the isolates Iberian and Basque. More than twenty languages have been cited as recipients of VpN, and around fifteen as donors. I am confident that much more material from all regions and linguistic families of the world could be added to the collection.[33] I am furthermore confident that – how ever limited – the sample is representative enough to allow the drawing of some preliminary generalisations concerning the phenomenon of VpN:

1.   VpN occurs particularly often in language contact, i.e. language-externally, but it can also be found, albeit with less frequency, in non-contact situations, i.e. language-internally. Some of the cited language-internal cases are ambiguous, however, e.g. British (14.1.), Old English (13.), Slovene (10.6.), or difficult to assess, e.g. Old Novgorodian (10.4.).

2.   Language-external VpN typically happens when the donor language possesses a morphologically marked vocative and the recipient language does not.[34] The reason for this is obviously that, given the token frequency of vocatives, especially of personal names, in natural conversation when calling for the attention of the

partners in conversation, speakers of languages without vocatives would not be able to expect that the very frequently used form of a name was not actually the base form. It is noteworthy that the possible, but ambiguous language-internal cases of British, Old English and Slovene occurred in languages that have lost the vocative; they are thus equivalent to external loans into languages without vocative.

3. VpN seems to be restricted to the singular. There are two obvious reasons for this: vocatives are typically used in the personal address of individuals, and, intimately connected with this, morphologically marked vocatives of non-singular numbers are lacking in many languages. The alleged case of VpN of three dual nouns in Tocharian B (15.) is peculiar in that it would be the only such non-singular example in the sample. This fact casts some doubt on the explanation, but does not falsify it. Maybe better examples for non-singular VpN will be discovered elsewhere in the languages of the world.

4. VpN typically affects personal names. Names of humans make up the bulk of the material, names of gods are far behind in second place.[35] This tendency finds a natural explanation in the frequency of vocatives of personal names in natural speech, whereas the use of theonyms is restricted to much more specific contexts.

5. VpN of names of humans occurs mostly language-externally, whereas VpN of names of gods tends to occur predominantly language-internally (e.g., 4. Etruscan which borrowed Italic theonyms in the nominative). The reason for this lies perhaps in the fact that situations that entail the invocation of deities are rarer in language-contact scenarios than those which entail direct interpersonal contact.

6. Much rarer are cases of VpN of non-anthroponymic or non-theonymic nouns. Where certain examples can be found, these typically involve referents high up on the animacy hierarchy, e.g. titles (e.g., 8.1. Latin *domine* 'master' in various languages, 10.3. Bosnian-Croatian-Serbian *bane* 'lord'), agent nouns (e.g., Greek 9.2. ἱππότα (*hippóta*) 'rider', 11. Finnish *pappi* 'cleric', 13. Old English *scepen*) or terms for classes of people (6.3. Basque *agure* 'old man'), which in natural discourse would have a reasonably

high token frequency in forms of direct address. If the explanation of the three Tocharian B duals *ñaktene* 'pair of gods', *eṅwene* 'pair of men', *pacere* 'parents' (15.) should be correct, it is noteworthy that they also fall in this class of words. Isolated instances of VpN of non-human referents are very uncertain (e.g., 6.1. Iberian *seśte* as a numismatic term). The possible case of Finnish *risti* 'cross' (11.) is only an apparent exception since it ultimately goes back to the name of Christ.

7.   The only systematic exception to the restriction against VpN of inanimate nouns are the Old Novgorodian nouns and participles in *-e* (10.4.), but it must be noted that their explanation as continuing vocatives is only a possibility. It is possible that VpN was one or *the* factor that created the starting base among personal names, from which the nominative ending *-e* eventually spread to all masculine *o*-stem nouns in an analogical extension which as such has nothing to do with VpN. I therefore draw the tentative conclusion from the case of Novgorodian that where VpN of common nouns seems to be attested, it is best ascribed to a secondary, analogical overgeneralisation that has to do with language-internal morphological rules, but not with VpN proper. This could also apply to 13. Old English *scepen* 'creator', if it belongs here at all.

The more general conclusion of the foregoing survey is that instead of being a rare phenomenon, the re-interpretation of vocatives of one language as nominatives in another language seems to be rather the rule in situations where languages with morphologically encoded vocatives come into contact with languages without it, and that similar things can occur, albeit under slightly different conditions, in language-internal developments. VpN tended to be treated as a marginal, if not exotic aberration in that it seemed to disregard the inflectional morphology and the grammatical categories of the donor languages. I hope to have demonstrated in this paper that quite to the contrary VpN is a widespread and – if I may say so – trivial phenomenon. In situations of language contact, not the category as such is borrowed in VpN, but a categorial marker of L1 is re-interpreted by speakers of L2.[36] This type of re-interpretation is more likely to occur when knowledge of L1 is limited or lacking (which in itself is indicative of not very intensive bilingualism; e.g., 4. Etruscan, 12. Old Prussian, 14.2. Gaelic). A situation where VpN obtains does not preclude the possibility that at the same or in a different period under sociolinguistically different circumstances nominatives can be borrowed as base forms as well (e.g., 7.2. Neo-Punic, 9.4. Syriac). For situations of language contact about which only insufficient historical information is available these broad tendencies may allow to make inferences about the level of knowledge of the target languages.

Notes

*   The work on this paper was undertaken as part of the project P20755-G03 'Old Celtic language remains in Austria' (http://www.univie.ac.at/austria-celtica/), funded by the FWF (Austrian Science Fund). I thank Anna Adaktylos, Joaquín Gorrochategui, Anders Jørgensen, Corinna Scheungraber, Stefan Schumacher, Rex Wallace and Paul Widmer for help and input.
      The following abbreviations are used:
      X = reconstructed form; X = reconstructed form that as such happens not to be attested in the historic corpus of a language but which can be generated with great confidence by synchronic grammatical rules; †X = wrong form (re)constructed for the sake of making a point; gen. = genitive, Gr. = Greek, Lat. = Latin, nom. = nominative, PIE = Proto-Indo-European, voc. = vocative, VpN = Vocatiuus pro Nominatiuo.

1.   'And Thyestes left it in turn to Agamemnon to carry', a quote from *Iliad* 2, 107. *T^{h}yest'* is for unelided *T^{h}yesta*, the vocative of nominative *T^{h}yéstēs*, which would be expected here. Note that Priscian's text below, although quoting the same passage, differs in the verb.

2.   (i) *censor-em=ue*   *tu-um*   *uel   quod*
      censor-acc.sg=or   2sg.poss-acc.sg   or   because
      trabeat-e   *salut-as*
      wearing a trabea-voc.sg.pred   greet-2sg
      'or because you, wearing a trabea [a knight's robe], (can) greet your censor'

3.   (ii) *mact-e*   *uirtut-e*   *es-to*
      blessed-voc.sg.pred   excellence-abl.sg   be-2sg.imp
      'be blessed by excellence!'

4.   (iii) *tu*   *quam*   *grat-us*   *erga*   *me*
      2sg.nom   how   grateful-nom.sg.pred   towards   1sg.acc
      fueri-s
      be.pst.subj.-2sg
      'how grateful you were towards me' (Cicero, *ad Atticum* 9, 11, A, 3)

5 .   There is a conceptual overlap of vocatives and imperatives. Littmann (1916: 110–111) draws attention to a number of cases where borrowing of the im-

perative as stem form of verbs has taken place (e.g., Greek loan verbs in Coptic). Cp. also Svennung (1958: 411).

6. Including zero-endings, as long as they are distinct from nominatives or the stem forms of the words.

7. Naturally, the reverse may also happen, that is, a nominative of the donor language being re-interpreted as a vocative in the recipient language because of surface similarity. A new nominative could then be backformed, like Oscan nom. *Herklos** ← Etruscan *Hercle* (Devoto 1928: 321).

8. One subtype of this is the typically language-internal generalisation of 'internal shortening' ("innere Kürzung", Kretschmer 1905: 132–134; Fraenkel 1956: 82–83). It involves the extension of originally intimate hypocoristics to general use, like German *Kurt* < *Kuonrât*, Italian *Dante* < *Durante*, French *sire* < *seniorem* etc.

9. The vocative-like status of this form can for example be seen in the fact that it cannot be used as the subject of a sentence.

10. Matters are complicated by the fact that the word for 'god' may itself be a loan from a Sabellic language (Wallace 2008: 128), originally perhaps an *o*-stem **aisos* (Untermann 2000: 68–69). If this is the case, Proto-Etruscan **aise* could again be due to the borrowing of a vocative.

11. There may have been a variant nominative singular of Latin gentilic names ending in *-i* instead of *-ius*, but its exact assessment is difficult. See Kaimio (1970) for a study of the phenomenon.

12. Etruscan had no vowel *o*, it is substituted by *u* in loans. The fact that the final nasal in Greek words shows up as *-m* in Etruscan may be due to an Italic language as mediator.

13. Schürr (2003) ascribes the origin of *Esimne* to Euganean, an otherwise unknown language in the Alps. For a different, more cautious assessment of *Essimnus/Essibnus* see Stifter forthc.

14. Untermann (1980: 48) mentions four possible instances of retention of Gaulish *-os*, viz. *anaioś* [B.1.36, .37], *biulakoś* [A.33–13], *botilkoś* [A.100–10,–11], *noukoś* [B.5.1.]. The first of these is surely to be connected with the Latin(ised) gentilic name *Annaeus*, for *botilkos* Untermann compares Gaul. *Bodilicus*; the others are without obvious parallels.

15. A longer list of Celtic names in Iberian texts from Ensérune in southern France was compiled by Ruiz Darasse (2010), but this article came to my attention too late to be fully included here. For a fuller treatment of the topic see also Stifter forthc.

16. On the picture of the inscription (http://www2.uah.es/imagines_cilii/fotos_cilii/14/cilii14,0301.jpg), I am only able to make out the final *ŕ*.

17. At the same time, these loans show that the involved Old Celtic languages had no *s*-less vocative in the consonantal-stem declension, i.e. the vocative of this declension did not consist of the plain stem.

18. Cp. section 8.1. on Latin below.

19. In particular, Karen Larsdatter's website *Basque Onomastics of the Eighth to Sixteenth Centuries* (http://larsdatter.com/basque/) records no instance of *Martie*.

20. For example:
    (iv) *C.   Fuf-i   Maxim-e   uix-it   an(nos)   XXXV*
         Caius Fufius-voc.sg Maximus-voc.sg live.pst-3sg year-acc-pl 35
         'C. Fufius Maximus lived 35 years' (CIL 8 1,2110).
    See also Svennung (1958: 395).

21. As such, the *signa* themselves appear to represent instances of VpN; cp. Adams (2003: 512 fn. 295).

22. Szemerényi (1977: 153–154) wants to derive the basic kinship terms of Indo-European from vocatives, too, but his etymological proposals strain credulity on formal grounds and will therefore not be included in this survey.

23. Incidentally, in the corresponding Vedic vocative *dyauḥ pitar* exactly the opposite happened: the vocative was supplanted by the form of the nominative.

24. Latin *deus*, unlike all other *o*-stem nouns, has no vocative distinct from the nominative.

25. Where Ethiopian sources have forms that look more vocatival, e.g. *Anṭōnā* and *Anṭōnī* beside regular *Anṭōniōs*, Littmann (1916: 105) suspects Coptic, Arabic or Syriac intermediaries.

26. Note also that some of the vocative forms used in Russian texts do not conform with Russian morphophonology, but are rather borrowed as such from Greek, cp. the vocative архистратиге (*arxistratige*) < ἀρχιστράτηγε (*arkʰistrátēge*) instead of expected архистратиже (*arxistratiže*) with palatalised guttural, or Тимоѳеѥ (*Timoθeje*) < Τιμόθεε (*Timótʰee*) instead of Тимоѳею (*Timoθeju*) with the ending appropriate to the 'soft' stem (Straxov 2004: 120–121).

27. This is not the place to go into the details of the fundamental problems besetting the reflex of Proto-Indo-European *-os* in Slavic. An extensive literature devoted to this question exists, as do alternative accounts of the developments; see, e.g., Vermeer (1991: 280–281), Kwon (2009: 46–47), and Majer (2011: 353) for further literature and for weighty arguments in favour of the assumption presented above. I want to add a further argument, apparently not mentioned in the literature so far: whereas in early loans from Slavic into Finnic the ending of the *o*-stem masculine nominative singular *-ъ* is usually represented by *u* (cp. *Turku* [name of a town] < Sl. *tъrgъ* 'market-place'), in some loanwords this ending is reflected by *-a* which points to early

Slavic *-ă (later > -o), i.e. *pakana* 'pagan' < Sl. *păgānă/ъ (later *poganъ*), *kuoma* 'godparent, friend' < Slavic *kōmă/ъ (cp. Old Russian кумъ [*kumъ*] 'godfather'), unless the feminine form *kōmā (cp. Old Russian кума [*kuma*]) was borrowed. This Slavic *-ă could be the inherited vowel *-o, before it was replaced by -ъ.

28. Regarding the frequent use of *Марко* (*Marko*) instead of the expected *Маркъ* (*Markъ*) for the name of the evangelist Mark in Church Slavonic literature, Straxov (2004: 128–129) ascribes it to 'hellenising' orthography, i.e. spelling Μάρκος (*Márkos*) with omission of the final -ς.

29. I had independently suggested something similar in Stifter (2008: 289), but I now regard this hypothesis as false and adopt the explanation at the end of section 10.5.

30. Zimmer (1997: 1038–1039) calls it "[d]ie traditionelle Erklärung" ('the traditional explanation'), but he does not specify the sources for this traditional explanation. Morris-Jones (1931: 42) explains this behaviour as being due to the fact that "[t]he epithet probably formed a compound with the name in Brythonic, so that its initial was softened, and this became the rule". However, the sequence of elements in British compounds is usually the reverse, the determinor preceding the determinate. Morris-Jones' explanation can therefore not account for the facts.

31. Morris-Jones goes on to qualify the previous statement by saying that the "adventitious addition […] is, however, often mutated, especially when vocative" (i.e. in situations of address), e.g. *o Dduw gwyn, feddyg einioes* 'oh fair God, doctor of life' (< *meddyg*) or *Daniel, ŵr anwyl* 'Daniel, bold man' (< *gwr*). This tendency in Welsh for lenition in the "vocative" cannot, however, continue the old morphosyntax of the Proto-British vocative, as the lack of lenition on *gwyn* 'fair' (not †*wyn*), the attribute immediately following *Duw* 'God', betrays.

32. I want to add that German names like *Otti, Edi, Gusti, Willi*, cited by Zimmer (1893: 197) as examples of a particular type of hypocoristic formation, but derided as entirely alien and unfamilar to himself and to all of his acquaintances in the following volume of the same journal by Kretschmer (1895: 269), are perfectly normal formations for my German *Sprachgefühl*, and are indeed all well-known to me.

33. E.g., Vondrák (1906–1908, 1: 401) mentions Aleksej I. Sobolevskij who provides Old Indic examples in *Лекции по истории русского языка*, *Москва* 1903, 148 ('Lessons on the history of the Russian language, Moscow'). I was not able to follow up this reference.

34. Strictly speaking, in the case of fragmentary or ill-understood languages like Iberian and Raetic it cannot be said with certainty whether they possessed morphologically marked vocatives or not.

35. The particular factors obtaining in the languages chosen for this study do not provide a large enough basis to make wide-sweeping generalisations in the regard of theonyms. Names of gods may be underrepresented in the sample, either because of insufficient evidence (e.g. in the case of the very fragmentary Raetic language) or because of the historico-religious contexts (in Christian societies, names of non-Christian gods are unlikely to be borrowed in the forms of address; on the other hand, the name of the Christian god is notoriously vocative-less in Latin *deus*).

36. This suggestion builds on the hypothesis that in natural situations of contact speakers of L2 are exposed to the vocatives of names of L1 in a particularly high frequency. This needs to be tested in empirical studies.

References

Adamik, Tamás
    1987   *Romaniane vivat* – Bemerkungen zum Gebrauch des Vokativs und zur afrikanischen Latinität. In *Latin vulgaire – latin tardif. Actes du Ier Colloque international sur le latin vulgaire et tardif (Pécs, 2–5 septembre 1985)*, József Herman (ed.), 1–9. Tübingen: Max Niemeyer.

Adams James N.
    2003   *Bilingualism and the Latin Language.* Cambridge: Cambridge University Press.

Adams James N.
    2007   *The Regional Diversification of Latin 200 BC–AD 600.* Cambridge: Cambridge University Press.

Bloomfield, Leonard
    1933   *Language.* London: George Allen & Unwin.

Brugmann, Karl
    1903–1904   *Kurze vergleichende Grammatik der indogermanischen Sprachen. 2. und 3. Lieferung. Von den Wortformen und ihrem Gebrauch und Lehre von den Satzgebilden.* Strassburg: Trübner.

Brugmann, Karl and Berthold Delbrück
    1892   *Grundriss der vergleichenden Grammatik der indogermanischen Sprachen. Zweiter Band. Zahlwortbildung, Casusbildung der Nomina, Pronomina, verbale Stammbildung und Flexion (Conjugation). Zweiter Theil.* Strassburg: Trübner.

Brugmann, Karl and Berthold Delbrück
1893   *Grundriss der vergleichenden Grammatik der indogermanischen Sprachen. Dritter Band. Vergleichende Syntax der indogermanischen Sprachen. Erster Theil.* Strassburg: Trübner.

Bülbring, Karl
1896   Vokativformen im Altenglischen. *Indogermanische Forschungen* 6: 140.

Correa, José Antonio
1993   Antropónimos galos y ligures en inscripciones ibéricas. In *Studia Palaeohispanica et Indogermanica J. Untermann ab amicis hispanicis oblata*, Ignacio-Javier Adiego Lajara, Jaime Siles, and Javier Velaza (eds.), 101–116. Barcelona: Universidad de Barcelona.

de Hoz, Javier
2008   A Celtic personal name on an Etruscan inscription from Ensérune, previously considered Iberian (MLH B.1.2b). In *Celtic and Other Languages in Ancient Europe*, Juan L. García-Alonso (ed.), 17–27. Salamanca: Publicaciones Universidad de Salamanca.

de Simone, Carlo
1970   *Die griechischen Entlehnungen im Etruskischen. Zweiter Band. Untersuchung.* Wiesbaden: Otto Harrassowitz.

de Simone, Carlo
1980   Gallisch *Nemeti̯os* – etruskisch *Nemetie. Zeitschrift für vergleichende Sprachforschung* 94: 198–202.

de Vaan, Michiel
2008   *Etymological Dictionary of Latin and the other Italic Languages.* (Leiden Indo-European Etymological Dictionary Series 7.) Leiden/Boston: Brill.

Devoto, Giacomo
1928   L'Etrusco come intermediario di parole greche in latino. *Studi etruschi* 2: 307–341.

Dunkel, George
1998   On the short vowel in the name Ἡρακλῆς. *Museum Helveticum* 55: 76–83.

Evans, Daniel Simon
1964   *A Grammar of Middle Welsh.* Dublin: Dublin Institute for Advanced Studies.

Ferrer i Jané, Joan and Francesco Giral Royo
2007   A propósito de un semis de **ildiŕda** con leyenda **erder**. Marcas de valor léxicas sobre monedas ibéricas. *Palaeohispanica* 7: 83–99.

Fraenkel, Ernst
1956 Zur griechischen Wortforschung. *Glotta* 35: 77–92.

Hakulinen, Lauri
1957 *Handbuch der finnischen Sprache. 1. Band.* Wiesbaden: Harrassowitz.

Hemon, Roparz
1975 *A Historical Morphology and Syntax of Breton.* Dublin: Dublin Institute for Advanced Studies.

Hedberg, Torsten
1935 *Eustathios als Attizist.* Inaugural-Dissertation. Uppsala: Almqvist & Wiksells.

Hermann, Eduard
1937 Zwei Analogiebildungen. *Zeitschrift für vergleichende Sprachforschung* 64: 72–75.

Hoffner, Harry and H. Craig Melchert,
2008 *Grammar of the Hittite Language. Part 1. Reference Grammar.* Winona Lake, Indiana: Eisenbrauns.

Hofmann, Johann B. and Anton Szantyr
1965 *Lateinische Syntax und Stilistik.* München: C.H. Beck'sche Verlagsbuchhandlung.

Jiriczek, Otto
1912 *Scepen* in Caedmons Hymnus Hs. N. *Indogermanische Forschungen* 30: 279–282.

Kaimio, Jorma
1970 The nominative singular in *-i* of Latin gentilicia. *Arctos* N.S. 6: 23–42.

Kallio, Petri
2006 On the Earliest Slavic Loanwords in Finnic. *Slavica Helsingiensia* 27: 154–166.

Kretschmer, Paul
1895 Die boiotischen kosenamen auf *-ει*. *Zeitschrift für vergleichende Sprachforschung* 33: 268–272.

Kretschmer, Paul
1905 Etymologien. 2. *Mavors, Mars, Mamers*. *Zeitschrift für vergleichende Sprachforschung* 38: 129–134.

Kwon, Kyongjoon
2009 The early development of animacy in Novgorod: Evoking the vocative anew. In *Grammatical Change in Indo-European Languages. Papers Presented at the Workshop on Indo-European Linguistics at the XVIIIth International Conference on Historical Linguistics, Montreal, 2007*, Vit Bubenik, John

Hewson, and Sarah Rose (eds.), 43–53. (Current Issues in Linguistic Theory 305.) Amsterdam, Philadelphia: John Benjamins.

Lapesa, Rafael
1951   La apócope de la vocal en castellano antigo. Intento de explicación histórica. *Estudios dedicados a Menendez Pidal* 2: 185–226.

Lapesa, Rafael
1975   De nuevo sobre la apócope vocálica en castellano medieval. *Nueva revista de filología hispánica* 24 (1): 13–23.

Leskien, August
1870   über den dialekt der russischen volkslieder des gouvernements Olonec. *Beiträge zur vergleichenden Sprachforschung auf dem Gebiete der arischen, celtischen und slawischen Sprachen* 6: 152–186.

Leumann, Manu
1939   Literaturbericht für das Jahr 1937. Lateinische Laut- und Formenlehre. *Glotta* 28: 1–21.

Littmann, Enno
1916   Anredeformen in erweiterter Bedeutung. In *Nachrichten von der Königlichen Gesellschaft der Wissenschaften zu Göttingen. Philologisch-historische Klasse*. Berlin: Weidmann, 94–111.

Löfstedt, Einar
1956   *Syntactica. Studien und Beiträge zur historischen Syntax des Lateins. Erster Teil. Über einige Grundfragen der lateinischen Nominalsyntax. 2. erweiterte Auflage*. Lund: Gleerup.

Majer, Marek
2011   PIE *so*, *seh₂*, *tod* / PSl. *tъ*, *ta*, *to* and the development of PIE word-final *-os* in Proto-Slavic. In *Indogermanistik und Linguistik im Dialog. Akten der XIII. Fachtagung der Indogermanischen Gesellschaft vom 21. bis 27. September 2008 in Salzburg*, Thomas Krisch and Thomas Lindner (eds.), 352–360. Wiesbaden: Ludwig Reichert Verlag.

Malzahn, Melanie
2000   Toch. B *ñaktene* 'Götterpaar' und Verwandtes. *Tocharian and Indo-European Studies* 9: 45–52.

Marx, Friedrich
1894   *De ratione dicendi ad C. Herennium*. Leipzig: Teubner.

Meyer-Lübke, Wilhelm
1935   *Romanisches etymologisches Wörterbuch. 3. vollständig neubearbeitete Auflage*. Heidelberg: Carl Winters Universitätsbuchhandlung.

Michelena, Luis
1961   A propósito de *done* 'santo'. *Boletín de la Real Sociedad Vascongada de los Amigos del País* 17: 222–224.

Morris-Jones, John
1931   *Welsh Syntax. An Unfinished Draft.* Cardiff: The University of Wales Press Board.

Orduña Aznar, Eduardo
2005   Sobre algunos posibles numerales en textos ibéricos. *Palaeohispanica* 5: 491–506.

Petersmann, Hubert
1998   Gab es ein afrikanisches Latein? Neue Sichten eines alten Problems der lateinischen Sprachwissenschaft. In *Estudios de lingüística latina. Actas del IX Coloquio Internacional de Lingüística Latina. Universidad Autonóma de Madrid, 14–18 de abril de 1997*, Benjamín García-Hernández (ed.), 125–136. Madrid: Ed. Clásicas.

Rix, Helmut
1963   *Das etruskische Cognomen. Untersuchungen zu System, Morphologie und Verwendung der Personennamen auf den jüngeren Inschriften Nordetruriens.* Wiesbaden: Otto Harrassowitz.

Rix, Helmut
1981   Rapporti onomastici fra il panteon etrusco e quello romano. *Gli Etruschi e Roma: Atti dell'incontro di studio in onore di Massimo Pallottino. Roma, 11–13 dicembre 1979*, 104–126. Roma: Bretschneider.

Rix, Helmut
1994   *Die Termini der Unfreiheit in den Sprachen Alt-Italiens.* (Forschungen zur antiken Sklaverei 25.) Stuttgart: Franz Steiner Verlag.

Rix, Helmut
1995   Etruskische Personennamen. In *Namenforschung. Ein internationales Handbuch zur Onomastik*, Ernst Eichler, Herold Hilty, Heinrich Löffler, Hugo Steger, and Ladislav Zgusta (eds.), 719–724. (Handbücher zur Sprach- und Kommunikationswissenschaft 11.1.) Berlin/ New York: Walter de Gruyter.

Rix, Helmut
1998   *Rätisch und Etruskisch.* (Innsbrucker Beiträge zur Sprachwissenschaft. Vorträge und kleinere Schriften 68.) Innsbruck: Institut für Sprachwissenschaft der Universität Innsbruck.

Ruge, Hans
1997   *Grammatik des Neugriechischen. Lautlehre, Formenlehre, Syntax. 2. Auflage.* Köln: Romiosini Verlag.
Ruiz Darasse, Coline
2010   Les ibères en Languedoc: L'onomastique celtique d'Ensérune en écriture paléohispanique. *Palaeohispanica* 10: 335–354.
Schumacher, Stefan
1998   Sprachliche Gemeinsamkeiten zwischen Rätisch und Etruskisch. *Der Schlern* 72: 90–114.
Schumacher, Stefan
2004   *Die rätischen Inschriften. Geschichte und heutiger Stand der Forschungen.* 2d. ed. (Innsbrucker Beiträge zur Kulturwissenschaft 121 = Archaeolingua 2.) Innsbruck: Institut für Sprachen und Literaturen der Universität Innsbruck.
Schürr, Diether
2003   *Esimne*: Ein alpiner Name und seine Verbreitung. *Beiträge zur Namensforschung* N.F. 38 (4): 379–399.
Schwyzer, Eduard
1939   *Griechische Grammatik. Erster Band. Allgemeiner Teil. Lautlehre. Wortbildung. Flexion.* München: C.H. Beck.
Sihler, Andrew L.
1995   *New Comparative Grammar of Greek and Latin.* New York/ Oxford: Oxford University Press.
Solier, Yves and Henri Barbouteau
1988   Découverte de nouveaux plombs, inscrits en ibère, dans la région de Narbonne. *Revue archéologique de Narbonnaise* 21: 61–94.
Solmsen, Felix
1906   Review of Brugmann 1903–4. *Berliner philologische Wochenschrift* 26: 176–185.
Steinbauer, Dieter
1993   Untersuchungen zu Texten und Grammatik des Etruskischen. Habilitationsschrift. Universität Regensburg.
Stifter, David
2008 [2010] OPr. *kelleweʃze* 'Driver of a Cart'. *Historische Sprachforschung* 121: 281–296.
Stifter, David
forthc.   Two Continental Celtic studies: the vocative of Gaulish, and *Essimnus.* In *Continental Celtic Word Formation. The Onomastic Data*, Juan Luis García Alonso (ed.). Salamanca: Ediciones Universidad de Salamanca.

Strachan, John
1909   *An Introduction to Early Welsh.* Manchester: Manchester University Press.

Straxov 2004 = Страхов, Александр Б.
2004   О вокативе и номинативе в древнерусских текстах и языке [On the vocative and nominative in Old Russian texts and the Old Russian language]. *Palaeoslavica* 12 (1): 111–136.

Svennung, Josef
1958   *Anredeformen. Vergleichende Forschungen zur indirekten Anrede in der dritten Person und zum Nominativ für den Vokativ.* (Skrifter utgivna av K. Humanistiska Vetenskapssamfundet i Uppsala 42.) Uppsala/Wiesbaden: Almqvist & Wiksells Boktryckeri/Otto Harrassowitz.

Szemerényi, Oswald
1977   Studies in the Kinship Terminology of the Indo-European Languages, with special references to Indian, Greek and Latin. *Acta Iranica* 16 (Acta Iranica: Série 3, Textes et mémoires 7): 1–240.

Trask, Robert Lawrence
1997   *The History of Basque.* London/New York: Routledge.

Trask, Robert Lawrence
2008   *Etymological Dictionary of Basque.* Edited for web publication by Max W. Wheeler. Sussex: University of Sussex. www.sussex.ac.uk/english/documents/lxwp23-08-edb.pdf, 14.10.2012.

Untermann, Jürgen
1980   *Monumenta Linguarum Hispanicarum 2. Die Inschriften in iberischer Schrift aus Südfrankreich.* Wiesbaden: Reichert.

Untermann, Jürgen
2000   *Wörterbuch des Oskisch-Umbrischen.* Heidelberg: Universitätsverlag C. Winter.

Vaillant, André
1977   *Grammaire comparée des langues slaves. Tome V: La syntaxe.* Paris: Klincksieck.

Vermeer, Willem
1991   The Mysterious North Russian Nominative Singular Ending *-e* and the Problem of the Reflex of Indo-European **-os* in Slavic. *Die Welt der Slaven* 36: 271–295.

Vermeer, Willem
1994   On explaining why the Early North Russian nominative singular in *-e* does not palatalize stem final velars. *Russian Linguistics* 18: 145–157.

Vondrák, Václav
  1906–1908   *Vergleichende Slavische Grammatik. 1. Band: Lautlehre und Stammbildungslehre. 2. Band: Formenlehre und Syntax.* Göttingen: Vandenhoeck & Ruprecht.

Vottero, Guy
  1985   Procedes d'expressivite dans l'onomastique personelle de Beotie. In *La Beotie antique. Lyon – Saint Etienne. 16-20 mai 1983*, Gilbert Argoud and Paul Roesch (eds.), 403–417. Paris: Éditions du CNRS.

Wackernagel, Jacob
  1920   *Vorlesungen über Syntax mit besonderer Berücksichtigung von Griechisch, Lateinisch und Deutsch.* Basel: Emil Birkhäuser.

Wallace, Rex E.
  2008   *Zikh Rasna. A Manual of the Etruscan Language and Inscriptions.* Ann Arbor, Mich.: Beech Stave Press.

Williams, Ifor
  1938   *Canu Aneirin gyda rhagymadrodd a nodiadau* [The Poems of Aneirin with introduction and notes]. Caerdydd: Gwasg Prifysgol Cymru.

Zaliznjak 2004 = Зализняк, Андрей А.
  2004   *Древненовгородский диалект. 2. изд., переработ. с учетом материале находок 1995–2003 гг.* [The dialect of Old-Novgorod. 2d ed., supplemented with material from the 1995–2003 excavations]. Москва: Языки славянской культуры.

Zimmer, Heinrich
  1893   Keltische studien. *Zeitschrift für vergleichende Sprachforschung* 32: 155–240.

Zimmer, Stefan
  1997   Archaismen in *Culhwch ac Olwen. Zeitschrift für celtische Philologie* 49–50: 1033–1054.

The vocative and its kin: marking function through prosody[*]

Aslı Göksel and Markus A. Pöchtrager

Abstract

This paper discusses the prosodic vocative and other tunes expressing various functions that are superimposed on names in Austrian German and Turkish, two languages with different word level stress. We observe that in both languages name-tune pairs have prosodic patterns that are robust, systematic and in their definition crucially rely on linguistic notions (syllable, word length, boundary). We therefore conclude that these tunes must be seen as part of the language system, not merely as sound symbolism or as paralinguistic features manifested in language use. We also provide arguments from both languages showing the differences between names used as arguments/adjuncts and names used as propositions, supporting the views in the literature that a vocative name is not a case-marked noun but a proposition.

1. Introduction

In this paper we discuss vocative contours in light of other prosodic contours that occur with names in Austrian German and Turkish. Neither language has overt segmental markers to indicate vocatives, leaving prosody as the only means to express an address (with various subclasses). Our investigation focuses on how languages with different word level stress systems behave and how stress systems interact with the various prosodic contours. Our findings point to the following:

(i)   Although Austrian German and Turkish differ with respect to the position of word level stress in nouns, there are striking parallels in the prosodic contours associated with names in the two languages. Following Anderson (2007), we claim that the vocative constitutes its own propositional form with a particular prosodic contour, which we discuss below, rather than being *part* of the propositional form of a sentence.

(ii)   This proposal entails that the vocative is not a typical case marker. Case markers express the relation between a noun and a verb/noun, and the vocative case marker, at best, marks the relation between two propositions. We suggest that other means can be used for expressing the vocative function, in this case prosody.

(iii)   We identify various types of prosodic contour superimposed on names and claim that the vocative is only one such contour. In this context we look at other tunes; the calling address, the surprise address and the 'is-it-you' address.

(iv)   We suggest that the vocative should therefore be categorized as a member of the set that includes other name-tune pairs. We define a tune as a prosodic contour with an identifiable pragmatic meaning (see Liberman and Sag 1974, Pierrehumbert and Hirschberg 1990 among many others). These tunes are the expression of various functional types of clause. The kin of the vocative, from a functional point of view, therefore, are other name-associated tunes, as we will explore below.

(v)   Both Austrian German and Turkish are illustrative examples that use tunes to mark various functional types of clause. It will be seen that each particular functional type is marked in the same way in the two languages, the only difference being the anchoring point of a particular tune, i.e. the point where stress is realised, thus regulating the localisation of a tune. While the tunes are the same across the two languages, the anchoring point varies, following the difference in the position of stress in the two languages.

We begin our investigation by describing, in section 2, the usage of names as arguments and adjuncts on the one hand, and their usage as forms of address in the other. In section 3 we discuss the forms of the vocative in Austrian German and Turkish. Section 4 focuses on the 'kin' of the vocative, i.e. other prosodic contours superimposed on names and associated with various functions. In section 5 we describe the stress pattern of the two languages, followed in section 6 by a detailed description of the prosodic contours under scrutiny. Section 7 focuses on the issue of paralinguistic and universal patterns of prosodic contours. The article concludes with further avenues for research.

2. Using names for different purposes: to speak 'of' and to speak 'to'

The difference between the referential usage of a name (i.e. a name used as an argument or an adjunct) and a name used for speaking to the hearer is highlighted in Zwicky (1974) and Anderson (2007).

> Names are used as either arguments with a role as participant or circum-stantial (complement or adjunct) in a predication, that is they are the means whereby an individual is 'spoken of', or they can be used as terms of ad-dress, vocatives, whereby an individual may be 'spoken to'.
>
> (Anderson 2007: 215)

Languages use various means to mark this difference. For example, some languages use the definite article with personal names when these function as arguments, e.g. Greek, Catalan or Seri, cf. Anderson (2007: 179ff.).[1] Austrian German is one of these languages. A name used when someone is spoken of, in other words a name used for referring to someone (abbrevi-ated as REF), must be used with the definite article (1a). Forms without the definite article sound literary, like forms borrowed from the written lan-guage (1b). Again similar to Greek, Catalan or Seri, the article is ungram-matical in forms of address (cf. 2a, b):

(1) a. *Der Florian kommt mit.*[2]   (REF)
        The Florian will.come.along
        'Florian will come along.'
     b. *Florian kommt mit.*

(2) a. *Florian, komm mit!*   (VOC)
        Florian   come(IMP).along
        'Florian, come along!'
     b. **Der Florian, komm mit!*

A further difference between the forms used as arguments as opposed to vocative forms is the unavailability of the first person plural pronoun in the vocative form:

(3) a. *Unser Florian spiel-t   hervorragend Schach.*   (REF)
        our   Florian play-3SG very.well   chess
        '[Our] Florian plays chess very well.'
     b. **Unser Florian!*   (VOC)

Turkish does not have a definite article, but similar to (Austrian) German the definiteness effect can be shown to occur in other forms. The word *bizim* 'our', literally the genitive form of the first person plural pronoun, can be used metaphorically when speaking of a person (or an object) of assumed familiarity, but it cannot be used when addressing a person:

(4) a. *Biz-im   Ahmet   çok iyi   tavla   oyna-r.*   (REF)
         we-GEN   Ahmet   very well backgammon play-AOR
         '[Our] Ahmet plays backgammon very well.'
     b. **Bizim Ahmet!*   (VOC)

The forms above indicate that the vocative and, as we shall see, any form of the 'speaking to'-function in the two languages are not expressed through segmental material and thus differ from case markers in the two languages. Rather, the bearer of the information relating to addressing forms in the two languages is, in the overwhelming case, prosody.[3]

3. The vocative forms in Turkish and Austrian German

While both Turkish and Austrian German have particles to indicate the vocative, these forms are confined to poetic usage and are not part of everyday spoken language. In fact the entire form in (5a) is frozen:

Turkish

(5) a. *ya Muhammed!* 'o Mohammed!'[4]
     b. *ey Meltem!* 'o Meltem!'

Austrian German

(6) *O Florian!* 'o Florian!'

In spoken Turkish, the only way to mark a name as a vocative is through shifting its stress from final position, which is the position of stress in names used as arguments. In Austrian German, the vocative usage of a name has no such shift of stress that would set it apart from referential usages.

(7) a. *Méltem* (Turkish)   (VOC)
     b. *Flórian!* (Austrian German)

While the prosodic marking of vocatives in Turkish has been noticed before (Zimmer 1970; Demircan 1975, 1996; Sezer 1981, among others), there has been very little research on the properties of the prosodic structure of this construction. Similarly in Austrian German, the prosody of names has received very little theoretical interest (with the notable exception for Ulbrich 2004; for Standard German intonation in general cf. Bierwisch 1966; Fox 1984; Jacobs 1982; Uhmann 1991; Wunderlich 1987, 1991).

In Turkish, there is a clear prosodic contrast between names used referentially on the one hand and names used as the vocative form of a name. Non-compound words in Turkish are usually finally stressed (Hameed 1985; Inkelas 1996, 1999; Underhill 1988). Referential usages of names (and other nouns functioning as names) also have the same (final) stress pattern, illustrated below.

(8)   a. *Meltém* (REF)   b. *Méltem* (VOC)

(9)   a. *Pembegül* (REF)   b. *Pembégül* (VOC)   c. cf. *pembé gül*
                                                                 ('pink rose')

(8) exemplifies the stress pattern of a name with underived internal structure used referentially (8a) and as a vocative form (8b). (9a–b) illustrate a name based on the phrase given in (9c) (*pembe* 'pink', *gül* 'rose'). As a noun phrase (9c) it would have been stressed on the adjective (*pembe* 'pink'), as Turkish has left-prominent stress in phrases (Kabak and Vogel 2001). Contrast this to its usage as a name: Used referentially, *Pembegül* has final stress, and when used as a vocative it has the stress pattern of ordinary three syllable words. These examples show that whatever the internal structure of a name may be, it conforms to the stress pattern of underived names in the language.

In Austrian German there is no comparable stress shift marking the vocative, neither is there segmental material (i.e. an affix) to indicate that the form is vocative. However, the differences in the use of definite articles (section 2) make clear that it is necessary to distinguish between the referential usage and vocative, just like in Turkish.

As indicated above in (8)–(9), at least for Turkish, the vocative form can immediately be identified on the basis of its prosodic structure. And although Austrian German does not display a differentiation of this sort among its forms at first glance, surprising similarities between the two languages exist. We therefore turn to some other types of address marked solely by prosodic contours. These show that the marking of names through prosody is not confined to the vocative, and that other forms which share pragmatic similarities to the vocative exist.

4. What is the kin of the vocative?

The vocative is not the only instance where a particular prosodic pattern is associated with a name. As shown in Demircan (1975, 1996) names can be associated with other semantic/pragmatic categories such as surprise, calling, exasperation, and other functions, all of which are expressed through prosody. What marks this group pragmatically is that its members have a common thread: that the person denoted by the name is, or is assumed to be, present, either in the same physical space or within hearing distance from the speaker. The vocative form is simply a form of address used specifically in the presence of the person who is addressed. The other prosodic contours used with names are associated with the following functions:

(i)   surprise at the presence of a person
(ii)   calling a person who is not in the immediate visual space
(ii)   checking the identity of a person whose presence is assumed/
        supposed ('is-it-you?')
(iv)   challenging the words of a person who is in the visual space ('oh
        come on!')

This is not an exhaustive list. Various emotive states can be expressed concurrently while using a name, in other words, a name can be associated with different tunes. We suggest that the vocative is simply one member of this group that has been studied to a larger extent, a fact maybe not so surprising given that the vocative may have segmental phonological material to mark it in many languages, as mentioned above (see also Stavrou 2010).

A question that immediately comes to mind is whether various tunes associated with different types of illocutionary force are simply sentence tunes superimposed on names, i.e. on smaller segmental material. While this may be true for some tunes, it is interesting to note that there is not a perfect fit. The various tunes associated with names may not be identical to the tunes associated with a particular type of functional sentence where that sentence contains other lexical material. In other words, one could assume that names are not special at all, and that they can carry any tune an utterance can be associated with. But that is not the case. For example, the intonational contour of a polar question may be seen as being superimposed on a name yielding the interpretation 'is-it-you?'. This is conceivable at least for Austrian German. However, Turkish illustrates that the tune that is superimposed on a name to indicate 'is-it-you?' does not have the intonation of a polar question. In polar questions in Turkish there is (a) a question particle *mi* and (b) this question particle is associated with the pitch pattern

H+L*, that is, a sharp fall on the particle *mi*. (Assuming that every prosodic contour has to end in a boundary tone, we posit the presence of an additional L%.)

(10) *Gel-di-n   mi?* (H+L* L%)
    Come-P-2SG INT
    'Did you come?'

If the position of *mi* shifts in the sentence, then so does the position of the sharp fall, as in (11):

(11) *Ahmét   mi   gel-di?* (H+L*L%)
    Ahmet INT   come-P
    'Is it Ahmet who came?'

In an 'is-it-you'-question, there is no *mi*. Now, crucially, if we remove the pitch marking contributed by *mi* from a polar question, we do *not* end up with the contour of an 'is-it-you'-question, which has a distinct rise towards the end:

(12) *Songül?* (L*H%)

The rise at the end of the 'is-it-you?'-tune in (12) therefore cannot be directly construed as the prosody associated with polar questions.[5] This further sets names aside as a special category (Anderson 2007).

    We therefore surmise that the vocative belongs to the set of items that are independent propositions, rather than the (vocative) case-marked form of a noun phrase.[6] Before we turn to the description of these tunes in detail in section 6, we briefly discuss the properties of stress.

5. Stress: evidence for (im)mobility

We will distinguish between stress (prominence relations) and intonational tunes (pitch contours), as is customary in intonational phonology (Ladd 1996; Liberman 1975; Pierrehumbert 1980). As is well known, stress can be cued independently of pitch, e.g. by duration, intensity, spectral tilt etc. (Gussenhoven 2004: 14). Furthermore, stress serves as an anchoring point for intonational tunes and regulates the text-to-tune matching.

    The two languages differ with repect to stress. In Turkish the stress in the referential usage of nouns is generally mobile (unless exceptionally marked, cf. Sezer 1981; Çakır 2000, 2006): it will always fall at the end of the word, i.e. it occurs on the last nucleus of the phonological word. (See Kabak and Vogel 2001; Inkelas and Orgun 2003; Charette 2008 for various analyses. See also Kamali 2011 for an alternative view.)[7]

(13) *Turkish*: mobile stress
    kitáp 'book'
    kitap-lár 'books'
    kitap-lar-ím 'my books'
    kitap-lar-ım-dá 'in my books', etc.

It is important to note that the position of stress can vary in the different categories under discussion here (referential usage, vocative etc.). In the cases we will look at, stress seems to depend on the choice of the particular word form. Since the position of stress can be different, this will also affect the 'anchoring' of the tunes.

In Austrian German (like in Standard German), on the other hand, stress is generally fixed on a particular syllable. (The literature on (Standard) German stress is rich, cf. amongst others Eisenberg 1991; Giegerich 1985; Kohler 1977; Vennemann 1991; Wiese 1996; Wurzel 1980.) The location of stress is, in the majority of cases, on the penultimate or antepenultimate syllable. Stress differences in morphologically related words are usually restricted to borrowed words, e.g. *Jápan* 'Japan' but *japán-isch* 'Japanese'. Usually, stress remains stable throughout the different categories, it does not seem to be defined by morphological category, but is assigned to a particular lexeme once and for all. (We will refer to this as 'lexically stressed' below, in opposition to 'morphologically stressed'.) In other words, whether a word is used vocatively or not will not have any bearing on the anchoring of the relevant tune.

(14) *Austrian German*: immobile stress
    záppel-n 'to fidget'
    záppel-ig 'fidgety'
    záppel-ig-e 'fidgety pl.' etc.

While there are differences in the position and flexibility of stress between the two languages, the intonational tunes are remarkably similar to each other. This parallel comes out clearly once stress is understood as the anchoring point of a tune. Though discussed below, we can immediately illustrate this by the surprise tune and how stress interacts with it. In both Turkish and Austrian German, the surprise address is marked by a rapid fall from a high pitch. Where this fall begins, however, is different in the two languages, because the location of stress is different. In Turkish, it begins right after the first syllable (which also is stressed).[8] In Austrian German, it begins right after the lexically stressed syllable.

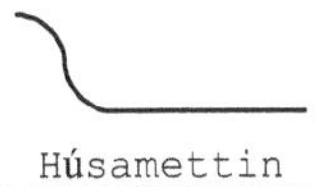 Húsamettin	 Alexánder
Surprise Address of Turkish *Hüsamettin*	Surprise Address of Austrian German *Alexánder*

Figure 1. Surprise address

With those preliminaries out of the way, let us now proceed to the patterns in detail. In order to make the differences and similarities between the two languages more obvious, the phonological characteristics of each category will be given in tabular fashion.

6. The patterns in detail

In this section we will look at some of the individual intonational patterns found in Austrian German and Turkish.[9] The different patterns are illustrated below over examples of different length, with a description of the details to follow:

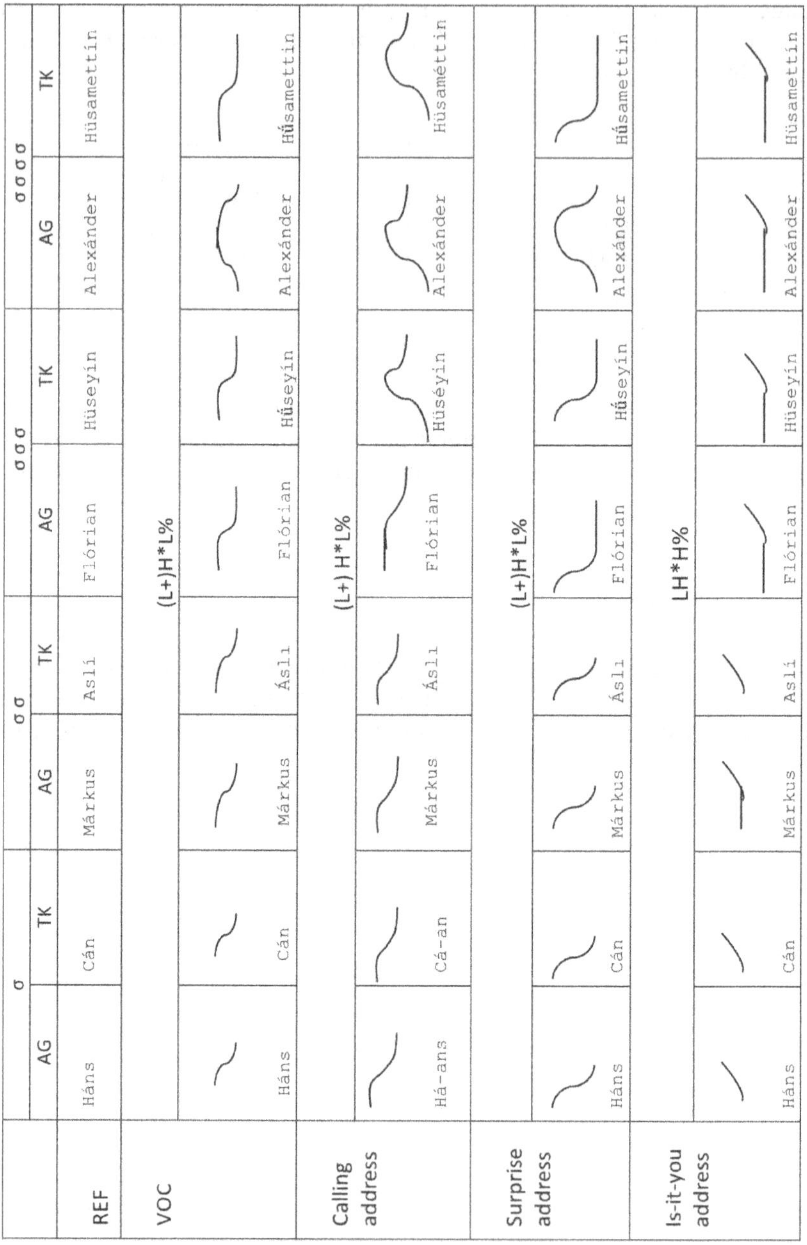

	σ		σσ		σσσ		σσσσ	
	AG	TK	AG	TK	AG	TK	AG	TK
REF	Háns	Cán	Márkus	Aslí	Flórian	Húseyin	Alexánder	Hüsamettin
VOC	Háns	Cán	Márkus	Áslı	Flórian	Húseyin	Alexánder	Hüsamettin
Calling address	Há-ans	Cá-an	Márkus	Áslı	Flórian	Húseyin	Alexánder	Hüsamettin
Surprise address	Háns	Cán	Márkus	Áslı	Flórian	Húseyín	Alexánder	Hüsamettin
Is-it-you address	Háns	Cán	Márkus	Áslı	Flórian	Húseyin	Alexánder	Hüsamettin

Intonation patterns by row: VOC — (L+)H*L%; Calling address — (L+) H*L%; Surprise address — (L+)H*L%; Is-it-you address — LH*H%

Figure 2. Intonational patterns

We now highlight the properties of each pattern in turn.

6.1. Names in referential usage

The properties of names that are used referentially are as follows:

Turkish	Austrian German
By default final stress (in names just like in common nouns, verbs etc.).	Stress lexical: Classic penulti-mate/ante-penultimate pattern (in foreign names); on the beginning of the stem in Germanic names.
Names based on compounds also have final stress and therefore over-ride compound stress, cf. (9).	
Stress usually marked by high pitch. Fall on following syllables if any.	

As stated before, the intonational tune is the same in the two languages. Where Turkish and Austrian German differ is in the anchoring of the tune, i.e. in the location of stress.

6.2. Vocative

Turkish	Austrian German
Stress usually penultimate.[10]	Stress lexical.
Stress marked by high pitch. Fall afterwards.	

In addition to the difference in the location of stress, the vocative seems to have a higher pitch than REF. This can be seen in monosyllabic names, where the location of stress trivially has to be identical in the REF and the vocative. At this point, we are not entirely certain if this difference is robust; if yes, one might wonder what its source could be. One potential answer could be the following: a REF form is (by definition) integrated, both intonationally and syntactically, into an entire sentence; whatever pitch it has will be part of the pitch contour of a larger unit. A vocative, however, is a proposition on its own and does not have to "share" the pitch contour with anything else, cf. Anderson (2007: passim).[11]

6.3. Calling address

The calling address is used when calling a person who is not in the im-mediate visual space; as opposed to a vocative that is used for addressing somebody close by. The properties of Turkish and Austrian German are given below:

Turkish	Austrian German
Stress on penultimate.	Stress lexical.
Imposes a template on the name that has to be minimally bisyllabic.	
The template has high pitch on its first syllable and a lowered (or down-stepped, according to Ladd 1996) pitch on its last syllable. If there are syllables in the middle they are also high.	
The individual syllables can be lengthened.	
Note that this involves breaking up monosyllabic names to conform to the template. Such an operation is unheard of in the rest of the language system. (But does occur in singing, of course, and, interestingly enough, in the calling contours of other languages, too: for English cf. Ladd 1978; 1996; for Hungarian cf. Varga 1989, 2008.)	

As already noted in Zwicky (1974), there is an affinity between calling and the vocative.[12] But note the difference in the location of stress as opposed to the vocative in Turkish: In the vocative, stress can be on the penultimate or antepenultimate. In the calling pattern, however, stress can only be on the penultimate. Given this difference, it will not be possible to interpret the vocative and the calling contour as ranging on a paralinguistic scale (cf. below, section 7).

6.4. Surprise address

By 'surprise address' we refer to the tune that accompanies a name when addressing someone unexpected. It can roughly be paraphrased as: 'Oh, you're here! (I didn't expect/know that.)'

Turkish	Austrian German
Stress initial.	Stress lexical.
Very high pitch on stress, rapid fall afterwards.	

We would like to add that the high pitch on the stressed vowel seems higher than in the vocative. It is unclear how this can be expressed in a model that only uses H and L as pitch properties. Again, like in the case of calling, the difference in stress between vocative and surprise address makes it impossible to treat the two as ranging on a paralinguistic scale (cf. below, section 8).

6.5 'Is-it-you'-question

This tune, which we mentioned above, is broadly associated with questioning whether a particular salient signal (e.g. a sound or shadow) belongs to a particular person, crucially, by addressing that assumed person.

Turkish	Austrian German
Stress final.	Stress lexical.
High pitch on the last vowel only.	
In this case, high pitch does not seem to follow stress but is assigned with respect to the end of the word. This would make the high pitch a boundary tone (Ladd 1996), and not a pitch accent.	

Now that we have discussed all the patterns in detail, we can investigate how these observations fit into a more general cross-linguistic picture.

7. Universal patterns, paralinguistic phenomena and sound symbolism?

To the extent that the parallel between Austrian German and Turkish is really as pervasive as we have found it to be, one will have to ask the question why there are such parallels. Are these tunes universally connected to specific speech acts? Are they derived from more general pragmatic principles? And are they paralinguistic?

It has been suggested that tunes are associated with designated speech acts and functional sentence types in various languages (Liberman and Sag 1974; Liberman 1979; Ladd 1996; Pierrehumbert and Hirschberg 1990; Göksel, Kelepir, and Üntak 2009). Pitch contours have also been linked to biology. For example Ohala (1997), among others, points out that high pitch (H*) is typical for the voices of children and small animals, thus high pitch is an icon of smallness, weakness, uncertainty. Therefore, according to Ohala, questions usually involve rising pitch.[13]

With respect to the universality of tunes, whether the explanation is etiological or not, the literature points out to some counterexamples, cases of 'unnatural intonation' as in 'Urban North English' where statements which should not involve uncertainty have rising pitch (Ladd 1996; Gussenhoven 2004; Chen 2005 etc.). This is also true of Hungarian, cf. Ladd (1996: 115): "[M]any Hungarian questions sound like emphatic statements to native speakers of English, which is *prima facie* something of a problem for a straightforward theory of intonational universals." Finally, polar questions in Turkish end in L% as indicated above (cf. 10, 11), a surprising fact under the assumption that L% is the marker for certainty or assertivity.

Given such problems with universals or sound symbolism, the parallels we have found in the tunes of Austrian German and Turkish should be approached with caution. As far as the data here is concerned, the only tunes that fit in with the generalizations above are the vocative, which ends in L%, and the 'is-it-you'-tune, which ends in H%. The L% at the end of the vocative signals assertivity, as the vocative is inherently a statement akin to an imperative. When one uses a vocative one is 'telling' the addressee to pay attention.[14] H% at the end of the 'is-it-you'-tune is also expected because it is a type of question. However, the generalizations cannot be said to extend naturally to the calling address and the surprise address. The calling address is used when searching for someone who is not present but who is assumed to be within hearing distance, so it is not clear how the L% at the end can be certainty or assertivity induced. This is even less clear with the surprise address: if L% indicates certainty, the unexpectedness flavor in the state of being surprised seems to be overridden.

In this context, another issue needs to be addressed, viz. that of paralanguage. We will follow the definition of paralanguage given by Ladd (1996: 36):

> The central difference between paralinguistic and linguistic messages resides in the quantal or categorical structure of linguistic signalling and the scalar or gradient nature of paralanguage. [. . .] If raising the voice can be used to signal anger or surprise, raising the voice a lot can signal violent anger or great surprise.

Within this formulation, the vocative and calling address could in principle be paralinguistically related, given that pitch seems to co-vary with distance (cf. 6). But if that is correct, we still have to resort to the linguistic properties of the signal for identifying the position of stress. Again, one cannot simply invoke pragmatic and paralinguistic factors in order to explain the difference in pitch height, given that there are other factors, such as the position that pitch anchors to, as we have tried to illustrate in this paper.

8. Conclusion

In this contribution we have tried to show that the vocative is not alone, but part of a family of tunes which are associated with names. The intonational patterns we have found can be understood in terms of stress and pitch. Despite parallels between the two languages, it is unclear if they can be explained by or derived from allegedly universal patterns of sound symbolism.

Given that the patterns we found are (i) robust, (ii) systematic and (iii) in their definition crucially rely on linguistic notions (syllable, word length, boundary etc.), they must be seen as part of the language system, not just as functional structures manifesting themselves in language use only. Insofar as morphology is the encoding of particular functions onto forms, prosodic contours (specialized tunes) are morphological items. The rich array of categories expressed only by prosody argues against a notion of morphology that relies on strict serialisation of morphological markers; rather, as indicated in the literature (see Gussenhoven 2004 among others), the phonological material representing different functional categories is superimposed over each other. We thus suggest that the exponents of certain functional categories, i.e the ones discussed in this paper, are suprasegmental, rather than segmental.

We do not expect that our findings are restricted to systems that have no overt segmental markers for addresses. There is no logical relationship to guarantee that overt segmental material excludes prosodic marking.

Notes

*   The contribution of Aslı Göksel was supported by Boğaziçi University Research Project BAP #5842 (11B04P1) and the contribution of Markus Pöchtrager was supported by Boğaziçi University Research Project BAP #5545 (10B04P3)

1.   Note that the article might have a special form when used with names, e.g. Catalan *el* for masculine proper nouns but *en* for masculine names. Note furthermore that in those languages the article is not used in 'acts of baptism' (Anderson 2007: 269), i.e. in constructions of the type "I am called *x*", even though they function as arguments.

2.   The abbreviations used in this paper are the following: ACC: accusative, AOR: aorist, CM: compound marker, GEN: genitive, REF: referentical usage, P: past, PL: plural, POSS: possessive, SG: singular, INT: interrogative, VOC: vocative.

3.   The same types of difference between 'speaking of' and 'speaking to' carry over to names given to professions where these are treated as names and used for referring to a person, not by their given name but by their profession.

Turkish
(i) a. *hemşire hanım*
     nurse   madam
     'nurse'
   b. *Hemşire   Hanım-ı   gör-dü-nüz   mü?*
      nurse   madam-ACC   see-P-2PL   INT
      'Have you seen the nurse?'
   c. *Hemşire   Hanım,   hasta-mız   nerede?*
      nurse   madam   patient-1PL.POSS   where
      'Nurse, where is the patient?'

Austrian German
(ii) a. *Schwester*
      nurse
      'nurse'
    b. *Haben   Sie   die   Schwester   gesehen?*
       have   you   the   nurse   seen?
       'Have you seen the nurse?'
    c. *Schwester,   schauen   Sie   mal   her?*
       nurse   look   you   once   here
       'Nurse, could you have a look?'

4.   This particular particle, borrowed from Arabic, is also used in colloquial speech to attract the attention of the hearer. Since this particle can be used without a name following it, we do not consider the informal *ya* a vocative marker. Furthermore there is a phonological difference between the formal and informal usages in that only the former forms a phonological unit with a following name, indicating that it might be cliticized to it.
5.   There is another prosodic contour associated with polar questions in Turkish used by some speakers (see Göksel and Kerslake 2005: 295). This has a H*L H% contour (identical to content questions in Turkish) but crucially this type of contour cannot be associated with the contour in (11) either, as this latter lacks H* as a separate tone.
6.   It is interesting to note that the vocative particles mentioned in (5) precede the stem in Turkish, unlike case markers which are suffixes. This brings further doubt to whether the vocative should be classified as a case marker.
7.   We leave aside certain clitics that do not figure in the computation of stress placement.

8. There may be an alternative form accepted by some speakers, where the second syllable is stressed. At this point it is unclear to us why this is so.
9. The curves in the chart are based on the recordings of our own speech. The forms were uttered in isolation. The pitch tracks of the recordings were analysed with the Wavesurfer software, produced by the Swedish Royal Institute of Technology. Recordings were made on a Marantz PMD661 Professional Compact Digital Audio Recorder. Further phonetic investigation of the speech of a larger number of informants is required to verify all the details of our work.
10. Stress may optionally be antepenultimate if there is a long vowel in this position, see fn. 8.
11. Pierrehumbert and Hirschberg (1990) point out that the vocative may have L* or H* depending on the pragmatic context.
12. What we call vocative here is referred to as 'address form' in Zwicky, and the term 'vocative' is used by him to cover the address form and the calling form.
13. Ohala (1997) extends his claim that high pitch correlates with smallness also to the inherent pitch of vowels: As an example of such sound symbolism he gives the Greek pair *mikros* 'small' as opposed to *makros* 'big'. The high vowel in *mikros* is iconic of smallness, while the low vowel in *makros* suggests bigness. It might be the case that when there is a semantic contrast in terms of size, there is also a tendency that the small or lesser entity is denoted by a word with a high vowel and the bigger one is denoted by a word with a low vowel. However, the pattern, if it exists, breaks down in other pairs, e.g. in Turkish *küçük* 'small' and *büyük* 'big', which have identical vowels.
14. In fact, the imperative flavour of a vocative is much more salient when it is placed at the end of the clause in the respective dialects of the two authors of this article.

References

Anderson, John
    2007   *The Grammar of Names*. Oxford: Oxford University Press.
Bartels, Christine
    1997   Towards a compositional interpretation of English statement and question intonation. Doctoral dissertation, University of Massachusetts.
Bierwisch, Manfred
    1966   Regeln für die Intonation deutscher Sätze. In *Untersuchungen über Akzent und Intonation im Deutschen*, Manfred Bierwisch (ed.), 99–201. (Studia Grammatica 7.) Berlin: Akademie-Verlag.

Çakır, M. Cem
2000   On non-final stress in Turkish simplex words. In *Studies on Turkish and Turkic Languages: Proceedings of the Ninth International Conference on Turkish Linguistics*, Aslı Göksel and Celia Kerslake (eds.), 3–11. Wiesbaden: Harrassowitz.

Çakır, M. Cem
2006   On stress, types of extrametricality and the phonological structure of the extrametrical syllable in Turkish simplex words. MA dissertation, Boğaziçi University, Istanbul.

Charette, Monik
2008   The vital role of the trochaic foot in explaining Turkish word endings. *Lingua* 118: 46–65.

Chen, Aoju
2005   Universal and language-specific perception of paralinguistic intonational meaning. Doctoral dissertation, Radboud Universiteit, Nijmegen.

Demircan, Ömer
1975   Türk dilinde vurgu: Sözcük vurgusu. *Türk Dili* 284: 333–339.

Demircan, Ömer
1996   *Türkçenin Sesdizimi*. Istanbul: Der Yayınevi.

Eisenberg, Peter
1991   Syllabische Struktur und Wortakzent: Prinzipien der Prosodik deutscher Wörter. *Zeitschrift für Sprachwissenschaft* 10: 37–64.

Fox, Anthony
1984   *German Intonation: An Outline*. Oxford: Clarendon Press.

Giegerich, Heinz J.
1985   *Metrical Phonology and Phonological Structure: German and English*. Cambridge: Cambridge University Press.

Göksel, Aslı and Celia Kerslake
2005   *Turkish: A Comprehensive Grammar*. London: Routledge.

Göksel, Aslı, Meltem Kelepir, and Aslı Üntak-Tarhan
2009   Decomposition of question intonation: The structure of response seeking utterances. In *Phonological Domains: Universals and Deviations*, Janet Grijzenhout and Barış Kabak (eds.), 249–286. Dordrecht: Mouton de Gruyter.

Gussenhoven, Carlos
2004   *The Phonology of Tone and Intonation*. Cambridge: Cambridge University Press.

Hameed, Jumah
1985   Lexical phonology and morphology of modern Standard Turkish. *Cahiers Linguistiques d'Ottawa* 14: 71–95.

Inkelas, Sharon
  1996   The interaction of phrase and word rules in Turkish: An apparent
                exception to the prosodic hierarchy. *The Linguistic Review* 13:
                193–217.
Inkelas, Sharon
  1999   Exceptional stress-attracting suffixes in Turkish: Representations
                vs. the grammar. In *The Prosody-Morphology Interface*, René
                Kager, Harry van der Hulst, and Wim Zonneveld (eds.), 134–
                187. Cambridge: Cambridge University Press.
Inkelas, Sharon, and Cemil Orhan Orgun
  2003   Turkish stress: A review. *Phonology* 20: 139–161.
Jacobs, Joachim
  1982   Neutraler und nicht-neutraler Satzakzent im Deutschen. In *Silben,
                Segmente, Akzente*, Theo Vennemann (ed.), 141–169. Tübingen:
                Niemeyer.
Kabak, Barış, and Irene Vogel
  2001   The phonological word and stress assignment in Turkish. *Phono-
                logy* 18: 315–360.
Kamali, Beste Aknoun Azad
  2011   Topics at the PF Interface of Turkish. Doctoral dissertation, Har-
                vard University.
Kohler, Klaus J.
  1977   *Einführung in die Phonetik des Deutschen*. Berlin: Erich
                Schmidt.
Ladd, D. Robert
  1978   Stylized intonation. *Language* 54: 517–539.
Ladd, D. Robert
  1996   *Intonational Phonology*. Cambridge: Cambridge University
                Press.
Liberman, Mark
  1975   *The Intonational System of English*. Doctoral dissertation, Mas-
                sachusetts Institute of Technology.
Liberman, Mark
  1979   *The Intonational System of English*. New York: Garland
                Publishing.
Liberman, Mark, and Ivan Sag
  1974   Prosodic form and discourse function. In *Papers from the tenth
                regional meeting of the Chicago Linguistic Society, April 19-21,
                1974*, 416–427. Chicago: Chicago Linguistic Society.
Ohala, John J.
  1997   Sound Symbolism. Talk given at Seoul International Conference
                on Linguistics, Seoul, Korea, August 11–15, 1997.

Pierrehumbert, Janet
1980   The phonology and phonetics of English intonation. Doctoral dissertation, Massachusetts Institute of Technology.
Pierrehumbert, Janet, and Julia Hirschberg
1990   The meaning of intonational contours in the interpretation of discourse. In *Intentions in Communication*, Philip R. Cohen, J. Morgan, and Martha E. Pollack (eds.), 271–311. Cambridge, MA: MIT Press.
Sezer, Engin
1981   On non-final stress in Turkish. *Journal of Turkish Studies*: 61–69.
Stavrou, Melita
2010   Vocative! Paper presented at Vocative! Bamberg, 10 December 2010 – 11 December 2010.
Uhmann, Susanne
1991   *Fokusphonologie: Eine Analyse deutscher Intonationskonturen im Rahmen der nicht-linearen Phonologie.* Tübingen: Niemeyer.
Ulbrich, Christiane
2004   Phonetische Untersuchungen zur Prosodie der Standardvarietäten des Deutschen in der Bundesrepublik Deutschland, in der Schweiz und in Österreich. Doctoral dissertation, Martin Luther University, Halle-Wittenberg.
Underhill, Robert
1988   A lexical account of Turkish accent. In *Studies on Turkish Linguistics*, Ayhan Sezer (ed.), 387–406. Ankara: Middle East Technical University.
Varga, László
1989   The stylized fall in Hungarian. *Acta Linguistica Hungarica* 39: 317–330.
Varga, László
2008   The calling contour in Hungarian and English. *Phonology* 25: 469–497.
Vennemann, Theo
1991   Skizze der deutschen Wortprosodie. *Zeitschrift für Sprachwissenschaft* 10: 86–111.
Wiese, Richard
1996   *The Phonology of German.* Oxford: Oxford University Press.
Wunderlich, Dieter
1987   Der Ton macht die Melodie – Zur Phonologie der Intonation des Deutschen. In *Intonationsforschungen*, Hans Altmann (ed.), 1–40. Tübingen: Niemeyer.

Wunderlich, Dieter
    1991   Intonation and contrast. *Journal of Semantics* 8: 239–251.
Wurzel, Wolfgang U.
    1980   Der deutsche Wortakzent: Fakten–Regeln–Prinzipien. Ein Bei-
                    trag zu einer natürlichen Akzenttheorie. *Zeitschrift für Ger-
                    manistik* 3: 299–318.
Zimmer, Karl
    1970   Some observations on non-final Stress in Turkish. *Journal of the
                    American Oriental Society* 90: 160–162.
Zwicky, Arnold M.
    1974   Hey, Whatsyourname. In *Papers from the Tenth Regional
                    Meeting of the Chicago Linguistic Society, April 19-21, 1974*,
                    Michael W. La Galy, Robert A. Fox, and Anthony Bruck (eds.),
                    787–801. Chicago: Chicago Linguistic Society.

On the structure of vocatives[*]

M. Teresa Espinal

Abstract

This paper analyses the structure of vocatives at the syntax-semantics inter-face, focusing mainly on data from Catalan. It postulates a distinction between "true" and "fake" vocatives, which combine in complex vocatives in different ways, similar to copular sentences. The output of this com-bination is that an identity, an identificational, or a predicational type of vocative can emerge.

1. Introduction

In this paper I will focus on the following two questions:

Q1.   What is the internal structure of a phrase interpreted as Vocative?
Q2.   Is it possible to find a syntactic correlation between vocatives and other syntactic structures available in the language?

Although it has been much debated in linguistic theory (Coene, D'hulst, and Tasmowski 1999; Moro 2003; Hill 2007; D'hulst, Coene, and Tasmowski 2007; Stavrou 2009), the first of these two questions remains to a certain extent still unresolved, at least if we try to account for new data such as those expressions that involve complex vocatives. The second question arises as an attempt to correlate the syntax of vocatives with the syntax of other structures, such as copular sentences (Higgins 1979), in order to challenge the common view that the study of vocatives is not a topic to be addressed as part of the core grammar.[1]

I will address these questions within a generative formal syntactic theory, the main ingredients of which are the following: (i) VocP is a functional projection (Moro 2003; Stavrou 2009) whose head Voc° is defined by a deictic [+DX] feature; (ii) Voc° can be specified by a vocative particle, and Voc° selects a DP (see the structure below in 1);[2] (iii) second person strong pronouns, which are standardly assumed to be generated in D°, are postulated to move from this position to Voc° in order to be valued appropriately as lexical items referring indexically to the hearer/addressee (see 2);[3] (iv) N° movement to D° in the syntax (Longobardi 1994) can be extended to Voc° in order to account for the syntactic and semantic properties of the nominal expression seen in (3a): the bare count nominal is incompatible with the D and denotes a property of the referred second person entity; and (v) a VocP can either occur at the left periphery of a sentential structure (assuming the split Comp field analysis of Rizzi 1997 and Moro 2003) (see 4), or alternatively, when vocatives occur isolated, a VocP is to be analysed as a disjunct or parenthetical constituent (Espinal 1991), with the structure in (1).

(1) $[_{\text{VocP}}$ Part $[_{\text{Voc'}}$ Voc° $[_{\text{DP}}$ $[_{\text{D'}}$ D° $[_{\text{NP}}$ $[_{\text{N'}}$ N° $]]]]]]$

           (iii)   (iv)

(2)   Eh   {*tu,*   *vosaltres,*   *vostè(s)*}!
      PART   you.SG.INFORMAL   you.PL.INFORMAL   you.SG/PL.FORMAL
      'Hey! You!'

(3)   a.   Ei   *company,*   com   va?
           PART guy   how   goes
           'Hey, man! How are things going?'
      b.   *Ei   *el*   *company,*   com   va?
           PART   the   guy   how   goes

(4)   C°= …Force° > (Top° > Foc° > Top° >) Fin°…

In the second part of the article I will turn my attention to some significant structural similarities that hold crosslinguistically between vocatives and copular sentences. Following Higgins' (1979) claim that copular sentences are not uniform, I will argue, based on data such as (2), (3), and (5), that vocatives are not a peripheral phenomenon in the syntax of natural languages, and that three of the four types of copular sentences postulated by Higgins are found among vocative structures as well, namely the identity, the identificational, and the predicational types. What these three types of structures have in common is that the subject (i.e., the vocative head) is always referential, while the predicate (i.e., the subsequent NP or DP) is either referential, identificational, or predicational, respectively (compare the three examples in 5).

(5)   a.   Tu!   *Joan!*   *identity*
           'You! Joan!'

b. Tu!   *el   noi   de   la   camisa   blava*!   *identificational*
   you   the   boy   of   the   shirt   blue
   'You! The boy in the blue shirt!'

c. Tu!   *noi*!   *predicational*
   'You! Boy!'

It will be shown that although vocatives are not arguments of verbal predicates (Longobardi 1994; Moro 2003; D'hulst, Coene, and Tasmowski 2007), they can be arguments of nominal predicational structures (5c), as is the case of copular sentences. However, vocative expressions differ from the latter in that they never show an overt copula verb. This parallel I will postulate between vocative structures and copular structures will allow me to extend the proposed analysis to additional data from English.

This paper is organized as follows. Section 2 presents the data, basically from Catalan, and the hypotheses that will be argued for in the rest of the article. Section 3 discusses the syntax of vocative structures and introduces a distinction, which is syntactically and semantically motivated between "true" deictic vocatives and "fake" vocatives. Section 4 is devoted to an analysis of complex structures, those that combine true and fake vocatives, and will show their parallel with copular sentences, from both a syntactic and a semantic perspective. Finally, Section 5 presents the conclusions and the predictions to be drawn from them.

2. The data: vocatives in Catalan

Vocatives are nominal expressions that sometimes designate straight-forwardly the hearer(s) or addressee(s) (see 2 and 6a), sometimes provide the identity or identification of the hearer(s) / addressee(s) (6b), and other times denote properties that call the attention of the hearer(s) / addressee(s) to whom the property denoted by N is attributed (see 3a and 6c,d).

(6) a. *Joan*!
        'Joan!'
     b. *Tu*,   {*Joan,   el   Joan*}!
        you.SG.INFORMAL   Joan   the   Joan
        'You, Joan!'
     c. *Senyor*!
        'Sir!'

> d. *Vostè,*   *senyor!'*
>   you.SG.FORMAL   sir
>   'You, sir!'

The problem with this set of examples is that intuitively we have different possible candidates for the category vocative, namely a second person pronoun, a proper name, and a common noun. We must therefore examine in some detail the constituents that can occur in these sequences as well as their properties in order to postulate a hypothesis about the structure of vocatives.

As already advanced in (2), one group of nominal expressions that occur as vocatives is made up of second person strong pronouns, optionally preceded by a vocative particle (Catalan *ei, eh*) which, according to Hill (2007), are particles of address that call the attention of the hearer.[4] Note that any of the possible sequences in (7c) are ungrammatical because the particle precedes either a first person or a third person strong pronoun, and (7d) vs. (7d') is ungrammatical because the particle cannot occur in postnominal position unless prosody indicates that the second person pronoun has moved further to the left periphery of the vocative particle. This last example also illustrates the fact that only one vocative particle per utterance is permitted.

(7) a. Ei   *tu*!
         PART   you.SG.INFORMAL
     b. Eh   *vosaltres*!
         PART   you.PL.INFORMAL
     c. *{Ei,eh}   {jo,   ell}
         PART   I   he
     d. *(Eh)   vosaltres   eh   d'. Vosaltres,   eh!
         PART   you.PL.INFORMAL PART   you.PL.INFORMAL PART

A second group of nominal expressions that may occur in vocatives is constituted by proper names, bare singulars, and bare plurals, optionally preceded by a vocative particle. As illustrated in (8), these vocative expressions are N heads that must be distinguished from full DPs (Longobardi 1994), whether definite or indefinite.[5] Regarding (8c,d) it should be noted that in Catalan, as in Greek (Stavrou 2009) and certain German dialects (Schaden 2010), a N in vocatives, in contrast to exclamatives and declaratives, cannot be preceded by a definite article. The contrast between (8c,d) and (8c',d') is due to the fact that the structural position of the DP in each pair of sequences is not the same. For the time being it should be noted that in (8c–e) the Voc particle is intended to specify the full DP and the sequence is fully ungrammatical, whereas in (8c'–d') the Voc particle specifies a null vocative and the full DP occurs in a complement position of Voc. In other words, (8c'–d') are well-formed only when the Voc particle and the DP correspond to two different syntactic and prosodic units (as represented by the symbol ##); note that a full DP cannot occur in Voc° (see below, structure (24), for the position of identificational DPs). Besides, nominal expressions in vocatives are not number-neutral since they either refer to an individual entity if singular or refer to a set of individuals if plural, and they neither accept an existential reading nor a kind-generic interpretation.

(8) a. Ei *Joan*!
         PART Joan
    b. Eh *company(s)*!
         PART guy(s)
    c. *Ei *el Joan*!   c'. Ei, ##*el* *Joan*!
         PART the Joan   PART the Joan
    d. *Eh *el company*!   d'. Eh, ##*el* *noi ros*
         PART the guy   PART the boy blond
    e. *Eh *un(s) company(s)*!
         PART {a, some} guy(s)

It should also be noted that these nominal expressions can be followed by a declarative, an imperative or an interrogative clause. Example (9c) differs from (9a,b) not only in the force of the host sentence, being interrogative, but also in having a collective noun instead of a common count noun in vocative position.

(9) a. Ei *tio*! M'agrada la samarreta que portes.
         PART pal me.likes the T-shirt that wears
         'Hey, man! I like your T-shirt.'
    b. Ei *nois*! Calleu!
         PART boys shut
         'Hey! Boys! Shut up!'
    c. Eh *canalla*! Què tal?
         PART kids how that
         'Hey, kids! How are things?'

All these examples make salient the fact that bare nominal vocatives introduce a series of mismatches at the syntax-semantics interface, because in spite of disallowing a Determiner they are well-formed in the initial position of the clause.[6] That is, count bare nominals can occur in vocative contexts even though they are not arguments of the verbal predicate of the host structure (Longobardi 1994; Moro 2003; Corver 2008), which suggests that being deictic, as the nominal vocatives in (9) are, should not be confused with being argumental. On the other hand, nominal vocatives have an ostensive-deictic interpretation, even though common count nouns, unlike proper names, are property-denoting expressions.

A third group of lexical items that can occur in vocatives are bare adjectives, optionally preceded by a vocative particle. These vocative expressions are A heads that denote properties of token individuals, and predicate deictically on the hearer(s) / addressee(s), quite similarly to the bare nouns in (8b) and (9a–c). See (10).

(10) a. Ei   *jove!*   On   vas?
     PART   young.SG   where   go
     'Hey, young man! Where are you going?'
   b. Eh   *desgraciats!*   Marxeu   de   casa   meva!
     PART   bastards.PL   leave   from   house   mine
     'Hey, you bastards! Get out of my house!'

Related to the abovementioned contrasts between (8c–c') and (8d–d'), in Section 4 I will provide an explanation for (11b), which shows a postnominal predicational adjective. The wellformedness of (11b), in contrast to (11a), is due to the fact that the A does not compete for the same position as the 2P pronoun.

(11) a. *Eh   *vosaltres*   *desgraciats!*
     PART   you   bastards.PL
   b. Eh   vosaltres,   *desgraciats!*
     PART   you   bastards.PL

It might also be the case that certain adjectives (such as *benvolgut, stimate, caro* in 12) occur as specifiers of DPs that are interpreted as non-deictic predicational vocatives. See (12).

(12) a. *Benvolgut*   amic   meu, ...   [CATALAN]
     dear   friend   mine
     'My dear friend'
   b. *Stimate*   cititorule, ...   [ROMANIAN]
     respected.VOC   reader.the.VOC   (Hill 2007: 2084, ex. 12e)
     'Dear reader'

c. *Caro* amico, vieni a trovarmi.   [ITALIAN]
   dear friend come to visit.me   (Longobardi 1994: 612, ex. 7a)

With these data in mind, I would like to put forward the following three hypotheses:

H1. A distinction should be made in the syntax of vocative structures between "true" and "fake" vocatives.

H2. In "true" vocatives, second person strong pronouns, proper names, bare nominals, and bare adjectives, immediately specified by an optional Voc particle, occur in Voc° and are interpreted as deictic, either because 2P pronouns and proper names directly designate the hearer(s) / addressee(s), or because bare nominals and bare adjectives introduce a property predicated on the hearer(s) / addressee(s) that points to him/her/them.

H3. In "fake" vocatives a full DP (or QP), very exceptionally specified by a Voc particle, enters into a syntactic relationship with Voc° (either as Spec,VocP or as Spec,DP c-commanded by Voc°), and may be associated with either a predicational or a referential interpretation.

In the next section I will focus on the syntactic structures to be associated with these nominal expressions.

3. The syntax of vocative structures

VocPs can occur at the left periphery of a sentential structure, above Force (see the split Comp field analysis in Rizzi 1997 and Moro 2003) as seen in (4), repeated here.

(4) $C° = ...$ Force° > (Top° > Foc° > Top° >) Fin° ...

Alternatively, when vocatives do not occur with a host structure, they can be analysed as disjunct / parenthetical constituents (Espinal 1991). In this case the VocP is not integrated syntactically in any host structure as seen in (1), repeated here.

(1) $[_{VocP}$ Part $[_{Voc'}$ Voc° $[_{DP}$ $[_{D'}$ D° $[_{NP}$ $[_{N'}$ N° $]]]]]]$

The examples in (9) illustrate clearly that vocatives can co-occur at the left periphery of declaratives, imperatives, and interrogatives. Therefore, in this paper, regarding its external structure, a VocP is postulated in [Spec,ForceP] and the Voc particle in its turn is conceived as the Spec of Voc°.[7] Taking into account the data presented so far, I would like to postulate the structure in (13).

(13) [$_{ForceP}$ [$_{VocP}$ {*ei, eh*} [$_{Voc'}$ [$_{Voc°}$]...]] [$_{Force'}$ [$_{Force°}$ {decl, imper, inter}]...]]

With regard to its internal structure, I would like to claim that vocatives are nominal, since they are direct forms of address that take a DP with a canonical structure (Chierchia 1998; Longobardi 2001, 2005; Zamparelli 1995) as its complement. (14) differs from (1) only in the fact that it specifies the two lexical items that can be used as vocative particles in Catalan and the projection of Number between N and D.

(14) [$_{VocP}$ {*ei, eh*} [$_{Voc'}$ [$_{Voc°}$] [$_{DP}$ D° [$_{NumP}$ Num° [$_{NP}$ N°]]]]]

An argument in support of this structure comes from Moro's (2003: 259) coordination test. See the data in (15), which show that Voc particles cannot be conceived as heads of Voc° (technically speaking, the head of X is the constituent which determines the category of X) and must be postulated separately from the DP complement of Voc°.

(15) a. Ei,   *Joan i   Maria,* acosteu-vos.
      PART Joan and Maria come.closer.you
      'Hey, Joan and Maria, come closer to me.'
   b. *Ei Joan i   ei   Maria acosteu-vos.
      PART Joan and PART Maria come.closer.you

In accordance with what has been said in the literature about vocatives, I assume that Voc° is defined by a deictic interpretable feature [+DX], and that vocative particles specify a deictic expression, by default a 2P strong pronoun. Vocative particles can also specify a N (or an A) when this N (or A) has a deictic interpretation.

In order to account for the data I also assume an extension of N-raising (Longobardi 1994) to common nouns (Coene, D'hulst, and Tasmowski 1999). In fact, as has already been pointed out in the literature (Cabredo-Hofherr 2009), this N°-to-D° movement is relevant when considering French vocatives, which is something that we do not expect given the set of properties that we know from this Romance language: their nominal expressions being defined as [-arg, +pred] (Chierchia 1998), they should not occur unless in predicate position. The French examples in (16), just like the Catalan examples given above, show that simple vocative nominals in sentence-initial position must be bare, not only when the noun is a proper name but also when the noun is a common count noun.

(16)a. Le Seigneur est mon esperance. *Seigneur* vous êtes mon esperance. (Cabredo-Hofherr 2009: 2, ex. 6).

  b. *Françaises, français!* (Schaden 2010: 179, ex. 18a).

In addition to N°-to-D° movement, in this paper D°-to-Voc° movement is also postulated for vocative expressions.[8] In the case of second person strong pronouns, already defined as pro-D by Déchaine and Wiltschko (2002), they are assumed to move to Voc° in order to be interpreted as designators of the hearer(s) / addressee(s) (see 17a);[9] bare nominals and bare adjectives are also assumed to continue their movement from N°-to-D°-to-Voc° or from A°-to-N°-to-D°-to-Voc° in order to deictically refer to the addressee (see 17b,c). Catalan nominal vocatives are incompatible with Ds but are nonetheless referential and interpreted as familiar and unique; Catalan adjectival vocatives cannot be preceded by a D° either, but instead denote a property of the designated addressee, which suggests that a cyclic movement to Voc° is what accounts not only for its syntactic behaviour but also for its semantic interpretation. Therefore, we assume that bare nominals and bare adjectives follow a head-to-head movement from their basic positions to the final Voc°. Romanian nominal and adjectival vocatives (either proper names, count nouns, or adjectives) support this analysis, since they show an overt definite article in postnominal position.[10]

(17) a. $[_{Voc°} tu_i [_{D°} t_i]]$ a'. *Tu!*
   b. $[_{Voc°} \{Joan, noi, nois\}_i [_{D°} t_i [_{N°} t_i]]]$ b'. *{Joan, noi, nois}!*
   c. $[_{Voc°} desgraciat_i [_{D°} t_i [_{N°} t_i [_{A°} t_i]]]]$ c'. *Desgraciat!*

(18) a. *Băsescule,*   vezi   ce   faci!
       Băsescu.the.MASC.VOC   see.2P.SG.IMP   what   do.2P.SG.IND
       'Mind what you're doing, Băsescu!'   (Hill 2007: 2084, ex. 12b)

   b. *Copilule,*   nu   mai   striga!
       Child.the.VOC   no   more   shout
       'Child, don't shout any more!'

   c. Hei,   *frumosule!*
       PART   beautiful.the.MASC.VOC
       'Hey, beautiful!'

In order to account appropriately for the data described in Section 2, I would also like to introduce a structural distinction between "true" and "fake" vocatives. In "true" vocatives a Voc°, optionally preceded by a vocative particle, is filled either by a 2P strong pronoun moved from D° or by a nominal expression moved from an N° or A° position lower than D°; a semantic characteristic of "true" vocatives is that they are always deictic. In "fake" vocatives a DP (or QP), very exceptionally specified by a Voc particle, enters into a syntactic relationship with a null Voc° and is associated with either a referential / quantificational, or a predicational interpretation.

Consider the structure of "true" deictic vocatives in (19).

(19)

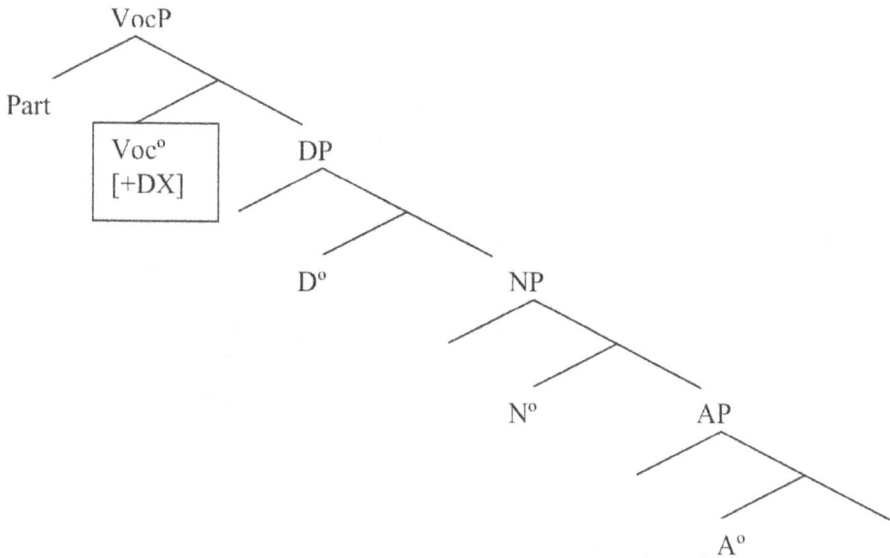

Unlike first and third person pronouns (see 7c), only 2P pronouns, specified by [+II,-I] person grammatical features and defective for a deictic feature [+DX], satisfy the requirement of being forms of direct address to the hearer / addressee (Hill 2007). Other nominal heads (proper names, common nouns) and adjective heads are assumed to move to a probe deictic Voc° in the process of the derivation in order to guarantee its deictic interpretation.

On the other hand, "fake" vocatives, which are full DPs associated with either a predicational or a referential meaning, as exemplified in (12) and (20) respectively, cannot occur in Voc°, since they are not heads.

(20) a. Au   travail, *les filles!*   [FRENCH]
       to   work   the   girls
       (Cabredo-Hofherr 2009: 3, ex. 12a)
   b. *I   protoetis   fitites,*   elate   edo.   [GREEK]
       the   first.year   students   come   here
       (Stavrou 2009: 16, ex. 57a)
   c. *Tots   vosaltres,* veniu!   [CATALAN]
       all   you   come

The example in (21a), represented in (21b), contains a null Voc° marked with the formal feature [+DX] c-commanding a full DP. In this Romanian example the Voc head is specified by a particle in VocP. A similar structure would be postulated for (8c'–d') in Catalan.

(21) a. Măi   *dragă băiatule /   băiete,*   nu   intelegi   nimic.[11]
       PART   dear   boy.the.VOC   boy.VOC   NEG   understand   nothing
       'My dear boy, you don't understand anything!'
   b.

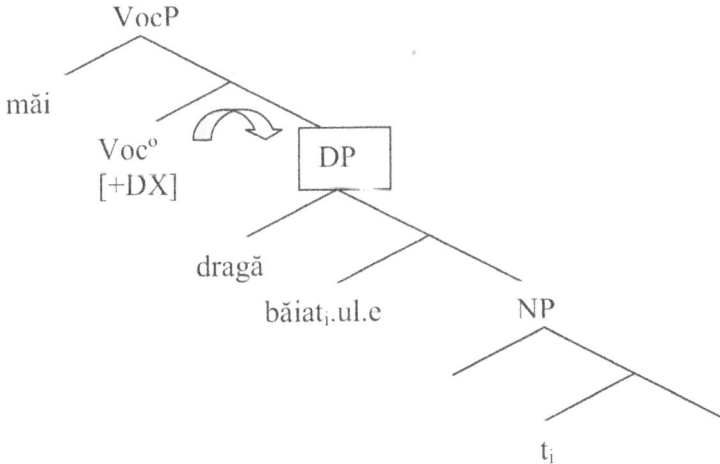

Once we have considered the basic structure of "true" and "fake" vocatives, in the next section we shall consider the structure that should be associated with more complex vocatives in which two nominal expressions combine in a specific order (see 6b,d).

4. Complex vocatives

The question that will be addressed in this section is Q2, but before addressing it we must consider which of the following nominal expressions in each example ought to be considered the "true" vocative, and what its interpretation must be.

(22) a. *Tu,   Joan!*   strong pronoun + proper name
       you   Joan
     b. *Tu,   el   noi   de   la   camisa   blava!*   strong pronoun + DP
       you   the   boy   of   the   shirt   blue
     c. *Tu,   {nen,   desgraciat}.*   strong pronoun + bare {noun, adjective}
       you   kid   bastard

According to what we have seen so far, the most immediate answer seems to be that the "true" vocative expression is precisely the 2P pronoun because it is the best candidate to deictically designate the individual entity it refers to. Only 2P pronouns, specified by [+II,-I] person grammatical features and deficient for a deictic feature [+DX] (see note 8 above), satisfy the requirement of being forms of direct address to the hearer / addressee and show the possibility of combining with other nominal expressions in complex vocatives.

Thus, following a 2P pronoun, the "true" vocative expression, proper names (22a) are no longer true vocatives but instead expressions that provide the *identity* of the entity associated with the addressee. Full definite DPs (22b) provide the *identification* of the entity associated with the addressee. Bare nominals and bare adjectives (22c) are NPs and APs that introduce *predicational* information on the addressee. Interestingly enough, this classification suggests that there is an important similarity between vocatives and copular sentences.

Let me remind the reader that, according to Higgins (1979), four types of copular sentences can be distinguished in English. See Table 1.

Table 1. Copular sentences in English

Type	Subject	Predicate
Identity	Referential	Referential
Identificational	Referential	Identificational
Predicational	Referential	Predicational
Specificational	Superscriptional	Specificational

English sentences that instantiate each type are illustrated in (23) (Alexiadou 2005: 815, ex. 67).

(23) a. The Morning Star is the Evening Star.   *Identity*
     b. That man over there is John Smith.   *Identificational*
     c. Paul is sick.   *Predicational*
     d. What I don't like about John is his tie.   *Specificational*

What I would like to do next is to extend this typology to vocative expressions, since in complex vocative structures we can identify a "true" vocative expression, usually the 2P pronoun, and an additional "fake" vocative, either a proper name, a DP, an NP, or an AP. It should be noted, however, that vocative constructions are distinct from copular sentences in (i) not having a copula verb, and (ii) lacking the specificational type since the head is not cataphoric but deictic. Nevertheless, they are similar in that they relate nominals in subject-predicate structures, as represented in (24).

(24)

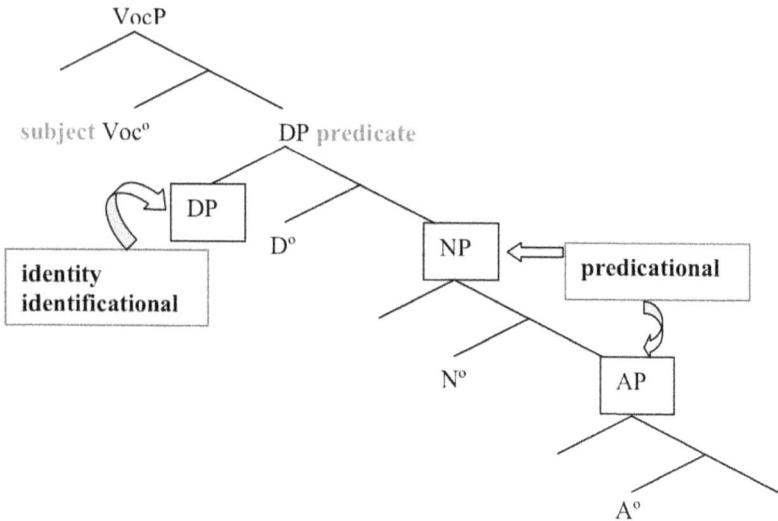

The extension from copular sentences to vocative expressions is illustrated in (25), (26), and (27). In (25a) we exemplify an identity complex vocative made up of a 2P pronoun followed by a bare proper name; according to the syntactic analysis put forward so far the structure associated with this example is represented in (25b), and (25c) gives an English example parallel to the Catalan one. The examples and structures in (26) correspond to an identificational complex vocative. Note that example (26b) differs from (25a) in that the proper name does not move to D^o, since an overt D is made explicit; therefore, in (26c,d), in contrast to (25b), the noun remains in N^o and D^o is overtly realized by a definite article. Finally, (27) contains examples of predicational complex vocatives, characterized by a 2P pronoun followed by either bare common count nouns (27a) or bare adjectives (27b); their structures are illustrated respectively in (27c,d). English correlates are given in (27e,f).

(25) a. *Tu, Joan!*   *Identity*
     b. $[_{VocP} [_{Voc^o} tu_i] [_{DP} [_{DP} [_{D^o} Joan_j] [_{NP} [_{N^o} t_j]]] [_{D^o} t_i]]]$
     c. You, John, come here!

(26) a. *Tu, el noi de la camisa blava!*   *Identificational*
     b. *Tu, el Joan!*   vs. (26a)
     c. $[_{VocP} [_{Voc^o} tu_i] [_{DP} [_{DP} [_{D^o} el] [_{NP} [_{N^o} noi] [_{PP} de la camisa blava]]] [_{D^o} t_i]]$

    d. [$_{VocP}$ [$_{Voc°}$ tu$_i$] [$_{DP}$ [$_{DP}$ [$_{D°}$ el] [$_{NP}$ [$_{N°}$ Joan]]] [$_{D°}$ t$_i$]]]

    e. You, the boy with the blue shirt, come here!

(27) a. *Tu, {noi, violí primer}!*   *Predicational*

    b. *Tu, {desgraciat, idiota}!*

    c. [$_{VocP}$ [$_{Voc°}$ tu$_i$] [$_{DP}$ [$_{D°}$ t$_i$] [$_{NP}$ [$_{N°}$ noi]]]]

    d. [$_{VocP}$ [$_{Voc°}$ tu$_i$] [$_{DP}$ [$_{D°}$ t$_i$] [$_{NP}$ [$_{N°}$] [$_{AP}$ [$_{A°}$ desgraciat]]]]]

    e. You, {boy, first violin}, come here!

    f. You, {bastard, idiot}, come here!

All these examples and representations illustrate the fact that complex vocatives combine a "true" vocative, hosted in Voc°, with a "fake" vocative, located either in a specifier DP position or in a subordinate NP or AP. See the structure in (24) for details on how the parallel between copular sentences and vocative structures must be understood.

In the following section we present the conclusions that must be drawn from this study and the predictions to be inferred from them.

5. Conclusions and predictions

The conclusions of this paper can be formulated as follows:

C1. A structural distinction should be made between "true" and "fake" vocatives.

C2. Three types of complex vocatives (i.e., identity, identificational and predicational) can be distinguished.

Let us now evaluate the predictions made from these conclusions.

Predictions from C1:

1.   We expect to find vocative particles with "true" vocatives, in which the particle specifies the vocative nominal expressions, but we do not expect them to be likely with "fake" vocatives, since in the latter no adjacent [Spec,Head] relationship is fulfilled. This is exactly what we find in examples such as (7), (8), (9), and (10) above, in comparison to (12) and (20). Examples (8c',d'), repeated here, are well-formed because they are structured in two prosodic units, one for the particle and one for the DP,

and the particle is assumed not to specify the DP. See also the structure postulated for the Romanian example in (21).

(8) c'. Ei,   *##el*   *Joan*!
   PART   the   Joan
  d'. Eh,   *##el*   *noi*   *ros.*
    PART   the   boy   blond

2.   Full definite and indefinite expressions are not expected as "true" deictic vocatives because they are not heads. This prediction is borne out.

(8) c. *Ei   *el*   *Joan*!
   PART   the   Joan
  d. *Eh   *el*   *company*!
   PART   the   guy
  e. *Eh   *un(s)*   *company(s)*!
   PART   {a, some}   guy(s)

3.   Full NPs that have a [N A] structure are not expected either in "true" vocatives because they are not heads. This prediction is also confirmed, as shown in (28).

(28) *Ei   noi   guapo!
  PART   boy   handsome

4.   Bare singulars and bare plurals must be distinguished from singular and plural indefinites in that they can move to Voc° and be interpreted as deictic (i.e., they provide a property of the individual identified as the addressee, either a singular entity or a set of individuals). See the contrast between the data in (9) and (8e).

(9) a. Ei   *tio*!   M'agrada   la   samarreta   que   portes.
   PART   pal   me.likes   the   T-shirt   that   wears
   'Hey, man! I like your T-shirt.'
  b. Ei   *nois*!   Calleu!
   PART   boys   shut
   'Hey, boys! Shut up!'

(8) e. *Eh   *un(s)*   *company(s)*!
   PART   {a, some}   guy(s)

5.   Two different interpretations must be associated with the bare plurals in (29a,a') (deictic vs. predicational), and also with the nominals in (29b,b')

(deictic vs. merely referential; Coene, D'hulst, and Tasmowski 1999: 8, exs. 26b,a and 29c,c') (deictic vs. generic; Schaden 2010: 179, exs. 18a, b).

(29) a. *Nois,* veniu aquí! a'. Vosaltres, *nois,* veniu aquí!
      boys come here you boys come here
   b. *Amis,* partons tout de suite. b'. Allons, *les amis.*
      friends let's.leave straight away let's.go the friends
   c. *Françaises, français!* c'. *Les français!*
      French.FEM French the French

Predictions from C2:

6.   In identificational vocatives we expect recursivity of DPs because it is expected that several DPs can occur in Spec,DP position. This prediction is also borne out by the data. See (30).

(30) a. Tu, *el Joan,* vés-te'n!
      you D Joan go.CL.CL
      'You, Joan, go away!'
   b. Tu, *el Joan, el Joan Ripoll,* vés-te'n!
      you D Joan D Joan Ripoll go.CL.CL
      'You, Joan, Joan Ripoll, go away!'

7.   In identificational vocatives we expect a 2P pronoun to be followed by an appositive nominal. This is exactly what we find in the possessive vocative pattern characteristic of Swedish (Corver 2008).

(31) Du, din idiot, borde vara försiktigare i framtiden.
     you your idiot should be careful.COMPAR in future.the
     (Corver 2008: 54, ex. 33a)

8.   In predicational vocatives neither bare nominals nor bare adjectives move to D^o since they are not referential, and they cannot move to Voc^o either since they are not deictic and this position is already filled by the 2P pronoun. Let me remind the reader that the structures postulated for (32) were given in (27c,d) respectively, which show that below the D^o a noun or adjective constrains the predicational interpretation.

(32) Tu, {noi, desgraciat}!
    You boy bastard
(27) c. $[_{VocP} [_{Voc^o} tu_i] [_{DP} [_{D^o} t_i] [_{NP} [_{N^o} noi]]]]$
    d. $[_{VocP} [_{Voc^o} tu_i] [_{DP} [_{D^o} t_i] [_{NP} [_{N^o}] [_{AP} [_{A^o} desgraciat]]]]]$

9.   "True" vocatives can be arguments of nominal (and adjectival) predicates in predicational complex vocatives (contra Coene, D'hulst, and Tasmowski 1999: 2, note 1). Thus, in (32) the 2P pronoun is the subject-external argument of the bare predicate, regardless of whether it is nominal or adjectival.

10.   A final prediction has to do with the sequence *You linguists* in English. I would like to propose a reinterpretation of the structure that should be attributed to this sequence.[12] When you is the head of VocP, the internal syntax of this sequence is predicted to be the same as the one corresponding to *you idiot!*.[13] Syntactically, it should be noted that these two complex vocative sequences are associated with a predicational vocative structure, in spite of the fact that the nominal heads are semantically different: a predicate of a set of entities in the first case and a gradable predicate (among which evaluative vocatives should be included) in the second case (Espinal 2011).

My analysis of this sequence consists in assuming that *you* is a pronoun that has moved from D° to Voc°, the subject of the complex structure according to (24). On the other hand, *linguists*, as predicate and head of the predicational NP, has moved from N° to Num°. This structure is represented in (33).

(33) $[_{VocP} [_{Voc^{\circ}} you_i] [_{DP} [_{D^{\circ}} t_i] [_{NumP} [_{Num^{\circ}} linguists_j] [_{NP} [_{N^{\circ}} t_j]]]]]$

By contrast, the English sequence *You the linguists* corresponds to an identificational vocative. As before, *you* is assumed to move from D° to Voc°, the subject of the complex vocative. The predicate definite DP is postulated to occur in the [Spec,DP] position complement of Voc°, a position from which it identifies the referent of the vocative head. See (34).

(34) $[_{VocP} [_{Voc^{\circ}} you_i] [_{DP} [_{DP} [_{D^{\circ}} the][_{NumP} [_{Num^{\circ}} linguists_j] [_{NP} [_{N^{\circ}} t_j]]]] [_{D^{\circ}} t_i]]]$

To sum up, in this paper I have focused on the internal syntactic structure of vocatives. I have postulated a distinction between "true" and "fake" vocatives, which can combine in complex vocatives in different ways. The output of this combination is that an identity, an identificational, or a predicational type of vocative can emerge.

Notes

*   This paper has benefited from comments and discussion with A. Gallego, V. Hill, C. Picallo, and M. Stavrou. Different versions were presented at the *Vocative!* Workshop (Bamberg, December 2010), *Journée d'étude Langues avec et sans articles* (Paris, March 2011), *Workshop on the Syntax and Semantics of Nounhood and Adjectivehood* (Barcelona, March 2011), and *International Workshop on Sentence-Initial Bare Nouns in Romance* (Tübingen, May 2011).

   Financial support for this research has been obtained from the Spanish Ministerio de Ciencia e Innovación (HUM2006-13295-C02-01FILO, FFI2011-23356) and the Generalitat de Catalunya (2009SGR-1073). The author also acknowledges an ICREA Acadèmia award.

1.   See also Hill (2007: 2078), who states explicitly this same goal.

2.   In the discussion that follows I have omitted reference to NumberP to keep my analysis simple, but I assume that the canonical structure of nominal expressions in languages with number morphology and determiners has the form in (i) (Chierchia 1998; Longobardi 2001; Zamparelli 1995).

     (i) $[_{DP}$ D $[_{NumP}$ Num $[_{NP}$ N $]]]$

3.   The data under study are Catalan unless otherwise specified.

     Most examples correspond to "call" vocatives (Zwicky 1974), although the analysis proposed here can be extended to vocatives that serve other "communicative" purposes.

4.   These particles are to be distinguished from exclamative particles (Catalan *ah, oh*).

5.   Moro (2003: 253) notes that vocatives "display anomalous behaviour both syntactically (absence of the article, presence of an interjection which immediately precedes the noun phrase, selective referential capacities) and phonologically (truncation and stress retraction)." Several studies deal with specific phonological processes (truncation, prosodic contours) that apply to vocative forms in languages both with and without articles (Floricic 2000, 2010; Cabré and Venrell 2008; Daniel & Spencer 2009; and others).

6.   It might also be the case that vocatives are reduced to the Voc particle, and that a postsentential nominal in the informational coda (Vallduví 1990) must be analysed as a topic constituent. See (i).

     (i) a. Ei!   M'agrada   la   samarreta   que   portes,   *tio*.
          PART   me.likes   the   T-shirt   that   wears   pal
          'Hey! I like your T-shirt, man!'
        b. Ei!   Calleu,   *nois*!
          PART   shut   boys
          'Hey! Shut up, boys!'

      c. Eh!   Què   tal,   *canalla?*
         PART   how   that   kids
         'Hey! How are things, kids?'

7.   According to Moro (2003: 258) a VocP is a full noun phrase containing both N° and D° projections that may display anomalous behaviour both syntactically and phonologically. He assumes that the VocP is hosted in the Spec of the head projected by a Voc° feature governing $Force^{\circ}$. See (i).

    (i) $C^{\circ} = ...Voc^{\circ} > Force^{\circ} > (Top^{\circ} > Foc^{\circ} > Top^{\circ} >) Fin^{\circ}...$

However, as will be shown shortly, it is not clear how this structure can be integrated with the internal structure of VocP, which is characterized by the fact that it selects DPs. See (1) in the text.

     According to Hill (2007: 2078) the VocP is a functional RoleP in which pragmatic Role markers select DPs and, depending on their morphological status, they merge either in the head or in the specifier of RoleP. She also postulates that RoleP is in the specifier position of a Speech Act Phrase above ForceP, whose head is assumed to be the particle *hai(de)* in Romanian.

    (ii) $[_{SAP}\ RoleP_{hearer}\ [_{SA'}\ [\ hai\ ][_{ForceP}\ ]]]$

When considering Catalan this structure must be simplified, since no item like *hai* seems to exist in this language.

     According to Stavrou (2009: 9) the specifier position of the pragmatic category Pragmatic Role Phrase$_{addressee}$ is the locus of a VocP of direct address. She postulates that the Voc particle is generated inside Voc°, whose complement is a NumberP, and that the second person addressee is generated in PR°.

    (iii) $[_{PRP}addressee\ [_{VocP}\ [_{Voc'}\ [_{Voc^{\circ}}\ ][_{NumP}]]]\ [_{PR'}addressee\ [_{PR^{\circ}}addressee][_{ForceP}]]]$

This analysis predicts a syntactic order such as (iv), which is ungrammatical in Catalan.

    (iv) *Ei   estudiants   vosaltres.
         PART   students   you.PL.INFORMAL

It also predicts that the particle is not a specifier and that the complement of Voc is not a DP, predictions that appear to be wrong when considering the data in Catalan.

8. We refer the reader to the notion of structural deficiency as the key to moti-vate the series of head-movements postulated here (Roberts 2010).

9. An argument in support of a distinction between a second person determiner and a second person pronoun is given in (i). Notice that in (i a), *vosaltres nois* is the subject of the sentence, and *vosaltres* is a D° head that cannot be specified by a vocative particle; by contrast, in (i b) *vosaltres* is a pronoun in Voc° that allows both a vocative particle in [Spec,VocP] position and a predicative nominal in complement position.

(i) a. (*Ei), vosaltres$_d$ nois   us   penseu
       PART   you.PL.INFORMAL boys   CL   think
       que   aprovareu sense   estudiar.
       that   pass   without   studying
       'You boys think that you will pass (the exams) without studying.'
   b. Ei,   vosaltres$_p$,   nois,   que   us   penseu
       PART   you.PL.INFORMAL boys   that   CL   think
       que   aprovareu sense   estudiar?
       that   pass   without   studying
       'Hey, you, boys, do you think that you will pass (the exams) without studying?

   See below, mainly (24), for details about the structure to be attributed to predicational complex vocatives.

10. I thank E. Ciutescu (p.c.) for discussion of Romanian data, and for providing me with examples (18b,c).

11. I owe this example to A. Mardale (p.c.).

12. Previous analyses include Déchaine and Wiltschko (2002: 421, ex. 33a), who postulate that *you* is a D° and *linguists* is a complement N°. For these authors φP is an intermediate functional projection that intervenes between N and D and encodes φ-features (where φ-features include number and gender, and in some cases person). See (i).

(i)   [$_{DP}$ [$_{D°}$ *you*] [$_{φP}$ [$_{φ°}$] [$_{NP}$ [$_{N°}$ *linguists*]]]]

   See also Payne and Huddleston's (2002) distinction between *you* determiner and *you* pronoun. An argument in support of the claim that *you* starts as a Determiner is that it can be preceded by *all*.
   A different proposal is given by Cowper and Hall (2009: 115, ex. 28a), who analyse *you* as the head of φP (in this case a functional projection that introduces an index), modified by #P (which introduces number features).

(ii)   [$_{φP}$ [$_{φP}$ *you*] [$_{#P}$ *linguists*]]

13. See Corver's (2008) study of the syntax of evaluative vocatives.

References

Alexiadou, Artemis
2005   Possessions and (in)definiteness. *Lingua* 115: 787–819.
Cabré, Teresa and Maria del Mar Vanrell
2008   Accent i entonació en els vocatius de l'alguerès. Paper presented at the XXXV *Colloqui de la Societat d'Onomàstica*, Sala del Consell Comunal, l'Alguer (Sardenya). May 10th and 11th. 2008.
Cabredo-Hofherr, Patricia
2009   Definiteness markers in vocatives. Ms. CNRS/Université de Paris 8, Paris.
Chierchia, Gennaro
1998   Reference to kinds across languages. *Natural Language Semantics* 6: 339–405.
Coene, Martine, D'hulst, Yves, and Tasmowski, Liliane
1999   Romance vocatives and the DP hypothesis. Paper presented at *CSSP*, Paris.
Corver, Norbert
2008   Uniformity and diversity in the syntax of evaluative vocatives. *Journal of Comparative German Linguistics* 11: 43–93.
Cowper, Elisabeth and Daniel Currie Hall
2009   Argumenthood, pronouns, and nominal feature geometry. In *Determiners*, Jila Ghomeshi, Ileana Paul, and Martina Wiltschko (eds.), 97–120. Amsterdam: John Benjamins.
Daniel, Michael and Andrew Spencer
2009   The vocative – an outlier case. In *The Oxford Handbook of Case*, Andrej Malchukov and Andrew Spencer (eds.), 626–634. Oxford: Oxford University Press.
Déchaine, Rose-Marie and Martina Wiltschko
2002   Decomposing pronouns. *Linguistic Inquiry* 33: 409–442.
D'hulst, Yves, Coene, Martine, and Liliane Tasmowski
2007   The Romance vocative and the DP hypothesis. In *Studii de Lingvistica si Filologie Romanica. Hommages Offerts à Sanda Reinheimer Rîpeanu*, Alexandra Cunita, Coman Lupu and Liliane Tasmowski (eds.), 200–211. Bucharest: Editura Universitatii din Bucuresti.
Espinal, M. Teresa
1991   The representation of disjunct constituents. *Language* 67: 726–762.

Espinal, M. Teresa
2011   Bare nominals, bare predicates: properties and related types. Paper presented at the *Workshop on the Syntax and Semantics of Nounhood and Adjectivehood.* Barcelona: Universitat Autònoma de Barcelona. March 24th and 25th.

Floricic, Franck
2000   De l'impératif italien *sii* (*sois!*) et de l'imperatif en général. *Bulletin de la Société de Linguistique de Paris* 95: 227–266.

Floricic, Franck
2010   Vocatives and the 'Minimal Word' syndrome. Paper presented at the *Vocative!* Workshop. Bamberg: University of Bamberg. December 10th 2010.

Higgins, Francis Roger
1979   *A Pseudo-Cleft Construction in English.* New York: Garland.

Hill, Virginia
2007   Vocatives and the pragmatics-syntax interface. *Lingua* 117: 2077–2105.

Longobardi, Giuseppe
1994   Reference and proper names: A theory of N-movement in syntax and logical form. *Linguistic Inquiry* 25: 609–665.

Longobardi, Giuseppe
2001   Reference and proper names. *Linguistic Inquiry* 25: 609–665.

Longobardi, Giuseppe
2005   How comparative is semantics? A unified parametric theory of bare nouns and proper names. *Natural Language Semantics* 9: 335–369.

Moro, Andrea
2003   Notes on vocative case. A case study in clause structure. In *Romance Languages and Linguistic Theory* 2001, Josep Quer and Jan Schroten (eds.), 247–261. Amsterdam: John Benjamins.

Payne, John and Rodney Huddlestone
2002   Nouns and nouns phrases. In *The Cambridge Grammar of the English Language*, Rodney Huddleston and Geoffrey K. Pullum (eds.), 323–524. Cambridge: Cambridge University Press.

Rizzi, Luigi
1997   The fine structure of the left periphery. In *Elements of Grammar: Handbook of Generative Syntax*, Liliane Haegeman (ed.), 281–337. Dordrecht: Kluwer.

Roberts, Ian
2010   *Agreement and Head Movement: Clitics, Incorporation and Defective Goals.* Cambridge MA.: MIT, LI monograph.

Schaden, Gerhard
    2010   Vocatives. A note on addressee-management. *University of Pennsylvania Working Papers in Linguistics* 16: 176–185.
Stavrou, Melita
    2009   Vocative! Ms. Aristotle University of Thessaloniki.
Vallduví, Enric
    1990   The informational component. PhD Dissertation. University of Pennsylvania. Published by Garland, Philadelphia, 1992.
Zamparelli, Roberto
    1995   Layers in the Determiner Phrase. PhD Dissertation. University of Rochester. Published by Garland, New York, 2000.
Zwicky, Arnold M.
    1974   Hey, whatsyourname! In Michael Galy, Robert Fox, and Anthony Bruck (eds.), *Chicago Linguistic Society* 10: 787–801.

Features and strategies: the internal syntax of vocative phrases

Virginia Hill

Abstract

This paper argues that vocatives are syntactically processed, as Vocative Phrases, by the same mechanism that generates Noun Phrases. The structure of Vocative Phrases differs from the structure of Noun Phrases only at the left periphery, where certain pragmatic features are encoded for the former but not for the latter. These pragmatic features are encoded as stable sets of functional features, namely: [specificity], which is central to the identification of the addressee; and [inter-personal], which qualifies the relation between the speaker and the addressee. Cross-linguistic variation follows from the available options for the checking of these two features during the syntactic derivation.

1. Introduction

The interpretation of vocative phrases involves, besides lexical semantics, pragmatic information, such as the degree of familiarity between the speaker and the addressee, the type of interaction between them, the speaker's designs on the addressee, and so on. This pragmatic input in the interpretation of vocatives arises systematically, irrespective of whether the vocative is related to an utterance, or whether it stands in isolation. For example, *Mr. Smith!* brings to the interpretation not only the lexical/referential information inherent to the word *Mister* and to the name *Smith*, but also pragmatic information, signalling the need for a respectful (versus condescending) 'call'.

The capacity of vocatives to generate compositional meaning goes hand in hand with syntactic and phonological peculiarities that make the vocative 'typed' for a specific interpretation, on par with exclamatives or interrogatives. What is the mechanism that triggers this 'typing'? From the perspective of generative grammar, the mechanism may apply at one of two levels: (i) only at the interface, in the Phonological Form (PF), after the completion (and independently) of the syntactic computation; or (ii) in the syntactic derivation, so the PF only spells out instructions issued during the syntactic computation. The current standard assumption in the Minimalist Program (Chomsky 1995 and further work) is that pragmatics related phenomena (which, in my understanding, also include vocatives) should be confined to point (i). In this paper, I will argue for point (ii), by bringing empirical evidence that vocatives are visible to syntactic computations. In my view, once the syntax of vocatives has been clarified, we can approach the syntax-PF interface from a better standpoint.

More precisely, in this paper I shall argue that the interpretation of a noun as a vocative arises from the way it is syntactically processed; and that the processing concerns pragmatic features encoded in syntax as stable feature sets. Thus, the first task of this paper is to identify the sets of pragmatic features that are syntactically relevant. The second step is to determine the syntactic strategies for computing these features within the vocative phrase, which must reflect the variations one may notice in the organization of vocative phrases.

2. The functional features

This section aims to demonstrate that vocatives arise from syntactic operations, and that they involve not only the vocative noun itself but also a functional field around this noun. Evidence comes from cross-linguistic data, as follows: (i) particles dedicated to vocative marking bring information on the type of functional field around the vocative nouns; (ii) the features of these particles, in addition to the morphology of vocative nouns, indicate two sets of functional features that trigger the syntactic operations: one set concerns the *addressee* (identification etc.) and one set concerns the *inter-personal relation* between speaker and addressee (familiarity, respect etc.). A formal representation of the vocative phrase is then proposed and generalized cross-linguistically, on the basis of the empirical observations.

2.1. Specialized particles

Various unrelated languages display particles that accompany or replace the vocative nouns, and this is their only function. Such vocative particles behave as in (1): they may stand by themselves (1a), or they may modify vocative nouns, on an optional (1b) or an obligatory basis (1c).

(1) a. ***măi,***   *vino-ncoa!*   (Romanian)
       MRK   come here
       'Come here!' – said to an addressee contextually identified
   b. ***(măi)***   *Ioane,*   *vino-ncoa!*   (Romanian)
       MRK   Ion.VOC   come here
       'Ion, come here!' – the addressee is named
   c. ***a***   *Maria,...* // **Maria,...*   (Umbundu)
       MRK   Maria.VOC // Maria.*VOC – *Maria* is addressee because of
       marker *a*

Hill (2007) presents a Table of such particles in three languages. The Table below expands that sample of data. The purpose is to show systematic patterns in the properties and the distribution of these particles.

Table 1. Vocative particles

Language	Particle*	Optional presence	Formality of address	Source
Arabic	ya+	+	-	http://corpus.quran. com/ documentation/ vocative.jsp
	+umma	-	+	
Bulgarian	(a)be/bre	+	-	O. Mladenova p.c.
	+le	+	-	
	ma	+	-	
Celtic	a	+	-	Mac Eoin (1993: 112)
Greek	vre	+	-	Stavrou (2010)
	(mo)re	+	-	
Korean	+(y)a	-	-	Sohn (2001: 134)
	+nim	-	+	
Portuguese	pá	+	-	Carvalho (2010)
	ó	+	-	
Romanian	măi (mă'/fă/bă)	+	-	Hill (2007)
	bre	+	-	
	tu	+	-	Zafiu (2003)
Telugu	+gA-rU	-	+	Arden
	E-mOy+/E-mma+	+	-	([1873]1905)
Toda	+(y)as	-	+/-	Emeneau (1984)
Umbundu	a+	-	+/-	F. Collins p.c.
	epa	+	-	

* '+' in front or after the particle indicates its prefix or suffix status, respectively.

The particles in Table 1 fall in two groups: (i) those that are obligatory and (ii) those that are optional. The obligatory particles indicate that the noun (common or proper) they affix to must be interpreted as a vocative (its referent is the addressee). Without them, the noun is interpreted differently (e.g., as a topic), not as a vocative. Since their main function is to mark the addressee role of the noun, these markers may be compatible with any formality value (e.g., Umbundu *a+*). Alternatively, some languages have separate obligatory addressee markers, one for formal and one for informal address (e.g., Korean).

Optional particles pattern together insofar as they are all associated with informality and need not be attached or co-occur with a noun. Their optionality is illustrated in (1a, b).

The interpretation of the particles in Table 1 indicates one basic property that applies to them all: they make an *addressee* out of a noun; hence, they *Role mark* it in the conversational setup. This property is intrinsically related to the interpretation (i.e., +/- formal), which may be further nuanced by types of (in)formality. Since the exact type of (in)formality can vary to a great extent, it is unlikely that every possible degree is encoded on the Role marker. What we rather detect is a general underspecified feature that allows for various values defining the relation between speaker and addressee. Let us call it the *inter-personal* [i-p] feature. The exact value of this feature arises from its semantic-syntactic environment. Therefore, irrespective of whether a Role marking particle co-occurs with a noun or not, it contributes two pragmatic ingredients to the compositional meaning of the utterance: the *addressee* and the [i-p].

2.2. Addressing the *addressee*

The nature of the inter-personal feature is self-explanatory. However, the concept of *addressee* needs further clarification. The *addressee* is a pragmatic role in the discourse set-up. As shown in Speas and Tenny (2003), pragmatic roles are converted to syntax in the same way thematic roles are converted from semantics to syntax. That is, thematic roles (e.g., 'agent', 'theme' etc.) are encoded as features of verbs, thus underlying the derivation of clauses (i.e., by determining the projection of corresponding argumental slots, such as 'subject' and 'direct object'). Along the same lines, pragmatic roles (i.e., 'speaker', 'addressee') are encoded as features of speech acts, deriving clause-like structures as well. Hence, our *addressee* feature, as a pragmatic role feature, should belong to a speech act head (i.e., predicative), not to the head of an argument (which is the status of nouns, vocatives included). So, what we perceive as the *addressee* feature must follow from the position of the entire vocative phrase in relation to speech acts (i.e., an external condition), rather than from the mapping of that feature within the vocative phrase (i.e., an internal condition). This is actually the analysis proposed in Hill (2007), Haegeman (2010), Haegeman and Hill (2012), Stavrou (2010) for integrating vocative phrases in the clause hierarchy.

However, the fact that the vocative phrase is computed as an argument saturating the *addressee* pragmatic role feature of a speech act indicates that there is an addressee related feature computed within the vocative phrase itself; that is, some feature of the vocative ensures compatibility between the vocative noun and the speech act carrying the addressee pragmatic role feature. I will identify that feature as [specificity], which is an intrinsic component of the *addressee* semantics.

Evidence for the obligatory presence of [specificity] on vocatives comes from the interpretation: Vocative nouns always have a specific reading even when they display indefinite forms, as in (2) (Hill 2007; Espinal this volume).

(2) a. *oameni   buni,...*   (Romanian)
         folks   good
         'Good folks, ...'
     b. *eh,   desgraciats,...*   (Catalan)
         PRT   swines[1]
         'Swines,...'

Languages like Romanian and Catalan have a one-to-one correspondence between definite articles and specific readings in common nouns. Thus, definiteness falls necessarily under semantic specificity.[2] Generic, non-specific noun semantics, on the other hand, is encoded through indefinite articles or lack of articles. In this system, vocative nouns come as a puzzle, since they lack definite articles (as in 2), but yield a specific interpretation at all times, irrespective of the context.

Related to this mismatch between semantics and morphology is the well-known observation that the use of definite articles is deviant in vocative phrases. For example, languages that have default processing of names with definite articles eliminate the article in vocative constructions; e.g., Albanian in (3) and Greek (see Stavrou 2010). On the other hand, languages that process names without article by default, may use them when the name comes in vocative; e.g., Romanian in (4).

(3) a. Default: *Azim*   vs.   *Azimi*   (Albanian)
                    Azim.NOM   Azim.the.NOM   (+article)
     b. Vocative: *Azim,..!*   vs.   **Azimi, ...!*   Albanian
                    Azim.VOC   Azimi.the.VOC   (-article)

(4) a. Default: *Ionel*   vs.   **Ionelul*   (Romanian)
                    Ionel   Ionel.the   (-article)
     b. Vocative: *Ionelu'*   lu' *mama,....* // *Ionelule,...*   (Romanian)
                    Ionel.the   of mother.the   Ionel.the.VOC   (+article)

Such examples show that the article is as much of a Role marker (i.e., marking the noun as *addressee*) as the particles are. From a syntactic perspective, the article is generated as D, which is, thus, the locus for [specificity] (associated with definiteness). Hence, vocatives must incorporate D, and/or the features associated with this head. Furthermore, a vocative that incorporates D in this sense may also co-occur with the Role marking particles of Table 1. These particles are also associated with [specificity], which is intrinsic to the *addressee* role. Consequently, vocative nouns have [specificity] encoded twice: once as D (or equivalent) and once on the Role marker. This feature composition is independent of the morphological Case marking.

Let us expand on this double specificity marking on vocatives: When we consider the Role markers in Table 1, each of them brings [specificity] to the interpretation of the vocative noun, or to the vocative phrase, even if the noun is non-lexical, since they unambiguously identify a referent as the addressee. In the absence of Role markers, double [specificity] is still operating, because there is change in intonation, which forces the specific interpretation. So [specificity] is associated with both D and Role in vocatives, irrespective of the lexical or non-lexical manifestation of these items. Technically, during the syntactic derivation, a competition arises for [specificity] checking between the definite article (or equivalents; e.g., demonstratives) and the element (e.g., Role markers) responsible for the vocative reading. Predictably, languages resolve this competition in different ways, and that must be reflected in a different internal structure in vocative phrases. However, given the processing constraints in syntax, in general, it is also predictable that the range of cross-linguistic variations is configurationally restricted, and that there must be one basic representation of vocative phrases that underlies these variations.

2.3. Formal syntax

Syntactic operations are driven by functional features (Chomsky 1995 and further work). Therefore, in order to formalize the syntactic derivation of the vocative phrase, one must first establish the functional features that may drive it.

So far, we have talked about [specificity] and [i-p] features as part of the lexical definition of the addressee Role makers. If these features count only as semantic properties of the particle, then we would expect the respective features not to be recoverable when there is no particle in the vocative phrase. Obviously, this is not what happens. As mentioned for (1b), the particle may be absent but the vocative noun is still interpreted for the values of the same features. Thus, cases as (1b) indicate the presence of a null counterpart to the particles in Table 1. For further illustration, consider the Romanian vocatives in (5), where no Role marking particle is present, and even the Vocative Case marking can be absent (e.g., *Ion* has the same form in vocative as in Nominative or any other Cases). The forms in (5) occur in free alternation with the forms in (4), which were shown to also display definite articles.

(5) *Ioane,... // Ion,...// Ionele,...*
    Ion.VOC // Ion // Ion.DIM.VOC

The name *Ion* is used with or without the vocative Case ending *-e*. Use of the ending signals an informal address, whereas dropping the ending means a more formal address. The addition of a diminutive [DIM] to the noun brings the address to a more endearing level. The point is that the speaker must make a morphological decision (i.e., whether to use the Vocative Case mark or not) according to the value of the [i-p] feature, although there is no particle indicating what the [i-p] value might be. The same goes for the [specificity]: either the particle or the noun or both satisfy the requirement for promoting a noun as a candidate for the *addressee* role; the absence of the particle does not block this feature, it only changes the [i-p] value (e.g., *măi Ion,...* is more informal than *Ion,...*).

Within the framework adopted in this paper, these facts indicate that [specificity] and [i-p] are encoded as functional features and are computed in the functional fields of substantive categories. In Minimalist terms (Chomsky 1995 and further work), these are *uninterpretable* features that have to be checked and eliminated before sending the derivation to the interface components. This is done either by merging items with interpretable features (i.e., the Role markers in Table 1) at the slot of feature computation or by having these features probe constituents that will move to the slot of feature computation (e.g., a nominal item or phrase). In other words, the particles in Table 1 do not cause "extra-structure" when they are inserted in the utterance, they only fill out structural positions that are systematically projected in that particular derivation. I formalize this finding in (6), following Hill (2007).

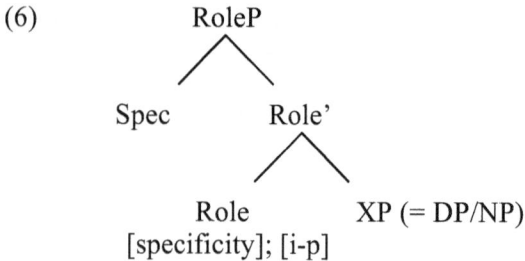

(6)

```
                    RoleP
                   /     \
              Spec        Role'
                         /     \
                     Role        XP (= DP/NP)
               [specificity]; [i-p]
```

The configuration in (6) means that there is a functional head associated with the uninterpretable features that triggers the vocative reading. Role markers, as in Table 1, merge either in the head (affixes) or in the Spec position (free morphemes) and check one or both of these features, depending on their semantics. If Role markers are not available, movement of the noun to Role may also accomplish the feature checking. A combination of Role marker merging and noun movement is also predictable.

There is evidence for the local relation indicated in (6) between Role markers (when they are available) and the vocative noun: a free morpheme Role marker is adjacent to the vocative noun, and may only precede (vs. follow) the noun, as in (7). The ungrammatical word order becomes acceptable if there are significant intonation breaks between the two items, the prosodic contour being completely different – which I consider to represent repetitions of the vocative phrases versus word order variation within the same vocative phrase. Graphically, such repetitions would be signaled by commas between the relevant items (e.g., *tataie, bre,…*).

(7) a. *bre   tataie,…*   vs. **tataie   bre,….* (Romanian)
        MRK grand'pa.VOC   grand'pa.VOC   MRK
    b. *(zău) bre   (*zău) tataie,   zău,…*
        PRT   MRK   PRT   grand'pa   PRT

Furthermore, the obligatory markers in Table 1 attach to the vocative noun as prefixes or suffixes, which also indicates that the noun moves to the Role head.

The presence of lexical Role markers allows us to see their relation with the vocative noun and to trace the movement of the noun. However, they may be invisible in the sentence, and yet the noun is processed in the same way, because there is a constant need to check [specificity] and [i-p] on the Role head. Thus, the analysis in (6) entails a generalization that holds cross-linguistically: vocative phrases are always RolePs, irrespective of whether the language has Role markers as in Table 1 or not (e.g., English).

3. Independent evidence for the syntactic status

So far, evidence for a syntactic status of vocative phrases came from constraints on the distribution and the interpretation of Role markers, and from the use of definite articles. One may still argue that such effects arise from pragmatics only, while the word order constraints follow from linearization at PF. After all, even the presence of Vocative Case ending on nouns is subject to debate as to its morpho-syntactic reality (see Donati, this volume). In this section, I bring further evidence for the syntactic status of vocative phrases by presenting constraints arising from morpho-syntactic agreement. Such agreement is necessarily the result of syntactic, pre-PF, operations.

3.1. Role markers and agreement

Some of the Role markers in Table 1 display different forms according to the number and the gender of the vocative noun. For example, Umbundu *epa* allows for masculine singular, but not for feminine or for plural (8). Furthermore, it applies only to informal addresses.[3] In the same vein, Romanian *măi* is spelled differently in sub-standard Romanian, according to whether the addressee is masculine or feminine (9).

(8) *epa a   Pedro,... // *epa   a   Maria,...* (Umbundu)
     MRK MRK   Pedro   MRK   MRK   Maria
(9) *bă   Marine,.... //   fă   Mario,...*   (Romanian)
     MRK   Marin.VOC   MRK   Maria.VOC

This type of agreement mimics the agreement we see between adjectives and nouns. Hence, it must also involve a similar configuration (i.e., Spec-head agreement), triggered by the features of the functional head (Role in 6).

3.2. Verb agreement

The Role markers listed in Table 1 for Umbundu are inherently specified for singular only. When the vocative involves a plural noun, it is licensed by the suffix *-ì* on the verb, instead of a Role marker on the noun. Schadeberg (1990: 29) provides the description for the string of verbal inflection in Umbundu, as in (10), illustrated with an assertive verb in (11).

(10)

1	2	3	4	5	6	7	8	9
PI+	I+	Fo+	Fo2+	preR+	VB+	Fi+	Fi2+	Cl
NEG	SCd	TAM	IT	OCd	LEX	TAM	PL	LOC

(11) *ka   tw   á   ka   vau   pandwíl   il   ì   kó*
not   we   PAST go   them.you thank.for PAST VOC.PL there
'we did not go there to thank them for you' (address to plural entity)

In (10), 1PI is the pre-initial negative marker; 2I the initial subject concord; 3Fo the formative tense marker for Tense/Aspect/Mood; 4Fo2 the formative 'itive' marker; 5preR the pre-radical object concord; 6VB the lexical verb base/root; 7Fi the final tense marker for TAM; 8Fi2 the final plural vocative marker; 9Cl is an enclitic locative complement. Importantly, the plural vocative morpheme is necessarily computed in the same way as the other morphemes of the verb string since it is embedded in the string.

3.3. Allocutive agreement

Haegeman and Hill (2012) point out the relevance of the allocutive agreement in Souletin (a Basque dialect) for the understanding of the syntactic processing of particles involved with the *addressee* pragmatic role feature. In particular, following the discussion in Oyharçabal (1993), Miyagawa (2012) shows that there are four ways to say 'Peter worked', depending on the gender/number of the addressee(s) and the inter-personal relation between the speaker and the addressee. The relevant patterns are given in (12), from Miyagawa (2012).

(12) a. To a male friend
Pettek   lan   egin   dik.
Peter.ERG work.ABS do.PRF AUX.3SG.ABS-2SG.C.MSC.ALLOC-3SG.ERG

b. To a female friend
   Pettek   lan   egin   din.
   Peter.ERG work.ABS do.PRF AUX-3.SG.ABS-2SG.C.FM.ALLOC-
   3SG.ERG
c. To someone higher in status (formal)
   Pettek   lan   egin   dizü.
   Peter.ERG work.ABS do.PRF AUX-3SG.ABS-2SG.F.ALLOC-3SG.ERG
d. Plural addressee
   Pettek   lan   egin   du.
   Peter.ERG work.ABS do.PRF AUX-3SG.ABS-3SG.ERG

Miyagawa demonstrates that allocutive agreement is authentic agreement, because it competes with the regular 2nd person agreement morpheme. If the sentence contains a 2nd person subject, object, etc., allocutive agreement does not arise:

(13) a. *(Nik   **hi**)   ikusi   **haut**.*
        (1SG.ERG **2SG.C.ABS**) see.PRF   aux-2SG.C.ABS-1SG.ERG
        'I saw you.'
    b. ***(Zuek**   ni)   ikusi   naiz**ue**.*
        (**2PL.ERG**   1SG.ABS) see.PRF aux-1SG.ABS-**2PL.ERG**
        'You saw me.'

Although these examples do not directly involve vocative phrases, they do involve the processing of the *addressee* feature, which is central to the vocative syntax. Proof that the *addressee* has morpho-syntactic impact supports the thesis of bringing the processing of vocatives into the syntax as well.

To conclude, there is strong evidence that vocative nouns and Role marking particles for the addressee constrain each other and/or the verb with respect to number and/or gender agreement. Agreement counts as an uninterpretable functional feature that drives checking operations in narrow syntax; in particular, it has to be eliminated before the derivation is sent to the interface. This process involves a probe (the uninterpretable feature) and a goal (the lexical item semantically specified for agreement). Since in our case the goal is a Role marker or a vocative noun, these items must be merged during the syntactic computation, or else the derivation would crash.

4. Licensing of vocative nouns within RoleP

This section explores the consequences of the RoleP configuration in (6) for the internal organization of the vocative phrase. First, I determine the conditions for feature checking, then I outline the patterns of variation allowed by the syntactic constraints.

The theoretical framework adopted here is that any noun projects a phrase (NP) reflecting its combinatorial possibilities, and that this phrase is extended with a functional field that inflects it (Abney 1987). The main functional element in this field is the D(eterminer) (e.g., article); so the structure is NP > DP. The head D carries uninterpretable features (basically [agreement] and [specificity]) and thus acts as an inflectional field for the noun, and ensures Case checking for this noun. In technical terms, D probes the items of NP for need of its feature checking; the probing results in the movement of the noun or the adjective to positions within DP (Giusti 1997 for Romanian). In (6), DP is the complement of Role and contains the vocative noun.

4.1. Noun movement to Role

The driving force for the syntactic operations in RoleP is the need to check its [specificity] and [i-p] features. As already mentioned, this may involve the merging of a Role marker or the movement of the noun to Role or both. This section brings evidence that nouns do indeed move to RoleP.

Evidence for noun movement to Role comes from examples as in (14). Bulgarian has the Role marker *-le*, which is an enclitic identifying the addressee, as in (14a). The Vocative Case is morphological. (14b) shows that the vocative noun follows the possessive adjective on par with the argumental use of this noun. However, when *-le* is introduced, the noun must precede the possessive adjective, which indicates movement (14c). Furthermore, this movement must be of the head-to-head type (i.e., N/D-to-Role) because the possessives occupy Specifier positions and would block any other constituent from moving across them to another Specifier position.

(14) a. *goro!* //   **le!* //   *gorole!*
          forest.VOC//   ROLE //   forest.VOC.YOU
   b. *moja*   *goro*
          my   forest.VOC
   c. *gorole*   *moja* //   **moja*   *gorole*
          forest.VOC.ROLE   my   my   forest.VOC.ROLE

The mechanics of (14) match the observation in Longobardi (1994) for Italian, where vocatives behave in the same way in relation to possessives:

(15) *Gianni mio,...*   vs.   **Mio Gianni,....*   (Italian)
    Gianni my.VOC   my Gianni.VOC

Italian does not have lexical Role markers, but the similarity in noun movement indicates that the head Role attracts the vocative noun at all times, irrespective of whether it is lexical or not. The mechanics of movement is shown in (16), where the arrows indicate the path of movement for the noun; the scored capital letters indicate the (memory) copies left behind by the moving noun.

(16)   [$_{RoleP}$ Role/D/N [$_{DP}$ ~~D/N~~ [$_{NP}$ ~~N~~]]]

The data in (14) and (15) confirm that nouns move to Role (with or without Role marker affixation). This movement crosses the DP level in response to probing from Role. Hence, we expect that the internal structure of vocative phrases must differ from the structure of regular NP/DP in all aspects related to Role probing for feature checking.

4.2. Checking within RoleP

The configuration for vocative phrases in (6) established that Role needs checking for two features: [specificity] and [i-p]. Movement within RoleP must be justified only by the need to check these two features.

The cross-linguistic examples in (3) and (4), showing deviant uses of definite articles in vocatives, signalled a competition between D and Role for [specificity] checking, since [specificity] is a feature on both heads. Hence, the checking operations within RoleP must allow for variations in [specificity] checking, in addition to the checking of the [i-p] feature. The operations are constrained insofar as they can only involve the head Role and the Spec, RoleP. Within these structural constraints, variation may arise from the presence or the absence of Role markers, either in Role or in Spec, RoleP. This is compounded by the movement of the noun, which may take the form of N/D-to-Role, as in (16), or it may occur as NP/DP to Spec, RoleP. Furthermore, adjectives may be nominalized and, so, they can alternate with genuine NPs for movement to Role or to Spec, RoleP. Therefore, the configuration in (6) allows for a considerable range of variation in the composition of vocative phrases, which may or may not all be available in one single language. A discussion of variation patterns follows, drawing, mostly, on Romanian data.

Pattern A: Lexical checking for informal [i-p]

Masculine singular vocatives in Umbundu provide the most complete set of lexical elements in RoleP, since it has two sets of Role markers: *epa* for informal [i-p]; *a* for [specificity]; the latter is an affix that attracts the noun irrespective of the [i-p] feature value in Role.[4] Thus, the representation of the vocative phrase is as in (17).

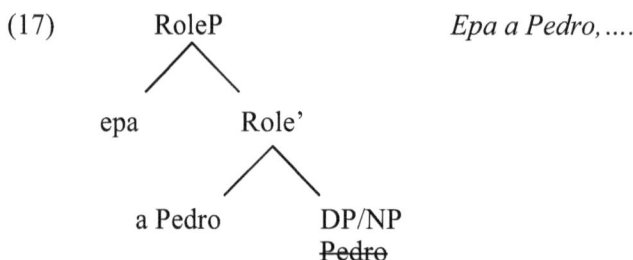

(17)   RoleP   *Epa a Pedro, ...*

         epa   Role'

             a Pedro   DP/NP
                            ~~Pedro~~

Romanian has Role markers for informal [i-p] (e.g., the free morpheme *măi*) but not for [specificity]. Hence, noun movement is expected to check [specificity] in Role. This movement, however, interferes with the checking within DP, since Role probes D before its [specificity] feature is deleted. Thus, restrictions on combinatorial possibilities arise which do not apply to DPs elsewhere. This is shown in (18).

(18) a. *Măi   fetiţo   (*isteaţă / mea), vino   mai   repede!*
        MRK   little.girl.VOC   smart   mine come.2SG.IMP more quick
        'Little girl, come quick!'
   b. *Măi   isteaţo   (*fetiţă), ...*
      MRK   smart.VOC   little.girl, ...
      'Smarty, ...'
   c. *(Isteaţa) (mea) fetiţă /   fetiţa   (mea) (isteaţă) a   venit.*
      smart.the my   little.girl / girl.the my   smart   has   come
      'The/my smart little-girl has come.'

In (18c), a regular DP allows for adjectives to precede or follow the noun. When the noun is vocative, only one phrase may occur, either the noun (18a) or the nominalized adjective (18b), but not both.

The restrictions in (18) follow from the need of movement to check [specificity] in Role. Thus, Role probes D (the nearest item) for [specificity]. As a free-ride,[5] D also checks its agreement features against Role instead of probing AP/NP for that purpose. The only feature for which D still probes down the tree is [D]-nominal (so the selected phrase is computed as a NP vs. e.g. an IP), for which only one item is necessary: i.e., either the noun, as in (18a), or the adjective, as in (18b), whichever is nearer. It has been established that D agreement checking on AP and/or NP is fundamental to license the agreement between A and N (e.g., Giusti 2005 establishes two agreement phrases for that purpose in Romanian). Since such an agreement fails, only one of these items can be a licit syntactic object (i.e., the item probed by D). The probed item (i.e., either N or AP) ends up as a portmanteau for the vocative morphology. This analysis explains why adjective nominalization is so common in vocatives. The checking variation arising in this context is that the operation is fulfilled either by N/D-to-Role, in which case the noun surfaces, as in (18a), or through AP to Spec,DP, Role being checked through distance 'Agree' with D, in which case we obtain the nominalized adjective in (18b). This variation is captured in (19a, b), respectively.

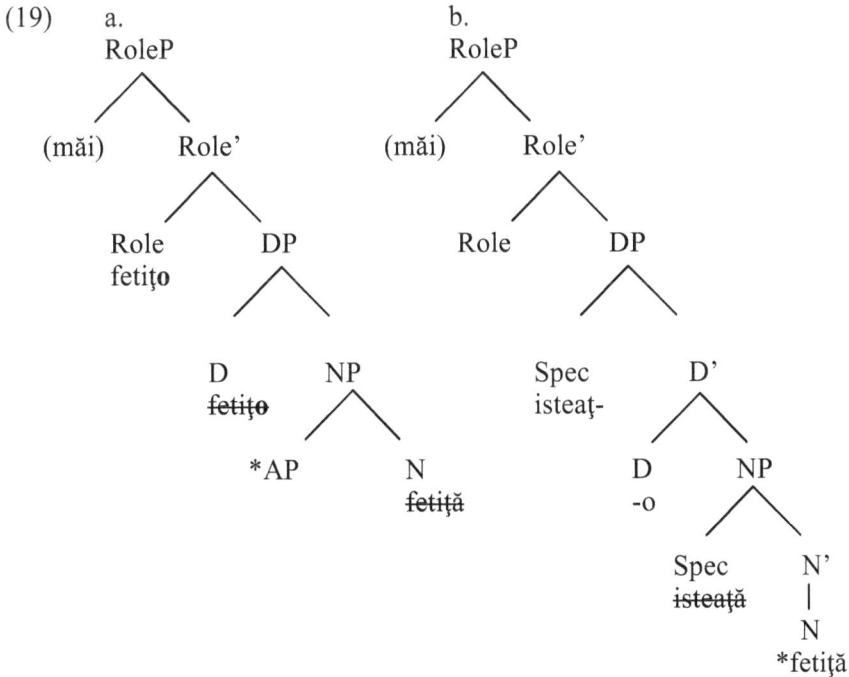

(19)   a.   b.
       RoleP   RoleP

  (măi)   Role'   (măi)   Role'

       Role   DP   Role   DP
       fetițo   Role

              D   NP   Spec   D'
              ~~fetițo~~   isteaţ-

                    *AP   N   D   NP
                           ~~fetiță~~   -o

                                              Spec   N'
                                              ~~isteață~~ |
                                                          N
                                                        *fetiță

(19) is a replica of the pattern in (17), and has the same interpretation as output: an informal address to a friend or a child.

Pattern B: Lexical checking for formal [i-p]

Formal address does not have dedicated particles in Table 1, but it may involve pragmaticized items. Thus, Romanian has *măi* for informal address, but resorts to certain adjectives for formality: *stimat* 'beloved', *drag* 'dear', etc. These adjectives have been semantically weakened and morpho-syntactically impoverished (e.g., *drag* lost some inflection). The syntactic behavior of these adjectives indicates that they have been re-analyzed as pragmatic/vocative markers. Consider the examples in (20): The re-analyzed form is in complementary distribution with *măi* (20a). In (20c), these forms do not allow for modifiers, whereas the same adjectives used elsewhere, do. In (20b), regular adjectives preceding the noun carry the definite article; the re-analyzed forms do not do that, the article remaining on the vocative noun. Hence, the adjective in (20a) is merged directly in Spec, RoleP (competing with *măi*), and is not subjected to the operations of the DP field. This is captured in the representation in (21).

(20) a. (*Măi) *stimate   cititorule,   publicaţiile   noastre*
         MRK   beloved   reader.the.VOC publications.the our
         îţi   stau   la dispoziţie.
         you.DAT remain   at disposal
         'Dear reader, our last publications are at your disposal.'
    b. *Stimatul   cititor*   vs.   **Stimat   cititorul*
         beloved.the   reader   beloved   reader.the
    c. *foarte stimat / mai   stimat*   vs.   **foarte/mai stimate cititor!*
         very   beloved more beloved   very/more   beloved reader

(21)

```
                    RoleP
                   /      \
            Spec           Role'
         Stimate/*măi     /    \
                      Role       DP
                    cititorule   /  \
                              D        NP
                         cititor-(u)le  |
                                        N
                                      cititor
```

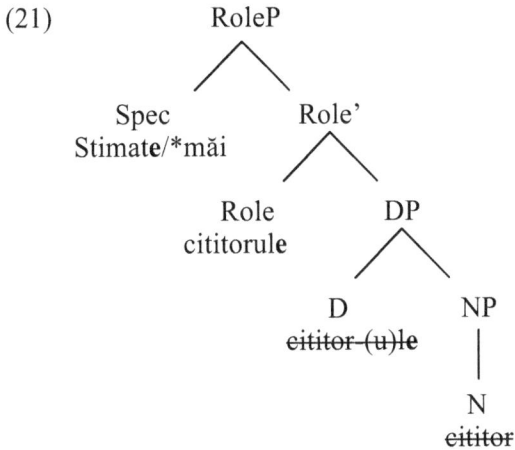

The representations in (19) and (21) are identical, the variation consisting only in the lexical items that check the [i-p] feature: Role marker in (19) versus pragmaticized adjective in (21). Then the value of the [i-p] feature is informal or formal, respectively.

Pattern C: Deletion of the DP field (+/- formal [i-p])

The main argument in this analysis is that [specificity] is a feature of both Role and D, and that affects the way feature checking is implemented around the vocative noun. One consequence is that Role may subsume the functions of D in relation to the noun. That takes place when the DP field is deleted, and Role probes the noun (N) directly. The deletion of the DP field is signalled by obligatory deletion of the definite article, as shown in (22), with the configuration in (23).

(22) a. *Măi oameni (*i) (*mei) buni,... // *Măi   oamenilor   buni,...*
       MRK folks *the my   good   MRK   folks.*the.VOC good
       'Good folks,...'
   b. *Carte frumoasă, cinste cui   te- a   scris!*
       book   beautiful   hail   to.whom you has   written
       'Beautiful book, homage be paid to whom wrote you!' (T. Arghezi)

(23)

```
                    RoleP
                   /      \
        Spec           Role'
        (Măi)          /    \
               Role          NP
            oameni 'folks'   /  \
                         Spec      N'
                         buni 'good'  |
                                      N
                                    o̶a̶m̶e̶n̶i̶
```

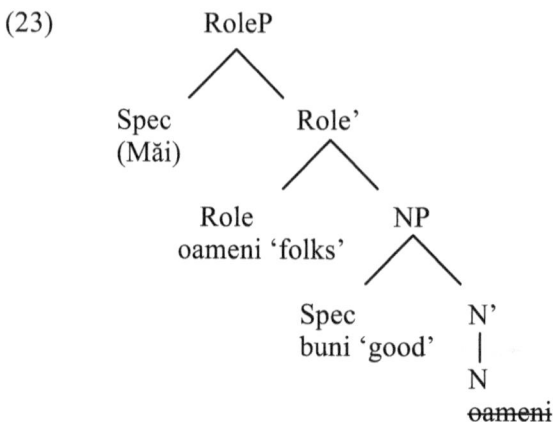

In (23), the [i-p] feature is checked either by a marker in Spec, RoleP (e.g. *măi*) or just by N-to-Role (in which case, the reading is more formal). The noun moves to Role without the intermediate step in D. This allows for the checking of the complete set of features between N and Role, which involves not only [specificity], but also gender/number, and this allows N to license an adjective. Thus, the main difference between Pattern C in (23), and Patterns A, B (19/21), is that the former does not have to choose between noun and adjective, but it can license both. Predictably, (23) does not allow for nominalization of adjectives (e.g., *Măi buni,...*'MRK good.MASC.PL') since the nominalization can be implemented only by the definite article.

Pattern D: Phrasal roll-up

Constructions as in (24) allow for either formal or informal interpretation, the reading depends on the context. The optional reading is enhanced by the fact that the Role marker *măi* is disallowed, even if the interpretation is [+familiar] (24). Furthermore, the vocative noun displays a definite article – which signals the presence of D – and it may co-occur with an adjective, contrary to the cases in (19). These properties indicate that this DP is computed as in the default (non-vocative) configurations, so Role probes the entire DP, and attracts it to Spec, RoleP, as shown in (25). This variation in the checking configuration follows from the possibility of having phrasal movement to Spec position, which, in (25), can check both features of Role (i.e., [i-p] and [specificity]) in this local structural relation.

(24) *(*măi) (toţi) băieţii   înalţi,   (toţi) treceţi   (toţi) la dreapta!*
   PRT   all   boys.the tall   all   go.2PL.IMP all   at right
   'The tall guys – move all to the right!'

(25)

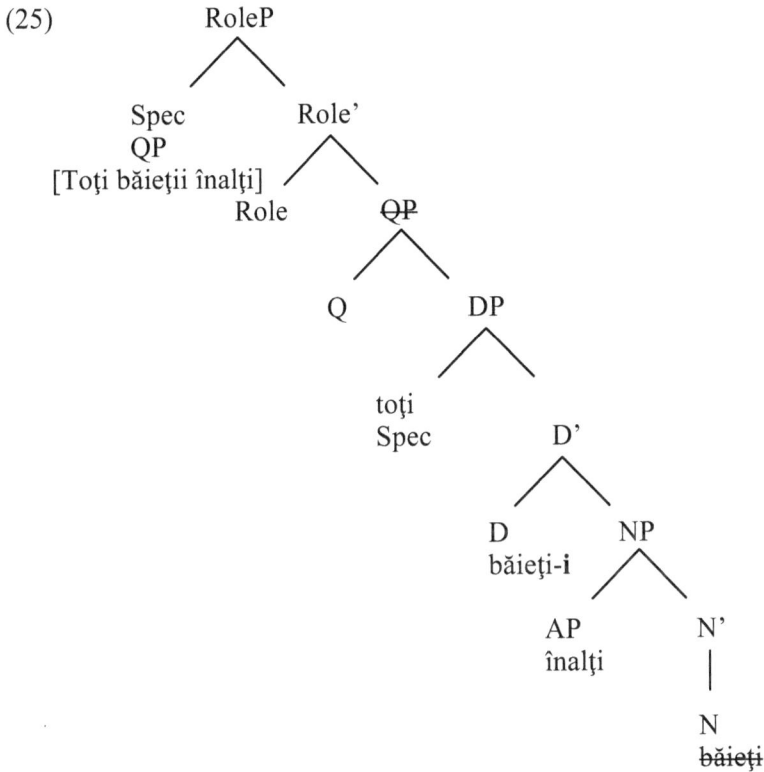

In (25), *măi* is impossible because the DP is merged in its place. The floating quantifier 'all' marks the possible positions for the DP it modifies. It appears that the DP originates lower in the clause – i.e., in the subject position of the imperative verb – and moves up to Spec, RoleP. In Romanian, this option applies only to vocative phrases that also qualify as subjects to imperative verbs. We can, thus, say that these are obligatorily intradeictic addresses, in terms of Stavrou (2010), or 'fake' vocatives in Espinal (this volume).

To sum up this section, the configuration in (6) underlies a whole range of variations we may see in vocative phrases, and which occur inter- or cross-linguistically. In this light, the theory does not have to chose between analyses that argue for bare nouns (NP) in vocatives (Longobardi 1994) or those that argue for DPs in vocatives (D'hulst, Coene, and Tasmowski

2007), as both patterns may arise, their derivation being restricted only by the conditions on syntactic checking of the [i-p] and the [specificity] features of Role.

5. Conclusions and cross-linguistic comments

This paper provided arguments for a syntactic status of vocative phrases. The main thesis is that the pragmatic features of vocatives are converted to a two-member set of functional features (i.e., [i-p] and [specificity]) associated with a functional field above DP/NP. Once this generalization is in place, then the ensuing syntactic configuration (i.e., RoleP > (DP) > NP) can account for any variation occurring in the vocative phrases, these variations reflecting the range of possible operations that achieve the checking of [i-p] and [specificity] in the domain of RoleP.

Romanian was shown to present the whole range of checking variations. However, not all languages do so, and, even those that do, show preferential patterns. English, for example, displays three patterns, as in (26), but (26a, b) are the most productive. In (26c), *you* can be replaced with *the* as modifier to the nominalized adjective, which would also make the switch between and address and an exclamation.

(26)   a. *John, ...!; Driver, ...!*   = Role > NP (23)
      b. *Old boy, ...!*   = Phrase roll-up (25)
      c. *you idiot!*   = nominalization (19b)

On the basis of the examples in this paper, it is reasonable to predict that the 'preference' for one pattern or another is constrained by certain parameters in the language; for example, lack of Role markers in the language and/or the type of definite article (clitic or non-clitic). Especially the latter may decide on the RoleP > DP versus RoleP > NP variation, since a free morpheme in D blocks the movement of N to Role. My analysis predicts a typology along these lines but further investigation in this respect is needed.

Notes

1. PRT stands for 'particle' in general, which is distinct from MRK 'marker', the later being exclusively used in vocatives.
2. Generally, morphological definiteness yields a specific reading. There are, of course, turns where this is not the case (e.g., Engl. non-specified 'this' in *There was this man there, and he said...*). Such uses, however, do not invalidate the relevant contrast between morphology and interpretation that is so pervasive in vocatives.
3. For more information on word order and embedding in the Umbundu sentence, we refer the reader to Hill (2007).
4. Umbundu does not have morphological Case marking. Thus, the marker *a* has the function to endow the noun with a vocative reading (i.e., [specificity] related to *addressee* identification), not to encode the Vocative Case.
5. Free-ride checking is a 'side-effect' checking when two probe and goal meet for the purpose of checking some feature. Here, the probing feature is [specificity]. Agreement features and Case for the noun or the nominalized adjective are the side effect of this main operation.

References

Abney, Steven Paul
  1987   The English Noun Phrase in its Sentential Aspect. Doctoral dissertation. MIT, Cambridge, MA.
Arden, Albert Henry
  1873/1905   *A Progressive Grammar of the Telugu Language*. Madras: The Society for Promoting Christian Knowledge. Available online: http://www.learningtelugu.org/files/.
Carvalho, Ana Sofia
  2010   Functions of the vocative in European Portuguese. Paper presented at Vocative! Bamberg, 10 December 2010–11 December 2010.
Chomsky, Noam
  1995   *The Minimalist Program*. Cambridge, MA: MIT Press.
D'hulst, Yves, Martine Coene, and Liliane Tasmowski
  2007   Romance vocatives and the DP hypothesis. In *Studii de lingvistică şi filologie romanică. Hommages offerts à Sanda Reinheimer Rîpeanu*. Cunita, Alexandra, Coman Lupu, and Liliane Tasmowski (eds.), 200–211. Bucharest: Editura Universităţii din Bucureşti.

Donati, Margherita
  this vol.   The vocative case between system and asymmetry.
Emeneau, Murray Barnson
  1984   *Toda Grammar and Texts*. Philadelphia: American Philosophical
              Society.
Espinal, Maria Teresa
  this vol.   On the structure of vocatives.
Giusti, Giuliana
  1997   The categorial status of determiners. In *The New Comparative
              Syntax*, Liliane Haegeman (ed.), 95–123. London: Longman Lin-
              guistics Library.
Giusti, Giuliana
  2005   At the left periphery of the Romanian Noun Phrase. In *On Space
              and Time in Language*, Coene, Martine and Liliane Tasmowski
              (eds.), 23–49. Clusium: Cluj.
Haegeman, Liliane
  2010   The cartography of discourse markers in West Flemish. *Cam-
              bridge Occasional Papers in Linguistics* (to appear).
Haegeman, Liliane and Virginia Hill
  2012   On speech acts and syntax. In *Le Verbe en Verve,* Marleen Van
              Peteghem, Peter Lauwers, Els Tobback, Annemie Demol,
              Laurence De Wilde (eds.), 571–590. Ghent: Academia Press.
Hill, Virginia
  2007   Vocatives and the pragmatics-syntax interface. *Lingua* 117:
              2077–2105.
Longobardi, Giuseppe
  1994   Reference and proper names: A theory of N-movement in syntax
              and Logical Form. *Linguistic Inquiry* 25: 609–665.
Mac Eoin, Gearóid
  1993   Irish. In *The Celtic Languages*, Martin J. Ball (ed.), 101–140.
              London: Routledge.
Miyagawa, Shigeru
  2012   Agreements that occur mainly in the main clause. In *Main Clause
              Phenomena: New Horizons*, Lobke Aelbrecht, Liliane Hae-
              geman, and Rachel Nye (eds.), 79–112. Amsterdam: John
              Benjamins.
Oyharçabal, Bernard
  1993   Verb agreement with non arguments: On allocutive agreement. In
              Generative Studies in Basque Linguistics, Jose Ignacio Hualde
              and Jon Ortiz de Urbina (eds.), 89–114. Amsterdam: Benjamins.
Sohn, Ho-Min
  2001   *The Korean Language*. Cambridge: Cambridge University Press.

Schadeberg, Thilo
1990   *A Sketch of Umbundu*. Köln: Ruediger Koeppe.
Speas, Peggy and Carol L. Tenny
2003   Configurational properties of point of view roles. In *Asymmetry in Grammar*, Anna Maria Di Sciullo (ed.), 315–344. Amsterdam: John Benjamins.
Stavrou, Melita.
2010   Vocative! Paper presented at Vocative! Bamberg, 10 December 2010 – 11 December 2010.
Zafiu, Rodica
2003   «Tu» generic în limba română actuală. In *Aspecte ale dinamicii limbii române actuale*. Vol. 2, Gabriele Pană Dindelegan (ed.), 233–256. București: Editura Universității din București.

Addressing changes in the Bulgarian vocative

Cammeron Girvin

Abstract

The contemporary Bulgarian language allows for a great deal of flexibility in speakers' use of vocative forms. Descriptive grammars present a fairly straightforward set of rules for the formation of the Bulgarian vocative, which can be used instead of the unmarked general form with both impersonal nouns and personal names. Use of these forms today is generally regarded as optional, especially for personal names, and even a brief examination of informal communication among Bulgarian speakers reveals vocative-like morphological forms other than those described in grammars. It appears that the system of morphologically marking the addressing of others by name is more complex than what is described in grammars and, furthermore, that the various possible morphological markers on names carry different connotations. The goal of the present work is to assess exactly what grammatical endings exist for formation of the vocative for personal names, what pragmatic coloring is imparted by each of these forms, and also to see whether variation exists among speakers of different demographics. Analysis is based primarily on data gathered from an online survey, but also from examples of written Bulgarian. Ultimately, it is shown that the system of the vocative in Bulgarian is currently in a state of flux, with a situation more complex than what is typically presented.

1. Standard morphology of the vocative

Traditional vocative markings in Bulgarian are a remnant of the morphologically richer Common Slavic system of nominal inflection.[1] Standard Bulgarian does not mark case on noun stems, and I use the term 'general form' in the present work to refer to forms without a marked vocative ending. In general, vocative forms can be created from singular masculine and feminine nouns, both common nouns and personal names, but only the latter are of primary interest to the present study.

Contemporary reference grammars typically present several rules explaining the morphological formation of the vocative. Although they generally agree on the major points, none mentions every possible distinction, nor do they explicitly separate names into different classes. For a more thorough delineation of the patterns of vocative formation, then, I have designated two male (M1–M2) and five female (F1–F5) discrete classes of names. They are illustrated in Table 1.[2]

Table 1. Classes of personal names

	Male Names			Female Names	
Class	General Ending	Vocative Ending	Class	General Ending	Vocative Ending
M1	**-C**	**-Ce**	F1	**-Ca**	**-Co**
	Ivan	*Ivane!*		*Ana*	*Ano!*
				-Vja	**-Vjo**
				Marija	*Marijo!*
M2	**-V**	**-V**	F2	**-ka / -ca**	**-ke / -ce**
	Dobri	*Dobri!*		*Radka*	*Radke!*
				Elica	*Elice!*
			F3	**-C'a**	**-Ce**
				Kat'a	*Kate!*
			F4	**-i**	**-e**
				Mimi	*Mime!*
			F5	**- a (folk names)**	**-e**
				Cona	*Cone!*

Clearly, the rules for the formation of masculine vocatives are simpler than those for feminine vocatives. For names that end in a consonant (M1), the ending /-e/ is added. If /-ŭ/ is between two consonants, the latter of which is a sonorant, this /ŭ/ is dropped (Nicolova 2008: 75), as in:

(1) *Petŭr*   *Petr-e!*
      Petŭr   Petŭr-VOC
      'Petŭr'   'Petŭr!' (Krŭsteva 2003: 72)

Masculine names ending in a vowel (M2) are generally not described as having a special vocative form.

  Grammarians sometimes mention that words ending in /-k/, /-g/, /-x/, /-ž/, /-č/, /-š/, /-c/, and the suffix /-in/ add a vocative ending of /-o/. Only Krŭsteva, however, gives an example of this occurring with a personal name:

(2) *Mark*   *Mark-o!*
     Mark   Mark-VOC
     'Mark'   'Mark!' (Krŭsteva 2003: 72)

Because I have found this rule to be marginal and rarely applied, it has not been treated as a separate class.

Furthermore, although common nouns ending in /-j/ and consonants that are historically 'soft' take the ending /-u/, this is said not to apply for names (Rå Hauge 1999: 33). For example, as a common noun, *slavej* takes a vocative ending, but as a personal name it should not:

(3) a. *slavej*   *slavej-u*
        nightingale   nightingale-VOC
        'nightingale'   'nightingale!'

     b. *Slavej*   **Slavej-u*
        Slavej   Slavej-VOC
        'Slavej'   'Slavej!'

Of course, some common nouns are listed as exceptions to the above, but the inflection of masculine personal names is determined essentially by whether the name ends in a vowel or consonant.

For feminine names, the system is somewhat more complex. Class F1 is the most straightforward. For names ending in /-Ca/ (with the exception of /-ka/ and /-ca/, or /-C'a/) or /-Vja/, the /a/ is replaced by /o/, and general orthographic rules determine the spelling of any palatalization.

Classes F2–F5 form their vocative with /-e/ rather than /-o/. I have designated class F2 based on Nicolova's (2008: 76) assertion that feminine names ending in <-ka>, <-ička>, and <-ica> take the /-e/ ending. Names in class F3 end in /-C'a/ in the general form, but, as palatalization is neutralized before /e/ in Bulgarian, these names take a /-Ce/ ending in the vocative. Class F4 describes nicknames ending in /-i/ in the general form. Although Nicolova (2008: 76) claims such names usually do not have a special vocative form, examples of an /e/ ending for such names are quite widespread, and, when a vocative is marked, this would be the most common ending. Finally, I have separated class F5 given Nicolova's (2008: 76) statement that some 'folk' (*narodni*) names ending in <-a> (i.e., /-Ca/) take an /-e/ ending in the vocative, although she does not explain what qualifies a name as 'folk'. This, then, is the only class of name designated with semantic criteria rather than phonology.

Thus, personal names can be divided into these seven classes based on their rules for standard vocative formation. In following sections, I will refer to these classes in my analysis of patterns of vocative formation and use.

2. Changing use of the vocative

The vocative endings just described are encountered widely in written and spoken Bulgarian. The first writings in modern Bulgarian show almost universal use of vocative forms. They are used invariably in folk lyrics, which presumably reflect an older form of the language. Examples can be seen in traditional songs in which one lover is addressing another, such as:

(4)   a.   *Bre, **Stojane**, mlat **Stojane!**³*
           'Hey, **Stojan**, young **Stojan**!' (Arnaudov 1976: 496)

      b.   *Daj, **Bonke**, da te celunem!*
           '**Bonka**, let me kiss you!' (Arnaudov 1976: 499)

      c.   *Mari **Todoro**, t'onka **Todoro!***
           'Hey, **Todora**, thin **Todora**!' (Arnaudov 1976: 505)

The language in such songs is typically marked as old-fashioned and dialectal by contemporary standards, but it is noteworthy that the vocative is used consistently for addressing both males and females. Written literature up to the middle of the twentieth century also shows regular use of the vocative. The following example consists of selections from Jordan Jovkov's 1930 play *Albena*. All characters use the vocative consistently in addressing both males and females, and in both emotively marked and neutral lines:

(5)   *SAVKA (otvŭn). **Albeno!** [...] **Albeno**, tuka li si?*
      *ALBENA. Tuka sŭm, **Savke**. Ela de. [...]*
      *ALBENA. Az ne znaja, **Kucare**. [...]*
      *ALBENA. (otiva kŭm nego). **Kucare**, zašto praviš tŭj? [...]*
      *ALBENA. Ne šte da e zatuj, babo **Mito**. Ne vjarvam. [...]*
      *ALBENA. Ah, **Njagule!** Koga dojde? [...]*

      SAVKA (from outside). **Albena!** [...] **Albena**, are you there?
      ALBENA. I'm here, **Savka**. Come on in. [...]
      ALBENA. I don't know, **Kutsar**. [...]
      ALBENA. (walks toward him). **Kutsar**, why are you doing it like that?
      [...]

ALBENA. It can't be because of that, Granny **Mita**. I don't believe it.
[…]
ALBENA. Ah, **Njagul**! When did you come? […]'
(Jovkov [1930] 1971: 54–65)

Many more examples of the vocative can be found throughout this play and other works of literature fairly consistently up until around this time period. Overall, it is clear that, from the period of the standardization of the modern Bulgarian literary language until the early twentieth century, use of vocative forms for personal names was the norm.

However, the marked vocative form for names began to give way to unmarked forms in the first half of the twentieth century. Grammarians protested this trend and repeatedly placed the blame on female speakers.[4] This is first noted by Mladenov, who writes:

> I pri vse tova mnozina «obrazovani» bŭlgari, pisateli i nepisateli, i ne po-malko takiva bŭlgarki misljat, če bilo «grubo» i «prostaško» upotreblenieto na starite formi za zvatelen padež i če naj-mnogoto možela da se dopusne formata Eleno, kogato imalo da se obŭrneme kŭm sluginja s ime Elena. No kŭm drugarkata si, kojato e krŭstena Elena, «obrazovanata» bŭlgarka trjabvalo da se obŭrne ne s obidnoto Eleno, ami s «po-priličnoto» – Elena! […] I toku-reči vsički po-novi, «moderni» bŭlgarski pisateli započnaxa da zanemarjavat formite na zvatelnija padež.

> [And, even so, many "educated" Bulgarian men, writers and non-writers, and just as many such Bulgarian women think that the use of the old forms for the vocative case is supposedly "rude" and "vulgar," and that the form "Eleno" could for the most part be permitted when one is addressing a servant with the name "Elena." But her friend, who is named "Elena," the "educated" Bulgarian woman would have to address not with the offensive "Eleno," but with the "more proper" – "Elena!" […] And nearly all the newer, "trendy" Bulgarian writers began to neglect the forms of the vocative case.] (Mladenov 1927–1928: 215–216)

Notably, he remarks that vocative forms are becoming pragmatically marked, ostensibly restricted to addressing individuals of lower status. Further on, Mladenov (1927–1928: 216) attributes this to influence from Russian and Western European languages, which do not typically mark vocatives. Maslov makes a similar statement in 1956, noting that the standard form of a name has become preferred, and vocative forms have come to be perceived negatively:

Esli obraščenie predstavljaet soboju ličnoe imja, osobenno ženskoe, to v
reči, pretendujuščej na intelligentnost' i na nekotoruju izyskannost', sejčas,
nesmotrja na protivodejstvie škol'noj grammatiki, predpočitaetsja obščaja
forma (zvatel'naja forma, rekomenduemaja grammatikoj, vosprinimaetsja v
etix slučajax kak neskol'ko famil'jarnaja ili daže vul'garnaja).

[If a form of address occurs as a personal name, especially a female one,
then in speech purporting to be sophisticated and refined, now, despite the
opposition from school grammars, the general form is preferred (the vocative form, recommended by the grammar, is taken in such situations as
somewhat folksy or even vulgar).] (Maslov 1956: 97)

Pŭrvev (1978: 226) also cites many instances in which the general forms of
names are used in vocative contexts in mid-twentieth-century fiction, such
as in Dimov's 1951 novel *Tjutjun*. Thus, over the twentieth century, it is
clear that vocative forms began to acquire a marked semantic meaning.

Observations by current grammarians attest to the continuation of this
process in the present. Pašov (1999: 79–80) states that the vocative form is
'in decline' ("v upadŭk"),[5] and that in recent decades it is being abandoned,
especially for female names but also for masculine ones. Pašov, Staneva,
and Pašova (2003: 20) claim that the vocative forms are perceived
'primarily by the intelligentsia' ("predimno ot inteligencijata") as 'dis-
respectful, vernacular, rude, and almost offensive' ("neuvažitelni,
prostorečni, grubi, edva li obidni"). Ivanova and Nicolova (1995: 26–27)
give a slightly more detailed examination. They state that, for female
names that take the ending /-o/ in the vocative, the general form is used for
expressing 'an official relationship or distancing in relation to the
addressee' ("oficialno otnošenie ili distanciranost po otnošenie na
adresata") and the vocative expresses 'closeness, intimacy, or informality'
("blizost, intimnost, neoficialnost"). For female names that end in /-e/ in
the vocative, however, this form carries a 'diminutive or adulatory'
("umalitelno-laskatelen") nuance. Masculine names can take either the
general form or the marked vocative with, it is said, little difference in
meaning. Overall, however, grammarians make little further inquiry into
pragmatic nuances of the vocative.

It should also be noted that the vocative's fall from use is still being
lamented. Pašov (1999: 390) states, 'But the vocative forms are a richness
in our language, and we must strive to use them in addressing' ("No
zvatelnite formi sa edno bogatstvo na ezika ni i nie trjabva da se stremem
da gi upotrebjavame kato obrŭštenija"). He also writes that their use makes
language 'clearer' ("po-jasni") (Pašov 1999: 80). One could argue, though,
that the change in pragmatic value of the vocatives has actually enriched

the language. Rather than carrying a simple case-like meaning indicating only that a person is being addressed, vocative forms have developed pragmatic distinctions to put a wider variety of nuances at a speaker's disposal. In any case, it is clear that the functions of the vocative have been changing over the past century.

In addition to the evolving pragmatics of these inherited vocative forms, however, morphological changes may be occurring as well. There are many examples of endings on names other than those inherited from Common Slavic that seem to function as vocatives. For example, one encounters plenty of vocative forms with an /-e/ ending for names ending in /-o/ in the general form; this would be unexpected for class M2 names. A simple Google search for potential minimal pairs demonstrates this, yielding 177 results for 'Hi Sasho' in the general form (*Zdrasti Sašo*) and 73 results for a marked vocative form (*Zdrasti Saše*).[6] No grammars would predict the latter form, yet it occurs here with almost half the frequency of the expected form. It is also possible to find online examples of the /-e/ ending occurring after masculine names ending in vowels. Nicolova (1984: 49) lists vocatives such as *Metodie* (from *Metodi*) and says that they sound 'archaic' ("arxaično"), but they do appear to be at least marginally grammatical. One finds an example of this form in the line of a joke intended to parody ecclesiastical writings:

(6) – *iz "Panonski hroniki" – versija 2.0: "Poradi kompjutŭrna negramotnost, brate **Metodie**!*
' – from the "Pannonian Chronicles" – version 2.0: "Because of computer illiteracy, Brother **Metodi**!'[7]

Also, in some dialects, masculine names ending in /-i/ can replace the ending with /-e/ as in:

(7) *Dobri*   *Dobr-e!*
    Dobri   Dobri-VOC
    'Dobri'   'Dobri!' (Nicolova 1984: 49)

These examples all run counter to what appears in grammars of the modern standard language, yet it appears that they are very much alive in parts of the spoken language.

Feminine names also show the possibility for variation. Ivanova and Nicolova (1995: 27) claim that, for names (presumably mostly nicknames) ending in /-i/ (i.e., my class F4), the vocative can also be formed with /-o/ in order to impart 'closeness and intimacy' ("blizost, intimnost") in the same way that the /-e/ ending is usually described. One may even wonder whether it might simply be possible to form two types of vocatives with all female names, one with /-e/ and one with /-o/. Additionally, no current grammar addresses the issue of female given names and nicknames that end in a consonant, such as *Nikol* or *Aleks*, and whether there exist vocative forms for such names. These questions regarding female names were also examined in the survey.

Finally, there exists the issue of articulated personal names. Female names can form a diminutive with the suffix /-če/, which necessarily takes an article in non-vocative roles. This can be seen with the given name *Gergana*:

(8) *Gergana*   *Gergan-če*
     Gergana   Gergana-DIM
     'Gergana' (general)   'Gergana!' (diminutive vocative)

     Gergan-če-to
     Gergana-DIM-DEF
     'Gergana' (diminutive general)

However, one occasionally encounters articulated female names used in a vocative sense. The following online post, written by one friend to another, articulates the name of the addressee, Eva:

(9) *ohh, **ewata**... tuka wsichkoe edin golqm wic...*
     [Ox, **Evata**... tuka vsičko e edin goljam vic]
     'Oh, **Eva**, here everything is a big joke.'[8]

One assumes from the content of such a message that this form is intended to imply friendliness or possibly gentle teasing. But such forms have simply not been described, and it is uncertain to what extent speakers would find such a form valid.

Given these various considerations, it is clear that actual vocative usage has changed significantly from that which is described by grammarians. There is the possibility for innovated morphological forms, and the connotations of such forms would be expected to vary as well. These connotations might differ according to a speaker's age, since the vocative has clearly been undergoing a gradual change over the past several decades. There are also hints that the sex of the speaker may be a factor, such as Pŭrvev's assertion that some vocative forms are used 'particularly amongst girls' ("osobeno meždu devojki") (1978: 230). Finally, Kovačev's (1987: 150) description of dialectal variation in the formation of personal names leads one to suspect that a speaker's dialect could influence his perception of vocative forms. In addition, it is not clear even which forms would be considered possible for various classes of names, since examples can be found of vocatives that do not appear in grammars. These uncertainties all point to a vocative system full of many more complexities than what is described by grammarians.

3. Description of survey

In an effort to address the issues described above, I created an online survey (see Appendix A) to assess speakers' perceptions and uses of various vocative forms.[9] The survey was accessed by 112 respondents, but only 93 went beyond providing their demographic information. An introduction explained the goals of the survey and asked respondents to answer quickly, without thinking for a long time over the answers; this was to ensure that they gave answers that reflected their own linguistic perceptions rather than what they might expect to be "correct" according to a supposed authority on the language. Respondents were then asked to answer demographic questions. In addition to their sex, they were asked for their age as well as the areas in which they were born, grew up, and now live, including the number of years they had lived there. This information was later used to analyze potential linguistic differences depending on the social backgrounds of speakers.

The bulk of the survey consisted of a section in which respondents were asked to assess various vocative forms. In one section of female names and then another of male names, speakers were given the full name of a hypothetical individual, such as *Radoslava Stojkova*, with a proposed vocative, such as *Radoslave!*, and a set of terms they could select to describe how each vocative form sounded to them.[10] They were told to assume that they 'knew' (*poznavate*) the individual and spoke with her/him 'using informal pronouns' (*na 'ti'*).[11] From each class of names of those described at the end of section 1, an unmarked name was given along with a vocative ending with all suffixes that might be possible for that class of names. For example, for F4 names, possibilities given were *Stili* (a nickname for *Stiljana*), *Lile* (from *Lili*, a nickname for *Liljana*), and *Vilo* (from *Vili*, a nickname for *Viljana*). The order of prompts was automatically randomized for each respondent in order to minimize the influence of similar forms on each other. When describing vocative prompts, if speakers felt such a form did not exist, they were asked to indicate that it was 'impossible' (*nevŭzmožno*) by marking the corresponding box for the prompt.[12] Otherwise, they were asked to select all of the possible descriptors for the way each vocative form sounded. Options included 'neutral' (*neutralno*), 'slightly rude' (*leko grubo*), 'very rude' (*mnogo grubo*), 'affectionate/ tender' (*gal'ovno/nežno*), 'friendly' (*prijatelski*), 'respectful' (*uvažitelno*), and 'modern/cool/fashionable' (*moderno/gotino/modno*). While other descriptors could certainly have been included, this collection of terms seemed to be semantically broad enough to capture most connotations of how a form could sound.

Before arriving at a final page signifying completion, respondents were presented with a box in which they could provide any personal ob-servations regarding the vocative. They were asked, 'What connotations does the vocative of personal names have for you? Does the sex of the speaker/addressee matter? Do you have any other comments regarding this topic?' ("Kakvi konotacii za Vas ima zvatelnata forma za lični imena? Ima li značenie polŭt na govoreštija/adresiranija? Imate li drugi komentari vŭrxu tazi tema?"). This section was marked as optional, but 26 respondents provided some additional feedback.

4. Results of survey: possible forms and pragmatic implications

Based on responses to the survey, it appears that many speakers permit a range of potential vocative forms, particularly for female names. For prompts with male names, most forms received either a very high or very low percentage of respondents selecting 'impossible'; this indicates relative stability in the choices available for male vocative forms. For female names, on the other hand, almost all forms had several descriptors that were chosen by at least a few respondents. The pragmatics of the vocative are evidently in a greater state of flux for female names.

The instability surrounding female vocative forms can be seen in the fact that, of all of the prompts given, the only one that was found to be al-most universally impossible was *Kamelie!* (*Kamelija*),[13] which 92% per-cent of respondents marked as 'impossible'. It is unclear why this form alone would be so unlikely. Even it, however, was considered by 7% of respondents to sound 'friendly', which is one connotation this /-e/ ending is said to have when used with names from other classes. Other forms that a majority of speakers found impossible were: *Nikole!* (*Nikol*); *Mišelo!* (*Mišel*); *Radoslave!* (*Radoslava*). The first two names are non-Slavic borrowings (i.e. *Nicole* and *Michelle*) that have consonantal endings in their general forms. Rå Hauge (1999: 32) claims that foreign names cannot take a vocative, and it may be that these names do not work within the framework for Bulgarian female names because of their atypical consonantal endings. *Radoslave!* may also not be possible for a woman because it would be homophonous with the normal vocative for the masculine name *Radoslav*. All other prompts for female names were considered by the majority of respondents to be possible, indicating that the system for female vocative forms allows for much flexibility.

Among the female names, vocatives ending in /-e/ were much more commonly attributed with positive descriptors than were those ending in /-o/. The forms with the highest percentages of respondents indicating 'very rude' all ended in /-o/. Interestingly, this even included the form *Mišelo!*, which a majority of speakers did not find possible. Those who did, however, characterized it as highly rude, which likely indicates that this ending carries an implicit marking of rudeness, no matter to what name it is attached.

Female names with vocatives ending in /-e/, however, were received much more positively. They were among the forms most consistently described as sounding friendly, along with nicknames such as *Aleks* and *Kleo*. They were also typically regarded as sounding affectionate, although not as much as were the general diminutive forms *Gerganče!* and *Polinka!*. This result differs considerably from Pŭrvev's (1978: 49) statement that the /-e/ ending 'is not perceived of as so rude' ("ne se vŭzpriema kato tolkova grubo") as is the /-o/ ending, because, in fact, forms ending in /-e/ are described fairly positively.

For male names, fewer forms were permitted, and respondents were in greater agreement as to which forms were possible. Besides names ending in consonants (class M1), the only type of names for which grammars would predict a different vocative form, only three other non-articulated forms were found to be possible by more than half of the respondents: *Saše!* (*Aleksandŭr*); *Pepo!* (*Petŭr*); *Ilijo!* (*Ilija*). The first prompt was found possible by all respondents, and the second, by most respondents, who largely described these forms as affectionate and friendly. This is likely due to the fact that the underlying forms, *Sašo* (for *Aleksandŭr*) and *Pepi* (for *Petŭr*) are already nicknames; nonetheless, it is interesting that these forms are not mentioned in grammars but are clearly accepted by most speakers. The form *Ilijo!* (*Ilija*), however, was found to be rude by most respondents who found it valid. This form comes from the sole masculine /-Vja/ name in the survey, *Ilija*, so many respondents probably treated it as they would a feminine name with a similar ending, such as *Viktorija*.

In general, those masculine forms ending in the typical vocative ending /-e/ were described largely as neutral or with modest percentages of various other descriptors. As with female names, it appears that the /-e/ ending has positive connotations for some speakers. For example, *Andree!* (*Andrej*) is a form not expected to exist, and most speakers regard it as impossible. However, the majority of respondents who claimed that it does exist characterized it as sounding friendly. Also parallel to women's names were responses to specifically vocative forms ending in /-o/. Such an ending as a vocative marker does not exist according to most grammars, and most respondents agreed with this. However, those who did find such forms legitimate characterized them as rude. For *Valerio!* (*Valeri*), for example, 88% of respondents found the form impossible, but 11% described it as rude.

Therefore, it appears that there may be some convergence taking place between masculine and female vocative markers. For both male and female names, when /-e/ vocative endings are considered possible, they are typically not described as rude; instead, they may indicate friendliness or a sense of playfulness. The /-o/ ending is, however, when found to be possible, typically considered rude. All forms with a vocative /-o/ ending (of which the underlying name form did not already end in /-o/) that were found by the majority of speakers to be grammatical were classified most commonly as 'rude'; the one exception to this is *Dejanko!*, which is formed from a diminutive, *Dejanka*. This suggests that /-e/ and /-o/ may be acquiring similar pragmatic values regardless of the sex of the name with which they are used. As Schulz (1975: 64–75) observes, linguistic forms associated with women are more likely to develop a negative connotation, and something of this process may be happening here. If /-e/ is the most common marker for male names, it may be not treated as negatively when used for female names. Conversely, the /-o/ ending generally only occurs with female names, and is therefore marked specifically for that gender. This is likely why *Ilijo!* (from the male name *Ilija*) was found to be rude by almost every respondent who permitted it. I would not claim that the possible morphological endings are the same for male and female names, but it does appear that when either /-e/ or /-o/ endings are possible, the positive or negative connotations may be similar for a name of either sex.

The survey also examined the issue of articulated names, which consist of a given name or nickname with the definite article attached. For both sexes, five names with the expected definite articles were listed among the prompts: *Evata!* (*Eva*); *Didito!* (*Diljana*); *Ivanŭt!* (*Ivan*); *Ilijata!* (*Ilija*); *Sašoto!* (*Aleksandŭr*). *Didito!* (from the nickname *Didi*) was accepted by 87% percent of respondents as a vocative, most of whom described it as 'friendly'. The other articulated forms of names with vowel endings were also accepted by between 47% to 69% of respondents and were characterized in a similar manner. The only form found impossible by most (88%) of speakers was *Ivanŭt!*, the lone consonantal name. Thus, it seems that for many speakers, the addition of an article to a name ending in a vowel can serve a vocative role, adding a tone of friendliness, as was observed in example 9.

Full tables of all prompts given and the percentages of responses attributed to descriptors for each name can be found in Appendix B and Appendix C. Overall, it should be noted that every form in the survey was accepted as possible by at least several respondents, which indicates that almost any combination of name class and vocative ending is possible for some speakers.

5. Results of survey: demographics

In addition to testing the feasibility of various potential vocative forms, the survey also looked at the connotations of vocative forms based on the demographic information collected. Responses to the standard vocative forms given in Table 1 from the M1, F1, and F3 classes (the most representative of common personal names) were compared against responses to general forms. The following prompts were analyzed in this way:

(10) *Rumjano!*   (*Rumjana*)   (F1 vocative)
   Albena!   (*Albena*)   (F1 general)
   Kate!   (*Katja*)   (F3 vocative)
   Nadja!   (*Nadja*)   (F3 standard)
   Petre!   (*Petŭr*)   (M1 vocative)
   Ivan!   (*Ivan*)   (M1 standard)

By comparing responses to the marked and unmarked forms of each of these classes of names, it was possible to note differences in how speakers from different demographics felt about use of the vocative.

Data were first analyzed in terms of the sex of respondents. Overall, there were 52 female respondents and 41 male respondents. When comparing responses to the F3 names, one sees little difference between how men and women describe the marked vocative (/-e/) and unmarked forms of such names; in general, both find the marked vocative to sound friendly or affectionate in comparison with the standard name. However, there was a noticeable difference in the way the sexes described the marked vocative forms of the other two name classes. For the marked F1 and M1 vocative prompts *Rumjano!* and *Petre!*, men were slightly more likely to consider the vocative to sound friendly, while women found it more rude. In the table that follows, one can see the percentages of female and male respondents who chose 'slightly rude', 'very rude,' and 'friendly', as well as the percentages of those who chose at least one of the two 'rude' descriptors:

Table 2. Assessments in terms of sex of respondents

	'slightly rude'	'very rude'	'slightly rude' and/or 'very rude'	'friendly'
Rumjano! (F1 vocative)				
% female	42	67	96	2
% male	59	34	83	10
Petre! (M1 vocative)				
% female	35	8	38	31
% male	27	2	29	44

Thus, it appears that men may perceive the marked vocative in a slightly more positive light. This could indicate a slight difference in the usage of vocative forms between male and female speakers, but it could also simply be the result of a subset of men being less attuned to the full nuances of such forms. Nonetheless, this does appear to be an interesting point. Other than this, no major differences were found between men and women's responses.[14]

The next factor to be examined was age. Respondents' ages ranged from 20 to 66 years, with an average age of 32. As the goal of this examination was to see whether older respondents had different feelings about the vocative, it was hoped at first that the cutoff age between 'younger' and 'older' respondents could be 60. However, this would have left only five respondents in the older group, so 50 was made the cutoff age. The younger group, then, consisted of 77 respondents, and the older group had 15. (One respondent did not provide his age, and his data were ignored in this analysis.)

Overall, there was only a marginal difference between older and younger speakers. Unfortunately, it is possible that the sample set was too small to see many striking results, and also that by now even the oldest of speakers may have grown up attributing marked status to vocative forms. However, there does appear to be a slight difference: Although older and younger speakers described marked vocative prompts similarly, the older group was somewhat more likely to describe unmarked forms, *Albena!*, *Nadja!*, and *Ivan!*, as modern or fashionable, and less likely to describe them as neutral. These points of data are presented here:

Table 3. Assessments in terms of age of respondents

Assessments by age	'neutral'	'modern/cool/fashionable'
Albena! (F1 general)		
% 50 and younger	83	4
% 51 and older	40	20
Nadja! (F3 general)		
% 50 and younger	74	1
% 51 and older	53	20
Ivan! (M1 general)		
% 50 and younger	71	3
% 51 and older	53	13

This would be consistent with what one would expect based on the changes in status of the vocative noted by grammarians earlier. Older speakers are more likely to see use of the unmarked name as trendy, whereas younger speakers are more likely to perceive it as neutral. One respondent to the survey shared this observation, stating, 'I've noticed that older people use the vocative form much more often and that it has a neutral connotation for them' ("Zabeljazala sŭm, če po-vŭzrastnite xora mnogo po-često uportebjavat [sic] zvatelni formi i za tjax te sa s neutralna konotacija"). If more data could be gathered from older individuals, one might expect to see even sharper contrasts. Still, this point shows that slight variation may still be present in perception and use of the vocative between the generations.

An attempt was also made at comparing speakers of different dialects. For the purposes of this study, dialects from locales west of the isogloss dividing modern reflexes for the historical *jat*-vowel were considered 'western', and those to the east were considered 'eastern'. Because many contemporary Bulgarians live as adults in dialect regions different from those in which they grew up, an effort was made to identify speakers whose language would reflect mostly western or mostly eastern traits. As such, respondents were identified as 'consistently western' if they had both grown up in and had now lived in an area to the west of the *jat* -isogloss for at least the past five years, and 'consistently eastern if the opposite was true.[15] Data from 17 respondents were ignored for this part of the survey, because these respondents had grown up in and now lived on opposite sides of the isogloss,[16] and several other respondents were also not included because they had given insufficiently specific answers. All together, there were 29 eastern speakers and 42 western speakers.

Of the three variables analyzed, dialect seemed to be the least influential in determining a speaker's reaction to vocative forms. Percentages between the two groups were very close for almost every prompt and descriptor. The sole noteworthy point is that for masculine names, western speakers were more likely to regard the standard name as positive, as more respondents characterized *Ivan!* as friendly. The marked vocative, *Petre!*, however, was described the same way more by eastern speakers:

Table 4. Assessments in terms of dialectal region

	'friendly'
Petre! (M1 vocative)	
% eastern	41
% western	33
Ivan! (M1 standard)	
% eastern	3
% western	12

This could make sense in that respondents from Sofia, i.e., western speakers, are perhaps more likely to speak other European languages, which do not typically have a separate vocative form. Mladenov (1927–1928: 215–216) claims that this was the impetus for the initial decline in marked vocative use. Overall, though, the dialect variable was the least telling. There likely exist greater dialectal differences in vocative morphology and pragmatics than an online survey was able to capture, but from the data gathered here, it appears that the Bulgarian-speaking territory is mostly unified on this point.

Unfortunately, given the small sample size inherent in a survey of this nature, none of the differences in terms of the sex, age, and dialect variables are statistically significant. Although my expectation was not necessarily that large differences would be found, these small imbalances are apparent, and with more respondents I would expect to see these patterns hold up. Certainly, more extensive testing would be fruitful in examining the significance of age, sex, and dialect in terms of vocative use. Additionally, one could go further and also examine other classes of names against these or other variables. It might be possible, for example, that articulated forms of names are more often considered possible by a certain section of the population. However, the scope of this work does not permit such extrapolation, and these differences in vocative use of speakers of different sexes, ages, and dialectal regions do at least hint at minor sociolinguistic variation.

6. Conclusion

The most straightforward and authoritative statement one can make on the Bulgarian vocative is that it is a system in flux. As one respondent remarked in the optional comments section of the survey, 'Recently I have been thinking that when I have to address an acquaintance, it's difficult for me to decide whether to use 'Kiril' or 'Kirile.' The former sounds to me somewhat un-Bulgarian, and the latter sounds somewhat archaic' ("Naposledŭk se zamisljam, če kogato trjabva da se obŭrna kŭm svoj poznat, mi e trudno da reša dali da izpolzvam 'Kiril' ili 'Kirile'. Pŭrvoto mi zvuči malko nebŭlgarsko, vtoroto mi zvuči malko arxaično"). Another indicated that a Bulgarian language teacher might use the marked vocative form, but a mathematics teacher might prefer the unmarked form. The fact that no responses to either male or female name forms were universally considered impossible shows that there are a wide variety of morphological possibilities at a speaker's disposal when addressing others by name.

A very important point not covered by the survey is that vocative forms can take on different connotations in different contexts. One respondent mentioned 'tone' (*tonŭt*) as a factor in determining how a particular vocative form will sound. Several others also mentioned other descriptors they would have included in the survey, such as 'silly' (*glupavo*), 'teasing' (*podigravatelna*), 'ironic' (*ironično*), 'affected' (*manierno*), and 'coddling' (*razglezvašta*). None of these terms are typically mentioned in grammars, but they could all certainly apply to particular vocative forms depending on context. As one respondent stated about the survey, '[I]t would have been more precise if concrete situations had also been indicated – in the local pub, in the village, at a board meeting, an exchange of lines between friends, and so on...' ("[P]o-precizno šteše da bŭde, ako bjaxa posočeni i konkretni situaciji – v mestnata krŭčma, na selo, na sŭbranie na borda na direktori, razmjana meždu prijateli, i t.n."), and several other respondents remarked on the relevance of context as well. While I had considered this matter in creating the survey, I ultimately decided that describing different scenarios would make the survey too long and complex and could lead to a high rate of attrition of respondents. Further investigation with more focus on the context of the speech act, however, would surely prove highly telling.

Given these observations and the overall responses to different forms, it might be more appropriate to conceive of vocative forms as operating in a mode similar to that of formal and informal personal pronouns; that is, a vocative form could mark a certain level of intimacy between interlocutors, which may only be appropriate in certain situations. Many vocative forms are ranked highly for both rudeness and friendliness. For example, *Petre!*

(an M1 vocative form) was considered by 40% of respondents to be rude, by 40% of respondents to be friendly, and by 52% of respondents to be neutral; obviously, some respondents were willing to attribute multiple connotations to this form. One respondent alluded to the idea of there being an appropriate level of intimacy for the use of vocatives, stating, 'Often, vocatives that are used among a group of friends can be taken negatively if they come from a less well-known individual' ("Često zvatelnite, iz-polzvani ot prijatelskija krŭg xora, mogat da bŭdat vŭzpriemni negativno ako idvat ot po-malko poznat čovek"). Another informant claimed, 'Some-times the rude form can be used 'backwards,' i.e., as the most affectionate' ("Ponjakoga grubata forma može da se upotrebjava 'naobratno', t.e. naj-gal'ovno"). Though the choice between vocative and non-vocative forms is not exactly congruent with that of formal and informal personal pronouns, the related idea of intimacy between two interlocutors determining the ap-propriateness of a vocative form does seem relevant.

The pragmatics of the Bulgarian vocative, then, began to change in the twentieth century, and data show that these forms are continuing to develop. In terms of possible forms, speakers typically find legitimate a wider variety of vocative markings than appear in grammars. For female names especially, /-e/ endings are generally perceived positively, and /-o/ endings are perceived negatively. Most speakers make less of a distinction between marked and unmarked vocatives for male names, although for some the presence or absence of a form is significant. A new articulated form may also be gaining ground as a possible vocative for some speakers. Furthermore, there is evidence that slight differences may exist in as-sessments of vocative forms between men and women, older and younger speakers, and speakers of western and eastern dialects. For many, the vocative appears to imply a certain level of personal intimacy between speakers, which is only appropriate in some contexts. It is unclear what status marked vocative forms will have in Bulgarian for future generations. For now, however, it is apparent that not only are these forms more com-plex than general grammatical descriptions would indicate, but also that they have acquired pragmatic marking far richer than the neutral status they previously carried.

Appendix A. Survey

Celta na tazi anketa e da se proučat sociolingvističnite funkcii na zvatelnite formi v bŭlgarskija ezik. Šte Vi pomolim da razgledate različni formi na obrŭštenie, da posočite dali te sa vŭzmožni, i, izbirajki podxodjašti opisatelni dumi, da opišete konotaciite na vsjaka forma. Ne se zamisljajte, kogato otgovarjate. Razčitajte na intuicijata si i davajte otgovorite si bŭrzo. Kato cjalo, anketata ne trjabva da otneme poveče ot pet-deset minuti. Mnogo Vi blagodarim za učastieto!

[The goal of this survey is to investigate the sociolinguistic functions of the vocative forms in the Bulgarian language. You will be asked to examine the various forms of address, to indicate whether they are possible, and, selecting appropriate descriptors, to describe the connotations of each form. Do not ponder over the answers. Rely on your intuition and give your answers quickly. On the whole, the survey should not take more than five or ten minutes. Thank you very much for your participation!]

Pol (Sex)
( ) *žena* (female)
( ) *mŭž* (male)

Molja, popŭlnete slednata informacija (Please fill in the following information):
Vŭzrast (Age) _____
Roden/a sŭm v (I was born in) _____.
Izrasnax v (I grew up in) _____.
Sega živeja v (I have now lived in) _____
ot _ godini (for _ years). _____

Po-dolu šte vidite pŭlnite imena na ženi s različni formi na obrŭštenie. Kato priemem, če poznavate sŭotvetnata žena i si govorite na 'ti', molja, izberete *vsički* opredelenija, s koito bixte opisali kak može da zvuči vsjaka forma na obrŭštenie. Ako smjatate, če tazi forma na obrŭštenie ne sŭštestvuva, posočete 'NEVŬZMOŽNO'.

[Below you will see the full names of women with various forms of address. Assuming that you know the corresponding woman and you speak to each other with informal pronouns, please select *all* descriptors with which you would describe the way each form of address sounds. If you feel that this form does not exist, select 'IMPOSSIBLE'.]

	neutralno (neutral)	leko grubo (slightly rude)	mnogo grubo (very rude)	gal'ovno/nežno (affectionate/tender)	prijatelski (friendly)	uvažitelno (respectful)	moderno/gotino/modno (modern/cool/fashionable)	*NEVŬZMOŽNO* (*IMPOSSIBLE*)
Radoslava Stojkova: 'Radoslave!'	( )	( )	( )	( )	( )	( )	( )	( )
Nikol Xristova: 'Nikole!'	( )	( )	( )	( )	( )	( )	( )	( )
Nadja Boteva: 'Nadja!'	( )	( )	( )	( )	( )	( )	( )	( )
Petja Dikova: 'Pet'o!'	( )	( )	( )	( )	( )	( )	( )	( )
Kleopatra Boseva: 'Kleo!'	( )	( )	( )	( )	( )	( )	( )	( )
Diljana Tomova: 'Didito!'	( )	( )	( )	( )	( )	( )	( )	( )
Gergana Dimova: 'Gergančе!'	( )	( )	( )	( )	( )	( )	( )	( )
Cona Ruseva: 'Cone!'	( )	( )	( )	( )	( )	( )	( )	( )
Albena Ivanova: 'Albena!'	( )	( )	( )	( )	( )	( )	( )	( )
Elen Dimitrova: 'Elen!'	( )	( )	( )	( )	( )	( )	( )	( )
Kamelija Radoeva: 'Kamelie!'	( )	( )	( )	( )	( )	( )	( )	( )
Liljana Staleva: 'Lile!'	( )	( )	( )	( )	( )	( )	( )	( )
Radostina Milkova: 'Radostinke!'	( )	( )	( )	( )	( )	( )	( )	( )
Temenužka Stojčeva: 'Temenužka!'	( )	( )	( )	( )	( )	( )	( )	( )

Temenužka Martinova: 'Temenužko!'	( )	( )	( )	( )	( )	( )	( )	( )
Mišel Kostova: 'Mišelo!'	( )	( )	( )	( )	( )	( )	( )	( )
Stiljana Doreva: 'Stili'	( )	( )	( )	( )	( )	( )	( )	( )
Nona Pejčeva: 'Nono!'	( )	( )	( )	( )	( )	( )	( )	( )
Rumjana Peneva: 'Rumjano!'	( )	( )	( )	( )	( )	( )	( )	( )
Aksinija Goleva: 'Aksinijo!'	( )	( )	( )	( )	( )	( )	( )	( )
Eva Tomova: 'Evata!'	( )	( )	( )	( )	( )	( )	( )	( )
Dejana Živkova: 'Dejanko!'	( )	( )	( )	( )	( )	( )	( )	( )
Katja Mileva: 'Kate!'	( )	( )	( )	( )	( )	( )	( )	( )
Bona Georgieva: 'Bona!'	( )	( )	( )	( )	( )	( )	( )	( )
Viktorija Slavčeva: 'Viktorija!'	( )	( )	( )	( )	( )	( )	( )	( )
Viljana Simova: 'Vilo!'	( )	( )	( )	( )	( )	( )	( )	( )
Temenužka Mateeva: 'Temenužke!'	( )	( )	( )	( )	( )	( )	( )	( )
Polina Dimčeva: 'Polinka!'	( )	( )	( )	( )	( )	( )	( )	( )
Aleksandra Petkova: 'Aleks!'	( )	( )	( )	( )	( )	( )	( )	( )

Po-dolu šte vidite pŭlnite imena na mŭže s različni formi na obrŭštenie. Kato priemem, če poznavate sŭotvetnija mŭž i si govorite na 'ti', molja, izberete *vsički* opredelenija, s koito bixte opisali kak može da zvuči vsjaka forma na obrŭštenie. Ako smjatate, če tazi forma na obrŭstenie ne sŭštestvuva, posočete 'NEVŬZMOŽNO'.

[Below you will see the full names of men with various forms of address. Assuming that you know the corresponding man and you speak to each other with informal pronouns, please select *all* descriptors with which you would describe the way each form of address sounds. If you feel that this form does not exist, select 'IMPOSSIBLE'.]

	neutralno (neutral)	*leko grubo* (slightly rude)	*mnogo grubo* (very rude)	*gal'ovno/nežno* (affectionate/ tender)	*prijatelski* (friendly)	*uvažitelno* (respectful)	*moderno/gotino/modno* (modern/cool/fashionable)	*NEVŬZMOŽNO* (*IMPOSSIBLE*)
Ilija Senkov: 'Ilijata!'	( )	( )	( )	( )	( )	( )	( )	( )
Petŭr Zlatanov: 'Pešo!'	( )	( )	( )	( )	( )	( )	( )	( )
Andrej Javorov: 'Andree!'	( )	( )	( )	( )	( )	( )	( )	( )
Nikola Angelov: 'Nikola!'	( )	( )	( )	( )	( )	( )	( )	( )
Damjan Marinov: 'Damjano!'	( )	( )	( )	( )	( )	( )	( )	( )
Martin Goranov: 'Marti!'	( )	( )	( )	( )	( )	( )	( )	( )
Andrej Jovkov: 'Andreju!'	( )	( )	( )	( )	( )	( )	( )	( )
Nikola Točev: 'Nikolo!'	( )	( )	( )	( )	( )	( )	( )	( )
Ivan Mitev: 'Ivanŭt!'	( )	( )	( )	( )	( )	( )	( )	( )

Valeri Markov: 'Valerie!'	( )	( )	( )	( )	( )	( )	( )	( )
Petŭr Grigorov: 'Pepo!'	( )	( )	( )	( )	( )	( )	( )	( )
Ivan Simov: 'Ivan!'	( )	( )	( )	( )	( )	( )	( )	( )
Genadi Vasilev: 'Genadi!'	( )	( )	( )	( )	( )	( )	( )	( )
Ilija Velkov: 'Ilijo!'	( )	( )	( )	( )	( )	( )	( )	( )
Ivajlo Milanov: 'Ivajlo!'	( )	( )	( )	( )	( )	( )	( )	( )
Aleksandŭr Pašov: 'Sašoto!'	( )	( )	( )	( )	( )	( )	( )	( )
Nikolaj Kanev: 'Nike!'	( )	( )	( )	( )	( )	( )	( )	( )
Petŭr Mitov: 'Petre!'	( )	( )	( )	( )	( )	( )	( )	( )
Slavej Velikov: 'Slavej!'	( )	( )	( )	( )	( )	( )	( )	( )
Ivajlo Damjanov: 'Ivajle!'	( )	( )	( )	( )	( )	( )	( )	( )
Kamen Ivanov: 'Kamenčo!'	( )	( )	( )	( )	( )	( )	( )	( )
Nikolaj Genčev: 'Nik!'	( )	( )	( )	( )	( )	( )	( )	( )
Ilija Kŭnev: 'Ilija!'	( )	( )	( )	( )	( )	( )	( )	( )
Valeri Milev: 'Valerio!'	( )	( )	( )	( )	( )	( )	( )	( )
Genadi Petrov: 'Genadiju!'	( )	( )	( )	( )	( )	( )	( )	( )
Nikolaj Božilov: 'Nikolajo!'	( )	( )	( )	( )	( )	( )	( )	( )
Nikola Borisov: 'Nikolae!'	( )	( )	( )	( )	( )	( )	( )	( )
Ilija Tŭrnev: 'Ilie!'	( )	( )	( )	( )	( )	( )	( )	( )
Aleksandŭr Jordanov: 'Saše!'	( )	( )	( )	( )	( )	( )	( )	( )

(Ako imate dopŭlnitelni nabljudenija) – Kakvi konotacii za Vas ima zvatelnata forma za lični imena? Ima li značenie polŭt na govoreštija/ adresiranija? Imate li drugi komentari vŭrxu tazi tema?

[(If you have additional observations) – What connotations does the vocative form of personal names have for you? Do the sexes of the speaker/addressee matter? Do you have any other comments about this topic?)]

Appendix B. Descriptors attributed to each female name form

Under each descriptor is given the percentage of total respondents who selected it. Classes describe the underlying form for each name prompt, and vocative endings are given in parentheses. Terms selected by at least 15% of respondents are in boldface, and the most common descriptor for each prompt is highlighted.

Female Name Prompts	Class (Ending)	'neutral'	'slightly rude'	'very rude'	'affectionate/ tender'	'friendly'	'respectful'	'modern/ cool/fashionable'	'IMPOSSIBLE'
Albena! (Albena)	F1 (-a)	**77**	7	1	1	**20**	**45**	7	1
Viktorija! (Viktorija)	F1 (-a)	**78**	11	0	1	**20**	**43**	4	1
Radoslave! (Radoslava)	F1 (-e)	12	11	3	9	12	2	1	**67**
Kamelie! (Kamelija)	F1 (-e)	2	3	0	2	7	0	4	**92**
Rumjano! (Rumjana)	F1 (-o)	10	**52**	**54**	0	7	1	0	1
Aksinijo! (Aksinija)	F1 (-o)	3	**33**	**68**	0	5	1	0	3
Temenužka! (Temenužka)	F2 (-a)	**66**	8	1	3	**15**	**40**	3	7
Polinka! (Polina)	F2 (-a)	2	0	0	**67**	**58**	1	5	11
Temenužke! (Temenužka)	F2 (-e)	**42**	11	0	**25**	**59**	4	2	0
Radostinke! (Radostina)	F2 (-e)	10	13	1	**48**	**63**	1	1	0
Temenužko! (Temenužka)	F2 (-o)	9	**44**	**19**	12	**21**	0	3	**16**
Dejanko! (Dejana)	F2 (-o)	0	10	4	**40**	**39**	0	2	**29**
Nadja! (Nadja)	F3 (-a)	**72**	3	1	2	**28**	**47**	4	4

Kate! (Katja)	F3 (-e)	12	1	0	**52**	**85**	8	5	0
Petjo! (Petja)	F3 (-o)	7	**40**	**40**	5	**16**	1	1	8
Stili! (Stiljana)	F4 (-i)	2	0	0	**36**	**61**	0	**29**	11
Lile! (Liljana)	F4 (-e)	9	2	0	**54**	**67**	4	5	8
Vilo! (Viljana)	F4 (-o)	3	**26**	**49**	1	13	0	1	**28**
Bona! (Bona)	F5 (-a)	**75**	12	3	1	13	**30**	3	3
Cone! (Cona)	F5 (-e)	**19**	9	1	**30**	**70**	2	1	4
Nono! (Nona)	F5 (-o)	8	**43**	**45**	0	9	0	2	9
Elen! (Elen)	– (-C)	**68**	8	2	4	**22**	**35**	12	7
Aleks! (Aleksandra)	– (-C)	**26**	2	0	**21**	**71**	8	**46**	2
Kleo! (Kleopatra)	– (-o)	**15**	2	2	**36**	**67**	3	**40**	7
Nikole! (Nikol)	– (-e)	1	3	4	5	11	0	2	**77**
Mišelo! (Mišel)	– (-o)	0	**17**	**31**	2	5	0	0	**57**
Evata! (Eva)	F1 (DEF)	3	13	13	3	**29**	1	**20**	**31**
Didito! (Diljana)	F4 (DEF)	4	2	0	37	**65**	1	**22**	13
Gergančе! (Gergana)	F1 (DIM)	4	2	0	**63**	**61**	4	2	2

Appendix C. Descriptors attributed to each male name form

Under each descriptor is given the percentage of total respondents who selected it. Classes describe the underlying form for each name prompt, and vocative endings are given in parentheses. Terms selected by at least 15% of respondents are in boldface, and the most common descriptor for each prompt is highlighted.

Male Name Prompts	Class (Ending)	'neutral'	'slightly rude'	'very rude'	'affectionate/ tender'	'friendly'	'respectful'	'modern/ cool/fashionable'	'IMPOSSIBLE'
Ivan! (Ivan)	**M1 (-C)**	**77**	1	0	0	12	**41**	5	6
Nik! (Nikolaj)	**M1 (-C)**	7	0	0	12	**55**	0	**78**	2
Slavej! (Slavej)	**M1 (-C)**	**87**	1	0	2	**19**	**36**	2	2
Petre! (Petŭr)	**M1 (-e)**	**52**	**34**	6	1	**40**	8	1	1
Andree! (Andrej)	**M1 (-e)**	5	8	2	5	**18**	0	2	**71**
Damjano! (Damjan)	**M1 (-o)**	1	6	4	0	7	0	1	**85**
Nikolajo! (Nikolaj)	**M1 (-o)**	0	7	13	2	8	1	0	**81**
Andreju! (Andrej)	**M1 (-u)**	2	5	1	0	6	1	2	**89**
Nikola! (Nikola)	**M2 (-a)**	**87**	2	0	0	**25**	**46**	2	0
Ilija! (Ilija)	**M2 (-a)**	**84**	1	0	0	**22**	**41**	2	4
Nike! (Nikolaj)	**M2 (-e)**	2	1	0	**17**	**34**	1	13	**57**
Nikole! (Nikola)	**M2 (-e)**	11	8	1	4	11	2	0	**75**
Ilie! (Ilije)	**M2 (-e)**	2	1	0	6	5	0	1	**88**

Valerie! (Valeri)	**M2 (-e)**	2	4	0	0	1	1	0	**95**
Ivajle! (Ivajlo)	**M2 (-e)**	2	7	1	8	8	1	0	**80**
Saše! (Aleksandŭr)	**M2 (-e)**	6	1	0	**74**	**78**	0	6	0
Genadi! (Genadi)	**M2 (-i)**	**87**	1	0	0	**25**	**43**	2	0
Marti! (Martin)	**M2 (-i)**	7	0	0	**55**	**82**	0	**24**	0
Nikolo! (Nikola)	**M2 (-o)**	2	7	2	4	11	0	6	**80**
Ilijo! (Ilija)	**M2 (-o)**	5	**25**	**36**	0	10	0	0	**38**
Valerio! (Valeri)	**M2 (-o)**	1	5	6	0	2	0	2	**88**
Ivajlo! (Ivajlo)	**M2 (-o)**	**86**	4	0	0	**27**	**44**	2	0
Pepo! (Petŭr)	**M2 (-o)**	8	5	2	**35**	**68**	1	13	13
Pešo! (Petŭr)	**M2 (-o)**	**21**	6	0	14	**89**	4	6	1
Genadiju! (Genadi)	**M2 (-u)**	1	1	5	0	1	0	0	**94**
Ivanŭt! (Ivan)	**M1 (DEF)**	1	1	7	1	5	0	2	**88**
Ilijata! (Ilija)	**M2 (DEF)**	0	8	7	2	**34**	1	12	**49**
Sašoto! (Aleksandŭr)	**M2 (DEF)**	3	6	3	5	**29**	0	16	**53**
Kamenčo! (Kamen)	**M1 (DIM)**	1	8	0	**77**	**51**	0	1	1

Notes

1. Despite tendencies in the earlier part of the twentieth century to refer to the vocative as a 'case' (e.g. Andrejčin 1942: 135), most contemporary grammarians find it more accurate to describe vocative 'forms'. This term is preferred due to the fact that some other Slavic languages, such as Russian, which have otherwise preserved their case systems, have lost these vocative forms, and, more importantly, that the vocative does not serve a syntactic function within the sentence (Nicolova 2008: 74). Instead, the vocative works '[…] to secure contact with the addressee by indicating that the speaker is addressing a particular appeal precisely to him' ("da osiguri kontakt s adresata, kato posočva, če imenno kŭm nego govoreštijat otpravja njakakŭv priziv") (Nicolova 1984: 42).
2. I use 'V' to indicate vowels and 'C' to indicate consonants. Examples in this table reflect phonology, but further examples in the paper, except for those explicitly marked as phonological, reflect transliteration.
3. Here and in following examples, vocative forms are in boldface.
4. Such assertions coming from prescriptive grammarians should not be taken as a definitive account of the origin of such forms. Coates (1993) states that, in descriptions of language change, "[m]en will be seen to behave linguistically in a way that fits the writer's view of what is desirable or admirable; women on the other hand will be blamed for any linguistic state or development which is regarded by the writer as negative or reprehensible" (Coates 1993: 17).
5. This and all further translations are my own.
6. Search conducted March 21, 2011 at <www.google.com>.
7. Dimitrovgrad4u.com. 2008. *Smeški* [Jokes]. Retrieved March 17, 2010 from <http://dimitrovgrad4u.com/viewtopic.php?p=6036>.
8. Georgieva, Eva. 2010. *Facebook* [posting on personal profile]. Retrieved March 8, 2010, from <http://www.facebook.com/#!/eva.georgieva?ref=ts >. The first line is the original spelling (as it appeared in the Latin alphabet) and my normalization follows.
9. Survey conducted throughout April 2010 with SurveyMonkey, <www.surveymonkey.com>.
10. Full names were given in order to lead the speaker to conceptualize potential vocative forms as belonging to a real Bulgarian individual and also so that the surname, which is marked for sex, would subtly reinforce to the speaker that the proposed vocative was intended to denote either a woman or man.
11. While this latter instruction might appear to have lead respondents to conceptualize an unnecessarily friendly or close relationship with the imaginary individuals, I believe it was necessary. The informal pronoun *ti* is used relatively liberally in Bulgarian, and I was hoping to avoid an excess number

of 'rude' responses: Since it would be improper to address by first name anyone with whom one would use formal pronouns, I was concerned that some speakers might otherwise have indicated 'rude' for each prompt.

12. The phrase 'does not exist' (*ne sŭštestvuva*) was included to ensure that speakers would not select 'impossible' (*nevŭzmožno*) for forms that would simply be too infelicitous for them to use themselves; rather this descriptor was intended solely for ungrammatical forms.

13. In these examples drawn from the survey, vocative forms are presented first, and the personal names from which they are derived are given in parentheses.

14. The survey perhaps could have been more telling had it specified for each prompt whether a male or female was speaking, rather than simply analyzing in terms of a respondent's own sex. However, I decided that such a factor would have made the survey overly long and complicated.

15. Admittedly, such a method would not account for the possibility of speakers having moved to the opposite dialect region and then back at some earlier point in their life. However, the survey specifically did not ask for detailed personal history in an effort to avoid requiring complicated answers. Furthermore, the goal of the survey was to see general trends, and while any potential respondents who could have moved across the isogloss and back might make differences between eastern and western speakers appear less distinct, they would certainly not be expected to produce any 'false positives' by showing stronger dialectal features than would those living consistently on one side of the isogloss.

16. It is interesting to note that all 17 respondents whose data were ignored for this analysis had moved from an eastern dialect zone to a western dialect zone, which is due to the high numbers of young people moving to Sofia.

References

Arnaudov, Mixail
    1976   *Vekovno nasledstvo: Bŭlgarsko narodno poetičesko tvorčestvo* [Age-Old Heritage: Bulgarian Poetic Folklore]. Vol. 1. Sofia: Nauka i izkustvo.

Andrejčin, Ljubomir
    1942   *Osnovna bŭlgarska gramatika* [Basic Bulgarian Grammar]. Sofia: Xemus.

Coates, Jennifer
    1993   *Women, Men and Language*. Harlow: Longman.

Jovkov, Jordan
1971 [1930]   Albena. In *Sŭbrani sŭčinenija v šest toma* [Collected Works in Six Volumes]. Vol. 5, 5–97. Sofia: Bŭlgarski pisatel.

Ivanova, Kalina, and Ruselina Nicolova
1995   *Nie, govoreštite xora* [We, the People Who Speak]. Sofia: Sv. Kliment Ohridski.

Kovačev, Nikolaj
1987   *Bŭlgarska onomastika* [Bulgarian Onomastics]. Sofia: Jusautor.

Krŭsteva, Vesela
2003   *Obšta bŭlgarska gramatika* [General Bulgarian Grammar]. Sofia: Skorpio.

Maslov, Jurij
1956   *Očerk bolgarskoj grammatiki* [Outline of Bulgarian Grammar]. Moscow: Izdatel'stvo literatury na inostrannyx jazykax.

Mladenov, Stefan
1927–1928   'Ubijstvoto' na zvatelnija padež i drugi ezikovi neuredici [The 'killing' of the vocative case and other linguistic confusion]. *Rodna reč* 5: 215–216.

Nicolova, Ruselina
1984   *Pragmatičen aspekt na izrečenieto v bŭlgarskija knižoven ezik* [The Pragmatic Aspect of the Sentence in the Bulgarian Literary Language]. Sofia: Narodna prosveta.

Nicolova, Ruselina
2008   *Bŭlgarska gramatika: Morfologija* [Bulgarian Grammar: Morphology]. Sofia: Sveti Kliment Oxridski.

Pašov, Petŭr
1999   *Bŭlgarska gramatika* [Bulgarian Grammar]. Plovdiv: Xermes.

Pašov, Petŭr, Xristina Staneva, and Marija Pašova
2003   *Praktičeska gramatika i stilistika na bŭlgarskija ezik* [Practical Grammar and Stylistics of the Bulgarian Language]. Plovdiv: Xermes.

Pŭrvev, Xristo
1978   Zvatelnite formi na sobstvenite ženski lični imena [The vocative forms of proper feminine personal names]. In *Pomagalo po bŭlgarska morfologija* [Handbook of Bulgarian Morphology], Petŭr Pašov (ed.), 223–237. Sofia: Nauka i izkustvo.

Rå Hauge, Kjetil
1999   *A Short Grammar of Contemporary Bulgarian*. Bloomington: Slavica.

Schulz, Muriel
    1975   The semantic derogation of woman. In *Language and Sex: Difference and Dominance*, Barrie Thorne, and Nancy Henley (eds.), 64–75. Rowley: Newbury House.

Du Idiot! Din idiot! **Pseudo-vocative constructions and insults in German (and Swedish)**

Franz d'Avis and Jörg Meibauer

Abstract

This article analyses the German construction *Du/Sie Idiot!* ('You idiot!') and its correlates in Swedish (*Din Idiot!*). This construction can be used in vocative function, conveying always an expressive, derogatory and insulting meaning. Drawing on a functional distinction between Calls and Confirmations, we argue that the respective vocative construction is only acceptable as a Confirmation. This constraint motivates its categorization as a pseudo-vocative. The overall derogatory and insulting function has several sources, among them its specific syntactic make-up. Hence the idea of a pseudo-vocative construction (a pairing of a specific form and function) is suggestive. The derogatory meaning of *Du Idiot!* ('You idiot!') and *Du Lehrer!* ('You teacher!') is also connected with its semantics and pragmatics, as a comparison with the German comparative construction *Du-als-NP* shows. German and Swedish pseudo-vocative constructions display functional similarities, yet we find also formal differences between them.

1. Introduction

Although there have been a number of studies dealing with functional aspects of vocatives (cf. Welte 1980; Zwicky 1974) or their proper location in the grammar-pragmatics interface (cf. Hill 2007; Predelli 2008), more detailed studies on the expressive power of vocatives are still rare (cf. Corver 2008). Here we will discuss a particular vocative construction in German, namely *Du/Sie Idiot!* ('You Idiot!') as in (1c) (previously discussed in Rauh 2004) and its correlates in Swedish. In German, these constructions show three typical properties that renders them attractive for linguistic analysis. First, they can be used as vocatives (at least in one of its functions), which can be seen by its exchangeability for the *bona fide* vocatives in (1a) and (1b):

(1)   a. *Du,   komm   mal.*
         You   come.IMP   PART
         'You, come here.'
      b. *Peter, komm   mal.*
         Peter come.IMP   PART
         'Peter, come here.'
      c. *Du Idiot,   komm   mal.*
         you idiot   come.IMP   PART
         'You idiot, come here.'

Second, they are partly expressive and thus do not contribute to the truth conditions of the utterance (cf. Chierchia and McConnell-Ginet 1990; Kaplan 2004). As expressive devices, they possibly contribute to the use-conditions or the 'contextual bias' (Predelli 2008) of the utterance. The speaker of (1c) not only addresses someone, but, in addition, expresses an attitude towards the addressee. Expressivity as a general property of linguistic expressions or constructions has come on the linguistic agenda in a number of publications (e.g. McCready 2010; Meibauer 2013; Potts 2006, Potts forthc.; Schlenker 2007); constructions that easily lend themselves for insulting someone are certainly a case in point.

Third, syntactic patterns like *Du Idiot!* appear to constitute constructions in the sense of construction grammar. Their special syntactic form, lacking a finite verb, is not easily analysed in a projectionist manner; according to Jacobs (2008: 27), constructions like 'Pro N', with first or second person for 'Pro', resemble other formal idioms or so-called 'Phraseoschablonen' (phrasal templates) (cf. Nunberg, Sag, and Wasow 1994). Moreover, they display a special 'insulting' meaning (cf. Havryliv 2009; Neu 2008). These two properties taken together lead to the general question whether there are special expressive vocative constructions. We will not discuss the question whether *du-X* is a construction in the sense of construction grammar, but we safely believe that our analysis will be helpful in this respect.

On closer inspection, it becomes clear that a seemingly simple construction as in (1c) is not easily analysed, all the more when it is compared with its Swedish counterpart. Here, we do not try to give a comprehensive analysis; instead we will focus on three aspects of the topic. First, we will differentiate between two functions of vocatives, the Call-Function and the Confirmation-Function. We will argue that *du-X* constructions are good as Confirmations, but bad as Calls. Therefore, we prefer to speak of them as 'pseudo-vocative constructions'. The second, more data-orientated topic is the *du-X* construction in German and Swedish and its relation to vocative functions. While the insulting function is the same on both languages, it can be shown that there are formal differences that call for an explanation. In addition, it becomes clear that the construction under focus is by no means an idiosyncratic structure restricted to one single language.

Our third point will be the expressivity of the *du*-X constructions and how expressivity is connected to possible analyses in different functions (vocative vs. argument). We will argue that the overall insulting effect of this construction stems from a number of sources, but has always to do with its syntactic make-up.

2. Different functions of vocatives

2.1. Communication situation

We work on the basic assumption that in communication, there are at least two participants. If we reduce the situation to spoken language, these participants are the speaker and the addressee.

For face-to-face communication to work, it is not sufficient that there exists someone who is a speaker, and that there exists someone other who could be the addressee. Both participants must be connected in a situation that defines one participant as the speaker and another one as the addressee; both must be aware of the role they play in this situation. We call that a Communication-Situation (or C-Situation for short):

(2) In a communication situation (C-Situation), there exists someone who is the speaker and someone else who is the addressee. Both must be aware of their respective roles. Speaker and addressee are only defined within a communication situation.

There are possible problematic scenarios which we will not go in to here, e.g.: (i) (internal) monologues; (ii) prayers (God as addressee); (iii) conversations with machines or animals (e.g. *Du blöde Karre!/You damned jalopy!*); (iv) certain announcements (e.g. *All passengers to Bamberg, please proceed to track 11.* What if there are no passengers to Bamberg?; *Herr Schmitt, please come to the entrance!* What if Herr Schmitt already went home?). In these situations, it is either not certain if there is an addressee or the addressee's awareness of his role in the C-Situation is questionable. Either way, they do not conform to (2).[1]

The point is: even if someone says something and there is someone who could function as the addressee, the C-Situation needs not to be fully established. The addressee must also be instantiated within the C-Situation. Suppose I talk to you, using a second person pronoun – if you want to identify the reference of this pronoun, namely you, it is necessary that you understand that I am talking to you and not to someone else.[2]

It is not always words we use to accomplish this addressee instantiation. We could use gestures, facial expressions, and eye-contact. But, of course, there are linguistic means, and vocatives seem to be a case in point.

2.2. Vocative functions I: establishing a communication situation/ Call-Function

If a speaker wants to establish a C-Situation, two actions have to be performed:

> (i) the speaker attracts the attention of the selected addressee,
> (ii) the addressee is instantiated in the C-Situation.

An addressee is instantiated in a C-Situation, if he knows that he is meant to be the addressee[3] and if the speaker knows that the addressee knows this.[4] In the act of addressee instantiation, the addressee is identified. These two steps are not always separated (cf. e.g Anderson 2007: 219; Lyons 1977: 214; Zwicky 1974). But there is evidence that we are indeed dealing with two different actions. There are linguistic and non-linguistic means we can use to attract attention, step (i), but by means of which we are not able to identify the addressee, step (ii), see the selection in (3).

(3) a. linguistic means
> – Interjections: *he* 'hey', *ey* 'ey', *hallo* 'hello',...
> – Pronouns: *du* 'you.SNG', *ihr* 'you.pl', *Sie* 'you.HON',...
> – Complex forms: *du da* 'you.SNG there', *Sie da* 'you.HON there', ...

>   b. non-linguistic means
> – whistling
> – throat clearing
> – gesticulation (waving,...)

By using for instance the means in (3), you can get the attention of a selected addressee. But it is obvious that this alone does not identify the addressee, and so it is not enough to establish a C-Situation. Now you could argue that, if you shout *hey* to someone and he is turning around and looking at you, perhaps with an enquiring look, a C-Situation is already established; or you could be in a room with just one other person and start to talk without explicitly establishing a C-Situation. In the first case, it is the eye-contact or other deictic support we would interpret as the point of identification and in the second case, it is the non-linguistic context that provides for the establishment of the C-Situation: there is obviously no other interlocutor available.

For an addressee to be instantiated in a C-Situation, he has to know that he is the one the speaker means; the speaker identifies or marks the addressee. This can also be done with linguistic or non-linguistic means, compare some examples in (4).

(4)   a.   linguistic means[5]
     –   first (+last) name: *Heinz, Maria Schmidt,...*
     –   (prefix+) last name: *Herr Schmidt* 'Mr. Schmidt', *Müller,...*
     –   titles (+last name): *Professor, Doktor Schmidt* 'Doctor Schmidt',...
     –   kintitle (+first name): *Mama* 'mum', *Onkel Peter* 'uncle Peter',...
     –   descriptions: *du/Sie mit der Brille* 'you.SNG/you.HON with the glasses', *der Junge mit der Mundharmonika* 'the boy with the blues harp',...

    b.   non-linguistic means
     –   eye-contact
     –   pointing gesture

Using elements of (4), a speaker can mark/identify an addressee. To take the two steps we need to establish a C-Situation, we first use one of the elements in (3), getting the attention of the selected addressee, and then an element of (4), marking/identifying the addressee.

We see the two actions as two different speech-acts. They can be used independently of one another.

You can use *hey* or *hallo* just to get someone's attention. You can actually use all kinds of utterances just to get the attention of someone. But the ones in (3a) seem to have this as one of their main functions. You can use these expressions even if you do not know if there is somebody around who may be able to hear you or if there are a lot of people and you just want somebody, whoever, to pay attention to you.

Just as well, you can use elements of (4) to identify a specific addressee, even if you already have the attention of a set of potential addressees. Imagine a teacher in a classroom talking to his pupils. They already listen to him and now he utters a pupil's name, say *Peter*, thereby marking him as the addressee, perhaps of a following question, or even as the addressee of a question already asked before.

There are also different reactions to an utterance which can be analysed as referring to the failure of different speech-acts in that utterance. Imagine a situation where a foreman calls in the direction of a few workers, supposing that getting-attention speech-act and identification are successful, cf. (5):

(5)   *Hey, you with the shovel, come here!*

But none of the men reacts and the foreman walks to one of them, the one he wanted to come to him, and asks him why he did not come. Possible reactions include those in (6):

(6)   a. *I did not hear you.*
    b. *I did not know that you called for me.*
    c. *I did not want to come.*

If the answer is (6a), the act of attention-getting failed. (6b) indicates that the act of identification failed, and (6c), however unlikely, suggests that the command speech-act failed.

With most of the expressions in (4), a speaker can perform both speech-acts needed to establish a C-Situation simultaneously. So, you can use *Hey Mary!* to first get Mary's attention and then identify her as the addressee, but you can also use just *Mary!* to get her attention and identify her as addressee at the same time.

Expressions that a speaker can use to establish a C-Situation are expressions that fulfil the Call-Function. In utterances like (7a,b) both involved speech-acts are performed explicitly and can be linked to different expressions. In utterances like (7c,d) the getting-attention and the identification-speech-act are performed simultaneously.

(7)   a. *He, du mit   der grünen Hose!*
       hey you with the green   trousers
       'Hey, you with the green trousers!'
    b. *Hallo, Herr Professor Schmidt-Grün!*
       hello   Mr.   Professor Schmidt-Grün
       'Hello, Professor Schmidt-Grün!'
    c. *Maria!*
    d. *Mama!*
       mum
       'Mum!'

Linguistic expressions that fulfil the Call-Function are vocatives in call-function (V_{CF}).

(8) An expression is a vocative in Call-Function (V_{CF}), if:
  (i) it is used to get the attention of a selected addressee,
  (ii) it marks/identifies the selected addressee.

2.2.1. Position

Vocatives in Call-Function are not integrated in a possible following sentence (cf. Duden 2005: 822; Zifonun et al. 1997: 917). A speech-act is performed that is independent from the following utterance, which in turn can be used for different speech-acts, cf. (9):

(9) a. Statement: *He Heinz, ich gehe jetzt nach Hause.*
            hey Heinz I   go   now to   home
            'Hey Heinz, I am going home now.'
   b. Question: *Hallo Herr Schmidt, soll ich Sie   mitnehmen?*
            hello Mr. Schmidt shall I   you.HON take-with
            'Hello Mr. Schmidt, can I give you a ride?'
   c. Request: *Du, Peter, hol   doch mal   die Katze rein!*
            you Peter fetch PART PART the cat   inside
            'Peter, please get the cat inside!'

The V_{CF} keeps its function, even so the following utterance is a statement, a question, or a request. V_{CF}s have an own intonation contour and are typically separated from the following utterance by an intonation break.

The position of V_{CF} before a relevant utterance makes, indeed, sense. If a speaker wants to get the attention of a selected addressee and wants to identify him, then, positioning the V_{CF} inside or after the related[6] utterance would be unnecessary or too late. The V_{CF} is unnecessary, if the C-Situation is already established, cf. (10):

(10) Speaker to Mary: *Lass uns heute ins   Kino   gehen.*
            let   us   today in-the cinema go
            'Let's go to the movies today.'
   Mary: *Oh ja, gute Idee. Wann denn?*
            oh yes good idea when PART
            'Okay, this is a good idea. When?'

Speaker: #*[He Maria,]*V_{CF} *am   besten jetzt.*
                 [hey Maria]V_{CF} at-the best   now
                 '[Hey Maria,] V_{CF} now would be best.'

The C-Situation is already established, the speaker makes a suggestion and
Mary reacts and asks a question. Using now the V_{CF} *He Maria* is at least
inappropriate.
    If a speaker starts with an utterance and uses a V_{CF} inside this utterance,
it may be too late, cf. (11).

(11) *Der Hund, #[he Maria,]*V_{CF} *ist draußen.*
      the dog   [hey Maria]V_{CF} is outside
      'The dog, [hey Maria,]V_{CF} is outside.'

If a speaker wants to establish the C-Situation after he started his utterance,
he must assume that the selected addressee did not hear or understand the
part before the V_{CF}. Here, some kind of repair seems to be suitable (cf.
Schegloff 1968: 1081).

(12) *Der Hund, [he Maria,]*V_{CF} *der Hund ist draußen.*
      the dog   [hey Maria]V_{CF} the dog   is outside
      'The dog, [hey Maria,]$V_{CF}$the dog is outside.'

To sum up, one function of vocatives is to get the attention of a selected
addressee and identify him. An expression used in this way is a vocative in
Call-Function (V_{CF}).

2.3. Vocative functions II: confirmation of the addressee-status/
A-Confirmation

Not all expressions that seem to possess vocative properties are committed
to the position before the sentence. If the C-Situation is established, utterances as the following are in order:

(13) *Die Müllabfuhr,   Maria / meine Liebe / du /   Frau Müller /*
the waste-disposal Maria / my   dear /   you / Frau Müller /
du   kleiner Schnuckel / du Dummkopf, kommt aber erst
you little   sweetie /   you fool,   comes PART PART
übermorgen.
the.day.after.tomorrow
'The waste-disposal, Maria / my dear / you / Frau Müller / you little
sweetie / you fool, is coming the day after tomorrow.'

We can see that certain forms of address also appear inside the sentence (cf.
Zwicky 1974: 797). More precisely, they can stand in so-called
parenthetical-niches (cf. Altmann 1981; d'Avis 2004), or before or after the
sentence (start- and end-parentheticals, cf. Schwyzer 1939). Even these
positions can be seen as suitable for vocative expressions.

(14) *(Maria,) die Müllabfuhr   (Maria) kommt aber   erst*
Maria   the waste.disposal (Maria) comes PART PART
übermorgen   (Maria).
the.day.after.tomorrow   Maria
'(Maria), the waste disposal (Maria) is coming the day after tomorrow
(Maria).'

Please keep in mind that the C-Situation is already established. The function of the vocative-expressions is to confirm the addressee-status of the
person spoken to. Consequently, we call this function confirmation of the
addressee status, short: *A-Confirmation*. A vocative that fulfils this function
we call V_{AC}.

Alongside the addressee confirmation other aspects can be reinforced,
e.g. politeness or social relations. See the list and appropriate examples in
Zwicky (1974: 795–796). What we describe as V_{AC}s, Nehring ([1933]
1977) calls 'Anrede' (address). He sees the main property of elements one
can use as address in characterising the addressee. This is also the main
difference to expressions used as 'Anruf' (call), our V_{CF} (cf. Nehring
[1933]1977: 128).

To sum up: We differentiate between V_{CF} and V_{AC}. V_{CF} establish a
communication situation by getting the attention of a selected addressee
and identifying him. V_{AC} on the other hand are used, when the C-Situation
is already established. Their main function is to confirm the addressee status, and they can "locate the speaker and the discourse in a particular social
world" Zwicky (1974: 795).[7]

3. *Du*-X and vocative functions

Imagine the following situation: We are at an exhibition. Three men are standing in front of a picture looking at it. The man in the middle is wearing a green jacket. A wants to talk to this man. If A simply shouts *Hey!* or says *Good day!* loud enough, possibly all three men will turn around. Suppose the man in the middle is called Heinz and A knows this, A could pick him out and start a conversation just with saying *Heinz!* A could even say:

(15) *Der Mann mit   der grünen Jacke! (Ihr   Auto wird*
      the man with the green jacket your.HON car is.being
      gerade   abgeschleppt.)
      just.now hauled.off
      'The man with the green jacket! (Your car is being hauled off just now.)'

What he can not use in this situation, are expressions like: *Sie Dummkopf, du Trottel* etc.

(16) #*[Sie   Dummkopf!]*V_{CF} *(Ihr   Auto wird   gerade*
      [you.HON fool]V_{CF} your.HON car   is being just.now
      abgeschleppt.)
      hauled.off
      '[You fool!]V_{CF} (Your car is being hauled off.)'

In the situation we described, it would not be clear who is meant. It seems that the communication situation has to be established before you can insult someone.

Proper names, on the other hand, can be used in a Call-Function (17a) and in Confirmation-Function, cf. (17b).

(17) a. *[Heinz,]*V_{CF} *dein Auto wird   abgeschleppt.*
        [Heinz]V_{CF} your car is.being hauled.off
        '[Heinz]V_{CF} your car is being hauled off.'
     b. *Dein Auto, [Heinz,]*V_{AC} *wird   abgeschleppt.*
        your car [Heinz]V_{CF} is.being hauled.off
        'Your car, [Heinz,]V_{AC} is being hauled off.'

Interjections like *he!* are good as Calls,[8] but seem to be not as good in Confirmation-Function.

(18) a. *He, dein Auto wird abgeschleppt.*
    hey your car is being hauled off
    'Hey, your car is being hauled off.'
  b. *Dein Auto, [#he,]V$_{AC}$ wird abgeschleppt.*
    your car, [#hey,]V$_{AC}$ is.being hauled.off
    'Your car; [#hey,]V$_{AC}$ is being hauled off.'

With *du*-X it is the other way round. As we have seen, it cannot be used in Call-Function.

(19) #*[Du Trottel,]V$_{CF}$ dein Auto wird abgeschleppt.*
    [you fool]V$_{CF}$ your car is.being hauled.off
    '[You fool,]V$_{CF}$ your car is being hauled off.'

But those expressions can easily be used as A-Confirmation. If it is clear who A is talking to, i.e. if the C-Situation is established, A could say:

(20) *Ihr Auto, [Sie Dummkopf]V$_{AC}$ / [du Trottel]V$_{AC}$,*
    your.HON car, [you.HON dumbhead]V$_{AC}$ / [you fool] V$_{AC}$
    wird gerade abgeschleppt.
    is.being just.now hauled.off
    'Your car, [you dumbhead]V$_{AC}$ /[you fool]V$_{AC}$ is being hauled off just now.'

This is an important property of *du*-X with respect to vocative constructions: With *du*-X, a speaker cannot establish a communication situation, that is, *du*-X cannot be used in Call-Function.

3.1. Some other properties of *du*-X

As we have seen, *du*-X behaves different with respect to possible uses as vocatives. But there are also differences to standard noun phrases. The *du*-X-construction occurs in different cases: nominative, dative, accusative but not genitive.

(21) *du kleiner Trottel*
    'you little sucker'
(22) NOM: *du – du kleiner Trottel*
    GEN: *deiner– ???*
    DAT: *dir – dir kleinem Trottel*
    ACC: *dich – dich kleinen Trottel*

(23) a. *Gestern   hast   du   kleiner Trottel   versagt.*
        yesterday have [you little   sucker].NOM screwed up
        'Yesterday, you little sucker screwed up.'
   b. *Gestern   habe ich dir   kleinem Trottel   geholfen.*
        yesterday have I   [you little   sucker].DAT helped
        'Yesterday, I helped you, you little sucker.'
   c. *Gestern   habe ich dich kleinen Trottel   gesehen.*
        yesterday have I   [you little   sucker].ACC seen
        'Yesterday, I saw you, you little sucker.'

There is a genitive form of the 3rd person pronoun, namely *deiner*, that appears in argument position as a genitive object,[9] cf. (24), or as argument of a preposition like *statt/instead*. But it cannot be expanded with a noun.

(24) a. *Ich kann mich deiner /   *deiner Trottel(s)   nicht* entsinnen.
        I   can   me   you.GEN / [you sucker].GEN not   remember
        'I can't remember you/you sucker.'
   b. *Wir bedürfen deiner /   *deiner Trottel(s).*
        we   need   you..GEN / [you sucker].GEN
        'We need you/you sucker.'
   c. *Bon Scott singt statt   deiner / *deiner Trottel(s).*
        Bon Scott sings instead you.GEN / [you sucker].GEN
        'Bon Scott is singing instead of you/you sucker.'

If used as a vocative, the 'du-X-construction' appears in nominative form.

(25) *Peter, du   kleiner Trottel /   *dir kleinem Trottel/*
     Peter, [you little   sucker].NOM /[you little   sucker].DAT/
     *dich   kleinen Trottel,   komm mal   her.
     [you little   sucker].ACC, come PART   here
     'Peter, you little sucker, come here.'

But even so, there are differences between the *du*-X-construction and normal noun phrases in the nominative case as well as with unexpanded 2nd person pronouns in nominative case.

(i) *du*-X and generic meaning

There is a generic meaning of 'du' that is not available for 'du-X'.

(26) a. *Hier   kannst du   dich   echt   entspannen.*
         here   can   you   you.REFL really relax
         'Here, you can really relax.'
         →*man/you*: generic or addressee
     b. *Hier   kannst du   Trottel dich   echt   entspannen.*
         here   can   you   fool   you.REFL really relax
         'Here, you fool can really relax.'
         →*du Trottel*: only addressee, no generic reading

'Du' can be used generically in (26a), but not in (26b), where it is expanded.

(ii) *du*-X and focus particles

Pronouns allow focus particles.

(27)   *Selbst / auch / nur / sogar du   hast   versagt.*
        even / even / only / even   you   have   failed
        'Even/only you failed.'

du-X allows focus particles only if it is in an integrated position.

(28) a. *Selbst / auch /nur / sogar du   kleiner Trottel hast   versagt.*
         even / even / only / even you little   sucker have failed
         'Even/only you little fool failed.'

In the vocative function, *du*-X does not accept focus particles.

     b. *Gestern, (*nur) du   Idiot, haben wir wegen   dir   das*
         yesterday (*only) you   idiot have   we   because you   the
         Spiel   verloren.
         match   lost
         'Yesterday, (*only) you idiot, we lost the match because of you'

(iii) *du*-X Predicative usage

With the verbs *sein, werden, bleiben; scheinen, dünken; heißen*, there is a
predicative usage of nominative NPs.

(29) a. *Du   bist und bleibst   ein   Trottel.*
         you   are and remain   a   fool
         'You are and remain a fool.'

b. *Du dünkst mich ein Trottel.*
you seem me a fool
'You seem to me to be a fool.'

A predicative usage is not possible for *du*-X phrases.

(29) c. **Du bist und bleibst du Trottel.*
you are and remain you fool
   d. **Du dünkst mich du Trottel.*
you seem me you fool

To sum up the properties: *du*-X can function as a vocative in the A-Con-firmation function, it can function as an argument, but it has not the same grammatical possibilities as other noun phrases. These idiosyncratic properties could suggest that we are indeed dealing with a construction in the sense explicated above. There are even language specific properties which are made clear by the differences found between *du*-X and the re-lated Swedish *din/ditt*-X construction, at which we now will have a short look.

3.2. Differences between *du*-X as vocative and in argument position in Swedish

In Swedish, the difference between the *du*-X-construction in vocative func-tion and in other syntactic functions is easier to see. There is a phrase with a 2nd person possessive pronoun that functions as the Swedish correlate of *du*-X, namely *din/ditt*-X. *din* and *ditt* are the utrum (common gender) and neuter forms of the 2nd person singular possessive pronoun, respectively.

(30) a. *din idiot, din dumbom*
you idiot you fool
   b. *ditt äckel, ditt pucko*
you stinker you asshole

In German we recognise the use of possessive pronouns in vocative phrases from 1st person singular possessives like the ones in (31).

(31) *mein Schatz, mein Lieber*
my treasure my dear

There are also conventionalised forms in the 2nd person plural like (32).

(32) *Euer/Eure Majestät*
    your   Majesty

The *din/ditt*-X-construction can be used as a vocative in all functions except the Call-Function.

(33) a. *Men här kan du ju   inte parkera, din   idiot!*
        but here can you PART not park   you   idiot
        'But here, you can not park, you idiot!'
    b. *Koka äggen   dindumbom!*
       cook the.egg you fool
       'Cook the egg, you fool!' (from the internet)
    c. *Tack ska   ni   ha   era   skitstövlar, svarade   jag* [...]
       thank shall you.PL have you.PL shitheads   answered   I
       'Thank you, you shitheads, I answered...' (SAG 4: 797)

The *din/ditt*-X construction cannot be used in argument position/as subject in Swedish.[10]

What you can use instead is a 2nd person pronoun with a nominal, like in German.

(34) a. *Vad   i   helvete gör   du   idiot?*
        what in hell   do   you idiot
        'What the hell are you doing, you idiot?'
    b. *...va   fan   tror   du   idiot jävel ...*
       ...what devil think you idiot bastard
       '...what the hell do you think, you idiot...'
    c. *...hoppas   du   idiot som gjorde det läser detta och...*
       ...hope.1SG you idiot that did   that read   this   and
       '...(I) hope you idiot who did that are reading this and...' (from the
       internet)

din/ditt-X can be adjoined to a personal pronoun in argument position as an apposition.

(35) a. *Och vem   är   du   din idiot för   att veta   hur ateister tänker?*
        and who   are   you you idiot for to know how atheists   think
        'And who are you, you idiot, for to know how atheists think?'
    b. *Du din idiot   vet   tydligen   inte vad   vetenskap   är...*
       you you idiot know obviously   not what science   is...
       'You, you idiot, obviously don't know what science is...'

   c. *...och du   din Dumbom gick på   hans lama   ursäkt ...*
     ...and you you fool   went on   his   lame   excuse ...
     '... and you, you fool, fell for his lame excuse ...' (from the
     internet)

Even if the *din/ditt*-X construction exists in most Scandinavian languages
(Old Danish, Old Scandinavian, Danish, Norwegian, Swedish), there is – as
far as we could make out – no generally accepted analysis. Søren Beltoft
(2001) compiled work that was done on this construction. This is mostly
research from the 19th and the beginning of the 20th century. Exceptions are
Kjellmer (1976) and SAG (1999). The newest analysis we know of is
Corver (2008). We will not go into the analyses here, but just notice that
differences can be found between a vocative use, which would be *din/ditt*-
X and a construction with similar meaning in argument position, which is
du-X.

4. *du*-X as pseudo-vocatives

The *du*-X construction has its peculiarities, but we think it can be safely
classified as having at least some of the functions a vocative can have. Or
let us put it the other way around. The *du*-X construction cannot be used in
the Call-Function. Since this seems to be the basic function of a vocative
phrase, the term Pseudo-Vocative seems to be justified.

    For the *du*-X construction to be used as vocative, the communication
situation must already be established. Recall the example we had in the
beginning (see 1c): If we try to get the attention of someone who is *not* in a
communication relation with us, we cannot use the *du*-X construction.

(36) *#Du Trottel, komm mal   her!*
      you fool   come PART here
      'Come here, you fool!'

Whereas in an already established communication situation, other vocative
functions like A-Confirmation can be fulfilled by *du*-X.

(37) *Gestern, du   Trottel, hast du   dich   ganz schön blamiert.*
     yesterday you fool   have you you.REFL PART PART blamed
     'Yesterday, you fool, you made a fool of yourself.'

Why is it that you cannot establish a communication situation with *Du
Trottel/you fool*? Whatever your analysis of the internal structure of this

construction, it seems to be clear that the noun is predicative. More precisely, an evaluation on the side of the speaker is involved. But such an evaluation seems only possible, when the relation between speaker and addressee is given, i.e. when the C-Situation is already established.

Since the nominal in the *du*-X construction is interpreted as an evaluation predication, it suggests itself that it cannot really be used to pick out an addressee. So it cannot be used to establish a communication situation. The evaluation is subjective, related to the speaker, and it does not denote a common class of elements. How is the putative addressee supposed to know that he is meant? A speaker cannot assume that his evaluations are automatically shared by other people he wants to address.

Expressivity is one of the hallmarks of the *du*-X construction and this will be our next point.

5. On the expressivity of *ich/du* NP-constructions

In this paragraph, we will analyse the *ich/du-NP* construction as an expressive construction, i.e. a specific form-meaning pair. It will be compared to the *ich/du als NP* construction. (Note that when we talk of 'constructions' here, we are not committed to the views of construction grammar. While there are good reasons to assume their status as constructions in the sense of construction grammar, we will propose a modular approach below.) These constructions have, according to Rauh (2004), different syntactic and semantic properties:

Table 1. Syntax and Semantics of *ich/du* NP vs. *ich/du (als)* NP

	Syntax	Semantics
ich/du NP	transitive determiner + NP complement	NP predicates over the referents of ich/du in a holistic way
ich/du als NP	intransitive determiner + als NP-apposition	NP picks out some relevant property of the referents of ich/du

While *ich/du NP* is best analysed as transitive determiner plus NP complement (cf. Vater 2000), *ich/du als NP* is an intransitive determiner plus a right-adjacent apposition. In X-bar-theoretic terms, an apposition does not lead to the projection of a further syntactic level. The main semantic difference between these constructions is that *ich/du NP* predicates over the referents of *ich/du* in a holistic way, while in the *ich/du als NP*-construction, the NP picks out some relevant property of the referents of *ich/du*. How ever this may be implemented formally into the truth conditions of the respective sentences, we assume that the truth conditions do not directly encode expressive content. Being predicated in a holistic way, so we will argue, leads to certain conversational implicatures.

(i)   *Ich/du-NP* constructions appear as a single speech act and as an argument within a sentence.

(38) a. *Ich   Idiot! Ich   Glückspilz!*
       I   idiot I   lucky.man
       'Stupid me! Lucky me!'
    b. *Du   Idiot! Du   Glückspilz!*
       you idiot! You lucky man
       'You idiot! You lucky man!'
    c. *Ich Idiot habe schon   wieder vergessen, das   Licht*
       I   idiot have already again   forgotten   the   light
       auszumachen.
       to.switch.out
       'Stupid me, I forgot to switch off the light again.'
    d. *Du   Idiot könntest auch besser aufpassen!*
       you idiot could   MP   better watch.out
       'Watch your step, you idiot!'

In (38c,d), *ich/du Idiot* appear in the prefield and as subject. However, their position in the middlefield and their status as an object is also possible. Hence the expressive effect is independent of the topological position and subject- vs. object-status.

(39) a. *Habe ich Idiot schon   wieder   vergessen, das Licht*
       have I   idiot already   again   forgotten   the light
       auszumachen?
       to.switch.out
       'Stupid me, did I forget to switch off the light again?'
    b. *Hast   du   Idiot schon   wieder   vergessen,   das Licht*
       have you idiot already again   forgotten   the light
       auszumachen?
       to.switch.out
       'Did you idiot forget to switch off the light again?'
    c. *Ich könnte mich Idiot auf   den Mond   schießen!*
       I   could   me   idiot to   the moon   shoot
       'Stupid me, I could launch me into outer space.'

d. *Ich könnte　dich　　Idiot auf den Mond schießen!*
　　I　could　you.REFL　idiot to　the moon shoot
　　'I could launch you idiot into outer space.'

In (39a,b), the utterances constitute expressive speech acts of blaming or praising the speaker himself or the addressee. In fact, utterances like *Du/Sie X*, with X as a swearword, make use of a common pattern for insulting someone else (cf. Havrilyv 2003, 2009).

(ii)　The NP-part of the *ich/du-NP* construction is more often a NP with expressive content than not.

(40) a.　*Ich　Idiot / Trottel / Arschloch!*
　　　　　I　idiot /　fool / asshole
　　　　　'I idiot / fool / asshole!'
　　　b.　*Du　Idiot / Trottel / Arschloch!*
　　　　　you idiot /　fool / asshole
　　　　　'You idiot/fool/asshole!'
　　　c.　Ich Lehrer / Angestellter / Mensch!
　　　　　I　teacher / employee /　human
　　　　　'I teacher/employee/human!'
　　　d.　*Du Lehrer /　Angestellter / Mensch!*
　　　　　you teacher / employee /　human
　　　　　'You teacher/employee/human!'

(41) a.　*Ich beschissener Lehrer /　Angestellter / Mensch!*
　　　　　I　fucking　　　teacher / employee /　human
　　　　　'I fucking teacher/employee/human!'
　　　b.　*Du beschissener Lehrer /　Angestellter / Mensch!*
　　　　　you fucking　　　teacher / employee /　human
　　　　　'You fucking teacher/employee/human!'

All the examples are, in principle, fine as insults. However, (40c,d) need a specific context where the insult makes sense, for instance someone hating teachers has become a teacher himself, etc. Note that the expressive touch may made visible by adding the expressive adjective *beschissen* 'fucking', as in (41a).

　　Since in (40c,d) the NP is not expressive, it must be the construction itself that contributes expressivity. Note that this assumption does not lead automatically to a constructional grammar analysis. Quite on the contrary, we will propose a modular (projectionist) analysis below.

(iii) As an argument within a sentence, the *ich/du-NP* construction competes with the *ich/du als NP* construction.

The *ich/du-NP* construction may also appear as an argument within a sentence. Rauh (2004) argues at length that it may appear here without any expressive flavour and presents the following examples:

(42) *[Ihr Literaturwissenschaftler] mögt den jetzigen Zustand für*
    [you literary scholars]   might the actual   state   for
    angemessen halten,
    adequate   hold
    aber [ich Linguist] halte die Linguistik für weit
    but   [I   linguist] hold the linguistics for widely
    unterrepräsentiert.
    underrepresented
    'You, as literary scholars, might consider the actual state as adequate,
    but I, as a linguist, consider linguistics as widely underrepresented.'

We suspect that the *ich/du als* NP construction is more common, as in (43):

(43) *[Ihr als Literaturwissenschaftler] mögt den jetzigen Zustand für*
    [you as literary scholars   might the actual   state   for
    angemessen
    adequate
    halten aber [ich als Linguist] halt die Linguistik für weit
    hold,   but   [I   as   linguist] hold the linguistics for widely
    unterrepräsentiert.
    underrepresented.
    'You, as literary scholars, might consider the actual state as adequate,
    but I, as a linguist, consider linguistics as widely underrepresented.'

In (43), the pronoun is an intransitive determiner, and *als N* is an apposition. Roughly, as Rauh (2004) points out, *ich/du NP* codes holistic properties of being X, while *ich/du als NP* denotes X with respect to the property of being an X. The point is that the latter construction is never expressive.

(iv) In isolation, as well as within the sentence, *ich/du als NP* with expressive meaning is ruled out.

(44) a. *Ich Trottel!*
      I   fool
      'Stupid me!'

b. *Du   Idiot!*
   you idiot
   'You idiot!'
c. **Ich als   Trottel!*
   I   as   fool
d. **Du als   Idiot!*
   you as   idiot!

Note that in certain contexts, exclamations showing the structural pattern in (44c,d) may occur, e.g. in the following dialogue: A: *Du könntest doch Literaturwissenschaftler werden!* 'You could become a literary scholar!', B: *Ich als Literaturwissenschaftler! Gequirlte Kacke!* 'I as a literary scholar! Bullshit!'. But here, *Literaturwissenschaftler* is not expressive. Moreover, the possibility of becoming a literary scholar is already mentioned in the previous utterance of A, hence yields an echo effect when taken up by B.

This presupposing effect is also seen with (45):

(45) a. *Du Idiot hältst   den Zustand sicher für   angemessen.*
     you idiot consider the state   surely as   adequate.
     'You idiot consider the state as surely adequate.'
b. *#Du als Idiot hältst den Zustand sicher für   angemessen.*
   you as idiot hold   the state   surely for   adequate.

Du als NP presupposes that the denotation of NP is correctly predicated with respect to the addressee. If such a predication is plausible in the context, such utterances become acceptable. This is in contrast to *du NP*, where the addressee is evaluated by the denotation of NP. Being an idiot cannot be presupposed as a general property of the addressee, thus ruling out (44c, d) and (45b). The case *ich als NP* vs. *ich NP* behaves in the same way.

(v)   Even if *ich/du NP* appears as an argument within a sentence, the NP not displaying expressive content, it inherits an expressive flair.

Rauh (2004) argues at length that the difference between (42) and (43) is purely semantic, having to do with the holistic versus specific reading. But we would like to argue that *ich/du NP*, even if it appears as argument within a sentence, still inherits its expressive flair.

Thus, (46) potentially is a more pejorative way to express the information that the addressee having the status as student is relevant to the discourse than (47). Recall that the insulting meaning is due to the construction, without being a part of the truth conditions.

(46) *Du Student   (du Idiot) hältst den Zustand sicher für*
angemessen.
you student (you idiot) hold the state   surely as   adequate
'You, as a student, surely consider the state as adequate.'

(47) *Du als Student (*du als Idiot) hältst den   Zustand sicher*
you as   student (you as idiot) hold the   state   surely
für angemessen.
for   adequate
'You, as a student, surely consider the state as adequate.'

In sum, we argue against the following hypotheses of Rauh (2004):

(H1)   Isolated occurrences of *Du Linguist!* or *Du Mensch!* are impossible
(Rauh 2004: 100).

(H2)   When embedded, these constructions have no expressive touch at all.
(Rauh 2004: 83–84)

Rauh (2004: 98–102) points out that (H1) may be explained by referring to
Grice's maxims. Since the maxims of Relevance and Quantity prescribe
that something relevant and informative should be uttered, isolated utterances like *Du Linguist!* or *Du Mensch!* are ruled out, because in every
discourse situation it can be presupposed that the addressee is a linguist or a
human being. Hence the information in these utterances is redundant.

Quite on the contrary, we would like to argue that these utterances still
have an expressive touch. For our explanation, we may partly rely on
Rauh's semantics for the *ich/du* NP-construction vis-á-vis the *ich/du-als-*
NP construction (see Table 1). She points out that with the intransitive
variants, the referent is characterized as relatively unspecified with respect
to the set of entities fulfilling the predicate PERSON (x). In contrast, the
transitive variant is characterized by a restriction to a more specific set of
elements, which comes about through the denotation of the NP-comple-
ment, for instance LINGUIST (x) (Rauh 2004: 97).

The holistic meaning connected with *du Student* fits well with insulting,
because many insults go together with abstracting away from individual
properties. (Focusing on individual properties is also possible, as an
anonymous reviewer remarks.) In fact, the addressee is reduced to having a
certain property. Moreover, it is not only a property, but the decisive
property. This explains also, why *du als Idiot* ('you as an idiot') is an impossible insult. An expressive attitude is dealt with as if it were a (presupposed or inalienable) property of the addressee.

As a parallel case, consider ethnic slur terms like *spic, boche, nigger*, etc. Their derogatory force general meanings like 'being part of the x-group & x-group-members being despicable because of belonging to the group' which obviously are abstracting away from any particular properties of the individual referent. By the same token, groups like teachers, linguists or human beings may be constructed as groups with despicable properties (cf. Hom 2007; Saka 2007).

The question is, whether this evaluative effect has to do with the construction proper, or is an implicated meaning.

Since it is unlikely that generalising attributions are evaluative per se, we propose to derive these expressive meanings as an implicature (see Meibauer 2006). At a first shot, we consider triggering the implicature by way of the M-maxim (Levinson 2000)

It could be argued that (46) and (47) roughly mean the same, because someone is addressed and a certain property is predicated. In *du Student* as well as in *du als Student* someone is addressed (the referent of *du*) and it is implied that the referent is a student. (As a parallel case, think of pairs like *Bill stopped the car* versus *Bill caused the car to stop*. Both sentences denote the same event.) Then the M-principle (in the sense of Levinson 2000) would apply, *du Student* being the (syntactically) more marked message in comparison with *du als Student*:

(48) *The M-Principle*

Speaker's maxim: Indicate an abnormal, nonstereotypical situation by using marked expressions that contrast with those you would use to describe the corresponding normal, stereotypical situation.

Recipient's corollary: What is said in an abnormal way indicates an abnormal situation, or marked messages indicate marked situations, specifically:

Where S had said „p" containing marked expression *M*, and there is an unmarked alternate expression *U* with the same denotation *D* which the speaker might have employed in the sentence-frame instead, then where *U* would have I-implicated the stereotypical or more specific subset *d* of *D*, the marked expression *M* will implicate the complement of the denotation, namely *d'* of *D*.

The problem with the application of the M-principle is whether *du Student* and *du als Student* have, strictly spoken, the same denotation. Following Rauh (2004), we argued that this is not the case.

However, in standard cases like causative constructions (*Bill caused to stop the car* vs. *Bill stopped the car*), it may be also questioned whether the criterion of 'the same denotation' would apply. What matters more is the observation that in certain contexts, there is indeed a competition between the two alternatives. Moreover, we suspect that *ich/du* is more syntactically marked, less frequent or usual, and less neutral in register in comparison to *ich/du als NP*. This has to be empirically investigated. If this approach is on the right track, we can account for the data in the following way.

For (49) versus (50), competition does not exist.

(49) *Du   Linguist/Idiot!*
    you linguist/idiot
    'You linguist/idiot!'

(50) **Du   als   Linguist/Idiot!*
    you as   linguist/idiot

Sentence (50) is ungrammatical because it does not fit into the pattern of an evaluative act: it is presupposed that the addressee is a linguist or idiot. In contrast, the utterance *Du Linguist!* in (49) gives new information on the speaker's evaluative attitude. This is in line with Rauh's assumption that relevance and quantity play a role (or a maxim that requires that one should not tell what may be presupposed).

In (51) versus (52), however, we have indeed a competitive situation, albeit only with respect to *du Linguist* versus *du als Linguist*. Here, the M-principle applies, yielding an evaluative interpretation for (51).

(51) *Du Linguist/Idiot hast da   bestimmt keine Ahnung von.*
    you linguist/idiot have PART definitely no   idea   of
    'You linguist/idiot are clueless about that.'

(52) *Du als Linguist/ *Idiot hast da   bestimmt keine Ahnung von.*
    you as linguist   idiot have part definitely no   idea   of
    'You as linguist/idiot are clueless about that.'

The different effect connected with *du Linguist* versus *du als Linguist* is a subtle one. It goes without saying that it lends itself to experimental corroboration, a task that we cannot go into here.

6. Conclusions

What we arrived at in this contribution, focusing on constructions like German *Du Idiot!* and Swedish *Din idiot!*, is the following. First, we have drawn a distinction between two functions of vocatives, namely the function of Call and the function of Addressee-Confirmation. What we found was that *Du NP!* never can be used in Call-Function. Since this seems to be the most basic function of a vocative phrase, the term Pseudo-Vocative seems to be justified. Second, we have pointed out that there are several differences between the German *Du Idiot!* and its Swedish correlate *Din idiot!* These data show that there are language-specific ways of conveying the evaluative force typically connected with these constructions. Third, we discussed German data showing the expressiveness of the *Du-NP*-construction. In comparison with the comparative construction *Du-als-NP*, it became clear that the derogatory force of constructions like *Du Idiot!* ('You idiot!') and *Du Lehrer!* ('You teacher!') is connected with its semantics as well as with pragmatic processes.

Notes

1. That we use language in cases like that at all has possibly other reasons. In prayers, we hope that there is someone hearing us, talking to machines is like expressing our thoughts or feelings analogue to ordinary interpersonal communication.
2. It is not obvious if this is part of the communicative intention described by Grice (1957) or if this is a condition that must be satisfied independently.
3. Cf. Nehring ([1933] 1977: 101): "So läßt sich für die Funktion des Vokativs eine erste Bestimmung geben: Er dient dazu, eine zweite Person auf sich selbst als den vom Sprecher Gemeinten hinzuweisen." [So we can give a first definition of the function of the vocative: It indicates to a second person that she/he is meant by the speaker.]
4. The requirement that speaker and addressee 'know' is probably too strong, but they should at least have good reasons to suppose that the mentioned relations hold.
5. Cf. the list in Zwicky (1974: 788).
6. Cf. Zwicky (1974: 797): "When calls occur within sentences, they signal the interruption of one discourse by another."
7. Cf. also Schaden (2010) who proposes three basic functions of vocatives: identification of the addressee, predication of a property w.r.t. the addressee, activation of the addressee.

8. That is the first part, getting attention. In this case, identification must be taken care of by non-linguistic means.
9. There are a few predicates in German that require an object in the Genitive case: *sich annehmen* ('minister to'), *bedürfen* ('need'), *beschuldigen* ('accuse'), *sich bewusst sein* ('be aware'), *bezichtigen* ('accuse'), *sich enthalten* ('abstain'), *entheben* ('depose'), *sich entledigen* ('dispose'), *entraten* ('lack'), *sich entsinnen* ('recall'), *sich erfreuen* ('rejoice'), *sich erinnern* ('remember'), *gedenken* ('commemorate'), *harren* ('await'), *kundig sein* ('know'), *verweisen* ('expel').
10. See also Corver (2008) who cites two other Swedish informants.

References

Altmann, Hans
    1981   *Formen der 'Herausstellung' im Deutschen. Rechtsversetzung, Linksversetzung, Freies Thema und verwandte Konstruktionen.* Tübingen: Niemeyer.
Anderson, John M.
    2007   *The Grammar of Names.* Oxford: Oxford University Press.
Beltoft, Søren
    2001   Din nisse [You fool]. *Nyt fra Sprognævnet* 3: 48–51.
Chierchia, Gennaro and Sally McConnell-Ginet
    1990   *Meaning and Grammar.* Cambridge, Mass.: MIT Press.
Corver, Norbert
    2008   Uniformity and diversity in the syntax of evaluative vocatives. *Journal of Comparative Germanic Linguistics* 11: 43–93.
d'Avis, Franz Josef
    2004   Über Parenthesen. In *Deutsche Syntax: Empirie und Theorie,* Franz Josef d'Avis (ed.), 259–279. (Göteborger Germanistische Forschungen 46.) Göteborg: Acta Universitatis Gothoburgensis.
[Duden] Dudenredaktion (eds.)
    2005   *Die Grammatik.* Mannheim: Dudenverlag.
Grice, Herbert Paul
    1957   Meaning. *The Philosophical Review* 66 (3): 377–388.
Havryliv, Oksana
    2003   *Pejorative Lexik. Untersuchungen zu ihrem semantischen und kommunikativ-pragmatischen Aspekt am Beispiel moderner deutschsprachiger, besonders österreichischer Literatur.* Frankfurt/Main: Peter Lang.

Havryliv, Oksana
2009   *Verbale Aggression. Formen und Funktionen am Beispiel des Wienerischen.* Frankfurt/Main: Peter Lang.

Hill, Virginia.
2007   Vocatives and the pragmatics-syntax interface. *Lingua* 117: 2077–2105.

Hom, Christopher
2007   The semantics of racial epithets. *Journal of Philosophy* 105: 416–440.

Jacobs, Joachim
2008   Wozu Konstruktionen? *Linguistische Berichte* 213: 3–44.

Kaplan, David
2004   The meaning of *ouch* and *oops*: Explorations in the theory of meaning as use. Typescript.

Kjellmer, Göran
1976   Du pacifist – din pacifist [You pacifist – you pacifist]. *Språkvård* 1: 8–14.

Levinson, Stephen
2000   *Presumptive Meaning. The Theory of Generalized Conversational Implicature.* Cambridge, Mass.: MIT Press.

Lyons, John
1977   *Semantics.* Vol. 1. Cambridge: Cambridge University Press.

McCready, Eric
2010   Varieties of conventional implicature. *Semantics & Pragmatics* 3: 1–57.

Meibauer, Jörg
2006   Implicature. In *Encyclopedia of Language and Linguistics*, 2nd ed., Vol. 5., Keith Brown (ed.), 568–580. Oxford: Elsevier.

Mcibaucr, Jörg
2013   Expressive compounds in German. *Word Structure* 6.1: 21–42.

Nehring, Alfons
1977   Anruf, Ausruf und Anrede. In *Festschrift Theodor Siebs zum 70. Geburtstag 26. August 1932*, Walther Steller (ed.), 95–144. (Germanistische Abhandlungen, begründet von Karl Weinhold, fortgeführt von Friedrich Vogt, herausgegeben von Walther Steller, 67. Heft.) Reprint. Hildesheim/New York: Georg Olms. Original edition, Breslau: M. & H. Marcus, 1933.

Neu, Jerome
2008   *Sticks and Stones. The Philosophy of Insults.* Oxford: Oxford University Press.

Nunberg, Geoffrey, Ivan Sag, and Thomas Wasow
1994   Idioms. *Language* 70: 491–538
Potts, Christopher
2006   The expressive dimension. *Theoretical Linguistics* 33 (2), 165–
            197.
Potts, Christopher
forthc.   Conventional implicature and expressive content. In *Semantics:
            An International Handbook of Natural Language Meaning*,
            Claudia Maienborn, Klaus von Heusinger, and Paul Portner
            (eds.). Berlin/New York/Peking: Mouton de Gruyter.
Predelli, Stefano
2008   Vocatives. *Analysis* 68 (2): 97–105.
Rauh, Gisa
2004   Warum "Linguist" in "ich/du Linguist" kein Schimpfwort sein
            muß. Eine konversationstheoretische Erklärung. *Linguistische
            Berichte* 197: 77–105.
[SAG] Andersson, Erik, Staffan Hellberg, and Ulf Telemann
1999   *Svenska Akademiens Grammatik*. In collaboration with Lisa
            Christensen, Helena Hansson, Lena Lötmarker and Bo-A. Wendt.
            Stockholm: Norstedts Ordbok.
Saka, Paul
2007   *How to Think About Meaning*. Dordrecht: Springer.
Schaden, Gerhard
2010   Vocatives: A Note on Addressee-Management. *University of
            Pennsylvania Working Papers in Linguistics*, Volume 16.1: Pro-
            ceedings of the 33rd Annual Penn Linguistics Colloquium, 176–
            185.
Schegloff, Emanuel A.
1968   Sequencing in conversational openings. *American Anthropologist*
            70: 1075–1095.
Schlenker, Philippe
2007   Expressive presuppositions. *Theoretical Linguistics* 33: 237–245.
Schwyzer, Eduard
1939   Die Parenthese im engern und im weitern Sinne. *Abhandlungen
            der Preußischen Akademie der Wissenschaften 1939, Philoso-
            phisch-Historische Klasse*. Nr. 6. Berlin: Verlag der Akademie
            der Wissenschaften, Walter de Gruyter in Kommission.
Vater, Heinz
2000   „Pronominantien" – oder: Pronomina sind Determinantien. In
            Deutsche Grammatik in Theorie und Praxis, Rolf Thieroff,

Matthias Tamrat, Nanna Fuhrhop, and Oliver Teuber (eds.), 185–199. Tübingen: Niemeyer.

Welte, Werner
    1980   Zur Syntax, Semantik und Pragmatik exklamatorischer Vokative. *Indogermanische Forschungen* 85: 1–34.

Zifonun, Gisela, Ludger Hoffmann, and Bruno Strecker
    1997   *Grammatik der deutschen Sprache*. Berlin, New York: Walter de Gruyter.

Zwicky, Arnold M.
    1974   Hey, Whatsyourname! In *Papers from the Tenth Regional Meeting of the Chicago Linguistic Society*, Michael W. LaGaly, Robert A. Fox, and Anthony Bruck (eds.), 787–801. Chicago: Chicago Linguistic Society.

Vocative and the grammar of calls

Tore Janson

Abstract

Vocative forms appear in calls, which constitute a type of utterances; other
types are statements, questions, and commands. Grammatical descriptions
usually focus on sentences, the grammatical form of statements. This paper
presents a sketch of the grammar of calls.

The basic form of a call is a noun phrase denoting a person. Calls may
include special marking to show the utterance type. There may be markers
outside the noun phrase (utterance marking) or marking within the noun
phrase (noun phrase marking). Some languages have one of the types and
some have both. The types typically do not interfere but occur independently of each other.

Utterance marking consists of special intonation or of an optional vo-
calic particle. Noun phrase marking may consist of suppletion, contraction
or apocope of the noun, or of addition of an affix. The noun then has a
special vocative form. In languages with obligatory case marking, noun
marking of calls and marking of case may interfere in complex ways.

1. The nature of the vocative

The term 'vocative' occurs regularly in grammatical descriptions of various
languages, but theoretically inclined linguists rarely use it. It does not even
figure as an entry in standard handbooks such as Trask and Stockwell
(2007), or even the 14-volume *Encyclopedia of Language & Linguistics*
(Brown 2006).

To see why this is so, one has to consider the history of the term. 'Vocative (case)' in English renders the Latin *(casus) vocativus* (which was in its
turn originally translated from the Greek *(ptosis) kletike*). The Latin term or
its variants in modern languages has been employed in Latin grammars for
a very long time, to denote certain forms of nouns and adjectives. The
relevant categories for nominal inflection in Greek and Latin are gender,
number and case, and vocative has been listed as one of the cases.

However, grammarians and linguists since antiquity have been aware of
the fact that there is a difference between vocative forms and the other case

forms. The other case forms, such as nominative, accusative and dative forms, mark relations within the sentence, and that has always been regarded as the basic function of case. Vocative forms do not do that. Still, the vocative forms fit neatly in with the other case forms in the paradigms of declension in Latin, Greek and several other languages. Therefore, the term stayed in general use in morphological descriptions.

But with the rise of serious interest in syntax and semantics in the 20th century, the situation changed. Functions of cases and meanings of cases have been investigated in depth, and there is now an extensive literature, as well as several competing views on many problems. An overview is provided in a massive recent handbook (Malchukov and Spencer 2009). In almost all these discussions, case is regarded as something that has to do with the relation between a noun phrase and other constituents. Some scholars regard cases as universally present in languages, regardless of marking, while others employ the term only to discuss languages with marking. A succinct definition according to the latter view is found in Blake (2001: 1): "Case is a system of marking dependent nouns for the type of relationship they bear to their heads." But even though linguists may have various views on the nature of case, almost all seem to agree that vocative does not belong there. Thus, it usually does not figure in linguistic discussions of case.

In my view, there is no doubt that this is reasonable. The vocative has been lumped with the cases because of the nature of nominal morphology in some Indo-European languages, but in a descriptive framework that is suitable for languages in general that is not a rational arrangement.

But if it does not fit in with the cases, where does it fit in? Remarkably few seem to have asked that obvious question. A new, well-informed paper on vocative (Daniel and Spencer 2009) revolves around the problem whether vocative is a case and quite convincingly shows that it is not like the other cases. There is little discussion, in that paper or elsewhere, about the general nature of the phenomena that are referred to by the term 'vocative'.

The reason seems to be that ever since Aristotle, grammatical description focuses mainly on the constituents of sentences. Typically, vocatives are found outside sentences. Linguists therefore tend to dismiss them altogether, or to take an interest only in the vocatives that can be regarded as embedded in sentences or related to sentences.

This is unfortunate, in my view. It is an incontrovertible observational fact that people produce many utterances that belong to language but are not formed as sentences. In any full descriptive grammar, several types of utterances are described, with varying terminology; reasonably adequate descriptions usually distinguish at least five types. There are statements, questions, commands, calls, and exclamations. The last one is really a cover term for various utterances of no relevance here. One may also distinguish some minor utterance types, such as greetings. These types appear in all or almost all languages. Statements and questions usually have the syntactic form of sentences, including a verb phrase with noun phrase argument(s). If they do not, they can be reasonably regarded as consisting of incomplete sentences. Commands and calls are not normally sentences, and can be analysed as sentences only by the questionable device of assuming that vital parts are obligatorily deleted. Typical commands consist of a verb phrase only, and typical calls of a noun phrase only. The term 'vocative (case)' has primarily been used to classify markers that are found in the noun phrases of calls.

The distinction made above between different types of utterances has to be made, in one way or another, in any full grammatical description of a language. In practice, much more attention has been accorded to the utterances that are sentence-formed than to the ones that are not. However, there are now several studies of commands and exclamatives; see for example Aikhenvald (2010), Michaelis (2001). There are relations between form and function, and between form and meaning, in calls too. The remainder of this paper is an attempt to describe the grammatical properties of calls.

2. The grammar of calls

Calls seem to be employed in all human languages. The function is primarily to address someone, that is, to get someone's attention in order to begin or continue a conversation.

The grammatical form of a call is just a noun phrase. Typically, it consists of a name or some other designation for a human. In English, calls are not marked in any special way:

(1)   *Martha!*

(2)   *Mother!*

It seems that such utterances can be made in all or most languages. Many languages, possibly most, lack overt markers just as English, for example Wari'. An example (Everett and Kern 1997: 218):

(3) *te*
     father.1SG
     'Dad!'

In some languages nouns may have an affix marking it as a call. Examples from Malayalam (Asher and Kumari 1997: 224):

(4) *nampyaar-ee*
     Nambiar-VOC
     'Nambiar!' (name)

(5) *moon-ee*
     son-VOC
     'Son!'

Sometimes a special particle marks the utterance as a call. An example form Hawaiian (Alexander 1968: 11):

(6) *e keoni*
     VOC.PART. John
     'John!'

Beyond the noun phrase there is normally nothing at all: no other noun phrases (except for coordination), no verb phrases, no adverbs. There may be exceptions, but they should be rather marginal. Thus, calls have a particular grammatical form, clearly different from the grammatical form of statements and questions, the sentence.[1]

The noun phrase in a call is semantically constrained, as it denotes someone the speaker has decided to address. Normally the addressee is a human being, but speakers may wish to address much else too: animals and gods, of course, but sometimes also an urn, a wall, the universe, and so on. When making such a call, the speaker at least temporarily entertains the fiction that the addressee is able to interpret utterances.

The noun phrase mostly has the same properties as other noun phrases in the language. This means, among other things, that it may consist of a pronoun and may include modifiers such as adjectives, relative clauses and so on. Some examples in English:

(7) *You!*

(8) *Little boy!*

(9) *You who called out!*

Thus, the grammar of a call is similar to the grammar of a part of a sentence. However, there are several restrictions on the content of vocative NPs. One of them is that the noun phrase is not normally indefinite. Thus, for example, this is a normal call in English:

(10) *Waiter!*

However, this utterance can hardly be interpreted as a call:

(11) *A waiter!*

It is not addressed to a specific person but is a request for the appearance of a person.

A call is distinguished from other utterance types by the absence of a verb phrase and any other constituents, but it can also be marked by other means.

That marking can be made in two ways. The call is an utterance that consists of a noun phrase, and normally nothing more. It is then possible to mark the whole utterance, for example by using special prosody, or by adding some content in addition to the noun phrase. It is also possible to modify the noun phrase itself, using morphological or other devices. That is, there are three possibilities: no special marking, utterance marking, and noun phrase marking. Mostly, it is easy to distinguish between them, although there may well be borderline cases. Anyhow, I will treat them separately here.

In the following, I make a brief survey of the types of marking that have been found so far, according to the distinction just made. It is followed by some conclusions. The survey is based upon earlier studies, Daniel and Spencer (2009) in particular, and additional data from various languages.

3. The marking of calls

3.1. No marking

In my view, the most remarkable fact about call marking is that it is often either non-existing or sporadic. In that, it differs from other grammatical marking, such as marking for gender, for number, for case, or for tense. If a language marks nouns for number, for example, the usual situation is that, in principle, all nouns are so marked. There may be exceptions (an obvious one is for mass nouns), but usually the markers are not just optionally applied or found just on nouns of a special formal type. Possibly, marking of utterances generally works in a different way than marking of constituents, but that remains to be investigated.

The large majority of the languages of the world seem not to employ any type of marking for calls. Unfortunately one cannot be very sure, as there are no good grammars for most languages, and reports about calls tend to be scanty or non-existent even in otherwise good descriptions. A full typological survey would certainly be much needed, although Daniel and Spencer (2009) is a good beginning. There is no strong reason to believe that there are many under-investigated languages with rich morphology for calls, for example, but in the absence of a systematic examination one cannot exclude the possibility.

3.2. Utterance marking

It seems that calls are often distinguished by special intonation. Unfortunately, the study of such linguistic aspects of intonation has not advanced very far, and Daniel and Spencer (2009: 628) make just a couple of hints; but see Göksel and Pöchtrager (this volume). Until further work has been done in that area, it is hard to know how important intonation is in this respect. However, a number of other prosodic devices are also used as general markers in various languages; Daniel and Spencer (2009: 628–629) provide examples of stress shift, tone alternation, and vowel lengthening. All those types of prosodic marking seem to operate as utterance markers only, without any relation to marking of noun phrases.

The other main type of utterance marking is by additional segmental information. A large number of languages have vocative particles that may occur with the noun phrase without being an integrated part of it. In most cases the presence of such markers is optional in principle, but is often related to such factors as style or the social relation between speaker and addressee.

Many early Indo-European languages may have *o* before the noun; in some languages, such as Sanskrit and Old Irish, it is *a*. It is generally reconstructed as **o* for Proto-Indo-European. It occurs before the noun phrase and is phonologically a full word rather than a clitic. It is still found in several languages of the family, such as English. The particle is more frequent in some languages and some periods than in others, but it seems that it has nowhere been obligatory. It may be used or not used, depending on such factors as style or level of formality.[2]

Similar particles occur in many languages of the world. Several Semitic languages, including Arabic, have *ya*. Zulu has *e* (Doke 1961: 281), and so have several Oceanic languages (Daniel and Spencer 2009: 630). Dongolawi, an Eastern Sudanic language with case inflection, has a prefix *wo-* or *w-* (Armbruster 1960: 161). Korean has prefixed or suffixed particles, most often *-ya* (Lee 1989: 69).

As for the formal properties of these markers, Daniel and Spencer (2009: 230) remark that they are always vowels or semivowels. In many languages they are phonologically independent, but at least in Dongolawi and in Korean, it seems clear that the particles are clitics. Most occur before the noun phrase, but there are exceptions. Both the Arabic and the Korean particles can be postposed, and so can the *o* in Albanian.[3]

3.3. Noun phrase marking

The call may also be marked by use of some special form or forms in the noun phrase. It seems that utterance marking is not correlated with noun phrase marking of calls: in a given call, both types may occur, or either, or none. If the noun has a special vocative form or not seems to have no relevance for the use of particle in Indo-European languages. For example, in ancient Greek, the name *Kratylos* (nominative) has the special vocative form *Kratyle*, while the name *Menon* (nominative) is *Menon* also in the vocative. Both can be used with or without particle in calls:

(12) *O Kratyle!*

(13) *Kratyle!*

(14) *O Menon!*

(15) *Menon!*

In Zulu, with obligatory marking of all nouns (see below), the use of the particle *e* is optional in any call.

The head of the noun phrase is normally a noun, and the most frequent form of marking is to use a special form of that noun. In some languages there is also marking of pronouns and of modifiers such as adjectives. For example, in Latin there is a special vocative form for masculine singular in one morphological class of adjectives:

(16) *Optim-e   amic-e!*
  best-VOC friend-VOC
  'Best friend!'

But I leave most of that aside here, and discuss mainly noun marking.

Noun marking is universal in very few languages; mostly, it is used only with a subset of the nouns, such as only names and kinship nouns, or only nouns with a special type of inflection. In some languages, both semantic and morphological restrictions apply.

In what follows, a sample of languages with non-universal noun marking is presented. After that, a few languages with universal noun marking are discussed.

In Modern Bulgarian, there is no case inflection, and most nouns have just a singular form and a plural form. But some names and other personal nouns have a non-vocative form and a vocative form in the singular, while plural vocative forms do not exist. See Girvin (this volume) and Daniel and Spencer (2009: 627). Historically, the vocative forms are remnants of the older Indo-European system to be discussed below, and it seems that they are now on their way out. The reference forms sometimes occur in calls, and names that are recently introduced in the language sometimes only have a reference form but no vocative form.

In a number of languages, vocative forms may be formed through contraction or apocope. A well-known example is the so-called neo-vocative in Russian. Nouns ending in *-a* or *-ya* drop the final vowel, for example non-vocative *Lena* vs. vocative *Len!* The forms are found with names and with some kinship terms, such as *papa* and *mama* (vocatives *Pap!* and *Mam!*, respectively). See Daniel and Spencer (2009: 628).

A very similar situation is reported from Seediq (Tsukida 2005: 301). There, names and some kinship terms have special vocative forms that consist just of the last syllable of the stem; the vocative for *Masaw* (a name) is *Saw!*

In Tariana, an Amazonian language, nominal inflection is generally quite complex. Relevant categories are gender, number, case, and noun class, but also nominal tense and extralocality. Kinship nouns are marked obligatorily in calls (Aikhenvald 2003: 68–72). A few tens of words have special forms. Interestingly, several different formal devices are used. Aikhenvald (2003: 68–72) lists a) full suppletion, such as non-vocative *nuwasádo* 'son of male ego's sister' vs. vocative *tesí*; b) partial suppletion, such as non-vocative *nuwédo* 'younger sister' vs. vocative *nuedú*; c) subtraction of gender suffix, such as *nuphéri* / *nuphéru* 'elder brother / elder sister' vs. *nuphé* 'Brother! / Sister!'; d) stress shift, such as non-vocative *nunídua* 'wife's sister' vs. vocative *nuniduá*.

In the same language, an important group of names also have vocative forms. "To create a vocative form of a personal name of Portuguese origin, the final syllable of the name (which is usually longer than two syllables) is omitted, and stress shifted onto the last syllable, e. g. *Olívia* – vocative *Olí*, *Cándido* – vocative *Candí*, […]" (Aikhenvald 2003: 71). A small number of other names also have similar formation (Aikhenvald 2003: 70).

Setswana belongs to the Bantu languages, which have no case marking; noun inflection consists almost exclusively of prefixes. The language mostly has no markers in calls, but a handful of nouns exhibit what looks like inflection by suffix (Cole 1967: 396–397). They are *mme* 'mother', *rre* 'father', *ngwanake* 'my child', *mogatsake* 'my spouse', and a few other words for close relatives. When used as calls, the final vowel of these words is *-a*: *Mma! Rra! Ngwanaka! Mogatsaka!*

Further, it is reported that "(i)n several Uralic languages, designations of near relatives (as father, mother) may have a kind of vocative" (Collinder 1960: 239). This marking consists of what was historically a possessive suffix for first person but has become obsolete in other contexts than calls. An example from Vote is *mu sõbrani* '(My) friend!'. The word/particle *mu*, with the (previous) meaning 'my', occurs only in calls.

As can be seen from the examples above, it is not uncommon for languages to have vocative forms for a restricted set of nouns, usually names and/or kinship nouns. They may be obligatory in calls, or optional. When the forms are optional, it seems that the choice is often dictated by such factors as style and emotional colouring.

Some languages have markers for a wider range of calls. The most well-known instances of such marking are found in old Indo-European languages and modern Slavic languages. As has already been mentioned, several early languages mark nouns in calls by inflection, and this device is reconstructed as emanating from zero marking in Proto-Indo-European (Szemerényi 1999: 159). Because of later developments, most languages actually have markers that consist of suffixes.

In these languages, a noun can be analysed as consisting of a stem and a suffix, and the form of the suffix indicates both number and case. For example, in Latin:

(17) *serv-orum*
     slave-GEN.PL
     'of (the) slaves'

and

(18) *serv-us*
    'slave'-NOM.SG
    'slave'

In calls, some nouns (and adjectives) have a special form in the singular that is not found in other contexts, the vocative form. In Latin:

(19) *serv-e*
    slave-VOC.SG
    'Slave!'

However, other nouns have no special form of that kind, but the form for the nominative case is used in calls. In Latin:

(20) *civ-is*
    citizen-NOM.SG
    'citizen'

and

(21) *civ-is*
    citizen-VOC.SG
    'Citizen!'

See (12)–(15) above for similar examples from Greek. In the plural (and in the dual, of which there are remnants in several early languages), the form used is always identical with that of the nominative case.

Whether a noun has special vocative singular inflection generally depends upon gender and inflectional class, or declension. Indo-European languages generally distinguish between three genders: masculine, feminine, and neuter. Neuters never have vocative inflection. The systems of declension differ in several ways between languages, but generally, masculine and feminine forms of some formal types have special vocative forms, while others have not.

There is a general problem here, though, that concerns both Indo-European languages and other languages with case marking in nouns. One may analyse the situation in two ways. The nominative forms may be regarded as an unmarked form; there are some reasons to do that, one of them being that it is often used as the reference form in metalinguistic contexts. If that is so, many calls lack noun phrase marking. This is the view of Daniel and Spencer (2009) and most other modern treatments. Alternatively, all forms occurring in calls may be regarded as vocatives, that is markers for calls, although some are homophonous with nominative forms. This latter form of analysis is implied by most traditional grammars.

Before turning to the question which analysis is preferable, other languages should be considered. The Indo-European languages discussed are case-marking languages, that is, they have a variety of morphological noun forms for marking of various cases. Now, if the case system of a language is pervasive and does not allow for the possibility of noun phrases in sentences that are unmarked for case, what form should be used in calls?

Obviously, there are two alternatives. A special vocative form, not found in sentences, may be used in calls, or one of the forms marked for case in sentences may have to do double duty. Both alternatives are found in some languages of the world.

In a few languages, the form used in calls is homophonous with some clearly marked case form, such as the oblique plural (Kati), the allative (Khanti), or the possessive (Udihe), and in Arabic the accusative is used in some contexts; see Daniel and Spencer (2009: 630–631).

A few case-marking languages have the other solution, universal noun marking of calls. Two rather different cases are Georgian and Turkana.

Georgian is treated in Abuladze and Ludden (this volume); see also Daniel and Spencer (2009: 627, 629, 633–634). It is a language with rich agglutinative morphology and obligatory case marking by suffixes for nouns. The system is unusually complete: there do not seem to exist any 'reference' or 'unmarked' forms of nouns. Paradigms for Georgian noun declension regularly include vocative as a case, just as paradigms for Latin and other Indo-European languages. However, it seems that in modern Georgian, the vocative form is always different from all case forms. The markers used are -*o*, -*v* (obsolescent), and zero marking. Both nouns and adjectives have vocative forms. Even the pronouns 'you (sg.)' and 'you (pl.)' have vocative and non-vocative forms. Thus, it seems that all kinds of noun phrases in calls are obligatorily marked in this language.

In Turkana, an Eastern Nilotic language, there is also a system of case marking, albeit of a different formal type. According to Dimmendaal (1983: 66), "case is marked by way of tonal inflection". There are different tonal contours for the various cases. Dimmendaal (1983: 67) includes vocative among the cases, remarking that "[t]his case differs from the others" in that it is used outside the context of a sentence. The tonal contours for pronouns and for nouns used in calls are described (Dimmendaal 1983: 260, 268). It seems that in this language, the tone contours of noun phrases in calls are consistently different from tone contours of noun phrases in sentences. In Turkana, too, it seems that all nouns are obligatorily marked for case and that a neutral or reference type of tone contour cannot be identified. At least that is how I interpret Dimmendaal's presentation.

It can be seen, then, that in case-marking languages, noun phrase marking in sentences and noun phrase marking in calls tend to interfere. If case marking in sentences is consistent, there are no forms of nouns that can be regarded as unmarked for case, and in calls one must use either a form marked for some case, or a special vocative form. Both solutions are found in some languages: a language such as Kati employs a case form (Daniel and Spencer 2009: 630), while Georgian and Turkana use a special vocative form.

To return to the situation in early Indo-European and Slavic, it seems to be a kind of compromise between the two different solutions. Some nouns, including many names, are clearly marked in calls, but many other nouns occur in the not fully distinctive nominative form. Thus, there is an unusually complex relationship between case marking and marking of calls in those languages.

There seem to be very few languages without case-marking that have universal noun phrase marking in calls. A rare instance is Zulu, which is a Bantu language and has no morphological marking of case.

In Bantu languages, nouns belong to noun classes, sometimes called genders as their grammatical role is somewhat reminiscent of that of gender in several Indo-European languages. However, the number of different noun classes in a Bantu language may be quite large. Noun stems carry prefixes that mark noun class and number, and there is an elaborate concordance system by which corresponding prefixes are attached to modifiers as well as to verbal forms.

The prefixes of nouns consist of a CV syllable in most Bantu languages. An example from Swahili:

(22) *ki-tu*   *vi-tu*
　　　PREFIX.SG-thing   PREFIX.PL.-thing
　　　'thing'   'things'

However, in Zulu and some other Bantu languages the noun prefix normally has the form VCV. The first vowel of the prefix in such forms is often called 'augment'; see Maho (1999: 60–63). An example:

(23) *u-mu-ntu*   *a-ba-ntu*
　　　AUGMENT-PREFIX.SG-man   AUGMENT-PREFIX.PL.-man
　　　'man'   'men'

In some Bantu languages, forms with and without the augment seem to occur without any clear pattern, but in others the distinction is used for various grammatical purposes. In Zulu, forms without augment are used in calls, and forms with augment are employed elsewhere (Doke 1961: 280–282). Thus, for example:

(24) *a-ba-fana*   *ba-fana*
    AUGMENT-PREFIX.PL.-child   PREFIX.PL.-child
    'children'   'Children!'

Consonant deletions and other phonological processes complicate this marking system to some extent (see Doke 1961: 281), but it seems that a head noun in calls always has a prefix that is different from the one used in sentences. However, the personal pronouns *wena* 'you (sg.)' and *nina* 'you (pl.)' do not vary in form.

A similar usage seems to exist in at least one other Bantu language, Kinyarwanda; see Kimenyi (2006: 221). However, the augment in that language is used also to mark definiteness, so the situation is somewhat less clear.

In Zulu, and perhaps other Bantu languages, a variation in the form of noun markers has been utilized for universal marking of calls. This seems to be an example of eliminating a type of free variation by associating it with a functional distinction.

4. Conclusions

From the investigation presented above one may draw some general conclusions.

In the first part of the paper, it was pointed out that markers often named 'vocative' are used for signalling not a case, but a type of utterance. Thus, the information they convey is that the utterance is a call, not a statement, a question, or a command.

Calls consist of a noun phrase only, and the head is a name or some other designation of someone who can be addressed. The difference between types of utterances is usually quite obvious to the interpreter even without special markers, as calls are normally easy to recognize. Therefore, special markers are rarely needed for information, and it is just to be expected that very many languages do quite well without such devices.

There may be marking, though. It may be of two types: marking of the whole utterance or marking within the noun phrase.

Utterance marking may be made by prosodic means or consist of a special marker, most often a vowel, which is added to the noun phrase. Such marking seems to be optional in all languages that have it.

Noun phrase marking, which occurs independently of utterance marking, usually consists of a special 'vocative' form of the head noun. Mostly it is restricted to some types of nouns. Names and kinship nouns figure most frequently.

In languages with universal marking for case, the morphology of calls tends to interfere with other noun morphology. Case markers may be homophonous with call markers, or calls may have universal morphological marking.

Except for case-marking languages, marking of calls is almost always optional and/or semantically restricted. The universal marking in Zulu (and perhaps other Bantu languages) is exceptional and is connected with a very unusual morphological structure.

Notes

1. This grammatical form could be called a vocative, if there is a need for a technical term. In a similar vein, the grammatical form of a command could be called an imperative. Both these terms would then refer to entities of the same theoretical status as that of sentences.
2. It should be noted that *o* is also used for other purposes in many Indo-European languages from early times and onwards, in particular as an interjection expressing surprise, grief etc. (Mallory and Adams 2006: 359). Something similar is true for *e* in Zulu (Doke 1961: 281); it may be used alone for drawing attention to the presence of the speaker. Possibly, those utterance markers are often related to other kinds of discourse particles.
3. Welsh used to have a marker that triggered the phonological process of mutation of the initial consonant of the following noun. The particle has now disappeared, so that calls are marked only by mutation: see Daniel and Spencer (2009: 629). This may be regarded as a transition from utterance marking to noun phrase marking.

References

Abuladze, Lia and Andreas Ludden
    this vol.   Der Vokativ im Georgischen.
Aikhenvald, Alexandra Y.
    2003   *A Grammar of Tariana, From Northwest Amazonia.* Cambridge: Cambridge University Press.

Aikhenvald, Alexandra Y.
2010   *Imperatives and Commands.* Oxford: Oxford University Press.
Alexander, William De Witt
1968   *A Short Synopsis of the Most Essential Points in Hawaiian Grammar.* Rutland, Vt: Tuttle.
Armbruster, Charles Hubert
1960   *Dongolese Nubian: A Grammar.* Cambridge: Cambridge University Press.
Asher, Ronald E. and T. C. Kumar
1997   *Malayalam.* London: Routledge.
Blake, Barry J.
2001   *Case.* 2d ed. Cambridge: Cambridge University Press.
Brown, Keith (ed.)
2006   *Encyclopedia of Language & Linguistics*, 2d ed. 14 Vols. Amsterdam: Elsevier.
Cole, Desmond T.
1967   *An Introduction to Tswana Grammar.* London: Longmans.
Collinder, Björn
1960   *Comparative Grammar of the Uralic Languages.* Stockholm: Almqvist & Wiksell.
Daniel, Michael and Andrew Spencer
2009   The vocative – an outlier case. In *The Oxford Handbook of Case*, Andrej Malchukov and Andrew Spencer (eds.), 626–634. Oxford: Oxford University Press.
Dimmendaal, Gerrit J.
1983   *The Turkana Language.* Dordrecht: Foris.
Doke, Clement Martyn
1961   *Textbook of Zulu Grammar.* 6th ed. Cape Town: Longmans.
Everett, Daniel L. and Barbara Kern
1997   *Wari'.* London: Routledge.
Göksel, Aslı and Markus Pöchtrager
this vol.   The prosodic vocative and its kin.
Kimenyi, Alexandre
2006   Kinyarwanda. In *Encyclopedia of Language & Linguistics*, 2d ed., Vol. 10, Keith Brown (ed.), 217–223. Amsterdam: Elsevier.
Lee, Hansol H. B.
1989   *Korean Grammar.* Oxford: Oxford University Press.
Maho, Jouni Filip
1999   *A Comparative Study of Bantu Noun Classes.* Göteborg: Göteborg University.
Malchukov, Andrej and Andrew Spencer (eds.)
2009   *The Oxford Handbook of Case.* Oxford: Oxford University Press.

Mallory, James P. and Douglas Q. Adams
    2006   *The Oxford Introduction to Proto-Indo-European and the Proto-Indo-European World*. Oxford: Oxford University Press.
Michaelis, Laura
    2001   Exclamative constructions. In *Language Typology and Language Universals*, Martin Haspelmath, Ekkehard König, Wulf Oesterreicher, and Wolfgang Raible (eds.), 1038–1058. Berlin: Mouton de Gruyter.
Szemerényi, Oswald J. L.
    1999   *Introduction to Indo-European Linguistics*. Oxford: Oxford University Press.
Trask, Robert L. and Peter Stockwell
    2007   *Language and Liguistics: The Key Concepts*. 2nd ed. Abingdon: Routledge.
Tsukida, Naomi
    2005   Seediq. In *The Austronesian Languages of Asia and Madagascar*, Alexander Adelaar and Nikolaus Himmelmann (eds.), 291–325. Abingdon: Routledge.

Mexican *güey* – from vocative to discourse marker: a case of grammaticalization?

Friederike Kleinknecht

Abstract

Today's Mexican Spanish is marked by the frequent use of the word *güey*, which may assume a broad variety of functions: noun, adjective, invective, solidarity marker and discourse marker. This paper traces the development from the noun to the discourse marker, with intermediate stages being ritual insult and expressivity marking. The development is explained in several steps: a process of semantic-pragmatic bleaching from the invective use of *güey* to its use as a solidarity marker, then a shift of the vocative's attention-getting function from the interpersonal to the discourse level, and finally, a communicative overuse of the expressive function leading to its reanalysis as a discourse structuring element. The original semantics are preserved only insofar as *güey* is used exclusively within a relationship of solidarity between the collocutors. Finally it will be argued that the development of *güey* is not an instance of grammaticalization, although there are many similarities: the term routinization is proposed as a hyperonym.

1. Introduction

Vocatives are a genuine element of spoken language. Their essence is directly addressing the hearer. In written language, where there is usually a spatio-temporal distance between the interactants, their use is necessarily different and rarer. Since linguists have only recently begun to investigate oral discourse systematically, vocatives have been treated marginally for many centuries. As a consequence, few authors explicitly discuss vocatives, and even fewer put it in the context of its natural place of occurrence, the spoken language.[1]

Interestingly, there are languages whose speakers make extensive use of a large number of vocatives, while in other languages, these elements are used far more sparsely (cf. Dickey 1996: 190). Speakers of Spanish (in all its varieties), for example, seem to feel a strong need to use a lot of vocatives in their everyday interaction. This observation (see Hasbún Hasbún

2003; Palacios 2002a, 2002b) is supported by the fact that in Spanish there are different routinized vocatives and vocative particles whose uses exceed the traditional vocative functions and which may be described more accurately in terms of discourse marking. Cases in point are the particle *che* in Rioplatense Spanish (Carranza 1996; Dishman 1982), *hombre* in peninsular Spanish (see Álvarez Menéndez 2005: 42) and *güey* in Mexico.

Güey [gwɛj] has become the most characteristic feature of Mexican Spanish since it started to be generalized 30 to 40 years ago. Originally an imprecation with the acceptation 'stupid', 'idiot', in the 1990s it became a vocative marker of solidarity in the address among adolescents (Palacios 2002a, 2002b; Zimmermann 1996). As such, it was subject to such frequent use that nowadays in the vast majority of occurrences there is nothing left of its original semantics or of its vocative function, and it should most appropriately be classified as a discourse marker.

The present paper intends to trace the development of *güey* from its origins until its present use, where we can observe a process of semantic and pragmatic bleaching as well as a drift from the interpersonal level to the text or discourse level. I am taking a diachronic approach, although synchronically the different stages of its evolution still coexist (an instance Hopper (1991: 22) describes as 'layering'). This makes it easier to understand and exemplify the functions it assumes at every stage of the process. In the second part of the paper I raise the question of whether the change *güey* undergoes can be classified as a case of grammaticalization or whether another approach might be more suitable for describing the features of this specific kind of language change.

2. The vocative *güey*

2.1. A working definition

What is a vocative? When are certain occurrences of a word interpreted as vocatives, and when must they be said to assume a different function? A working definition of the term 'vocative' is necessary in order to answer these questions for the purpose of this paper.

In languages with morphological cases, as in Greek, Latin, Russian or Rumanian, the vocative is usually individuated by morphological criteria in addition to its addressing function.[2] However, not only may even in these languages a nominative form be used for addressing instead of the 'correct' vocative form (see Bonnekamp 1971: 23; Svennung 1958; Dickey 1996: 5), but many languages do not even possess morphological means for marking vocatives. Still, these languages do have means of appealing to the addressee with expressions that share the syntactic properties (see Bañón Hernández 1993; Bonnekamp 1971; Haverkate 1978) and the functional spectrum of morphological vocatives. In my opinion, this syntactic-functional parallellism justifies the extension of the term in the sense of a functional vocative. Defining it this way complies with current linguistic custom; moreover, as far as I know, no better term has been suggested.

Following Braun (1988: 7–12), in this paper I shall define the vocative as a (A) nominal (B) free (C) form of address.

(A) Vocatives can be realized by any kind of nominal element, i.e. by nouns and adjectives as well as by pronouns and complex NPs (Braun 1988: 7–9 speaks of 'nouns of address' and 'pronouns of address'; see also Leech 1999: 107). Semantically, they may be (a) names, (b) kinship terms, (c) titles and other additions to given and last names, (d) words that describe a relationship between the collocutors (e.g. *neighbor*), (e) terms of endearment, (f) familiarizers or (g) invectives and similar (see the classifications in Braun 1988: 9–10, Leech 1999: 110–111 and Mazzoleni 1995: 398–402)[3] – with categories (f) and (g) being the most important for the case of *güey*.

(B) Braun (1988: 11–12) differentiates between bound and free forms of address. This is important because nouns and adjectives used for addressing are typically not integrated into the sentence structure (see Bañón Hernández 1993; Panhuis 1986), whereas pronouns are – but the contrary is also possible. For example, on the one hand, (full) pronouns may be used as syntactically unintegrated vocatives, as in

(1) *Qué   onda,   tú?*
     what   wave-3SG,   you-2SG?
     'What's up, **you**?'

while on the other hand, nominal forms of address may be used as bound forms, as in

(2) **Vuestra   merced**   *llega*   *en*   *el*
     your-F.SG   grace-F.SG   arrive-PRS.3SG   in   DET.DEF.M.SG
     momento   *oportuno.*[4]
     moment-M.SG   right-M.SG
     '**Your grace** arrives at the right moment.'

Following Svennung (1958), Braun (1988: 12) calls the bound use of nouns of address 'indirect address', as opposed to their free vocative use.

(C) According to Braun (1988: 7), forms of address are "words and phrases used for addressing. They refer to the collocutor and thus contain a strong element of deixis". They may denote the hearer, but not necessarily, for "their lexical meaning can differ from or even contradict the addressee's characteristics". The pragmatic functions of address will be dealt with in the next section.

Zwicky (1974: 795–796) points out that whenever a speaker chooses to use a vocative, his choice will always reflect several aspects of the interaction, specifically:
- the speaker's attitude toward the addressee
- the speaker's evaluation of the addressee
- the speaker's evaluation of the relationship between the collocutors
- the speaker's attitude towards the interaction
- the degree of politeness and intimacy the speaker considers appropriate
- the speaker's sociocultural background.

Apart from these pragmatic restrictions, vocatives are, to a certain point, interchangeable. Virtually all vocative occurrences could also be filled by some other vocative form. If in a given context a vocative expression cannot possibly be replaced by any other, for semantically and formally similar as it may be, this is an indication that the element in question has ceased to possess its full vocative qualities, and rather, is being subject to a process of desemantization, taking over other functions in discourse.

2.2. Vocative functions of *güey*

The first step to describing the development of *güey* is examining its literal meaning and the functions it assumes as a vocative. In this section, I first trace its origin. Then, I give an overview on the functions ascribed to vocatives by other researchers on the subject, and finally, I provide a classification of my own for the different functions of vocative *güey* parallelly to the functions of vocatives in general.

2.2.1.   Origin of the word

The origin of *güey* [gwɛj] is the word *buey* [bwɛj] 'ox' in its popular pronunciation, typical for lower class speakers in many varieties of Spanish,
with initial /g/ (see Gómez de Silva 2001: *buey*; Lara and Colegio de
México 1996: *buey*, *güey*; Nava Sanchezllanes 2006: 2, 50; Zimmermann
1996: 498). As the word began to be used massively among adolescent
speaker groups and gradually lost its pejorative connotation, this pronunciation was generalized: while invective *buey* and *güey* were still interchangeable, the solidarity or discourse marker *güey* cannot be pronounced
buey anymore.

The frequent, negligent pronunciation of *güey* may result in the
reduction or even omission of the initial consonant, leading to a realization
as [ᵍwɛj], [ɣwɛj] or [wɛj].[5] In the age of the internet and the growing dif-
fusion of English writing habits, youngsters have also started to write the
word as <wey>, thus making the reduced pronunciation explicit (see Nava
Sanchezllanes 2006: 68, 85, 91–93).

The semantic-pragmatic evolution of the word in the Mexican society is
depicted as follows by blogger Queretanita (Queretanita 2009):

> Cuando era pequeñita, por ahí de la década de los 70's, esta expresión
> empezaba a surgir y no era bien visto que alguien la pronunciara, mucho
> menos que la repitiera, porque tenía un sentido netamente ofensivo. [...]
>
> En mis tiempos infantiles, un "güey" era una persona analfabeta, tonta,
> bruta, medio tarada, con una ignorancia que podía equipararse a un
> mastodonte, como el buey. El buey es una bestia de carga; bueno, pues el
> "güey" era una bestia humana. Al más bestia de los bestias se le calificaba
> así. Entonces, no era muy grato que a alguien le pusieran este calificativo,
> claramente era un insulto.
>
> Luego, de los 90 para acá, ya todo mundo es "güey", y no, no es que
> nos hayamos hecho tarugos de repente, sino que la palabra ya tiene otro
> significado, conforme pasó el tiempo y la adoptaron las nuevas
> generaciones, la han hecho suya, modificándola, suavizándola y sí, a falta
> de más vocabulario "culto", surge el "güey" fácil y divertido, como
> paliativo de mocedades jocosas y posmodernas en nuestro México querido.

> [When I was a little girl, round about in the 70s, this expression began to
> arise and it wasn't well seen that somebody pronounced it, much less re-
> peated it, because it had a clearly offensive meaning. [...]
>
> In my childhood, a *güey* was an illiterate, stupid, brutish, nutty person,
> with an ignorance that could be compared to a mastodon, like the ox. The
> ox is a draft animal; well, so the *güey* was a human brute. The most brutish

of all brutes was denoted like this. So, it wasn't very nice to give this name to somebody; clearly, it was an insult.

Later, from the 90s on, the whole world is *güey*, and no, it's not that we've become batty all of a sudden, but the word has acquired a new meaning, as time went by and new generations adopted it, they made it theirs, modifying it, extenuating it, and yes, in default of more "educated" vocabulary, there arises the easy, jolly *güey*, like a palliative of comic and postmodern juvenescence in our beloved Mexico.]

As can be seen, the modification of the pragmatic rules that allow the use of *güey* was accompanied by an adjustment in its semantics. More precisely, we are dealing with a change in several stages. The first step is from the concrete meaning 'ox, castrated bull' to a metaphorical transfer of the ox's assumed qualities – stupidity, brutality, ignorance – to a human. The result is a strong invective with the meaning of 'stupid, idiot' or 'cornuted'.

The invective *buey/güey* may be used as a vocative or as a referential noun. The general quality of invectives, which are most commonly used to insult somebody, makes me suppose that the vocative use was the first to become conventionalized; still, the majority of dictionaries mention the referential use first. However, they also give examples for the vocative use like in the following idiomatic phrase:

(3) *¡Álzalas,*   ***buey/güey!***
     lift-IMP.2SG=DO.F.PL ox-M.SG
     'Look where you step, **stupid**!'
     (Gómez de Silva 2001: *buey*; RAE 2001: *güey*)

Güey may also be used as an adjective with the meaning 'stupid',[6] as in the following examples:

(4) *¡Qué* ***güey***   *soy,*   *no*   *traje*
     how   stupid-SG   be-PRS.1SG   not   bring-PST.PFV.1SG
     el   *pasaporte!*
     DET.DEF.M.SG   passport-M.SG
     'How **stupid** I am, I didn't bring my passport!'
     (Lara and Colegio de México 1996: *güey*)

(5) *Susana   es   bien **güey**,   siempre nos*
    Susana   be-PRS.3SG well stupid-SG always   REFL.1PL
    la   cotorreamos.
    DO.F.SG   chatter-PRS.1PL
    'Susana is really **stupid**, we always make fun of her.' (Company
    Company and Academia Mexicana de la Lengua 2010: *güey*)

As a vocative, *güey* began to be used as a ritual insult (Labov 1972) by adolescents. Ritual insults are a common feature of the language of certain speaker groups, namely of male adolescents, who use it to assure their mutual solidarity as members of the same group (see Bernal 2008; Palacios 2002a; Zimmermann 1996). Their function is similar to Leech's (1999: 110) 'familiarizers' used as solidarity markers between male speakers,[7] but with the difference that their original semantics are strongly pejorative.

The motivation for the solidarity function of invectives seems to be a combination of the preference for taboo words by which adolescents distance themselves from other groups of speakers (Palacios 2002a) with the function of mutual confidence and group solidarity, as if they were to say: 'You adults think 'bastard' is something you don't say, but we do say it, and we know each other so well that we can even call each other a bastard without losing our face.' Accordingly, Stenström and Jörgensen (2008: 655) analyze the use of "expressions that have been criticized by adults" as "highly motivated for phatic purposes". Similarly, Bernal (2008: 796) asserts "the existence of a marked use of expressions that do not fall within the territory of impoliteness, although it could apparently be such a case. These expressions are interpreted as an affiliative signal between interlocutors".

As a result, *güey* is used to assure mutual solidarity – an interpretation Palacios (2002a: 74) describes as follows: "'[H]ablarse de güey' implica identificarse, pertenecer al mismo grupo […] Los adolescentes se identifican con esta forma y están conscientes de su empleo, lo que se refleja en frases como 'nos llevamos de güey' o '¿puedo hablarte de güey?'" ['Talk as *güey*' implies identifying, belonging to the same group […] Adolescents identify themselves with this form and are conscious of its use, which is reflected in sentences like 'we get along as *güey*' or 'can I call you *güey*?']. Company Company and Academia Mexicana de la Lengua (2010: *güey*) give, for this use, the definition "coloq[uial]. Amigo inseparable, compañero: 'Oye, güey, ¿y cómo sigue tu jefa?'" [colloquial. Inseparable friend, fellow: 'Listen, mate, so how is your mother doing?'].

As the use of *güey* as a solidarity marker became conventionalized, the word started to lose its pejorative connotation: first in the context of the adolescent speaker groups that used to employ it as a ritual insult; later on, as the vocative *güey* gained acceptance in the Mexican society, it acquired an almost neutral meaning even in its referential use. The denotation of 'stupid' was lost; what remains is the reference to a '(male) individual'. This reference may still carry some remains of its negative connotation, which is recognized by the main dictionaries in the definitions "Persona desconocida y despreciada" [unknown, despised person] (Lara and Colegio de México 1996: *güey*) or "coloq[uial]/despect[ivo]. Individuo desconocido, fulano" [colloquial/contemptuous. Unknown individual, thingamabob] (Company Company and Academia Mexicana de la Lengua 2010: *güey*); see examples (6) and (7):

(6) *La   entrada   a   la   oficina*
    DET.DEF.F.SG   entrance-F.SG to   DET.DEF.F.SG   office-F.SG
    estaba   llena   de   güeyes
    be-PST.IPFV.3SG full-F.SG   of   ox-M.PL
    'The entrance of the office was full of **people**.' (Lara and Colegio de México 1996: *güey*)

(7) *Me   acordé   de   un   güey   de*
    REFL.1SG   remember-PST.PFV.1SG   of   DET.INDF.M.SG ox-M.SG of
    no   sé   qué   siglo   que   cerró
    not know-PRS.1SG what century-M.SG   REL   close-PST.PFV.3SG
    la   oficina   de patentes   porque   ya
    DET.DEF.F.SG   office.F.SG   of patent-F.PL because   already
    todo   se   había   inventado.
    everything.M.SG REFL.3   AUX.PST.IPFV.3.SG   invent-PTCP
    'I remembered a **guy** of I don't know which century who closed the patent office because everything had already been invented.' (Nava Sanchezllanes 2006: 53)

However, in some contexts, especially among adolescents, referential *güey* may even have a positive meaning, as Nava Sanchezllanes (2006: 72) points out: "[*Güey*] ya no tiene un sentido peyorativo de insulto, sino que por el contrario, puede ser hasta afectivo" [[*Güey*] does not have a pejorative meaning of insult any more, but to the contrary, it may be even affectionate]. An example is (8):

(8) *Se   voltea   bien tierno   este   güey.*
    REFL.3.SG   turn-PRS.3SG   well sweet-M.SG   this-M.SG   guy-M.SG
    'This **guy** turns around in a really sweet way.' (Nava Sanchezllanes 2006: 53)

In discourse, in its invective use, but even more in its bleached acceptation as a solidarity marker, *güey* assumes a variety of functions. In the next section, I investigate the functional spectrum of the vocative as proposed in other related investigations and how these functions may be fulfilled by *güey*, before turning to the question of how these functions change with the overuse of the vocative.

2.2.2. Research overview

In the literature about the vocative, the function most often referred to is the summoning of attention. With the words of García Dini (1998: 57): "[La función apelativa] desde siempre había sido reconocida por los gramáticos como un elemento lingüístico independiente y marginal respecto a la estructura oracional, otorgándole asimismo la función de mero llamamiento o llamada de atención de alguien." [(The addressing function) had always been considered by the grammarians as an independent and marginal linguistic item with respect to the sentence structure, granting it the mere function of calling or seeking somebody's attention.]

Nevertheless, those authors who explicitly deal with the vocative usually recognize at least one additional function. Zwicky (1974: 787) differentiates between 'calls' used for summoning attention and 'addresses' used to maintain the contact, a distinction taken up, amongst others – although with different terminology –, by Mazzoleni (1995: 377) and Dickey (1996: 6). Haverkate (1978: 47) speaks of obligatory 'attention-getting devices' and non-obligatory vocative uses that typically reinforce certain kinds of illocution, like promises or requests. Similarly, the *Esbozo de una nueva gramática de la lengua española* (RAE 1973: 407; cf. Bañón Hernández 1993: 19) mentions an attention-related initial vocative and a central or final vocative used to strengthen or mitigate the expressivity of an utterance – a characterization that is perfectly fitting for the use of *güey*, as will be shown below. García Dini (1998: 57–58) accompanies the appellative function with an emphatic function capable of conferring to the text a pragmatic connotation of joy, grief, anger or other emotions.

Leech (1999: 108) attributes three pragmatic functions to the vocative: summoning attention, addressee identification and establishing or maintaining a social relationship. McCarthy and O'Keefe (2003) take up these categories, expanding the classification on the basis of their own corpus to the following types: relational vocatives, topic management, badinage, mitigators, turn management, and summons – which, interestingly, represent only 4%.

Shiina (2007: 17) adduces the functions of interpersonal, conversational, information, and illocutionary force management, apart from the rare case of a highly dramatic stand-alone vocative. Bañón Hernández (1993) finally, enumerates, for stand-alone vocatives, the functions of greeting/showing of respect, exclamation, order, plea, turn management and evaluation (*vocativo axiológico*), whereas according to him, vocatives integrated in the utterance may have functions of context marking, directing the hearer's attention to a certain part of the speech act, and intensifying or mitigating the illocution or parts of the informational structure.

The functions of vocatives in languages that mark them morphologically (or otherwise) and in those that do not seem to be essentially the same. As pointed out above, even in languages with morphological vocatives, speakers do not always choose the actual vocative form for addressing their collocutor – while, on the contrary, vocative forms may be used in functions other than addressing (Dickey 1996: 5; Svennung 1958: 394–411). Fossilized vocative forms, recognizable or not by morphological features, are found to assume other functions in language such as nominative nouns (like French *monsieur*; see Svennung 1958: 396), interjections (English *gee* < exclamative *Jesus!*; see Gehweiler 2008) or discourse markers, like Spanish *hombre* or *güey*. Thus, vocative forms and vocative functions, though interrelated, do not always match completely and therefore must be treated separately.

In the next section, I attempt to summarize the functions ascribed to the vocative in the literature and provide a classification of my own, giving examples of vocative *güey* and of other vocative forms.

2.2.3. Güey *as a vocative*

All the functions that have been identified above for vocatives in general can also be accomplished by the word *güey*. In the following I illustrate the functional spectrum of *güey* as a vocative in discourse with some examples taken from the corpora of Nava Sanchezllanes (2006) and Palacios (2002a, 2002b). It must be pointed out that in each of the cited examples, another vocative form could fill the slot of *güey*.

As I see it, the different functions referred to in the relevant literature can be summed up in three major categories:

A) Relational functions
B) Functions of summoning attention
C) Functions of emphasis and expressivity

In what follows, I describe them in more detail.

A) Relational functions

The category of relational functions comprises vocatives whose main purpose is to define the relationship between the interlocutors. This function is explicitly mentioned as 'relational vocatives' in McCarthy and O'Keefe (2003) and as 'interpersonal management' in Shiina (2007). Other authors do mention the vocative's relationship-indicating force but without postulating a separate functional category restricted to this kind of use (Bañón Hernández 1993: 103–128; Carranza 1996: 6–7; Mazzoleni 1995: 393–395; Zwicky 1974: 795–796).

Since every given vocative always tells something about the speaker's attitude towards the addressee, towards the relationship between them, and towards the ongoing interaction, this function is inherent to virtually all vocatives. Accordingly, the mere fact of two persons being able to use the solidarity marker *güey* in their linguistic interaction accounts for a certain kind of relationship between them: one of solidarity and equality[8] on a colloquial level. So, every time the vocative *güey* appears in the dialogue (unless it is actually used as an invective), it (re)defines this special kind of relationship.

The function of relationship defining is especially frequent in combination with formulae and routines, such as greetings and other recurrent expressions (see Haverkate 1978: 48; Mazzoleni 1995: 379–380). Since the main function of these linguistic elements is politeness[9] – which implies knowing what kind of relationship there is with a given interlocutor and therefore, how to behave towards him/her – the vocative helps to construct, and reflects the existing relationship, as in (9). This holds for every kind of vocative, although in certain speaker groups *güey* is used almost routinely with this kind of formulae.

By adding a vocative to his utterance, the speaker recognizes and/or emphasizes his relationship with the addressee, as in (10), where *güey* is used to add a facet of empathy and solidarity to the politeness formula *de nada*. Furthermore, the speaker may feel the need to focus on the identity of his collocutor, which is very conveniently achieved by the use of a vocative, as in (11) (see Leech 1999: 108; Mazzoleni 1995: 380). In the case of *güey*, the addressee is identified not by his name but in his quality as a person with whom the speaker knows that it is possible to use *güey* in the interaction.

a)   Use with formulae and routines

(9)   *Cómo   estás   güey?*
       how   be-PRS.2SG   VOC
       'How are you, **güey**?'

b)   Definition of relationship

(10) *S1:   Gracias.*
            thanks
            'Thank you.'
     S2:   De   nada   güey.
            of   nothing   VOC
            'You're welcome, **güey**.' (Palacios 2002a: 81)

c)   Addressee identification and recognition

(11) *Ya   era   como   la   una   y*
     already   be-PST.IPFV.3SG   like   DET.DEF.F.SG   one-F.SG   and
     media,   o   sea,   tú   estabas
     half-F.SG or   be-PRS.SBJV.3SG   you-2SG   be-PST.IPFV.2SG
     despertando,   güey.
     wake_up-GER   VOC
     'It was already about half past one, that is, you were waking up, **güey**.'
     (Nava Sanchezllanes 2006: 62)

Finally, vocative *güey* may be used to mitigate potentially face-threatening speech acts, such as orders or jokes (cf. the 'badinage' function in McCarthy and O'Keefe 2003), by invoking the positive relationship existing between the interlocutors – see example (12):

d)   Mitigation of speech acts and badinage

(12) *Pareces   lavacoches   güey.*
     seem-PRS.2SG   car_washer-M.SG   VOC
     'You look like a car washer, **güey**.' (Nava Sanchezllanes 2006: 62)

B)   Summoning attention

Although the function of summoning attention (similar to Jakobson's [1960] 'phatic function') is usually the first in being mentioned when it comes to the vocative, it is by no means as frequent as one might expect. In fact, the pure summoning function is actually quite rare (see McCarthy and O'Keefe 2003: 165). *Güey* seems almost never to appear alone in this function, but is typically accompanied by the word *oye* 'listen' or another attention getter; see (13).[10]

a)   Summons

(13) *Oye*   **güey,**   *no   tienen   salsa?*
      listen-IMP.2SG   VOC   not   have-3.PL   salsa-F.SG?
      Porque   con   salsa   saben   bien.
      because   with   salsa-F.SG   taste-PRS.3PL   well
      'Listen **güey**, don't you have salsa? Because these taste good with salsa.' (Nava Sanchezllanes 2006: 62)

More common is the function Zwicky (1974) describes as 'calls': the one of maintaining and re-establishing the attention of an already given addressee. This may, on the one hand, strengthen the contact and the communication channel between the interlocutors; on the other hand, it marks as especially important what the speaker has to say (cf. Carranza 1996: 9 for the Rioplatense vocative particle *che*). This effect is conventionalized in the emphatic/expressive function of the vocative described below.

b)   Calls

(14) *Fíjate*   **güey,**   *lo*   *peor*
      notice-IMP.2SG=REFL.2SG   VOC   DET.DEF.N.SG   worst.n.sg
      de   todo   es   que...
      of   all-M.SG   be-PRS.3SG   REL
      'Look **güey**, the worst thing is that...' (Nava Sanchezllanes 2006: 62)

In other examples, the vocative is used to strengthen the contact between the interlocutors in order to assure the hearer's understanding, as in (15).

c)   Strengthening of contact, assuring of understanding

(15) *Sí   lo   quieres   **güey?** La   verdá(d).*
      yes   DO.M.SG   want-PRS.2SG   VOC   DET.DEF.F.SG   truth-F.SG
      'You do want it **güey**? Really.' (Nava Sanchezllanes 2006: 60*)*

Finally, an attention-getting vocative may be used to organize the turn structure of the discourse (a function Shiina (2007) describes as 'conversational management', together with the assuring of the addressee's under-standing), in order either to elicit a response from the selected next speaker (16) or to attract the attention necessary to get a turn, an intent *güey* fails to achieve for S2 in (17).

d)   Turn management

(16) *Tú   sabes   bien   inglés   **güey?***
     you-2SG   know-PRS.2SG   well   English.M.SG   VOC
     'Do you speak a good English ***güey***?' (Palacios 2002b: 229)

(17) *[S1:   Lo   más   cagado   es   que*
           DET.DEF.N.SG   most   shit-PTCP.N.SG   be-PRS.3SG   REL
     la   llamo   como   a   las   nueve   y
     DO.F.SG   call-PRS.1SG   like   at   DET.DEF.F.PL   nine   and
     media   y   colgamos   hasta las   once||
     half.F.SG   and   hang_up-PRS.1PL   until DET.DEF.3PL   eleven.
     'The coolest thing is that I call her about half past nine and we talk until eleven.'
     *[S2:   **Güey** –*
           VOC
           '***Güey*** –'
     S1:   *No   sientes   cuando   hablas   tanto.*
           not feel-PRS.2SG   when   speak-PRS.2SG so_much
           'You don't feel [the time] when you talk so much.' (Palacios 2002a: 79)

C)   Functions of emphasis and expressivity

The function of getting the addressee's attention may be redirected in order to draw the attention to parts of the utterance, of the turn or of the informational structure, thus adding emphasis or expressivity or reinforcing the illocution. Furthermore, vocatives may be even used in an exclamative way.

The function of illocutional reinforcement has been observed by Haver-kate (1978: 47), by Bañón Hernández (1993: 27) in his analysis of the vocative function as context marking – similar also Rendle-Short (2010: 1202) for the Australian solidarity marker *mate* –, by García Dini (1998: 57) as the emphatic function and by Shiina (2007) as 'management of illocutional force'. Typically, the vocative accompanies imperative or ad-hortative illocutions (18), but may also occur with speech acts of promising, swearing or similar (19). In these cases, by directly appealing to the interlocutor it confers more emphasis, more insistence to the illocution.

a)   Illocutional reinforcement

(18) *Vamos,*   ***güey.***
   go-IMP.1PL VOC
   'Let's go, **güey**.' (Nava Sanchezllanes 2006: 61)

(19) *Te lo   juro,*   ***güey.***
   io.2SG DO.3SG swear-PRS.1SG VOC
   'I swear it, **güey**.' (Nava Sanchezllanes 2006)

In other cases the vocative is used to reinforce and emphasize parts of the informational structure of the utterance rather than its illocution, as in (20), where *no* is used not so much as a negation of its own but is cited from what the speaker has said before.

b)   Emphasizing parts of the utterance

(20) *Es   que no,* ***güey!***
   be-PRS.3SG that no VOC
   'It's no, **güey**!' (Nava Sanchezllanes 2006: 68)

A last typical function is the exclamative use, in which a vocative – which may be modified by a possessive, an interjection (21) or an adjective (22) – carries expressivity of its own, denoting surprise, anger, or other emotions (see Zifonun, Hoffmann, and Strecker 1997: 153–159; Mazzoleni 1995: 382). This function may be accomplished by stand-alone as well as by initial vocatives; but contrary to the majority of other utterances accompanied by vocatives, here it often seems to be the vocative itself that carries the illocutionary force, while the rest of the utterance is a kind of appendix explaining the reason of the strong emotion expressed.[11]

c)   Exclamative use

(21) *Órale* ***güey!*** *Ya* *me* *agujereaste*
   INTERJ VOC already IO.1SG perforate-PST.PFV.2SG
   el   *otro*   *lado.*
   DET.DEF.M.SG other-M.SG side-M.SG
   'Wow **güey**! Now you got me a hole on the other side.' (Nava Sanchezllanes 2006: 64)

(22) *Pinche*   **güey,**   *soltaste*   *el*
damned-SG   idiot-SG   loosen-PST.PFV.2SG   DET.DEF.M.SG
volante.
steering_wheel-M.SG
'F*** **idiot**, you let go of the steering wheel.' (Palacios 2002a: 77)

While in the given examples one could still imagine some other vocative – especially some kind of familiarizer or endearment term – in the place of *güey*, there are many cases where no such substitution could be justified. This happens when speakers start to use *güey* with growing frequency, so that it not only replaces other vocative forms but suffers an 'overuse' (Givón 2001) which leads it to assume new functions and to lose some of its former properties. In the next section I analyze the changes which take place along with the overuse of *güey*.

3. Discourse marking functions of *güey*

3.1. Conversational implicatures

Every kind of language change originates in discourse, which speakers create out of the elements their language provides them. Following the discursive techniques of the language, they use these elements in order to be communicatively successful – i.e. to be informative, relevant, clear, and truthful, as stated by the Gricean Maxims of Quantity, Relevance, Manner, and Quality.[12]

I have shown above how *güey*, as well as other vocatives, is used to define the relationship between the collocutors, to summon or maintain the addressee's attention, and I have suggested that the function of summoning and directing the attention may be shifted from the interpersonal level to the discourse level in order to emphasize parts of the ongoing linguistic interaction. This implies that the vocative *güey* is highly effective in conferring more relevance to what the speaker has to say – an effect which, according to the Maxim of Relevance, is to be used only when it is actually justified by the importance of the utterance. Every language has its conventional means of marking particular relevance, and in Mexican Spanish the use of the vocative *güey* may be considered one of them.[13]

Sometimes, though, speakers start to use a certain expressive element in an 'inflationary' way, a fact Givón (2001: 421) describes as "communicative over-use, a strategy of 'buying extra insurance'". The overuse does not only imply a growing frequency of the element in question, but also an 'abuse' made of it by the speakers: they use the corresponding element more often than is actually reasonable in view of the relevance of the information they are giving.

So what happens when somebody overacts continuously? Hearers will economize their understanding and, prescinding of the elements that carry the information 'very important', extract only the relevant information. In a process of reanalysis (see Detges and Waltereit 2002), they will stop interpreting the element in question as particularly expressive and ascribe it a new reading more appropriate to its actual use. In a linguistic community, where everyone is alternately speaker and hearer, this leads to a semantic change and a new significance of the respective element which is losing – at least in certain kinds of usage – its expressive connotation. In a process of semantic and pragmatic bleaching, the semantic and/or pragmatic force of the formerly expressive element 'wears out' as the usual interpretation of its occurrences is modified. As pointed out by Detges (2001: 430), this tactic is one of the main factors for the rise of new grammatical elements, thus for processes of grammaticalization.

Regarding the overuse of the word *güey*, this reanalysis occurs in two steps. First, hearers prescind of the vocative interpretation – i.e. of analyzing the word as a nominal element directly referring to them – and restrict their reading to the emphatic meaning it carries. A sign of this reanalysis is the fact that it loses the morphosyntactic properties of a noun (see Palacios 2002a: 70, 77). In the referential use of *güey* as a noun or an adjective it is possible to form the plural *güeyes* or the (emphatic) feminine *güeya*; also, it may be preceded by a definite or an indefinite article (*el güey/un güey*), a demonstrative determiner (*ese güey*), a possessive determiner (*su güey*) or a number (*dos güeyes*). While Spanish does not admit a determiner for the vocative, the plural and feminine variation is possible (although not very common) for the invective use of *güey* with its original imprecative semantics, as well as for the vocative use. In contrast, no such alternation is admitted once the vocative interpretation has been replaced by the emphatic reading. Still, the relational function of *güey* is conserved insofar as it is not possible to use emphatic *güey* outside a relationship of solidarity.

In a second step, there is an overuse of emphatic *güey* that cannot be justified by the relevance of the given information anymore. As a result, hearers start to prescind of the attention-getting, emphasizing reading, leaving *güey* to assume new functions on the level of discourse: what remains of the former invective is a homonymous element used as a discourse marker.

3.2. New functions

As shown above, the conventionalized attention-getting function of the vocative is 'abused' by speakers in order to emphasize certain parts of the discourse and gives way to a routinization of the expressive use of *güey*. It is in this function where it begins to lose its vocative properties and to be employed in discourse related functions; the expressive use of the vocative, thus, constitutes the point of contact with the discourse marker that arises from the reanalysis of its inflationary use.[14]

Accordingly, there are occurrences of *güey* that could be described as expressive-interjectional (classified as 'interjectional use' by Nava Sanchezllanes 2006: 65–71): cases that cannot be interpreted as vocatives any more, although, just like the emphatic vocative, they confer a strong emphasis to the utterance they occur in. In (23) the speaker uses *ay güey* as an exclamation whose scope is not the appealing to the addressee but the expression of the speaker's emotions concerning the little accident.

a)   Expressive-interjectional functions

(23) *Ay **güey**, ya   me   quemé!*
     INTERJ   already   REFL.1SG   burn-PST.PFV.1SG
     'Ouch **güey**, now I got burnt!' (Nava Sanchezllanes 2006: 73)

As regards the relational functions (use with formulae and routines, definition of the relationship, addressee identification and recognition, mitigation of speech acts and badinage), they are still preserved in the discourse marker *güey* insofar as it may only be used between speakers when there is a relationship of solidarity on a colloquial level. Sociopragmatic criteria decide whether a speaker feels like using *güey* with his collocutor or not. So, when it is used as a discourse marker, it serves to establish or strengthen not so much the actual contact between the speakers, but their common ground that enables them to use *güey* in their interaction (Palacios 2002b: 228). This is the case for its expressive use as well as its functions as a discourse marker.

Actually, as the use of *güey* has been generalized as a typical feature of Mexican Spanish, it has passed from only being part of the language of adolescents to also being used by adult speakers – although to a smaller degree and usually only in relational and expressive functions. Here, it seems to be a stylistic choice rather than a question of the sociocultural background when e.g. two elderly upper-class sisters use *güey* in order to emphasize an utterance (my own observation).

On the contrary, especially in adolescent speaker groups *güey* has evolved still further, being subject to a strong overuse in its expressive acceptation and, later on, losing great part of its expressivity. Instead, it comes to serve functions of discourse structuring. Speakers employ *güey* to segment their utterances, to organize the turn structure and to strengthen their common ground in the interaction.

The functions assumed by *güey* vary according to its position in the turn (Palacios 2002b: 229–232). It rarely occurs in initial position, as in (24), where it is used to start the turn in a more expressive way, to reinforce what has been said and to connect it with what is going to be said – in fact, the speaker is repeating something he/she had already said before.

b)   Discourse marking functions

(24) **Wey**, *no*   *quiero*   *ensayar*   *con*   *Andrea.*
DM   not   want-PRS.1SG practice-INF with   Andrea-F.SG
'**Güey**, I don't want to practice with Andrea.' (Nava Sanchezllanes 2006: 69)

In central position, as in (25), it strengthens the contact between the interlocutors and indicates a segmentation of the turn structure, reinforcing the previously given information and relating it to the following.

(25) *Le*   *dije*   **güey** *que*   *cuando* *llegara*
IO.F.3SG   say-PST.PFV.1SG DM   that   when   arrive-PST.SBJV.1SG
que   *ya*   *estuviera*   *arreglada.*
that   already   be-PST.SBJV.3SG dress_up-PTCP.F.SG
'I told her **güey** to be ready when I arrived.' (Nava Sanchezllanes 2006: 82)

In final position – the most frequent one –, as in (26) and (27), it reinforces what has been said before, claiming the addressee's approval and continuous attention – a function that can also by fulfilled by final vocatives but with the difference that the discourse marker *güey* has much less weight in the utterance. Not only may it occupy positions where no semantic-pragmatically full vocative form would be possible, but also it is used with a frequency that exceeds by far the possible number of vocatives in a discourse segment as short as in the examples.

(26) *S1:*   *Tengo*   *güeva*   **güey.**
             have-PRS.1SG   laziness-F.SG   DM
             'I feel so lazy **güey**.'

    [S2:   *Sí*   **güey.**
             yes   DM
             'Right **güey**.'

    [S3:   *Pero*   *ya*   **güey.**
             but   enough   DM
             'It's enough **güey**.' (Palacios 2002: 228)

(27) *Siempre*   *que*   *llega*   *a*   *calificar*   **güey**...
     always   that   arrive-PST.3SG   to   grade-INF   DM...
     ya   *me*   *tenía*   *que*   *calificar*   **güey**...
     already DO.1SG   have-PST.IPFV.3SG   REL   grade-INF   DM...
     'gracias **güey**'...   *'de*   *nada*   **güey**'...   *y*   *ahora*   *quién*
     thanks   DM   of   nothing   DM   and   now   who
     es   *el*   **güey**...   *pues*   *tú*   **güey**!
     be-PRS.3SG DET.DEF.M.SG stupid-M.SG DM   you-2.SG   VOC
     'Every time he has to give grades **güey**... he already had to grade me
     güey... 'thanks **güey**'... 'you're welcome **güey**'... and now who's the
     idiot?... It's you, **güey**!' (Nava Sanchezllanes 2006: 81)

In (26), although the conversation is among three speakers, it is impossible
to use the plural form *güeyes* instead of any incidence of *güey*. The
speakers use *güey* in the first place to create proximity and solidarity
between each other, in the second place to delimitate their utterances,
adding emphasis to the given information and thereby claiming their collocutors' attention and approval – a function still very similar to the expressive use of *güey*.

The morphological invariability holds also for (27) as far as *güey* could
be read as a vocative form. In this example, *güey* is used as a referential
noun in *y ahora quién es el güey*; in *pues tú / güey* it can be said to identify
the addressee as a vocative, and in *gracias güey* and *de nada güey* its
position with the politeness formulae could be filled by another vocative
form. Still, in *siempre que llega a calificar güey* and *ya me tenía que
calificar güey* its function can only be interpreted as pure discourse
marking. Here, *güey* is used to delimit the segments of the utterance and to
confer a touch of solidarity and expressivity to the conversation as a whole.

4. What kind of language change?

The development of *güey* from vocative to discourse marker is similar to the rise of other discourse markers, especially those based on imperative forms. It is no coincidence that vocatives and imperatives are often treated together in the literature (see Bañón Hernández 1993: 24; Conte 1972; Dorian 1985; Downing 1969; van Schooneveld 1986; Winter 1969). An evolution in several steps can be observed. The first step is the shift from the invective *güey* to a ritual insult and the establishment of the almost neutral vocative use in the language of adolescent speaker groups. In succession, we find a change from the vocative in its different interpersonal functions (relational, attention summoning and expressive) to an element working on the text level, i.e. an expressivity marker. The last step is the loss of the expressivity and the assumption of new functions as a discourse marker: text coherence, discourse segmentation, strengthening of contact and assuring of understanding. It must be pointed out, though, that these functions may not always be clearly separable but that a given occurrence of *güey* may serve several purposes, e.g. the discourse marking functions may still go hand in hand with the conferring of expressivity.

In order to delineate this process, I have given a description of the original form and functions, furthermore depicting several intermediate grades of evolution up to the present-day final product – the discourse marker *güey*. Also, I have tried to explain the sociocultural and, above all, pragmatic factors that account for this evolution.

In scientific research, different terms have been proposed to describe the rise of discourse markers like *güey*. Probably the most common term is grammaticalization, but the same evolution has also been discussed as an instance of subjectification, lexicalization, pragmaticalization, degrammaticalization, invisible-hand-process and routinization – among others (cf. Traugott 1997; Degand and Simon-Vandenbergen 2011).

The notion of grammaticalization, introduced by Meillet (1912) and basically defined by Lehmann (1982), has been the subject of much discussion over the last decades. In its core notion, grammaticalization is the change of a given linguistic element with a lexical or grammatical function to a more grammatical status (for an overview of the most prominent definitions and positions see Campbell and Janda 2001). In the words of Hopper and Traugott (1993: XV): "Grammaticalization [...] is the process whereby lexical items and constructions come in certain linguistic contexts to serve grammatical functions, and, once grammaticalized, continue to develop new grammatical functions."

Several authors have proposed to extend the notion of grammaticalization to the rise of discourse markers (see Brinton 1996; Chodorowska-

Pilch 1999; Company Company 2004; Diewald 1999, 2006, 2011; Lewis 2011; Pinto de Lima 2002; Prevost 2011; Simon-Vandenbergen and Willems 2011; Traugott 1997, 2007; van Bogaert 2011; Wischer 2000). However, this approach presents some substantial problems. First, the evolution of discourse markers does not match all the criteria usually assumed for grammaticalization (attrition, paradigmatization, obligatorification, condensation, coalescence, fixation; see Lehmann 1982). This problem may be solved in two ways: either by declaring some of these criteria less important than others and therefore extending the notion of grammaticalization to all processes that match the most important criteria; or by postulating two (or more) kinds of grammaticalization: one that has as a result "highly constrained grammatical morphemes, which operate on the level of the proposition" (which actually matches the criteria listed above for prototypical cases of grammaticalization); and one that "operates on the textual or discourse level and concerns the development of textual or discourse markers" (Wischer 2000: 356).

Evidently, there is a difference between grammatical morphemes and textual or discourse markers. Still, can discourse markers be considered elements of grammar? This might be the core question of the terminological debate about grammaticalization, for calling 'grammaticalization' a process whose result is not grammar is pointless (see Waltereit 2002: 1004). As Traugott (1997: 5) puts it: "If it is grammaticalization, then we have to rethink not only the criteriality of morphosyntactic coalescence and fixation, but also the nature of grammar."

That discourse markers are part of the system of a language is no longer disputed since the first comprehensive works on their inventory and functioning (e.g. Gülich 1970; Fraser 1990). However, they operate differently from grammatical morphemes. While grammatical morphemes are "automatic processing strategies" (Givón 1979: 108) which "operate on the level of the proposition" (Wischer 2000: 356), discourse markers operate "on the textual or discourse level" (Wischer 2000: 356) and are used to structure the ongoing discourse (cf. Detges and Waltereit 2007).

Of course, it is possible to summarize every systematically-working part of language under the label 'grammar', as does Traugott (1997: 5). In this case, though, there would be no need to differentiate between lexicalization and grammaticalization either, since the outcomes of lexicalization usually belong to a certain word class, which definitely work as a part of the system (cf. Wischer 2000: 359–360). Instead, reserving the notion 'grammaticalization' for processes whose result is grammar in the narrow sense of the term opens the perspective to the different features that characterize every kind of language change.

On the other hand, there are authors who claim the rise of discourse markers to be a process fundamentally different from grammaticalization, as its result is not grammar, but discourse organization (Aijmer 1997; Blas Arroyo 2011; Detges and Waltereit 2007; Günthner and Mutz 2004; Ocampo 2006; Páez Urdaneta 1982). Among the most prominent, Aijmer (1997) advocates a definition as 'pragmaticalization': a process whereby an autonomous lexical element acquires pragmatic functions, as opposed to becoming a grammatical form in a process of grammaticalization.[15] The notion of pragmaticalization has been broadly received and accepted since; however, it has also been questioned, especially by those authors who consider the rise of discourse markers a case of grammaticalization in a wider sense.

As pointed out by Waltereit and Detges (2007), every kind of language change begins in discourse. Speakers use the elements and structures of their language in order to be communicatively successful, i.e. to be more expressive, more relevant, more informative, more polite – in summary, for pragmatic purposes. This means that every language change has its original motivation in pragmatics. The term 'pragmaticalization' is therefore misleading insofar as it invokes the picture of a static element of the lexicon coming to pragmatic use, when it is rather an element freely usable in discourse whose pragmatic functions are being routinized.

The notion of 'subjectification' (Traugott 1995) has been widely accepted to accompany the evolution of discourse markers (see Waltereit 2002: 987–988). The problem with this, as outlined by Waltereit (2002: 988) is that subjectification in itself only describes, but does not explain the "recurrent tendency of semantic change" whereby "forms denoting 'objective,' ideational meanings acquire more speaker-based, subjective, attitudinal meanings in the course of time" (Waltereit 2002: 987–988). Therefore, while we may accept the evolution of *güey* to be listed as a case of subjectification, it is questionable whether this diagnosis is of any value for its description and explanation.

The notions of 'lexicalization' and 'degrammaticalization' do not seem to apply for the case of *güey*. Neither is it a free, analytically interpreted syntagma, which is being lexicalized to an only, holistically interpreted element of the lexicon, as would be the case of lexicalization (cf. Lehmann 2002). Nor is the original vocative a more grammatical element than its outcome, the discourse marker, so as to match the criteria for degrammaticalization (cf. Ocampo 2006).

What can be observed is the *routinization* of an element of discourse through the efforts of speakers to be communicatively successful. As I outlined above, speakers use the elements of their language in order to fulfill pragmatic purposes. In the course of time, certain uses or constructions may achieve the preference of many speakers, thus being more frequently used than other semantically equivalent ones. This preference may lead to an expressive overuse of these constructions, whose result – in an invisible-hand-process (cf. Detges and Waltereit 2002: 184) – is a reanalysis by part of the hearers: the element in question loses its expressivity and comes routinely to serve new functions, in this case concerned with discourse structuring.

This routinization may go along with semantic and syntactic opacity, but the resulting elements operate on different levels of language. There are elements which are concerned with the structuring of the proposition, i.e. elements of grammar (in the narrow sense). The routinization of elements in this function is what is generally called *grammaticalization*. Another kind of routinization is *lexicalization*, i.e. the development of new elements of the lexicon out of the routinized use of certain syntagmatic constructions.

In the case of *güey*, instead, we find a shift of its functions from the interpersonal-interactional level to the discourse level, including its turn structure: the rise of a discourse marker through the semantic-pragmatical bleaching of an invective vocative form.

Routinization, thus, is a very frequent kind of language change that may occur on different levels of language. According to its domain, different terms should conveniently be used in order to avoid confusion and maintain in sight the differences as well as the similarities.[16]

5. Conclusion

As I have pointed out, today's Mexican Spanish is marked by the use of the word *güey* in its many variants: as an invective vocative, a vocative solidarity marker, a noun with pejorative, neutral, or even affectionate connotation, an adjective with pejorative meaning or an apparently meaningless discourse marker. From being sociolinguistically marked, it has passed to being marked rather on a stylistic level, since its use nowadays is common almost throughout the whole speaker community of the country.

As to how this evolution could be called, I have given reasons for it neither being an instance of grammaticalization nor of pragmaticalization. Instead, I have proposed to consider the development of discourse markers a particular kind of routinization, a notion which may be used as a hyperonym for different kinds of language change: it is a condition for processes of grammaticalization as well as lexicalization. In the case of *güey*, we can observe a shift of its sphere of action from the interpersonal level to the structuring of discourse through its expressive overuse, its reanalysis and its semantic and pragmatic bleaching during a process of routinization.

Notes

1. Analyses of the vocative in Spanish are provided by Svennung (1958), Bonnekamp (1971), Haverkate (1978), Bañón Hernández (1993) and García Dini (1998). Investigation of the vocative is also closely related to the work on the sociolinguistic phenomenon of address; see e.g. Brown and Ford (1961) and Braun (1988). Among the few investigations of vocatives in the oral discourse are Leech (1999), Hasbún Hasbún (2003), McCarthy and O'Keefe (2003), Rendle-Short (2010), and Burgos (2009).
2. Whether the vocative may be defined as a case or not has been questioned, among others, by Hjelmslev ([1935–1937] 1972). His case definition is based on the relationship between the arguments of the sentence (see Harweg 1967: 40). More than the other cases, the vocative is usually described with the aid of functional criteria on a pragmatic level, i.e. its addressing function (Bonnekamp 1971: 17–18).
3. It must be pointed out that vocatives of the different categories have different syntactic properties. While some are or behave like proper names, which identify the addressee in the form of an equation (x = John) and may be used almost in the same way as vocatives and referential NPs, most other vocative forms identify the addressee by assigning him/her to a category of which he/she takes part (x = a darling/idiot), thus behaving like count nouns. Still others, though, do not behave like either proper or count nouns (cf. Zwicky 1974: 789–790).
4. The generalization of the construction *vuestra merced* used as integrated in the sentence has given origin to the modern Spanish V-pronoun *usted*.
5. How close the pronunciations with and without initial /g/ are is shown by the high number of words with alternating orthography in Mexican Spanish: dictionaries list without a preference variants with <hu> or <gu> like *huarache/ guarache* 'sandal', *huevón/güevón* 'lazy' (see Company Company and Academia Mexicana de la Lengua 2010); and especially poorly educated people confound them a lot.
6. According to Nava Sanchezllanes (2006: 72), the adjective use, derived from the referential noun, preceded the vocative use. In my opinion, it is more likely a secondary development of the noun that derives from its referential *and* vocative use, in fact possibly triggered by the vocative use without a determiner.

7. The equivalent mainly used by female speakers are endearment terms (Leech 1999: 112).
8. The categories of power and solidarity used to explain the address behavior in a linguistic community goes back to the works of Gilman and Brown (1958), Brown and Gilman (1960), and Brown and Ford (1961). 'Equality' here is equivalent to the absence of a hierarchical power relation.
9. For the concept of politeness in its two interpretations – relative or context adequate vs. absolute or characterized by the use of objective politeness markers – see Braun (1988: 45–64).
10. One could argue that in these cases *güey* does not fulfill any attention-getting function, but is only used to support the element actually used for summoning attention. I have preferred to consider its function as attention-getting in so far as by identifying the addressee, it also contributes to summon his/her attention.
11. For the concept of illocution carrying units vs. appendixes and other supporting units see Cresti and Moneglia (2005).
12. Leech (1983: 141–142) adds a 'Phatic Maxim' to the ones mentioned by Grice, which implies to avoid silence by keeping talking (see Stenström and Jörgensen 2008).
13. In fact, in situations where the collocutors and the relationship among them are already defined, the use of a vocative might seem to violate the Maxim of Quantity insofar as its use is 'superfluous' from the point of view of information. But this should lead the addressee to search for an implicature which justifies the use of the appellative element and to find it precisely in the conferring of relevance.
14. See Waltereit (2002) for a similar process regarding the imperative.
15. Páez Urdaneta (1982) describes the same process as degrammaticalization.
16. Elements whose purpose is the structuring of the interpersonal relationship may develop into elements of politeness or solidarity, as described by Traugott and Dasher (2002: 226–278). The development of the routinely used vocative *güey* shows some similarities. What makes it different from the development of politeness markers is that it did not have an especially positive meaning in the beginning and afterwards came to serve more everyday functions, as is the usual way of development for politeness markers (see Braun 1988: 57–58), but on the contrary began as an invective element and gradually lost its negative connotation to give way to the rise of the solidarity marker.

References

Aijmer, Karin
1997   *I think* – an English modal particle. In *Modality in Germanic Languages. Historical and Comparative Perspective*, Toril Swan and Olaf Jansen Westvik (eds.), 1–47. Berlin/New York: Mouton de Gruyter.

Álvarez Menéndez, Alfredo I.
2005   *Hablar en español. La cortesía verbal, la pronunciación estándar del español, las formas de expresión oral*. Oviedo: Nobel/Ediuno.

Bañón Hernández, Antonio Miguel
1993   *El vocativo en español. Propuestas para su análisis lingüístico*. Barcelona: Octaedro.

Bernal, María
2008   ¿Insultan los insultos? *Descortesía auténtica* vs. *descortesía no auténtica* en español coloquial. *Pragmatics* 18 (4): 775–802.

Blas Arroyo, José Luis
2011   From politeness to discourse marking: The process of pragmaticalization of *muy bien* in vernacular Spanish. *Journal of Pragmatics* 43 (3): 855–874.

Bonnekamp, Udo
1971   Der Vokativ im Romanischen. In *Interlinguistica. Sprachvergleich und Übersetzung. Festschrift zum 60. Geburtstag von Mario Wandruszka*, Karl-Richard Bausch and Hans-Martin Gauger (eds.), 13–25. Tübingen: Niemeyer.

Braun, Friederike
1988   *Terms of Address*. Berlin/New York/München: Mouton de Gruyter.

Brinton, Laurel
1996   *Pragmatic Markers in English. Grammaticalization and Discourse Function*. Berlin: Mouton de Gruyter.

Brown, Roger W. and Albert Gilman
1960   The pronouns of power and solidarity. In *Style in Language*, Thomas A. Sebeok (ed.), 435–449. New York/London: Wiley.

Brown, Roger W. and Marguerite Ford
1961   Address in American English. *Journal of Abnormal and Social Psychology* 62: 375–385. Reprint in *Language in culture and society*, Dell Hymes (ed.), 234–244. New York: Harper & Row, 1964.

Campbell, Lyle and Richard D. Janda
2001   Introduction: Conceptions of grammaticalization and their problems. *Language Sciences* 23 (2–3): 93–112.

Carranza, Isolda
1996   *Contextualización y expresiones pragmáticas: che como señal de marco*. Paper presented at the 10th Annual Meeting of the Association of Philology and Linguistics for Latin America, Vera Cruz, Mexico, March 1993.
             http://www.eric.ed.gov:80/ERICDocs/data/ericdocs2sql/content_storage_01/0000019b/80/16/50/70.pdf, 03.06.2008.

Chodorowska-Pilch, Marianna
1999   On the polite use of *vamos* in peninsular Spanish. *Pragmatics* 9 (3): 343–355.

Company Company, Concepción
2004   ¿Gramaticalización o desgramaticalización? El reanálisis y subjetivización de verbos como marcadores discursivos en la historia del español. *Revista de filología española* 84 (1): 29–66.

Company Company, Concepción and Academia Mexicana de la Lengua (eds.)
2010   *Diccionario de mexicanismos*. Mexico: Siglo XXI.

Conte, Maria-Elisabeth
1972   Vocativo ed imperativo secondo il modello performativo. In *Scritti e ricerche di grammatica italiana*, Centro per lo studio dell'insegnamento dell'italiano all'estero (ed.), 159–179. Triest: Lint.

Cresti, Emanuela and Massimo Moneglia
2005   *C-ORAL ROM. Integrated Reference Corpora for Spoken Romance Languages*. Amsterdam/Philadelphia: John Benjamins.

Degand, Liesbeth and Anne-Marie Simon-Vandenbergen
2011   Introduction: Grammaticalization and (inter)subjectification of discourse markers. *Linguistics* 49 (2): 287–294.

Detges, Ulrich
2001   Grammatikalisierung. Eine kognitiv-pragmatische Theorie, dargestellt am Beispiel romanischer und anderer Sprachen. Professorial dissertation, Universität Tübingen.

Detges, Ulrich and Richard Waltereit
2002   Grammaticalization vs. reanalysis. A semantic-pragmatic account of functional change in grammar. *Zeitschrift für Sprachwissenschaft* 21: 151–195.

Detges, Ulrich and Richard Waltereit
2007   Diachronie prozeduraler Routinen. Die Entwicklung von Diskursmarkern, Modalpartikeln und grammatikalischen Elementen in vergleichender Perspektive. Unpublished project outline.

Dickey, Eleanor
1996   *Greek Forms of Address. From Herodotos to Lucian.* Oxford: Clarendon Press.
Diewald, Gabriele
1999   Die Entwicklung der Modalpartikel *aber*: ein typischer Grammatikalisierungsweg der Modalpartikeln. In *Internationale Tendenzen der Syntaktik, Semantik und Pragmatik. Akten des 32. Linguistischen Kolloquiums in Kassel 1997*, Hans Otto Spillmann and Ingo Warnke (eds.), 83–91. New York/Bern/ Berlin/ Bruxelles/Frankfurt a.M./Oxford/Wien: Lang.
Diewald, Gabriele
2006   Discourse particles and modal particles as grammatical elements. In *Approaches to Discourse Particles*, Kerstin Fischer (ed.), 403–425. Amsterdam: Elsevier.
Diewald, Gabriele
2011   Pragmaticalization (defined) as grammaticalization of discourse functions. *Linguistics* 49 (2): 365–390.
Dishman, Amalia C.
1982   Sobre el origen y uso del *che* argentino. *Hispania* 65: 93–97.
Dorian, Nancy C.
1985   Vocative and imperative in decline. In *Studia linguistica diachronica et synchronica. Festschrift für Werner Winter*, Ursula Pieper and Gerhard Stickel (eds.), 161–174. Berlin/New York: Walter de Gruyter.
Downing, Bruce T.
1969   Vocatives and third-person imperatives in English. *Papers in Linguistics* 1 (3): 570–592.
Fraser, Bruce
1990   An approach to discourse markers. *Journal of Pragmatics* 14: 383–395.
García Dini, Encarnación
1998   Algo más sobre el vocative. In *Lo spagnolo d'oggi: Forme della comunicazione. Atti del XVII Convegno, Milano 24–25–26 ottobre 1996.* Vol. 2, Associazione Ispanisti Italiani (ed.), 57–62. Rome: Bulzoni.
Gehweiler, Elke
2008   From proper name to primary interjection: The case of *gee!*. *Journal of Historical Pragmatics* 9 (1): 71–93.
Gilman, Albert and Roger W. Brown
1958   Who says 'tu' to whom. *ETC: A Review of General Semantics* 15 (3): 169–174.

Givón, Talmy
1979   *On Understanding Grammar*. New York: Academic Press.
Givón, Talmy
2001   *Syntax: An Introduction*. Amsterdam/Philadelphia: John
             Benjamins.
Gómez de Silva, Guido
2001   *Diccionario breve de mexicanismos*. Mexico: Fondo de cultura
             económica.
Gülich, Elisabeth
1970   *Makrosyntax der Gliederungssignale im gesprochenen Franzö-
             sisch*. München: Fink.
Günthner, Susanne and Katrin Mutz
2004   Grammaticalization vs. pragmaticalization? The development of
             pragmatic markers in German and Italian. In *What Makes Gram-
             maticalization? A Look from its Fringes and its Components*,
             Walter Bisang, Nikolaus P. Himmelmann, and Björn Wiemer
             (eds.), 77–107. Berlin/New York: Mouton de Gruyter.
Harweg, Roland
1967   Skizze einer neuen Theorie des Vokativs. *Linguistics* 33: 37–48.
Hasbún Hasbún, Leyla
2003   ¿Qué le vendemos, reina? El uso de los vocativos en la Feria del
             Agricultor. *Revista de Filología y Lingüística de la Universidad
             de Costa Rica* 29 (1): 201–220.
Haverkate, Henk
1978   The vocative phrase in modern Spanish. A contribution to the
             study of illocutionary functions. In *Linguistics in the Netherlands
             1974-1976*, Wim Zonneveld (ed.), 46–62. Lisse: Peter de Ridder.
Hjelmslev, Louis
1972   Reprint. *La catégorie des cas: étude de grammaire générale*.
             München: Fink. Original edition, Aarhus: Universitetsforlaget,
             1935–1937.
Hopper, Paul
1991   On some principles of grammaticalization. In *Approaches to
             Grammaticalization*. Vol. 1, Elizabeth Closs Traugott and Bernd
             Heine (eds.), 17–35. Amsterdam: John Benjamins.
Hopper, Paul and Elizabeth Closs Traugott
1993   *Grammaticalization*. Cambridge: Cambridge University Press.
Jakobson, Roman
1960   Linguistics and poetics. In *Style in Language*, Thomas A. Sebeok
             (ed.), 350–377. New York/London: Wiley.

Labov, William
1972   Rules for ritual insults. In *Language in the Inner City*, William
              Labov (ed.), 297–353. Philadelphia: University of Pennsylvania
              Press.
Lara, Luis Fernando and Colegio de México (eds.)
1996   *Diccionario del español usual en México (COLMEX)*. Mexico:
              Colegio de México.
Leech, Geoffrey
1983   *Principles of Pragmatics*. London: Longman.
Leech, Geoffrey
1999   The distribution and function of vocatives in American and
              British English conversation. In *Out of Corpora. Studies in
              Honour of Stig Johansson*, Hilde Hasselgård and Signe Oksefjell
              (eds.), 107–118. Amsterdam: Rodopi.
Lehmann, Christian
1982   *Thoughts on Grammaticalization*. München: Lincom Europa.
              Reprint 1995.
Lehmann, Christian
2002   New reflections on grammaticalization and lexicalization. In *New
              Reflections on Grammaticalization*, Ilse Wischer and Gabriele
              Diewald (eds.), 1–18. Amsterdam: John Benjamins.
Lewis, Diana M.
2011   A discourse-constructional approach to the emergence of dis-
              course markers in English. *Linguistics* 49 (2): 415–443.
Mazzoleni, Marco
1995   Il vocativo. In *Grande grammatica italiana di consultazione*.
              Vol. 3. *Tipi di frase, deissi, formazione delle parole*, Lorenzo
              Renzi, Giampaolo Salvi, and Anna Cardinaletti (eds.), 377–402.
              Bologna: Il Mulino.
McCarthy, Michael J. and Anne O'Keefe
2003   'What's in a name?': Vocatives in casual conversations and radio
              phone-in calls. In *Corpus Analysis. Language Structure and
              Language Use*, Pepi Leistyna and Charles F. Meyer (eds.), 153–
              185. Amsterdam: Rodopi.
Meillet, Antoine
1912   L'évolution des formes grammaticales. *Scientia* (Rivista di
              Scienza) 12: 384–400. Reprint in *Linguistique historique et
              linguistique générale*, Antoine Meillet (ed.), 130–149. Paris:
              Edouard Champion, 1921.

Nava Sanchezllanes, Nelisahuel
 2006   El proceso de gramaticalización de la palabra güey en el habla de
             la ciudad de México. Bachelor thesis, Department of Linguistics,
             Universidad Autónoma de México.
Ocampo, Francisco
 2006   Movement towards discourse is not grammaticalization: The
             evolution of *claro* from adjective to discourse particle in spoken
             Spanish. In *Selected Proceedings of the 9th Hispanic Linguistics
             Symposium*, Nuria Sagarra and Almeida Jacqueline Toribio
             (eds.), 308–319. Sommerville, MA: Cascadilla Proceedings
             Project.
Páez Urdaneta, Iraset
 1982   Conversational *pues* in Spanish: A process of degrammati-
             calization?. In *Papers of the 5th International Conference on
             Historical Linguistics*, Anders Ahlqvist (ed.), 332–340.
             Amsterdam/Philadelphia: John Benjamins.
Palacios, Niktelol
 2002a   La interdicción lingüística en el habla de los adolescentes
             mexicanos. Bachelor thesis, Department of Linguistics.
             Benemérita Universidad Autónoma de Puebla.
Palacios, Niktelol
 2002b   Algunos marcadores discursivos característicos del habla de los
             adolescentes mexicanos. *Iztapalapa* 18 (53): 225–247.
Panhuis, Dirk
 1986   The vocative is outside the sentence. *Studies in Language* 10 (2):
             443–447.
Pinto de Lima, José
 2002   Grammaticalization, subjectification and the origin of phatic
             markers. In *New Reflections on Grammaticalization*, Ilse Wischer
             and Gabriele Diewald (eds.), 363–378. Amsterdam: John
             Benjamins.
Prevost, Sophie
 2011   A propos from verbal complement to discourse marker: A case of
             grammaticalization? *Linguistics* 49 (2): 391–413.
Queretanita
 2009   ¿Ser o hacerse Güey?, Blog con M de Mexico,
             http://mdemexico.blogspot.com/2009/03/ser-o-hacerse-
             guey.html, 16.11.2012
RAE: Real Academia Española
 1973   *Esbozo de una nueva gramática de la lengua espanõla, R.A.E.*
             Madrid: Espasa Calpe.

RAE: Real Academia Española
  2001   *Diccionario de la lengua española, R.A.E.* 22nd ed. Madrid:
             Espasa Calpe, http://buscon.rae.es/drae/, 8.10.2012.
Rendle-Short, Johanna
  2010   'Mate' as a term of address in ordinary interaction. *Journal of
             Pragmatics* 42: 1201–1218.
Shiina, Michi
  2007   Positioning and functioning of vocatives: Casework in historical
             pragmatics (1). *Bulletin of Faculty of Letters, Hosei University*
             55: 17–32.
             http://www.hosei.jp/bungaku/museum/html/kiyo/55/articles/shiin
             a.pdf, 26.01.2011.
Simon-Vandenbergen, Anne-Marie, and Dominique Willems
  2011   Crosslinguistic data as evidence in the grammaticalization
             debate: The case of discourse markers. *Linguistics* 49 (2): 333–
             364.
Stenström, Anna-Brita and Annette Myre Jörgensen
  2008   ¿Una cuestión de cortesía? Estudio contrastivo del lenguaje fático
             en la conversación juvenil. *Pragmatics* 18 (4): 635–657.
Svennung, Josef
  1958   *Anredeformen. Vergleichende Forschungen zur indirekten
             Anrede in der dritten Person und zum Nominativ für den Vokativ.*
             Uppsala/Wiesbaden: Almqvist & Wiksell.
Traugott, Elizabeth Closs
  1995   Subjectification in grammaticalization. In *Subjectivity and
             Subjectivisation. Linguistic Perspectives*, Dieter Stein and Susan
             Wright (eds.), 31–54. Cambridge: Cambridge University Press.
Traugott, Elizabeth Closs
  1997   *The role of the development of discourse markers in a theory of
             grammaticalization.* Paper presented at ICHL XII, Manchester
             1995.   http://www.stanford.edu/~traugott/papers/discourse.pdf,
             8.10.2012.
Traugott, Elizabeth Closs
  2007   Discussion article: Discourse markers, modal particles, and
             contrastive analysis, synchronic and diachronic. *Catalan Journal
             of Linguistics* 6: 139–157.
Traugott, Elizabeth Closs and Richard B. Dasher
  2002   *Regularity in Semantic Change* (Cambridge Studies in
             Linguistics 97). Cambridge: Cambridge University Press.

van Bogaert, Julie
  2011   *I think* and other complement-taking mental predicates: A case of
              and for constructional grammaticalization. *Linguistics* 49 (2):
              295–332.
van Schooneveld, Cornelius H.
  1986   Is the vocative a case? In *Pragmatics and Linguistics. Festschrift
              for Jacob L. Mey on his 60th Birthday 30 October 1986*, Jørgen
              Dines Johansen and Harly Sonne (eds.), 179–186. Odense:
              Odense University Press.
Waltereit, Richard
  2002   Imperatives, interruption in conversation and the rise of discourse
              particles: A study of Italian *guarda*. *Linguistics* 40: 987–1010.
Waltereit, Richard and Ulrich Detges
  2007   Different functions, different histories. Modal particles and
              discourse markers from a diachronic point of view. *Catalan
              Journal of Linguistics* 6: 61–81.
Winter, Werner
  1969   Vocative and imperative. In *Substance and Structure of
              Language*, Jaan Puhvel (ed.), 205–222. Berkeley: Berkeley
              University Press.
Wischer, Ilse
  2000   Grammaticalization versus lexicalization: '*Met hinks*' there is
              some confusion. In *Pathways of Change. Grammaticalization in
              English*, Olga C. M. Fischer, Anette Rosenbach, and Dieter Stein
              (eds.), 355–370. Amsterdam: John Benjamins.
Zifonun, Gisela, Ludger Hoffmann, and Bruno Strecker (eds.)
  1997   *Grammatik der deutschen Sprache*. Berlin/New York: Walter de
              Gruyter.
Zimmermann, Klaus
  1996   Lenguaje juvenil, comunicación entre jóvenes y oralidad. In *El
              español hablado y la cultura oral en España e Hispanoamérica*,
              Thomas Kotschi, Wulf Oesterreicher, and Klaus Zimmermann
              (eds.), 475–514. Madrid: Vervuert.
Zwicky, Arnold M.
  1974   Hey whatsyourname! *Chicago Linguistic Society* 10: 787–801.

The vocative case between system and asymmetry

Margherita Donati

Abstract

Linguistic literature generally lacks deep analyses of vocative devices, which are classified either from a formal point of view as part of the "language system" or from a functional point of view as concerning "language use" only. However, this supposed dichotomy between language system and language use cannot actually exist (Coseriu 1955–1956), since language itself is based on the inseparability of system and use: on the basis of this main point Benveniste revised the Saussurean dichotomy *langue* (i.e. language as a sign system) vs. *parole* (i.e. individual utterances putting the language system into practice) by means of the notion of *discours*. In Benvenistean terms, discourse is language put into action, assuming that language is both a sign system and an activity between partners. Participants actualize the system itself in a given speech context and share an inventory of common knowledge. In this sense, system and discourse cannot be regarded as separate dimensions. Indeed, in several well-known papers Benveniste discusses the indissolubility of *langue* and *parole*, showing that the language system actually contains signs that operate only with reference to the speech act (e.g. 1st and 2nd person pronouns) and that one cannot set up the sign as a unique principle of language in its discursive operation (Benveniste 1946, 1956, 1969, 1970; Venier 2007, 2008), thus overcoming the Saussurean dichotomy. However, a misleading approach to the dichotomy *langue* vs. *parole* seems to be the main reason for the lack of satisfying theoretical analyses of the vocative case[1] or of vocative devices in general.

In this paper, we show first that the vocative case has been discussed in the Western metalinguistic framework since the ancient Stoa because of its special asymmetric status within case systems. Our aim is to underline that the vocative case is actually an interesting topic, mainly from a theoretical point of view, and a source of reflection on language. We briefly sketch the assumptions of particular authors (especially Apollonius Dyscolus, Priscian, Martin of Dacia, and Hjelmslev [1935] 1972[2]). Second, we argue that the vocative case can be defined as a person deictic and a "referentiality shifter"; that is, a linguistic tool linking the inherently non-deictic referentiality of nouns to the extra-linguistic context, in particular to the participants in the speech act. Finally, we account for the asymmetry created by the vocative within case systems by means of the Benvenistean notions of person vs. non-person and *discours* vs. *langue*.

1. A brief sketch of Western metalinguistic thought on the vocative case: functional specificity and formal systemic character

The vocative case, especially in the Classical languages, Ancient Greek and Latin, has been the object of many remarks from the ancient Stoa to today: its specific status within case systems is a topic of theoretical discussion that often arises in Western metalinguistic thinking. The vocative case has special status with respect to the category of case: it is an extra-relational item and it does not mark, as other case values do, the semantic-syntactic relationship between noun phrases and other elements in the clause (Daniel and Spencer 2009). Its function, rather, is pragmatic, placing an addressee in a given speech context. Despite this functional difference, however, it can be formally integrated into the nominal system. For this reason, the issue arises of whether or not the vocative can be considered a case. In other words, the vocative case actually shows a sort of "detachment" between form and function: it is functionally different from the case values of the other cases, but it can nonetheless be integrated with them from a formal point of view, being part of the nominal paradigm, as, for example, in the Classical languages. Because of this detachment between form and function, the vocative case is often seen as an anomaly, so that some authors exclude it from the cases because of its functional specificity, while others do include it among the cases by virtue of its formal systemic character. However, this inclusion forces them to introduce theoretical trick into their linguistic analysis. The actual membership of the vocative among the cases is often denied, or at least disputed by ancient as well as modern authors (Donati 2009, 2010a).

In the next sections we briefly analyse some examples of how this special status of the vocative case is accounted for in the approaches of some scholars, that are different from a chronological and a theoretical point of view. In this perspective, we discuss these authors in order to highlight the theoretical problems arising from their approaches.

1.1. Ancient grammarians: Apollonius Dyscolus and Priscian

The ancient grammarians Apollonius Dyscolus (2nd c. AD) and Priscian (6th c. AD) do include the vocative within the Greek and Latin case systems respectively. Nevertheless, they point out that it is clearly special and different with regard to the other cases. In particular, these two authors seem to be aware of what we would describe, in modern terms, as the extra-relationality and deictic nature of the vocative case.[2]

First of all, the peculiarity of the vocative case is noted: it is linked to the second person. Its specific feature of referring to the second person only is mentioned several times by both Apollonius and Priscian.

In the work Περὶ συντάξεως 'On syntax' Apollonius states, "ἀνάγκη οὖν πᾶσα εἰς τὰ τρίτα πρόσωπα χωρεῖν τὰ ὀνόματα κατὰ πᾶσαν πτῶσιν χωρὶς κλητικῆς· αὕτη γὰρ πρώτη ἐπιστρέφει τὴν ἐκ τῶν τρίτων προσώπων θέσιν εἰς τὸ δεύτερον [...]" [It is necessary that nouns head toward the third person in every case value but the vocative; in fact, it firstly converts the reference from the third person into the second person] (*Grammatici Graeci* II.2: 156.13–157.4). Apollonius identifies the vocative case as a linguistic device that changes the third person into second person. This remark implies the relevant point that the vocative case involves reference to the addressee and to the speech act participants: in modern terms, it catches the deictic nature of the vocative case. Furthermore, Apollonius states that the vocative case is a holophrastic element (*Grammatici Graeci* II.2: 372.7–8). He uses the term αὐτοτέλεια 'completeness' to describe its syntactic (and functional) position in the clause, thus demonstrating that he is metalinguistically aware of the extra-relationality of the vocative case.

Priscian, too, in his work *Institutiones Grammaticae* 'Grammatical foundations', refers in several passages to the issue of the particular status of the vocative case with regard to the category of person. In particular, the vocative case is seen as imperfect, since it can refer only to the second person (*Grammatici Latini* II: 186 lines 20–22): "Extremum apud graecos obtinuit vocativus, quippe cum imperfectior ceteris esse videtur: nisi secundae enim personae coniungi non potest [...]" [Among the Greeks the vocative fills the last place, since it seems to be less perfect than the other case values: it can be linked only to the second person] (cf. also *Grammatici Latini* II: 553, 582–583, 585). With this definition Priscian clearly highlights the specific and different nature of the vocative case with respect to the other case values: ultimately, it is represented as an asymmetric element. In the section *De personis* 'On person', Priscian argues that the first and second person are usually expressed by pronouns, unlike the third person (unless deixis or anaphora is requested). For this reason, every nominal form – except the vocative – is in the third person:

Prima enim et secunda, nisi figurate, adiunctione nominis non egent, cum et substantiam et qualitatem tam suam ipse qui loquitur, quam eius, ad quem praesens praesentem loquitur, videtur scire vel aspicere. Tertiae vero personae ideo congrue adiunguntur nomina, quia potest vel abesse persona vel spatio eius qualitas obscurari.

[On the other hand, the first and second persons, unless they are *in figura*, do not involve nouns, since the speaker knows or sees both his own essence and characteristic and the essence and characteristic of the addressee, since he is present. Nouns are instead rightly added to the third person, since it may happen that the person is absent or that his characteristic is not accessible because of the distance.] (*Grammatici Latini* II: 585 lines 14–28)

In modern terms, Priscian seems to be aware that noun referentiality is typically full and not deictic. Moreover, it is really remarkable how Priscian's idea recalls the Benvenistean *corrélation de personnalité* (Benveniste 1946, 1956) (cf. section 3), according to which within the category of person there is a semiotic split: first and second person are in opposition to third person, since the referentiality of the former is defined only by linking to the extra-linguistic context of the speech act (i.e. deictically), unlike the referentiality of the latter (Donati 2010b).

In conclusion, Priscian and Apollonius do realize the deictic nature of the vocative, even if only implicitly, and in their approach it remains an asymmetric, unexplained element. In contrast, in our opinion the second person deictic nature of the vocative case can resolve the problem of its apparent exceptionality: since nouns can be used, without a pronoun, not only to refer to a third person, but also to identify the second person speech act participant, placing the participant in a given speech act, this function is carried out by the category of the vocative case. In other words, the vocative can be defined as a deictic category linked to the semiotic split identified by Benveniste. This point will be developed in section 3. However, as far as Apollonius' and Priscian's approach is concerned, we can say that, although they definitely include the vocative case in Greek and Latin case systems, they clearly recognize its functional specificity.

1.2. Martin of Dacia

The localist case theory of the Scholastic grammarian Martin of Dacia (13th c.) shows a very interesting treatment of the vocative, since he includes it within the Latin case system by using a theoretical trick. In his work *Modi significandi* 'Modes of meaning' (Roos 1961), he accounts for the entire Latin case system with two parameters: first the spatial notions of *principium* 'source' and *terminus* 'goal'; and second the parameter for defining the spatial relation with respect to the substance and/or the act.[3] In this frame, Martin assumes that: "Vocativus enim se habet in ratione termini excitantis, quia vocativus terminus est excitationis" [The vocative exists by reason of the arrival point of the person who is exhorting to act, since the vocative is the arrival point of the exhortation to act] (Roos 1961: 42).

Table 1. Latin cases in Martin of Dacia

	respectu substantiae 'with respect to the substance'	*respectu actus* 'with respect to the act'	
principium 'source'	genitive	nominative	
	indifferenter respectu actus et substantiae 'indifferent with respect to the substance'	*respectu actus* 'with respect to the act'	
		actus significati 'represented act'	*actus excitati* **'urged act'**
terminus 'goal'	dative ablative	accusative	**vocative**

For Martin, the only difference between the vocative and accusative cases is that the vocative exists in connection with an act urged by someone (*actus excitatus*) – that is, the imperative verb – whereas the accusative is linked to a simply represented act, but both fall in the category *terminus respectu actus*. On this basis, we can affirm that Martin's interpretation and inclusion of the vocative among the Latin cases is grounded in a theoretical trick. The trick lies in the choice of inserting an *ad hoc* split between two different kinds of act, *actus significatus* and *actus excitatus*, in order to involve the level of pragmatics and discourse in the description of the vocative case. The level of pragmatics is implicitly identified as essential for the analysis of the vocative. In other words, in Martin's work there is clear reference to the level of discourse and the dimension of pragmatics: the concept of illocutive force is introduced in this localist approach to cases. In order to include the vocative in the Latin case system, Martin must insert an *ad hoc* distinction in his description, thus confirming that the definition of the vocative case must involve the level of discourse.

1.3. Hjelmslev

Hjelmslev's position is different yet again: within his structuralist frame of the category of case, the vocative is definitely ruled out, since its meaning and function are totally unrelated to those of the other case values (Hjelmslev [1935] 1972[2]: 96–97).

According to Hjelmslev (1972[2]: 23–24), the proposal put forward by Bernhardi in the 19th century (1805: 138) to consider the vocative case a second person case must be refused, since noun paradigms lack first person forms and consequently lack a first vs. second person opposition; moreover, pronouns lack vocative forms. In Hjelmslev's perspective, the vocative case introduces an unacceptable asymmetry into the noun system. However, the idea of a specific correlation between vocative and second person is not new, as we have noted with reference to Apollonius and Priscian. In any case, from Hjelmsev's point of view, the vocative creates an asymmetry within the nominal system and must be excluded from the category of case: according to Hjelmslev, "Est cas une catégorie qui exprime une relation entre deux objets" [Case is a category expressing a relation between two objects] (Hjelmslev 1972[2]: 96) and consequently "La définition qui vient d'être donnée permet à coup sûr d'exclure le vocatif de la catégorie casuelle. Par opposition à tout véritable cas, le vocatif a précisément ceci de particulier de ne pas exprimer une relation entre deux objets" [The definition just given certainly allows us to rule out the vocative from the category of case. Unlike every true case, the vocative has exactly the peculiarity of not expressing a relation between two objects] (Hjelmslev 1972[2] : 97).[4]

On the other hand, this theoretical assumption of Hjelmslev's raises a basic question: excluding the vocative from the cases is obviously controversial, since we cannot forget that the vocative case can be formally integrated into case systems; in particular, it is fully integrated into the case systems of Ancient Greek and Latin, to which Hjelmslev himself refers in this section of his work. Once again the peculiarity of the vocative case emerges, together with the problems of its collocation within case systems. As a consequence, the choice to exclude it from the cases is not free from theoretical difficulties.

1.4. Questions

In light of these remarks, we can say that there are fundamentally two questions to account for.

First, it seems to be necessary to outline a definition of the function of the vocative case in appropriate linguistic terms, since this point is often quite neglected from a strictly theoretical point of view. It is simply defined as the case by means of which someone is addressed.

Second, we argue that the interpretation of what we called the "form-function detachment" problem is the source of the questions about the inclusion of the vocative case in case systems. As we have seen, the vocative can be formally integrated among the cases, but on the other hand it is functionally different from them. As a consequence, two basic positions can be found among scholars. Some exclude it from the cases because of its functional specificity: we have seen the example of Hjelmslev. Conversely, others do include it among the cases by virtue of its formal systemic character: we have seen some examples with Apollonius Dyscolus, Priscian, and Martin of Dacia. By analysing of texts in the previous sections we have tried to underline how, in these authors' works, the inclusion of the vocative among the cases actually comes into conflict with the classification parameters adopted to define its function. In other words, the classification of the vocative as a case implies either some theoretical trick, as in Martin of Dacia, or at least special pleading about its exceptional status with regard to the other case forms, as in Apollonius Dyscolus and Priscian.

Thus the crucial question seems to be: how is the form-function detachment to be handled from a theoretical point of view? And furthermore, can the vocative be regarded as a case?

2. The vocative case as a "referentiality shifter"

In order to answer to these questions, we have to take into account person deixis and the level of discourse. As we have said, the notions of person deixis and discourse often recur, more or less explicitly, in the treatment of the vocative case by different authors and in different theoretical approaches. Can we put together person deixis and discourse with the form-function detachment problem? And, if so, how?

The same kind of form-function detachment is the object of several seminal works by Benveniste (1946, 1956, 1969, 1970). In these papers, the French scholar shows that such detachment exists because language is fundamentally an activity. In fact, Benveniste develops the idea of the opposition between person and non-person in the apparently uniform paradigm of the personal pronouns. The deictic category of person emerges as one of the interface areas which actually show the impossibility of separating language as a system (*langue*) from language as an activity (*dis-*

cours). In this section, we argue that the Benvenistean opposition between person and non-person is an explanatory notion for the vocative case as well.

It is well known that from 1946 on, Benveniste identified the opposition between person (i.e. first and second person) and non-person (i.e. third person) within the structure of the category of person: first and second persons are intrinsically different from third person, since the referentiality of the ones is defined only by linking to the extra-linguistic context of the speech act, unlike the referentiality of the latter. In fact, the third person is intrinsically different from the first and second persons, because its referent is not supposed to appear *in praesentia* during the speech act; for this reason, according to Benveniste, it is wrongly put on the same level as the first and second persons by the grammatical tradition. The facts that third person pronouns are actually derived from demonstratives and that the third person of the verb has a special expression in several languages (it is very often represented by zero marker or by a formally less marked element than first and second person) provide evidence for the completely different nature of the third person (Benveniste 1946, 1956). To sum up, the third person is completely different from the first and second persons, since its reference is not necessarily realized deictically and its referent can therefore be absent: it is the non-person. As a consequence, there is a semiotic split within the category of person: the first and second persons carry out their reference deictically, unlike the third person. This characteristic of the category of person is illustrated by personal pronouns:

> [...] les pronoms ne constituent pas une classe unitaire, mais des espèces différentes selon le mode de langage dont ils sont les signes. Les uns appartiennent à la syntaxe de la langue, les autres sont caractéristiques de ce que nous appellerons les "instances de discours", c'est-à-dire les actes discrets et chaque fois uniques par lesquels la langue est actualisée en parole par un locuteur. [Pronouns do not form an unitary class, but different kinds according to the model of language of which they are signs. Some of them belong to the syntax of language, others are typical of what we will call "instances of discourse"; that is, the discrete and always unique acts by means of which language is actualized in speech by a speaker]. (Benveniste [1956] 1966: 251)

As a matter of fact, within the personal pronoun paradigm, semiotic and functional inconsistencies allow us to claim that this word class, which is conveyed as homogeneous by the Western grammatical tradition, is only apparently uniform and shows a form-function detachment: "I" and "you" need to refer to the extra-linguistic context in order to carry out their reference; by contrast, third person pronouns are totally different, since they concern the non-person and are mainly anaphoric: "Il n'y a donc rien de commun entre la fonction de ces substituts et celle des indicateurs de personne" [There is nothing in common between the function of these substitutes and that of the person markers], but "la symétrie est seulement formelle [...]" [the symmetry is only formal] (Benveniste 1966: 256).

This semiotic split points out a basic feature of language: the presence, within the language system, of elements directly referring to the actualization of the system itself, i.e. to the dimension of discourse. These elements make it necessary to consider language both as a system ("répertoire de signes et système de leurs combinaisons" [set of signs and system of their combinations]) and as an activity ("activité manifestée dans des instances de discours qui sont caractérisées comme telles par des indices propres" [activity manifesting itself in instances of discourse defined as such by means of specific markers[5]]) (Benveniste 1966: 257, 1970).

To return to the vocative case, we said that it has no semantic-syntactic function, unlike other case values, but rather a pragmatic function: to place an addressee in a given speech context. In other words, the vocative case is a person deictic and can be defined as a "referentiality shifter", namely a linguistic device linking the inherently non-deictic referentiality of nouns to the extra-linguistic context, in particular to the dimension of the speech act participants. The function of the vocative case is to insert a second person deictic variable into the referentiality of nouns, shifting it to (at least partially) deictic referentiality. In our perspective, the semantic-functional gap between the vocative and other cases can be understood in Benvenistean terms, by means of the opposition person vs. non-person, in line with the analysis of the personal pronouns. Benveniste pointed out that the internal structure of this class shows the split between first and second persons (person) and the third person (non-person). Among nouns, on the other hand, the person vs. non-person split is outlined in a different way by the vocative case: only the second person is marked, and it is in opposition to the first and third persons, which are not marked on nouns. In other words, there is a split because only the second person can be marked on nouns, thus referring to the speech act participants (person); otherwise, nouns, as their referentiality is typically full, are not marked for the category of person and lack reference to the speech act participants (non-person).[6] Therefore, as only the second person is marked, nouns show an opposition of second vs. first and third person (which are not marked), unlike Benveniste's *corrélation de personnalité*.

Hence, we argue that the asymmetry created by the category of vocative case is twofold: on the one hand, the asymmetry is internal to the speech act participants, since the first person is not marked on nouns; on the other hand, the vocative establishes a person vs. non-person opposition with respect to the other case values.

One may ask why only the second person is involved; this means trying to answer to the question put forward by Hjelmslev. In our opinion, the answer is that within nouns only the second person needs to be marked, since inserting a deictic variable for the first person would be impossible: that function is performed by the deictic "I" (as regards the third person, it goes without saying that if there is a noun, there is no anaphora). Conversely, the addressee must be identifiable not only by means of the deictic "you", but also by means of a noun. As a consequence, we can say that the anomaly constituted by the vocative is only apparent: in fact, the form-function detachment can be interpreted and solved by means of the Benvenistean concepts of person vs. non-person and *discours* as language put into action (cf. also section 1), in parallel to Benveniste's remarks about personal pronouns: within language systems, there are items directly referring to the dimension of discourse, in order to enable the language system to be put into use.

3. Conclusion: can the vocative be regarded as a case?

In light of the previous remarks, we can try to answer the specific question as to whether or not the vocative can be regarded as a case. The analysis of personal pronouns by Benveniste shows that in the system language can organize functionally different elements within formally homogeneous grammatical paradigms: in this sense, the systemic character can indeed coexist with a semantic-functional split. As a consequence, the question as to whether the vocative is a case is actually a false problem. The vocative, being a deictic, is definitely different from cases as regards its function, but can be formally included in the case system in order to refer deictically to the addressee by means of a noun and can be interpreted in light of the person vs. non-person opposition. We have seen that because of this form-function detachment the vocative case is often seen as an anomaly, so that some scholars exclude it from the cases because of its functional specificity, while others include it by virtue of its formal systemic character by means of theoretical tricks.

In opposition to these mutually incompatible positions, following Benveniste we have tried to show that elements belonging to the system (*langue*) and elements belonging to the *langue* but at the same time directly referring to the *discours* necessarily coexist in the language system, in order to enable the language system to be put into use.

Notes

1. The terms "vocative" and "case" have many different interpretations in the literature (Donati 2010a). In this work, the expression "vocative case" means a morphologically marked nominal form of address which is integrated into the case paradigm of a given language (as in Latin and Ancient Greek) as well as the grammatical category, in line with Daniel and Spencer (2009: 626): "Sometimes, the form of address is integrated into the case paradigm of the language, and then we can say there is a vocative case". The notion of "case" itself is not unambiguous. "Case" here means the nominal inflectional category indicating the syntactic-semantic relationship between noun phrases and other elements in the clause. The term "vocative devices" refers, in general, to the coding strategies used to mark address on nouns: vocative devices can be morphological (e.g. in Latin and Ancient Greek) or prosodic (e.g. in English and Italian), and can also use specific particles (e.g. in Arabic the particle *yā*). It is worth noting that these three strategies may coexist.

2. It goes without saying that we do not intend to attribute a modern theory of syntactic relationality and deixis to Apollonius and Priscian: our aim is to point out how several remarks by these two grammarians actually appear to make reference to notions and concepts which are well known in modern linguistics, although obviously they are formulated in a very different way.

3. This second parameter, i.e. the relation to the substance and/or the act, is syntactic and can be understood, in modern terms, as the opposition between adnominal and adverbal. According to Martin of Dacia, nominative and genitive can be seen as cases of origin with regard to act and substance respectively. In contrast, dative, ablative, accusative, and vocative are characterized as cases of *terminus*, i.e. destination; dative and ablative are neutral as to the relation to the act and/or substance, while accusative and vocative relate only to the act.

4. Hjelmslev's approach to the category of case is universalistic and localist. In his view, case relations are basically grounded on spatial relations. His theory may be outlined, simplifying it to an extreme degree, in the following way. Cases and their meanings are structured by three hierarchically implied dimensions: direction, coherence vs. incoherence and subjectivity vs. objectivity. The third parameter implies the second, and the second implies the first. This happens because every language exhibits the first dimension, several languages exhibit the second, and only a few exhibit the third. The fundamental dimension is direction, in which the positive term is approach and the negative term is separation. The second dimension, i.e. coherence, is also local: coherence vs. incoherence is the spatial relationship where one of the objects is contained or not contained in the other. Finally, the third dimension is not local, but concerns the opposition between an objectively

and a subjectively conceived relationship (Hjelmslev 1972[2]). Anyway, the question is too broad to deal with fully here: for a thorough analysis of the complex case theory of Hjelmslev, with regard to other structuralist approaches as well, see Agud (1980: 275), Calboli (1972: 121), Serbat (1981: 97). As for the connection between the spatial nature of cases and the vocative in Hjelmslev, see Donati (2010c).

5.   At the same time, Jakobson (1957) called this kind of linguistic item "shifters", which directly refer to the speech act and its participants.

6.   As we have said, the awareness of connection between the second person and the vocative case can be found in different terms beginning with the ancient grammarians. More recently, Fink (1972) has argued that the Latin vocative case can be regarded as a form that conveys the feature of person but does not express case, assuming that vocative forms can be considered nominative as well as dative, accusative, etc., depending on the case value of the element with which they are coreferent. However, this assumption is hardly acceptable, especially since it seems to confuse coreference with syntactic agreement.

Latin and Ancient Greek sources

Hilgard, Alfred and Gustav Uhlig (eds.)
    1965   *Grammatici Graeci*. Reprint. Hildesheim: Olms. Original edition
                Lipsiae: in aedibus B. G. Teubneri, 1883–1901.
Keil, Heinrich (ed.)
    1961   *Grammatici Latini*. Reprint. Hildesheim: Olms. Original edition
                Lipsiae: in aedibus B. G. Teubneri, 1855–1880.
Lallot, Jean (ed.)
    1997   *Apollonius Dyscole. De la Construction*. Paris: Vrin.
Roos, Heinrich (ed.)
    1961   *Martini de Dacia Opera*. Hauniae: apud librarium G.E.C. Gad.

References

Agud, Ana
   1980   *Historia y Teoría de los Casos*. Madrid: Gredos.
Bernhardi, August F.
   1805   *Anfangsgründe der Sprachwissenschaft*. Berlin. Reprinted 1990,
             Stuttgart-Bad Connstatt: Frommann-Holzboog.
Benveniste, Émile
   1946   Structure des relations de personne dans le verbe. *Bulletin de la
             Société de Linguistique de Paris* 43: 1–12. Reprinted 1966 in:
             Émile Benveniste, *Problèmes de Linguistique Générale I*, 225–
             236. Paris: Gallimard.
Benveniste, Émile
   1956   La nature des pronoms. In *For Roman Jakobson*, Morris Halle
             (ed.), 34–37. The Hague, Mouton. Reprinted 1966 in: Émile Ben-
             veniste, *Problèmes de Linguistique Générale I*, 251–257. Paris:
             Gallimard.
Benveniste, Émile
   1969   Sémiologie de la langue. *Semiotica* 1: 1–12 and 127–135. Re-
             printed 1974 in: Émile Benveniste, *Problèmes de Linguistique
             Générale II*, 43–66. Paris: Gallimard.
Benveniste, Émile
   1970   L'appareil formel de l'énonciation. *Langages* 5 (17): 12–18. Re-
             printed 1974 in: Émile Benveniste, *Problèmes de Linguistique
             Générale II*, 79–88. Paris: Gallimard.
Calboli, Gualtiero
   1972   *La Linguistica Moderna e il Latino. I Casi.* Bologna: Patron.
Coseriu, Eugenio
   1955–1956 Dcterminación y cntorno. Dos problemas de una lingüistica del
             hablar. *Romanistisches Jahrbuch* 7: 29–54. Reprinted 1961 in:
             Eugenio Coseriu, *Teoría del Lenguaje y Lingüística General,*
             282–323. Madrid: Gredos.
Daniel, Michael and Andrew Spencer
   2009   Vocative: an outlier case. In *The Oxford Handbook of Case*,
             Andrej Malchukov and Andrew Spencer (eds.), 626–634.
             Oxford: Oxford University Press.
Donati, Margherita
   2009   La categoria del vocativo nelle lingue classiche: aspetti teorici,
             diacronici e tipologici. Ph.D. dissertation, Università Roma Tre.
Donati, Margherita
   2010a   Per una teoria del vocativo. Sistema, asimmetria e persona. *Lin-
             guistica e Filologia* 30: 11–47.

Donati, Margherita
  2010b   Vocative and Person in Priscian's metalinguistic reflections. In
               Latin Linguistics Today. Akten des 15. Internationalen Kol-
               loquiums zur Lateinischen Linguistik, Innsbruck 4.-9. April 2009,
               Peter Anreiter and Manfred Kienpointner (eds.), 525–535. (Inns-
               brucker Beiträge zur Sprachwissenschaft 137.) Innsbruck: Institut
               für Sprachen und Literaturen der Universität Innsbruck.
Donati, Margherita
  2010c   The space of address between deixis and metaphor. In *Space in*
               Language 2009. Proceedings of the Pisa International Con-
               ference, Giovanna Marotta, Alessandro Lenci, Linda Meini, and
               Francesco Rovai (eds.), 299–315. Pisa: Edizioni ETS.
Fink, Robert O.
  1972   Person in nouns: is the Vocative a case? *American Journal of*
               Philology 93: 61–68.
Hjelmslev, Louis
  1935   *La Catégorie des Cas. Étude de Grammaire Générale.* Aarhus:
               Universitetsforlaget I. Reprinted 1972. München: Fink .
Jakobson, Roman
  1957   Shifters, verbal categories and the Russian verb: Russian Lan-
               guage Project, Dep. of Slavic Languages and Literatures, Harvard
               University. Reprinted 1971 in: Roman Jakobson, *Selected*
               Writings, Vol. 2, 130–147. The Hague: Mouton.
Serbat, Guy
  1981   *Cas et Fonctions.* Paris: Presses Universitaires de France.
Venier, Federica
  2007   Per un superamento della dicotomia *langue/parole*: sentieri
               paralleli e intersezioni di retorica, linguistica testuale e
               pragmatica. *Acta Romanica Basilensia* 18: 9–52.
Venier, Federica
  2008   *Il Potere del Discorso. Retorica e Pragmatica Linguistica.*
               Roma: Carocci.

Vocatives as functional performance structures*

Patrizia Noel Aziz Hanna and Barbara Sonnenhauser

Abstract

The vocative is morphologically marked only in some languages; not infrequently, it merely occurs in a constrained set of paradigms. Unless they are morphologically marked, vocatives are classified as typical elements of performance; yet they are both signalled and interpreted in systematic ways by syntactic and/or prosodic non-integration. As a category of usage, the vocative challenges the polarity of system vs. performance. This paper offers a syntagmatic account of vocatives. To account for the two-sided nature of vocatives, they are analysed here as functional performance structures, i.e. as syntagmatic categories with indexical function

1. Phenomena of usage: grammatical theory and its consequences for vocative classification

Contrary to their importance in communication, and although they are amongst the most basic and earliest acquired structures of language, vocatives[1] are typically dealt with as peripheral aspects in grammatical theory. However, the communicative need to express direct forms of address is obvious. In European grammar tradition, the classification of the vocative is tied to the notion of the word 'paradigm', although call and address functions need not be signalled morphologically. In languages without morphological encoding of vocatives, vocatives are usually treated as phenomena of usage and thus not considered part of the language system. Yet, as systematic occurrences which emerge in language use, vocatives cannot be regarded as mere phenomena of performance – the more so since performance is often assumed to be defective as compared to competence.

(1)–(5) display various ways of encoding vocative calls;[2] they exhibit regular form-function pairing in morphologically, phonologically, and syntactically systematic ways. The examples demonstrate that morphological marking is only one way of signalling addressing.

(1) Polish: *Dariusz*   *Dariuszu*   *Drogi*   *Dariuszu*
                Dariusz:Nom.SG   Dariusz:Voc   dear:Adj Dariusz:Voc
(2) Uzbek: *Pulat*   *PuLAT*   *Hej*   *PuLAT*
                Pulat:Nom.SG   Pulat:Voc   Part   Pulat:Voc
(3) Baoulé: *Já*   *Jáè*
                Ja   Ja.Part:Voc
(4) Middle Bavarian: *der Hans*   *Hansä*
                      the Hans:Nom.SG   Hans:Voc
(5) Slovene: *drag*   *dragi*   *Matevž*
                dear:Nom.SG.indef dear:Nom.SG.def Matevž:Nom.SG

In Polish (cf. 1), the vocative can be marked morphologically, i.e. *Dariusz* (Nom) vs. *Dariuszu* (Voc). There are also syntagmatic usages with adjectives in combination with the morphologically marked vocative: *drogi Dariuszu*. Morphologically marked isolated vocatives, however, are considered both peripheral and affective (Berger 2001: 42; Anstatt 2005: 7).

In the Uzbek (Turkic) example (2), the vocative is marked intonationally: *PuLAT*. Special prosodic signalling of calls is also found in Standard German, English, French, and many other languages without morphological marking of vocatives. In Uzbek, the additional syntagmatic encoding of calls by a vocative particle, *Hej PuLAT*, is dependent on the community in which the vocative is used.[3]

In example (3) from Baoulé (Niger-Congo) the vocative particle is obligatory: The high tone proper name *Já* has to be combined with a vocative particle, resulting in a syntagmatic construction. This example illustrates that calls in tone languages are not necessarily combined with marked intonation patterns.

Middle Bavarian *Hansä* in (4) displays a morphologically marked vocative (Merkle 1975: 100). Paradigmatic encoding of vocatives is not the case for all Bavarian subdialects; all of them, however, mark the difference between referential and vocative usage by employing the definite article only in the first case. Referential vs. vocative usage are thus encoded syntagmatically.

An interaction between markers of definiteness and vocative function can also be found in Slovene, cf. (5). Slovene masculine adjectives in the nominative singular[4] show a subparadigm for the definite form indicated by the suffix *-i* and a subparadigm for the indefinite form lacking this suffix. In addresses, only the definite form can be used: *dragi Matevž*. While the vocative is not part of the Slovene nominal paradigm, it is here marked syntagmatically.

This short cross-linguistic sample of vocative encoding shows that a classification of the vocative as part of a morphological paradigm is not the first choice for a typological analysis. Clearly, the vocative is a performance phenomenon which is systematically regulated. Even in languages without morphological vocative marking, vocatives can be perceived 'online'. They can be indicated prosodically, for instance by pauses.

The functionalisation of pauses is a controversial topic in linguistic literature. In classical generative grammar, for instance, deviations from the expected temporal (and syntactic) pattern are analysed as performance errors: "A record of natural speech will show numerous false starts, deviations from rules, changes of plan in mid-course, and so on" (Chomsky 1965: 4).[5] However, pauses, as deviations in the sense of an unexpected interruption of utterance, can also be used deliberately. This kind of deviation is interpreted as intentional placement (cf. Bolden 2004 for citations), carrying specific functions. When functionalised, pauses refer to cognitive activities (e.g. Kentner 2007; Warren, White and Reichle 2009). After such functionalised pauses, the sentence does not simply continue; instead a "forward dialogical movement in time" (O'Connell and Kowal 2008: 64) is instantiated. In vocative signalling, prosodic as well as syntactic deviations caused intentionally by a speaker meet routinized hearer expectations.

Both prosodic and syntactic deviations follow certain language-specific patterns, e.g. in terms of correlations between intonation and syntactic position. For instance, vocative calls as one-word sentences can be marked by increased intensity, as in the Uzbek example in (2), or by special intonation contours as in German. Based on observations like these, vocatives are here considered part of the larger category of functional performance structures which also comprises structures such as parentheticals, citations and delocutive particles (Sonnenhauser and Noel Aziz Hanna ms.). These structures range from purely indexical signs (signs directing attention by the mere fact of being used and not because of their semantically encoded meaning, cf. sec. 2.2.) to fully conventionalized (lexicalised and grammaticalized) linguistic occurrences.

2. Vocatives as functional performance structures

Functional performance structures such as parentheticals, citations, and vocatives are deeply rooted in language use. Serving a specific function, they have always been acknowledged as structures. However, they lack core features of traditional linguistic categories, such as form-function mapping and paradigmatic oppositions. Furthermore, they also lack typical features of syntactic categories/parts of speech or specific inflectional and distributional properties characteristic of these structures. Because of their non-uniformity both across and within the various sub-types these structures can hardly be characterized in terms of paradigms;[6] thus their shared features remain unfocussed. Here, they are grouped together because of their similar signalisation (cf. sec. 2.1), their indexical function (cf. sec. 2.2), and their syntagmatic nature (cf. sec. 3).

2.1. Prosodic coding of vocatives

The term 'performance structure' is a psycholinguistic concept which relates to the temporal organisation of sentences. It is reflected in the length of pauses and specific mechanisms in language processing (Gee and Grosjean 1983). Zellner (1994: 50) defines performance structure as "psycholinguistic structure that captures the various degrees of cohesion between the words of an utterance"; cohesion results from the frequency of co-occurrence in usage, its consequential syntagmatic associations, and from syntactic relations (such as agreement). Cohesion can be signalled or modified by pauses; such functional pauses refer to cognitive activities (cf. Lampert 1992) and unlike regular pauses, e.g. physiologically conditioned pauses, contribute to comprehension (Zellner 1994: 47). Zellner (1994: 49) contrasts these functional pauses with "abnormal pause insertion", which has a different effect. In addition, performance structures are not necessarily congruent with syntactic structures. Experiments revealed that they correlate more frequently with prosodic structures (Abney 1992).

In analysing vocatives as performance structures, the psycholinguistic concept is supplemented by a functional dimension. The subclasses of functional performance structures display a high amount of variability; this variability is, however, not arbitrary – functional performance structures are systematic elements of language. They are not necessarily signalled by inherent classificatory features, but by prosodic phenomena like intonation, intensity, pauses, etc. and syntactic non-integration, setting them apart from the surrounding syntactic and prosodic environment (cf. Figure 1).

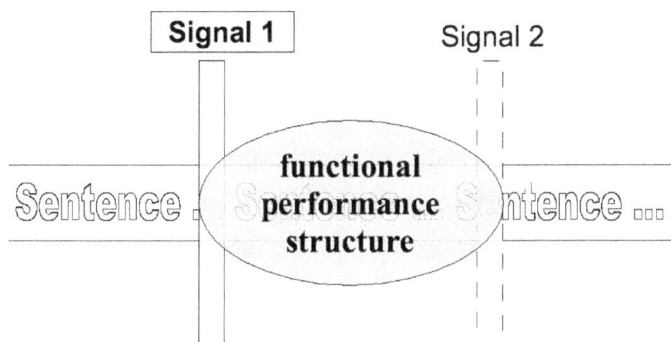

Figure 1. Signalisation of functional performance structures

Figure 1 shows the prosodic and syntactic non-integration of functional performance structures. Signal 1 marks the beginning of the functional performance structure, signal 2 marks its end. As will be illustrated, the specific ways of prosodic marking by signal 1 and 2 depend on the syntactic position of the functional performance structure: The systematicity of functional performance structures is indicated by the correlation of prosodic signalling and syntactic position. Furthermore, for their specific interpretation, pragmatic and contextual factors play a distinctive role as well.

For vocatives, both the signalling and their syntactic position at the beginning, the end, or in the middle of the sentence are crucial. This can be seen in (5), where the prosodic signalling distinguishes *Peter* as indirect object from *Peter* as address:

(5) a. *Was*   *hast*   *du*   Peter   *gesagt?*
          what   have:2.Sg   you   Peter   said:Pstptcp
     b. *Was*   *hast*   *du,*   Peter, *gesagt?*
          what   have:2.Sg   you   Peter   said:Pstptcp

Relevance of position is illustrated in (6); while *Peter* in clause-initial position functions as establishment of address, it serves as a pragmatically enriched continuation in clause-final position:

(6) a. Peter, *was*   *hast*   *du*   *gesagt?*
          Peter   what   have:2.Sg   you   said:Pstptcp
     b. *Was*   *hast*   *du*   *gesagt,*   Peter?
          what   have:2.Sg   you   said:Pstptcp   Peter

The encoding of vocatives can be represented as a language-specific inter-action of syntax and prosody (or as the reflection of prosodically and syn-tactically signalled functions by punctuation in written texts, cf. Noel Aziz Hanna and Sonnenhauser 2013). Depending on where and under which pragmatic or syntactic conditions a vocative is placed, its embedding has to be signalled prosodically. The signal of the beginning (signal 1) and end (signal 2) of functional performance structures can differ. For a vocative introducing a sentence, signal 1 coincides with a sentence-initial pause; signal 2 occurs under special conditions. While the German example in (7a) represents the default in which the ending of the vocative is not signalled by a subsequent pause and is simply used in addressing function, (7b) with a pause as signal 2 is interpreted in relation to this default temporal organi-sation. Deviating from this default, (7b) is thus interpreted as a warning, a joke and so on, depending on context information. As for pragmatic en-richment in the French example in (8a), the use of the imperative can be perceived as more direct than in German and thus can be understood as an authoritarian command. The insertion of a pause (8b) was interpreted by our informant as being more polite, since the speaker awaits the attention of the listener.

(7) a. no pause
    Anna,   *gib*   *mir*   *eine*   *Praline.*
    Anna:Voc give:2.Imp.SG me:Dat.SG a:Acc.SG.F praline:Acc.SG

b. pause
    Anna (.),   *gib*   *mir*   *eine*   *Praline.*
    Anna:Voc give:2.Imp.SG me:Dat.SG a:Acc.SG.F praline:Acc.SG

(8) a. no pause
    Madame,   *tenez-vous*   *droit.*
    (*Nouveau dictionnaire de la langue française*: s.v. droit)

b. pause
    Madame (.),   *tenez-vous*   *droit.*

Syntactic non-integration is explicitly marked by prosody when the inter-pretation of the NP as a vocative is at stake. While the dative *Anna* in (9a) is prosodically integrated in the sentence, the vocative in (9b) is prosodi-cally marked when spoken and also marked by comma insertion when written.

(9) a. *Hast*   *du*   *Anna*   *eine*
      have:2.SG.Ind.Prs you Anna:Dat.SG a:Acc.SG.F
      Praline   *weggenommen?*
      praline:Acc.SG   taken:PSTPTCP

b. *Hast*   *du,   Anna,   eine*
   have:2.SG.Ind.Prs   you   Anna:Voc   a:Acc.SG.F
   Praline   *weggenommen?*
   praline:Acc.SG   taken:PSTPTCP?

Estimations as to whether ambiguous constructions are grammatical or acceptable (cf. 10) are not just language-specific, but also dependent on the grammatical concept at the bottom of these considerations (cf. Haider 2011 on 'grammatical illusions'). As acceptable but ungrammatical constructions, they are not systematically comprised in a number of reference grammars.

(10) $^{?}$*She beat, my friend, everyone who challenged her at chess.*
       (Zwicky 1974: 798)

One fact leading to the marginal status of vocatives in reference grammars is the focus on the morphological paradigm. However, in languages which do not encode vocatives overtly by means of morphology, vocative particles, etc., the signalling of vocatives lies in the domain of usage. Vocative usage is indexical in nature.

2.2. Indexicality of vocative usage

The communicative function of functional performance structures is based on their indexical character. This function is abduced from a 'deviation' from what is expected, i.e. the prosodic and syntactic continuation expected at any given time in the online-process of utterance. Thus the kind of expectation related to functional performance structures is not an expectation primarily related to its internal structure (e.g. to the proper name which is called or to the parenthetically inserted material); instead, it is linked to its external structure, i.e. its syntagmatic embedding. The process leading to its decoding is abduction.

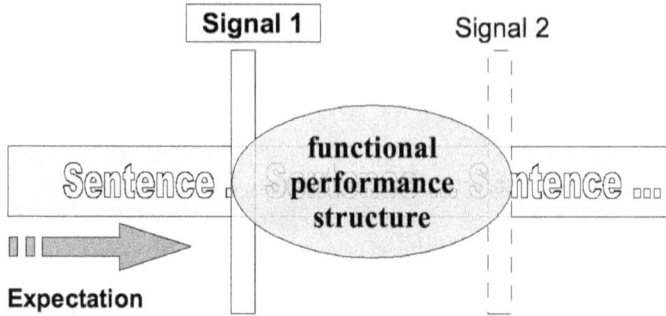

Figure 2. Perception of functional performance structures

Figure 2 illustrates functional performance structures from the recipient's perspective. The functional performance structure does not agree with the recipient's syntactic and/or prosodic expectation. It is perceived as a deviation from the likely pattern; thus the recipient interprets the functional performance structure by forming an explanatory hypothesis for its being used. Abduction is activated by a moment of surprise caused by systematically exploited non-integration.

The logical procedure of abduction has been elaborated by Peirce, who defines it as "the process of forming an explanatory hypothesis" (EP 2: 216). Abductive reasoning proceeds as follows: some surprising fact is observed, but if a specific assumption were true, this surprising fact "would be a matter of course" – and hence, there is reason to suspect this assumption to be true (EP 2: 231). With respect to functional performance structures, the deviation from the expected constitutes the 'surprising fact', the inference of a function the 'explanatory hypothesis'. This inferred function is best described in terms of indexicality, i.e. in a specific direction of attention and in relating different levels of (con)text.

We take functional performance structures to be interpreted by abduction as indexical signs. The notion of 'index' is here employed in its broader Peircean sense. Whereas in linguistic analyses the term 'index' is frequently employed as a synonym of deixis (cf. e.g. Bühler 1934; Nunberg 1993), Peirce conceives the index in more general terms as a "reactional sign, which is such by virtue of a real connection with its object" (EP 2: 163). Indices can thus be conceived as basically relational phenomena. They are context-dependent and cause the focussing of attention. In addition, Peirce stresses that indices, unlike symbols, need not be conventionalised. They are phenomena of 'existence' (e.g. EP 2: 277) and, as such, manifest themselves only within an actual context of usage.

As specific type of functional performance structures, vocatives are recognizable in the actual usage of language. A German proper name, for instance, can be used referentially or vocatively, cf. (9) above. Syntactic and/or prosodic non-integration runs counter to default pattern expectation, i.e. referential usage. The most plausible hypothesis to account for this deviation from expectation is vocative usage; under these conditions, the non-integrated proper name is most likely to refer to the actual context. This indexical relation to the actual context is abduced in a routinized way; it is interpreted as 'vocative' function.

In addition, the relational character of Peircean indices is capable of capturing the relation between signs as well as between sign and situation of utterance. The pragmatic dimension is fundamental to definitions of the vocative such as Lambrecht's (1996: 267): "Vocatives serve to call the attention of an addressee, in order to establish or maintain a relationship between this addressee and some proposition."

The systematic employment of functional performance structures can lead to individual habits or even new grammatical conventions, e.g. the emergence of new vocative forms in Russian, Romanian, Irish and Scottish-Gaelic (cf. the survey in Anstatt 2008). Naturally, the unambiguous signalling of non-integration can also introduce abduction processes. Examples of such unambiguous signals leading to abduction are 'sung' calls in languages such as Dutch or German and marked stress patterns in Turkish vocatives (Zimmer 1970; Göksel and Pöchtrager this volume).

Functional performance structures in general and vocatives in particular cannot be captured paradigmatically in their entirety. In the next section, a syntagmatic analysis of these structures will be proposed.

3. Paradigm vs. syntagm

Traditionally, vocatives are categorized paradigmatically. Saussure's distinction between syntagmatic and associative/paradigmatic relations also brings in the issue of system vs. performance (de Saussure 1916 [1959]: 123):

> In discourse, on the one hand, words acquire relations based on the linear nature of language because they are chained together. [...] Combinations supported by linearity are syntagms. [...] In the syntagm a term acquires its

value only because it stands in opposition to everything that precedes or follows it, or to both.

Outside discourse, on the other hand, words acquire relations of a different kind. Those that have something in common are associated in the memory, resulting in groups marked by diverse relations. [...]

We see that the co-ordinations formed outside discourse differ strikingly from those formed inside discourse. Those formed outside discourse are not supported by linearity. Their seat is in the brain; they are a part of the inner storehouse that makes up the language of each speaker. They are associative relations.

Syntagmatic relations pertain to the level of combination; they form a mechanism *in praesentia*. Associative or paradigmatic relations, in contrast, pertain to the level of selection, of substitutivity. This mechanism is one *in absentia* (de Saussure 1916 [1959]: 123). In structuralist terms, the value of an element in its paradigmatic dimension depends on the values of those elements that are associated with it but have not been chosen. Consequently, the value of an element from a paradigmatic perspective presupposes knowledge about its possible alternatives. And this in turn presupposes the set of alternatives to be closed and hence be definable prior to usage.[7] The value of an entity in its syntagmatic sense, however, cannot be determined in advance. It manifests itself online, i.e. in the actual usage of that entity. Thus the crucial distinction here is not one between paradigmatic and non-paradigmatic constituents, but between conventionalised (paradigmatic) and less or non-conventionalised (syntagmatic) co-occurrences, including not only constituents of certain classes, but also prosodic marking and syntactic position.

This distinction is fundamental for the analysis of functional performance structure such as vocatives. Traditionally, vocatives are classified in paradigmatic terms. It is this paradigmatic perspective that impedes cross-linguistic analyses of vocatives; as will be argued here, vocatives are more efficiently analysed as syntagmatic phenomena.

3.1. A paradigmatic perspective on vocatives

Although cross-linguistic data as in (1)-(5) demonstrate that a paradigmatic classification of vocatives is problematic, the categorization in European grammatical accounts centres on paradigmaticity. As a consequence, vocatives are integrated in reference grammars and handbooks if they are morphologically encoded in a paradigm, whereas the same is not true to the same extent for morphologically unmarked vocatives. Many Eastern European languages have old morphological vocative endings, e.g. Latvian, Lithuanian, Polish, Upper Sorbian, Czech, Ukrainian, Croatian, Serbian, Bulgarian, Macedonian, and Greek. There is, however, a tendency in many of those languages to non-obligatory vocative usage (Anstatt 2008: 9, 11). This is the case also for Standard German, in which vocative marking by *du* as in (11) is non-obligatory:

(11)   *Du*   *Hans,*   *gibst*   *du*
       you:2SGL.Nom   Hans   give:2SGIndPrs   you:2SGNom
       mir   *die*   *Zeitung?*
       me:1SG.Dat   the:Acc.SG   newspaper:Acc.SG
       'Hans, can you give me the newspaper'

The classification of a language as 'vocative language' is arbitrary to a considerable extent. Standard German is not usually classified as a language with vocative marking, although Schottelius, in the 17th century, listed vocative case for German in combination with particles: "Rufendung (Vocativus) ist die fünfte/wodurch man einen rufft/beklagt/begrüsset/als: *O du Mensch/Hör du Mann/O du Hauß*" (*Ausführliche Arbeit von der Teutschen HauptSprache* [1663]: 296; cf. Häcki Buhofer 1987: 138) ['The call ending (Vocativus) is the fifth by which one calls, bewails, greets, e.g. 'Oh you mankind, Hear you man, Oh you house']. The vocative is not always classified as a case, but even then, the argument is based on the notion of paradigm. Trubetzkoy (1937: 43), for instance, notes:

> Der Vokativ ist ja kein eigentlicher Kasus. Man ersieht es schon daraus, dass er in einer Sprache, wie das Bulgarische, wo die Nominaldeklination zugrunde gegangen ist, weiter bestehen bleibt, und andererseits den besonders kasusreichen finnischugrischen und ostkaukasischen Sprachen unbekannt ist. Übrigens, haben sich die meisten großrussischen Mundarten einen neuen Vokativ geschaffen.

> [The vocative is not a case proper. This can be learned from the fact that it persists in a language like Bulgarian in which nominal declension was lost, and then again is not known in languages with rich case systems like the Finno-Ugric and East Caucasian languages. Furthermore, Great Russian dialects have created new vocatives.]

The paradigmatic perspective on vocatives is obvious in Trubetzkoy's statement. From a different angle, Kuryłowicz acknowledges the vocative as a case, but notes that it would be a methodological error to classify it together with other cases. His argument is functional and in its core also paradigmatic (1949: 147):

> Mettre le vocatif sur un seul et même plan avec les autres formes casuelles serait un lapsus méthodique comparable à une confusion de l'emploi expressif des interjections avec la valeur symbolique des autres parties du discours. La première dichotomie, quand on procède à classer les cas, détachera donc le vocatif de tout de reste.

More frequently, however, nominative and vocative case are classified together in terms of syncretism. The defining criterion of syncretism, identity of form but not of function, again means a paradigmatic evaluation of the vocative. Yet the aspect of identical form can be questioned both for vocative and nominative, depending on whether form is understood in merely paradigmatic or also in syntagmatic terms, i.e. including its external structure (cf. sec. 2.2).

The fact that nominative case marking is an option of expressing the address function, however, does not imply that an explicit morphological marking of the vocative remains without impact for the morphological system. In colloquial Polish, for instance, subjects can have vocative form; thus, apart from its affectionate meaning, the vocative has syntactic function: *Mój misiu* (Voc.) *już śpi* 'My teddy bear is already asleep' (Kottum 1983: 140; cf. also Stifter this volume). In reverse, in languages in which the vocative is not marked morphologically, the paradigm is not necessarily a crucial factor for its classification.

The indexical function of functional performance structures and its being abduced from prosodic and syntactic deviations cannot be captured in paradigmatic terms. Deviation and indexicality, which are both fundamental to the concept of functional performance structures, are dependent on the syntagm.

3.2. A syntagmatic perspective on vocatives

Functional performance structures cannot be defined extensionally by enumerating an extensive list of members of this category, since they do not constitute a closed class. Instead, the syntagmatic perspective on the vocative involves the interaction of linguistic subsystems.[8] The syntagmatic signalisation of the vocative is language-specific because the interacting subsystems are language-specific.

Vocatives are characterised by an internal and an external structure. While morphological marking as well as special intonation (e.g. Ladd 2008 for English, Gussenhoven 1993 for Dutch, Varga 2008 for Hungarian intonation of calls) fall into the category of internal structure, the external structure is linked to actual performance. The vocative is a category of usage and is signalled as such (cf. Figure 1); its structure is marked by special intonation in relation to the surrounding syntactic structure as well as by means of syntactic non-integration.

(12)   *He tries Peter at court.*
(13)   *He tries, Peter, at court.*
(14)   *Ich*   *erkläre*   *Mika*   *gleich,*
       I:1SG.Nom   eplain:1SG.Prs.Ind   Mika:Dat.SG   immediately
       worum   *es*   *geht.*
       what   it   goes:3SG.Ind.Prs.
       'I'll explain immediately to Mika what this is all about.'
(15)   *Ich*   *erkläre,*   *Mika,*   *gleich,*
       I:1SG.Nom   eplain:1SG.Prs.Ind   Mika:Voc   immediately
       worum   *es*   *geht.*
       what   it   goes:3SG.Ind.Prs.
       'I'll explain immediately, Mika, what it is all about.'

Differences in intonation are easily perceptible and can be obligatory. The meaning of (12) with *Peter* as a direct object is clearly different from (13) with *Peter* as a vocative. The same is true for the intonational encoding of the proper names in relation to the surrounding structure. In these syntactic positions, the vocative has to be signalled unambiguously.[9] In (13) and (15), unlike (12) and (14), signal 1 as well as signal 2 are employed, e.g. as pauses. The vocative as a syntagmatic category is only perceivable under these 'concatenated' conditions of usage. In this way, the temporal organisation contributes to the encoding of the vocative. A laxness in marking vocatives may necessitate a tedious reanalysis of a sentence; cf. e.g. the following interview (wdr5 Presseclub, 16.10.2011[10]):

(16)   Ähm, aber das Witzige ist, der Anlass ähm über dieses über das System nachzudenken, äh aus meiner Sicht, wäre die Finanzkrise vor zwei Jahren gewesen, als Frau Hermann die Banken sich verspekuliert haben [...].

       [Um, but the funny thing is the occasion ahem to think about this system, er, from my point of view, would have been the financial

> crisis two years ago when Frau Hermann the banks speculated and lost.]

In the discussion in (16), the addressing of Frau Hermann is not marked prosodically (which in the transcription is represented by missing commas). The result is an ambiguous structure, a garden path phenomenon, since the most likely interpretation is incorrect. The default interpretation is that *Frau Hermann* is the subject of the sentence, because of the placement and prosodic integration of the constituent. The reanalysis is introduced by the predicate *verspekuliert haben* 'speculated-and-lost:PstPtcp have:Inf', which does not agree with a singular subject *Frau Hermann* and reveals *die Banken* 'the banks' as subject of the sentence. Expectations as to the likely continuation of a structure are predictions about possible following constituents. If these expectations are not fulfilled, the result is (temporal) ungrammaticality (a 'surprising fact', cf. sec. 2.2). The grade of expectedness and hence the required efforts in reanalysis depends on individual linguistic experiences (cf. Gibson, Desmet, Grodner, Watson, and Ko 2005: 337–338 on the relation between an individual's experience with language and its expectations on the continuation of the linguistic input).

The prosodic marking favours a classification of vocatives as a syntagmatic instead of a paradigmatic category. The distribution in the sentence points in the same direction. As has been shown (cf. sec. 2.1), vocative placement has an impact both on vocative and sentential meaning. A vocative placed in first position introduces the selection of the next speaker. A vocative in last position may serve as a signal of reassurance. The vocative in second position is part of the group of Wackernagel 'enclitics' since it was a low tone element following the first word in the oldest Indo-European languages (cf. Wackernagel 1892). Low tone in combination with second position placement again provides evidence for an interaction between syntax and prosody (Noel Aziz Hanna 2009) and thus for the multi-dimensional and syntagmatic nature of vocatives.

Vocatives are signalled by a deviation from the syntactically or prosodically expected default pattern. This deviation is made use of in an economic way. In (17), the vocative *Susi/Susie* is not signalled by a pause after the vocative NP.

(17) without pause
      German: *Susi gib mir noch 5 Minuten.*
      English: *Susie give me 5 more minutes.*

Since (17) is a verb-first imperative, *Susi/Susie* is unambiguously a vocative. In addition, there is no morphological agreement between the NP and the finite verb. Any misinterpretation is thus excluded. If, however, in this environment the vocative is realised in a prosodically non-integrated way, the result is pragmatic enrichment. Signal 1 (cf. Figure 2) is usually present at the beginning of a sentence. Thus signal 2, the pause, is critical for pragmatic enrichment; in this case, the second boundary signal is functionalised (cf. 18).

(18)   pause following the vocative
       German: *Susi (.) gib mir noch 5 Minuten.*
       English: *Susie (.) give me 5 more minutes.*

The internal marking of vocatives also has a syntagmatic dimension. Here, the factor of formulaicity plays a crucial role, i.e. conventionalised co-occurrences, related to vocatives. Forms of address are frequently syntagmatic, e.g. French *Madame le Professeur*, Arabic *'ammu Sa'eed* 'uncle Saeed', and Polish *drogi Dariuszu* 'dear Dariusz'. As formulaic expressions, they display a faster and less distinct articulation (Wray 2002: 261).

Another phenomenon which demonstrates the syntagmatic contribution to inner vocative marking is the fact that vocative calls show special prosodic patterns. In German and English they are sung in a definable intonation contour. However, if a sentence is not entirely sung, the embedded call cannot be sung. The whole German utterance in (18), for instance, can be sung; however, to provide only the proper name with special intonation is not conventional. Thus the deviation from the expected which constitutes functional performance structures is language-specific not only in its paradigmatic but also in its syntagmatic dimension.

4. System vs. performance

Vocatives as syntagmatic categories of usage challenge the separate treatment of language as system vs. language as performance. The answers of various theoretical frameworks concerning categories between system and performance are part of a larger current discussion. Vocatives may serve as a testing case for these positions. Functional performance structures capture the assumption that 'the system' is to be found not *behind* but *in* performance.

'Performance' is a notational term – there is more than one accepted definition. In de Saussure's *Cours de linguistique générale*, performance is conceived as instantiation of *langue*. Chomsky's (1965) differentiation of competence and performance postulates competence as "the speaker-hearer's knowledge of his language" and performance as "the actual usage of language in concrete situations" (1965: 4). In contrast to de Saussure, Chomsky's performance cannot reflect competence because performance is regarded as deficient.

Both approaches to the language system and its realisation have been criticized. Stetter (2005: 19) argues against an equation of 'Können' and 'Wissen' (ability/skill vs. knowledge) and locates the system in performance (2005: 12). This view is also held in more recent psycholinguistic approaches: "spontaneous spoken discourse [...] generally reflects an underlying orderliness that derives from the psychology of the speakers and listeners themselves" (O'Connell and Kowal 2008: 77).

Vocatives are tied to the situations in which they are used. Their place in grammatical literature seems to be owed to the fact that they are morphologically marked in a number of languages. Morphological marking is the reason for their classification as system-level elements – any notion of a performance phenomenon signalled by a suffix is undesirable from a theoretical point of view in grammatical traditions which rely on inflectional morphology. Yet, as this article has demonstrated, morphological marking is just one of many possible markings of vocatives, both language-internally and in a cross-linguistic perspective.

In order to deal with the various possibilities of signalling vocative functions, the concept of functional performance structures has been proposed in this paper. These structures are neither unambiguously assignable to the language system nor to performance. Functional performance structures 'break rules', but are not arbitrary. They develop certain language-specific regularities. It is their position between an assumed dichotomy of system vs. performance which makes them relevant for grammatical theory. Therefore vocatives, which are usually regarded as peripheral phenomena, quite on the contrary provide a chance to investigate in detail fundamental axioms in linguistic theory.

5. Summary

It has been argued that the paradigm as a criterion for vocative classification is a highly problematic benchmark. The paradigmatic approach to vocatives is not only tied to the morphological paradigm, it also obscures the fact that even morphological vocative marking can be optional. Vocative marking in a cross-linguistic perspective relies on a much larger inventory of signals. Cross-linguistically, vocatives are part of a class of linguistic phenomena which are signalled by sentential temporal organization and by prosodic and syntactic non-integration. Categories which are signalled in this way are classified here as functional performance structures. A model for both the signalisation and the interpretation of these phenomena has been suggested; it is based on the notions of abduction and indexicality. The model enables the representation of the default signalling of vocatives and a vocative signalling which is pragmatically enriched. Facing the fact that morphological marking of vocatives is only one among many possibilities, vocatives – and performance structures in general – are analysed as syntagmatic categories. This allows us to capture the two-sided nature of vocatives as elements of usage, and at the same time as systematic elements of language.

Notes

* We would like to thank Firmin Ahoua (Université de Cocody, Abidjan), Laurence Bourgeais (Paris), Olga Dioubina-Reubold (University of Bamberg), Kristina Mochar (University of Vienna), Pulat Nazarov (Samarqand Davlat Universiteti), Christiane Nessmann (University of Vienna), and Iwona Woźniczko (University of Bamberg) for examples and native speaker judgements, the anonymous referees, and William Tayler (University of Bamberg) for native speaker judgements as well as correcting our English.
1. The term 'vocative' is used here in its pre-theoretical reading, i.e. as an utterance used for calling and addressing.
2. For a differentiation between calls and addresses cf. Zwicky (1974).
3. According to our informant, it is unusual using the particle in Samarkand.
4. There is no such distinction for adjectives ending in consonant clusters (Greenberg 2008: 42).
5. More recently, deviations have been treated in context with grammaticality judgements which are not binary but gradual; Sternefeld et al. (1999–2008), for instance, propose to extend generative grammar with a parameter 'constraint violation cost strength' in order to include deviations into the grammatical model.
6. Cf., for instance, Isačenko's (1995: 614–620) attempt to classify Russian parenthetically inserted words as separate parts of speech. However, almost none of the examples he considers can be judged as parenthetical word outside usage, since most of them may be used as adverbials as well. This can be seen, for instance, in *očevidno* 'obviously' which can be used both parenthetically (*oni, očevodno, ugovorili ego* 'they, obviously, managed to con-

vince him'), and as an adverb (*očevidno, čto* 'it is obvious that'). The specific function manifests itself in the actual usage only.

7. The concept of a priori knowledge of alternatives is not affected by actual contexts of usage which may render specific alternatives more or less salient.

8. In the syntagmatic perspective on vocatives, syntax is included in the argumentation but not considered in isolation (for a syntactic analysis of vocative in which the vocative is analysed as a functional head like mood, force, topic and focus cf. Stavrou ms., Hill this volume).

9. The context can render such an utterance unambiguous. If Mika is the only person present in the situation, the dative reading is unlikely which means that an explicit prosodic signalling of the vocative is not crucial.

10. <http://www.podcast.de/episode/2872458/WDR_5_Presseclub%3A_ Vollgas_oder_Vollbremsung_-_Deutscher_Wirtschaftsboom_am_Ende%3F_ Sendung_vom_16.10.2011> (02.12.11)

References

Abney, Steven
  1992   Prosodic structure, performance structure and phrase structure. *Proceedings of the 5th DARPA Workshop on Speech and Natural Language*. http://www.vinartus.net/spa/92d.pdf, 19.11.2012.

Anstatt, Tanja
  2005   Der polnische Vokativ: Aussterbende Kasusform oder produktiv verwendetes Wortbildungsmittel? *Zeitschrift für Slawistik* 50: 328–347.

Anstatt, Tanja
  2008   Der slavische Vokativ im europäischen Kontext. In *Linguistische Beiträge zur Slavistik: XIV. JungslavistInnen-Treffen*, Ljudmila Geist and Grit Melhorn (eds.), 9–26. München: Sagner.

Berger, Tilman
  2001   Semantik der nominalen Anrede im Polnischen und Tschechischen. In *Studies on the Syntax and Semantics of Slavonic Languages: Papers in Honour of Andrzej Bogusławski on the Occasion of his 70th Birthday*, Viktor S. Chrakovskij, Maciej Grochowski, and Gerd Hentschel (eds.), 39–50. Oldenburg: Bibliotheks- und Informationssystem der Universität Oldenburg.

Bolden, Galina
  2004   The quote and beyond: defining boundaries of reported speech in conversational Russian. *Journal of Pragmatics* 36: 1071–1118.

Bühler, Karl
    1934   *Sprachtheorie*. Reprinted 1999. Stuttgart: Lucius und Lucius.
Chomsky, Noam
    1965   *Aspects of the Theory of Syntax*. Cambridge/Massachusetts: MIT Press.
[EP 2]
    1998   *The Essential Peirce. Selected Philosophical Writings*, edited by the Peirce Edition Project, Vol. 2 (1893–1913). Bloomington, Indiananpolis: Indiana University Press.
Gee, James Paul and François Grosjean
    1983   Performance structures: A psycholinguistic and linguistic appraisal. *Cognitive Psychology* 15: 411–458.
Greenberg, Marc L.
    2008   *A Short Reference Grammar of Slovene*. Munich: Lincom.
Gibson, Edward, Timothy Desmet, Daniel Grodner, Duane Watson, and Kara Ko
    2005   Reading relative clauses in English. *Cognitive Linguistics* 16: 313–353.
Göksel, Aslı and Markus A. Pöchtrager
    this vol.   The vocative and its kin: Marking function through prosody.
Gussenhoven, Carlos
    1993   The Dutch foot and the chanted call. *Journal of Linguistics* 29: 37–63.
Häcki Buhofer, Annelies
    1987   Die Kasus des Deutschen – Wissenschaftsgeschichtliche und methodologische Überlegungen. *Deutsche Sprache* 2: 137–150.
Haider, Hubert
    2011   Grammatische Illusionen – Lokal wohlgeformt – global deviant. *Zeitschrift für Sprachwissenschaft* 30: 223–257.
Hill, Virginia
    this vol.   Features and strategies: the internal syntax of vocative phrases.
Isačenko, Aleksandr V.
    1995   *Die russische Sprache der Gegenwart. Formenlehre*. München: Hueber.
Kentner, Gerrit
    2007   Length, ordering preference and intonational phrasing: Evidence from pauses. *Proceedings of Interspeech 2007*. Antwerpen. http://www.ling.uni-potsdam.de/~gerrit/KentnerInterspeech07.pdf, 19.11.2012.
Kottum, Steinar E.
    1983   In defense of the vocative: The case of modern Polish. *Scando Slavica* 29: 135–142.

Kuryłowicz, Jerzy
 1949 Le problème du classement des cas. In *Esquisses linguistiques*, 131–150. Reprinted 1973. München: Fink.
Ladd, Dwight Robert
 2008 *Intonational Phonology*. Cambridge: Cambridge University Press.
Lambrecht, Knud
 1996 On the formal and functional relationship between topics and vocatives. Evidence from French. In *Conceptual Structure, Discourse and Language*, Adele Goldberg (ed.), 267–288. Stanford: CSLI Publications.
Lampert, Martina
 1992 *Die parenthetische Konstruktion als textuelle Strategie*. München: Sagner.
Merkle, Ludwig
 1975 *Bairische Grammatik*. Heimeran: München.
Noel Aziz Hanna, Patrizia
 2009 Wackernagels Gesetz im Deutschen: Zur Interaktion der linguistischen Subsysteme Phonologie, Syntax und Informationsstruktur. Habilitationsschrift, LMU Munich.
Noel Aziz Hanna, Patrizia and Barbara Sonnenhauser
 2013 Verschriftlichung zwischen System und Rede: Zur interpunktorischen Kodierung von funktionalen Performanzstrukturen. *Sprachwissenschaft*.
[Nouveau dictionnaire de la langue française]
 1835 Edited by François Noël and Charles Pierre Chapsal. 5th ed. Bruxelles: J.P. Meline.
Nunberg, Geoffrey
 1993 Indexicality and deixis. *Linguistics and Philosophy* 16: 1–43.
O'Connell Daniel C. and Sabine Kowal
 2008 *Communicating with One Another. Toward a Psychology of Spontaneous Spoken Discourse*. New York: Springer.
Saussure, Ferdinand de
 1916 *Course in General Linguistics*. Edited by Charles Bally and Albert Sechehaye. In collaboration with Albert Reidlinger. Translated from the French by Wade Baskin. Reprinted 1959. New York: Philosophical library.
Schottelius, Justus Georg
 1663 *Ausführliche Arbeit von der Teutschen HauptSprache*. Reprinted 1967. Tübingen: Niemeyer.
Sonnenhauser, Barbara and Patrizia Noel Aziz Hanna
 ms. Funktionale Performanzstrukturen.

Stavrou, Melita
    ms.   About the vocative phrase.
Sternefeld, Wolfgang, Sam Featherston, Tanja Kiziak, Anca Weimer, and Tim
            Friedrich
    1999–2008   Suboptimal syntactic structures. Projekt A3 in the SFB 441 Lin-
                guistic data structures: on the relation between data and theory in
                linguistics. Tübingen. http://www.sfb441.uni-tuebingen.de/a3/
                index-engl.html, 19.11.2012.
Stetter, Christian
    2005   *System und Performanz: Symboltheoretische Grundlagen von
                Medientheorie und Sprachwissenschaft.* Weilerswist: Velbrück
                Wissenschaft.
Stifter, David
    this vol.   Vocative for nominative.
Trubetzkoy, Nikolai Sergejewitsch
    1937   Gedanken über die slovakische Deklination. *Sbornik Matrice
                Slovenskej* 15: 39–47.
Varga, Lázló
    2008   The calling contour in Hungarian and English. *Phonology* 25:
                469–497.
Wackernagel, Jacob
    1892   Über ein Gesetz der indogermanischen Wortstellung. *Indoger-
                manische Forschungen* 1: 333–436.
Warren, Tessa, Sarah J. White, and Erik D. Reichle
    2009   Investigating the causes of wrap-up effects: Evidence from eye
                movements and E–Z Reader. *Cognition* 111: 132–137.
Wray, Alison
    2002   *Formulaic Language and the Lexicon.* Cambridge: Cambridge
                University Press.
Zellner, Brigitte
    1994   Pauses and the temporal structure of speech. In *Fundamentals of
                Speech Synthesis and Speech Recognition*, Eric Keller (ed.), 41–
                62. Chichester: John Wiley.
Zimmer, Karl E.
    1970   Some observations on non-final stress in Turkish. *The American
                Oriental Society* 90: 160–162.
Zwicky, Arnold
    1974   "Hey, Whatsyourname". In *Papers from the Tenth Regional
                Meeting. Chicago Linguistic Society. April 19-21, 1974*, Michael
                La Galy, Robert Fox, and Anthony Bruck (eds.), 787–801.
                Chicago: Chicago Linguistic Society.

On the case of the vocative

Christian Stetter

Abstract

In traditional grammar, the vocative has been described as a case within the morphological system of certain languages, e.g. of ancient Greek or Latin. As a category of syntax, however, it cannot be treated in the same way within the parameters of what W. von Humboldt called the "third-person-perspective" of traditional theories of syntax. Within this theoretical framework, its systematic status cannot be described. This will be demonstrated by discussing the description of the vocative given by Helbig and Buscha in their grammar of contemporary German. In the following sections, an alternative view of the problem will be developed on the basis of the so-called "second-person-perspective", described by W. von Humboldt in his essay on the dualis. Within that theory of grammar, a "first-" and "second-person-perspective" has been added to the traditional "third-person-perspective". Within this framework, the vocative can be described as a category of syntax.

1. The vocative – a problematic case

The vocative is a special case among cases in every way. Shakespeare has a dying Caesar say to his adoptive son *Et tu, Brute,*[1] *Thou too, Brutus, auch Du, Brutus,*[2] while Brutus is stabbing him with a dagger. That this case is not morphologically marked in English or German does not mean that there is no vocative in these languages. What is then the vocative? It cannot be a case in these languages. Many grammarians resort to a "rule": vocative = nominative. But this is clearly nonsense. This would be tantamount to giving Chinese, which has no cases but rather words that can be described with good reason as nouns or pronouns, an accusative case. On the other hand, the speech act of direct address, for which the vocative is always and only used, in the languages in which it exists, belongs to the universal repertory of speech acts which people use in oral communication. From this perspective one has to understand the vocative as a universal form of human speech. The vocative must therefore be categorically different from what is taught in school grammars of Greek or Latin.

As simple as the vocative appears, it is apparently a case, in both senses of the word, in which traditional grammatical standards easily seduce us into making category errors.[3] Let us focus first on a description of the phenomenon in a grammar of German language that is as simple as it is clever, that namely the nominative can "serve the address (vocative)" and does so "as a constituent external to the sentence".[4] This description skirts around the dangers by first avoiding a grammatical categorization of the vocative and second emphasising that the vocative is a special use of the nominative that cannot be captured through a syntactic description of the clause. The kind of use is thereby left open. But clearly the vocative is being treated as a performance phenomenon here. So the case of the voca- tive in fact poses a question of categories: whether the difficulties that it causes traditional grammatical, that is, systematic treatment, is a result of its failure to fit into the basic schema of post-Saussurian linguistics, which has dedicated itself to the study of language systems, in which – especially under the influence of generative linguistics – the more or less vague con- cept of language system was often equated with that of a grammar and still is today conceived of as a hierarchically ordered system of articulation levels or schemata: syntax, morphology and phonology.[5]

This confronts us with two questions or problems:

(1) Where is the vocative located in the whole of language articulation systems?
(2) Does it belong to the language system or to performance – or isn't it an either-or in this case?

The first question can only be answered if its material and formal charac- teristics have been described thoroughly enough. We begin with a brief assessment.

Even in the introductory remarks the vocative was referred to in three dif- ferent respects:

• as a formal case in certain languages – that is, as a morphological cate- gory; this is the traditional categorisation.
• as a "free", i.e. sentence external constituent; the question is then "con- stituent of what?"
• as a speech act of address.

This last categorisation is undoubtedly the most comprehensive. So let us begin there: Wherever the vocative is used as a case, it is used as a morphological marking of a word or a phrase with which one person approaches another to address him or her. In the Caesar quotation above the address is *et tu, Brute*, or *thou too, Brutus*. The word 'vocative' apparently refers to the entire act of address. In contrast, in an expression like *Paul, come here*, the vocative would be part of a speech act which we would understand as a request or command or something similar. In a structural grammar this speech act would be expressed as something like

(1) *[Command]*[6] → *VOC(ative) + VP*

with the following development

(2) *VP → V(erb) + ADV*

(3) *ADV → here*

(4) *V→ come*

(5) *VOC → Paul*

In accordance with the formal rules of such a grammar, "VOC" functions here as the name for a lexical category. The speech act function would be filtered out of this account, because in this kind of formal expression, the initial symbol "Command" signifies that and only that which the projection of this symbol by the subsequent C-rules signifies, here merely that a single word can also be used as a vocative or in the function as such, and that this word used in this manner exhibits no special morphological features as does *Paul's address* or *the present Pauls*, etc.

So nothing is gained by such an account. However, a simple permutation test shows the syntactic distinctiveness of a vocative expression or phrase:

(6) *(?) come Paul here*

(7) *come here Paul*

(6) would only be acceptable with a special intonation, something like: *come Paul 'here* (not over there); in contrast, (7) is as syntactically well-formed as *Paul come here*.[7] Does this mean that the description offered by Helbig and Buscha is correct, that the vocatively used word is external to the sentence? Let us consider some other examples:

(8) *Paul kannst Du mir eine neue Parkmarke zuweisen*
     Paul can you issue me a new parking permit

(9) *kannst Paul Du mir eine neue Parkmarke zuweisen*
     can Paul you issue me a new parking permit

(10) *kannst Du Paul mir eine neue Parkmarke zuweisen*
     can you Paul issue me a new parking permit

(11) *kannst Du mir Paul eine neue Parkmarke zuweisen*
     can you issue me Paul a new parking permit

(12) *kannst Du mir eine Paul neue Parkmarke zuweisen*
     can you issue me one[8] Paul new parking permit

(13) *kannst Du mir eine neue Paul Parkmarke zuweisen*
     can you issue me a new Paul parking permit

(14) *kannst Du mir eine neue Parkmarke Paul zuweisen*
     can you issue me a new parking permit Paul

(15) *kannst Du mir eine neue Parkmarke zuweisen Paul*
     can you issue me a new parking permit Paul[9]

Examples (8), (9), (10), (11) and (15) are possible as uses of the (address act) vocative without special intonation marking;[10] in (9)–(14) the vocative *Paul* can be understood as the rheme-marking of the previous word. In all of these cases the vocative thus has a uniquely identifiable semantic function.[11] One can speak of a position "external to the sentence" in the narrow sense only in reference to (8) and (15). But since in (8), (9) and (15) *Paul* and *you* have the same co-reference to the person addressed as in all of the other cases, one will hardly be able to refer to the position of Paul in (8) and (15) as "external to the sentence", if one views each expression as a whole. More accurate might be a description to the effect that the vocative – always understood as an act of address – can always fill the position after the appropriate rheme, and that the positions before the first and after the last constituent of the phrase can be regularly filled by an act of address.[12] This characteristic of the vocative act can be called its "syntactic indefiniteness" – a hardly satisfactory description that requires further interpretation.

2. 'Dual' reference and rheme marking

How can this result be reconciled with the traditional grammatical view of treating phrases, which apparently is based on assuming a kind of "normal form" of phrases, in which a function like rheme marking doesn't play a role or need not be taken account of. If the assumption is correct that the vocative, understood as an act of address, has the above-described property that in addition to the "null positions" in front of and behind the phrase in question it can take the position after the rheme as a sign of markedness, then its semantic properties are at issue. As already hinted at above, these are based on the special character of its reference: in each act of address, the speaker does not make reference to a situation – be it asserting, questioning or in another way – but rather, to say it with W. von Humboldt, refers as an "I" to another person, a "you" with which a specific subject, an "it", is negotiated.[13]

In contrast, the perspective of the grammar theory from the beginning with the Greeks up to today is characterised by the fact that, in coming from Aristotelian logic, it proceeded from the level of the situation from the outset, that is the level of the "it". The prototype of that which still today is called a sentence, the verbal phrase, is a sentence that is constructed, today the same as 2000 years ago, in the schema of subject + predicate (+ object$_1$ + object$_2$ + ... + object$_n$) – a schema that can be adjusted to the most diverse sentence forms by categories like "statement" or "adverbial".

With these sorts of phrases one refers invariably to an "it" in the suggested Humboldtian sense. In contrast, with a vocative – always understood as an expressive act or a part thereof – one invariably makes reference to a person being spoken to, a 'you'. If I say in a certain situation at ... in ... "Paul, can you ... issue...", I am referring with "Paul" to a 'second person', whether that person is present or not; with the rest of the utterance to a 'third person'. This reference to a 'second person' who is addressed – spoken to as a person – in a speech act or a literal text will be designated in what follows as the 'dual' reference. This can only be realised in actu, that is, in performance. If the speech act or written text in question is cited in a report, the dual reference is rescinded, as in:

(16) *He said, "Paul, can you ... issue."*

With "he", the speaker or writer of this report makes reference to a person, but not at all so with "Paul" – he does not even have to know who or what "Paul" means. He refers solely to the situation that at some point this and that was said or written by so and so.[14]

This dual reference is thus the characterising semantic feature of the vocative as a speech act in the sense of Austin, and this act is subject to – as are all speech acts – certain success conditions: the speaker or writer must know the addressed person, e.g. know that the person is still alive, how to address this person, etc. These are success conditions exclusively for the effective execution of the relevant action, here a request. In contrast, the act of quotation is subject to very different conditions and different types of success conditions, primarily of course sufficiently exact information about who said or wrote exactly what under which conditions. A quotation is only correct when the wording of the quoted utterance or text exactly matches the words of the quotation.[15] The references made in the quoted text are obliterated by the act of quotation, as shown above.

Let us now return to the question posed above, of what the syntactic indeterminacy rests on: clearly there is a connection between this property and the dual reference that occurs in every vocative act. For the various positions that the vocative can occupy in the sentence – with the exception of the two "null" positions in front of and behind the phrase as in (8) and (15) and position (9) – there is a corresponding specific rheme marking. Even these can only be determined in the moment of the speech act: What the theme and the rheme of a phrase are depends exclusively on the prior thematised context of the conversation. The reference area to which the expression "the prior thematised context of the conversation" refers remains indeterminate, or more precisely must remain indeterminate. For in every discourse, the extension of this expression is "discoursively" determined by the persons involved in the discourse: as we go along.

A discourse element can only become a rheme of the particular discourse fragment relative to the corresponding thematised fragment. What that is, is something that only the persons taking part in the discourse and their listeners know, if anyone. And they also decide what new discourse element gets introduced hic et nunc. Of course a third person C can enter into a discourse between A and B and return to a previously thematised element. Person C could join the discourse about the allocation of a parking permit from the example above and ask:

(9‘)   *Kannst Paul Du ihm eine neue Parkmarke zuweisen*
       Can Paul you issue him a new parking permit

namely in the sense of:

(9'') *Kannst Paul Du ihm [tatsächlich o. ä.] eine neue Parkmarke*
zuweisen
Can Paul you [really or something similar] issue him a new parking
permit

where the modal *can* is rhematised. Semantically *can* is part of the verbal
segment of the logical predicate "x issues y a z", and plays the role of the
discourse rheme in what in logic is assumed to be the "normal case" of
linguistic communication, while the theme role is played by one of the
verbal complements.[16] The rhematisation of the other part of the verb *issue*
would accordingly be noted as

(15') *kannst Du mir eine neue Parkmarke 'zuweisen Paul.*
can you 'issue me a new parking permit Paul

Thus the syntactic indeterminacy of the vocative described above can be
explained: It is clearly related to the function of determining the rheme of a
new phase in the discourse. This can also only be done – as shown above –
in the actual performance of the discourse participants, in that they mention
what emerges from what was earlier thematised. The discourse participants
can certainly have different views of what that may be. In the course of the
discourse, each can bring up something already thematised and add something new to it. The rules of phrase construction are basically neutral in
regard to such discourse aspects.[17]

Within this approach the vocative act can be understood as a speaker
function which explicitly augments the linguistic act of the articulation of a
text sequence or a phrase as an element of parole by means of the "dual"
address act, the addressing of the person being spoken to. This act usually
has the additional function of the rheme-marking within the theme-rheme
structure, in as far as this is present. Thus there are two times two
possibilities:

First, the addressing can be made explicit through the use of a vocative
word such as "you", "Paul", "Brutus", etc., or it is implicit in the course of
the dialogue, as in:

(17)　A: 　*Ich glaube [Anne], wir müssen diesen Punkt heute*
entscheiden.
'I think [Anne] we have to decide this point today.'

　　　B: 　*Der Meinung bin ich nicht [Paul].*
'That is not what I think [Paul].'

Second, the rheme marking can refer to an element of the conversation that was already thematised, or it refers to a theme that is new for one or all of the discourse participants.[18] The referential field of the already thematised, compared to which an element of the conversation in each case is described as "new", is nothing objective in the current discourse, but rather is likewise – explicitly or implicitly – determined in each discourse, and changed again and again ... The possibilities here range from the formal decision-taking of an agenda to the conversation with guests during dinner, where the subjects of the conversation come from the guests themselves – an extreme contrast to the formalised proceedings in a court process, for example.

3. Concepts of type

The name "vocative" can be used for different things: as the description of a morphological category as well as of a speech act. But here we are confronted with the situation that the traditional categorisation of the vocative as a system category – and a morphological one at that – contradicts the speech act theory understanding of the vocative as an actual executed address of a person, that is, a performance category. So the question emerges: is this contradiction really a contradiction? If one follows linguistic orthodoxy, then yes – because the system dictates the system of rules for performance.[19] According to this perception, the language system is a collection of units – phrases, words, morphemes – subject to the operation of combinatory rules: a noun as the head of a phrase can bind an article in the left null position, left and right attributes, etc.; an adjective that heads a phrase can ..., a verb ..., etc. Under such an understanding of the relationship between system and performance, the use of the conjunction *weil* 'because of' as a subordinating conjunction, for example, would disobey a certain rule and that use would be wrong: *Ich bin zu spät, *weil ich hab' den Bus verpasst*[20] 'I am too late, because of I missed the bus'.[21] This ignores the fact that this is often used in colloquial (German) language today, at least in non formal spoken contexts, by persons whose "native speaker" status can hardly be denied by a particular slant of the same orthodoxy. This paradox results from a notion of language type whose provenence out of a certain understanding of alphabetic writing is by now barely controversial.[22] The type is conceived there extensionally as a quantity of replicas, that is tokens of this type, which not only are similar but are equal in the sense that minimal differences between the shape or form of two replicas R' and R" of the same type T are negligible in terms of both R' and R" being tokens of type T. An example of in this sense not only similar but equal tokens of a type could be the letters of this text. That is, the rules for the production of one replica are also the rules for the production of all replicas of the same set.[23] Thus, the rules that account for the replica-of relation for any tokens A, B, C of a group M are:

(18)   *A is a replica of itself.*

(19)   *If A is a replica of B, then B is also a replica of A.*

(20)   *If A is a replica of B and B is a replica of C, then A is a replica of C.*

In other words: the replica-of relation is reflexive, symmetric and transitive.[24] Each word written in an alphabet whose sequence of letters is uniquely identifiable in the described sense can be thus considered a replica of, for example, the entry of the same word in the Duden dictionary and thus of each identically spelled literal word of the German language. I call a type that is based on the replica-of relation in the described way a 'realistic' (type of) type.

Other conditions obtain for the copy-of relation:

(21)   *If A is a copy of B, then B is not a copy of A.*[25]

(22)   *If A is a copy of B and B is a copy of C, then A is under no circumstances a copy of C.*[26]

Thus the copy-of relation is neither symmetric nor transitive and – trivially – also not reflexive.[27] I call a type that is based on the copy-of relation a 'nominalistic' (type of) type.[28]
   The oral words of every natural language are one and all nominalistic types in the described sense: groups not of equal but rather of similar tokens in terms of form and meaning. A glance at Grimms' dictionary shows this. The same thing is true mutatis mutandis for the abstract units of a natural language, be they morphological units like case or syntactic units such as phrase types. And this is true not only diachronically but also synchronically: What we call a noun phrase is a type that can only be described by a rule of alternation, consisting of a noun as head of the phrase and complements like articles or article phrases, right and/or left attributes, and each of these type can themselves have different forms – that is basic linguistic knowledge. And a formal grammar must even allow a "null projection" of the form XP → X, as in NP → N.[29]

In each case it is categorically true that what a word or phrase is – no matter what language – is true always and only relative to a theory of syntax in which that which we call a "word" is depicted as an end or basic category.[30] This phenomenon cannot be captured with a realistic notion of type, but it does work with a nominalist(ic) notion. With this notion of type synchrony can even be represented as the borderline case of diachrony.[31]

Thus the syntactic type noun phrase, for example, is in the light of these facts always representable only as a group of phrases that have a noun as head and are similar to each other, but are certainly not equal to each other.

The same principle works for the vocative, if it is understood as a speech act in the sense described above. The criterion that makes it possible to collect all of these acts into one set is the function of the 'dual' address. The rest of the functions described above usually serve the rhematisation function, and in fact this is also a collective title for more or less similar functions. All of them have something to do with the function of 'dual' address, and some of them can only be understood as a borderline case of the rhematisation function.

Their common feature is in fact the function of the 'dual' address. This shows that the vocative cannot be a syntactic category, since the address, like the rhematisation, is a semantic, not a syntactic function.[32] On that account it is a performance category par excellence, as this function can only be realised in performance, as shown above.

The vocative, understood as an act of address, that is as a speech act, must be viewed both as a universal type of speech act as well as a literal executed act, similar to the constative or certain classes of performatives. If one uses the name "vocative" for the description of a certain case, that is, a morphological category, this is simply an equivocal use of this name. This is not a problem of the theory, but in the best case one of the cultivation of theoretical vocabulary.

With this position of "neither fish nor fowl" in the traditional menu of linguistic theory, the vocative is undoubtedly a not only materially highly interesting object of linguistic inquiry but at the same time one which, when discussed – as suggested – leads to the center of current questions of theoretical linguistics and philosophy of language.

4. Conclusion

To conclude, it seems to be evident that the vocative can, in fact, be described as a category of syntax within a theory of syntax which is not restricted to the "third-person-perspective" of traditional grammar.

Notes

1. According to another version: „Tu quoque, Brute".
2. Act III, Scene 1.
3. For the concept of 'category error' cf. Ryle (1949: Ch. 1).
4. Helbig and Buscha (2001: 261).
5. Based of course on the doctrine of double articulation: syntax and morphology as the two "semantic" articulation systems and phonology as the "sub-semantic" system; cf. Martinet (1963).
6. The initial symbol in brackets is characterised here as "command" only for the purposes of the exposition, since what it means syntactically emerges exclusively from the subsequent projections through the constituency rules (C-rules) of the form A → B + C + ... + D. Because this is the description of an effectively completed expression, only C-rules and not lexicon rules are used. Cf. Stetter (2005: 221–223) and Stetter (2009).
7. I have left out the commas in these examples.
8. *one* corresponds with the meaning of *eine* in this example.
9. Identical with the translation of the German example (14).
10. The interpretation given here only holds for the German language examples. Without specific intonation (9) is certainly a rare case, but an address after the first words of a phrase does occur often in normal conversation. With the intonation *'kannst Paul* 'can Paul'... *kannst* 'can' would be the rheme; cf. below also p. 310–311. (15) could also be possible with the following intonation: *kannst Du mir eine neue Parkmarke 'zuweisen Paul* 'can you 'issue me a new parking permit Paul'; here the rheme would be *zuweisen*.

    Also cf. Noel Aziz Hanna (2009: 217–225), for the vocative in second position.
11. I consider the rheme marking to be a semantic function, since it serves to identify a new logical subject within the reference area to which the so-called theme refers. One could also speak of a rhetorical or pragmatic function, but essentially it is about the behavior just described, and that is without a doubt reference. The reference area of a discourse is the whole of the situation to which the discourse refers.
12. This last case is apparently not unambiguous. Cf. (15') below.
13. Cf. for this Humboldt (1827) *Ueber den Dualis*; and further Stetter (1997: Ch. 10, 400–415).
14. This constellation is similar to the problem of so-called belief-sentences, which may not occur in a truth-functional language, as discussed by Wittgenstein in his "Tractatus". The expression marked in " ..." in (16) is taken to be the name for a discourse subject through the function of citation, rather than an expression with which an action is taken – in the same way as the sentence "On the Ides of March Caesar was murdered" can be summarised in the

nominal "The murder of Caesar on the Ides of March" which no longer refers to Caesar but to the fact that he was murdered. Cf. Wittgenstein, *Tractatus* (5.54–5.542).

15. Word orders of the things cited can be left out under certain circumstances, in as far as they are irrelevant to the purpose of the quotation and if the ommission is identified as such. In contrast, meaning-changing or omissions left unidentified are falsifications, so to speak.

16. At least this is the case for the verb complement 1, traditionally called "subject". The basic meaning of the word "subject" is of course: that which is the basis of the discourse, that which is assumed to be its theme. But other verbal complements and free adjuncts can also be rhematised.

17. From this perspective, a theory of syntax that is not oriented towards the traditional syntactic categories 'subjec't, 'object', 'predicate' etc., but rather on structural aspects of the language, such as the distinction between 'head' and 'complement' is of course better suited to the presentation the of the problems discussed here.

18. This should explain the above-mentioned cases without particular intonation marking (8)–(11) and (15). With this a new theme is opened: the logical borderline case of a rheme-marking.

19. This has led in part to the equating of language system with grammar in theoretical linguistics. Logically, however, this is problematic, because a grammar is based on constitutive rules of the form $A \rightarrow K_1 + K_2 + \ldots + K_n$, and the operation by means of the operator "+" is logically understood as conjunction, while statements about the language system are based on paradigmatic relations, which are logically alternations. Cf. on this Stetter (2009).

20. In written German: *Ich bin zu spät, weil ich den Bus verpasst habe.*

21. This example too only holds for German.

22. Concerning this cf. the discussions about the so-called scripticism: Stetter (1997), Krämer (1998), Dürscheid (2006) among others. The logical problems connected with this position are treated in Stetter (2005, Chs. 6 and 7).

23. This is even true of hand-written texts, as long as each letter of the particular text, e.g. the original text of the *Nibelungenlied*, can be uniquely distinguished from every other letter of the same text.

24. The definition of "equal" given above is assumed: (1) Every element X of M is equal to itself. (2) If A is equal to B, then B is also equal to A. (3) If A is equal to B and B is equal to C, then A is also equal to C.

25. Otherwise there would be no difference between original and copy.

26. Rather, it is a copy of B and only of B, and B is here relative to A the original which gets copied.

27. The copy is always a copy of an object that is not itself.

28. I am of course referring to familiar distinctions here.

29. This follows from the implications of the head principle.
30. This is the prerequisite for the various types of word to be described in a morphological theory. Cf. Stetter (2009).
31. Cf. Stetter (2005: 289–291).
32. This also explains the feature of the syntactic indeterminacy of the vocative act described above.

References

Dürscheid, Christa
    2006   *Einführung in die Schriftlinguistik.* 3rd revised and supplemented ed. 2006. With 31 illustrations. Göttingen: Vandenhoeck and Ruprecht.

Helbig, Gerhard and Joachim Buscha
    2001   *Deutsche Grammatik. Ein Handbuch für den Ausländerunterricht.* München: Langenscheidt.

Humboldt, Wilhelm von
    1827   Ueber den Dualis. In *Werke in fünf Bänden*, Andreas Flitner and Klaus Giel (eds.), 113–143. Reprinted 1960–1981. Darmstadt: Wissenschaftliche Buchgesellschaft.

Krämer, Sybille
    1998   Das Medium als Spur und als Apparat. In *Medien, Computer, Realität. Wirklichkeitsvorstellungen und neue Medien*, Sybille Krämer (ed.), 73–94. Frankfurt a. M.: Suhrkamp.

Martinet, André
    1963   *Grundzüge der Allgemeinen Sprachwissenschaft.* 2nd ed. Authorised translation from French by Anna Fuchs in collaboration with Hans Heinrich Lieb. Stuttgart: Kohlhammer.

Noel Aziz Hanna, Patrizia
    2009   Wackernagels Gesetz im Deutschen – zur Interaktion von Syntax, Phonologie und Informationsstruktur. Habilitationsschrift, LMU München.

Ryle, Gilbert
    1949   *The Concept of Mind.* Reprinted 1963. London: Peregrine Books. (German: *Der Begriff des Geistes.* Stuttgart: Reclam 1969.)

Stetter, Christian
    1997   *Schrift und Sprache.* Frankfurt a. M.: Suhrkamp.

Stetter, Christian
    2005   *System und Performanz. Symboltheoretische Grundlagen von Medientheorie und Sprachwissenschaft.* Weilerswist: Velbrück

Stetter, Christian
  2009   Die Logik der Linguistik. In *Oberfläche und Performanz.*
                Untersuchungen zur Sprache als dynamischer Gestalt, Angelika
                Linke and Helmuth Feilke (eds.), 51–76. Tübingen: Niemeyer.
Wittgenstein, Ludwig
  1984   *Werkausgabe in acht Bänden.* Vol. 1, Tractatus logico-
                philosophicus, Tagebücher 1914-1916, Philosophische Untersu-
                chungen. Revised ed. by Joachim Schulte. Frankfurt a. M.:
                Suhrkamp.

Language index

Subject index

www.ingramcontent.com/pod-product-compliance
Lightning Source LLC
Chambersburg PA
CBHW070018100426
42740CB00013B/2544